THE RECOVERY OF MISSION

THE RECOVERY
OF MISSION

Beyond the Pluralist Paradigm

Vinoth Ramachandra

Wipf and Stock Publishers
EUGENE, OREGON

Wipf and Stock Publishers
199 West 8th Avenue, Suite 3
Eugene, Oregon 97401

The Recovery of Mission
Beyond the Pluralist Paradigm
By Ramachandra, Vinoth
©1996 Paternoster Press
ISBN: 1-59244-064-9
Publication date: October, 2002
Previously published by Paternoster Press, 1996.

Contents

PART III

Author's Preface

There is a scene in a film by the late Benagli film-maker Satyajit Ray in which a group of children are playing in the fields outside their village. Skipping their way through the fields they move further and further from the village. They suddenly hear a loud roar and crouch, terrified, in the long grass. A train screams past. As the train disappears over the horizon, the children wend their way home, silent and awe-struck. When they left home that morning, their village was their world. Now, not only have they seen with their own eyes an extraordinary new machine, but they have come to understand that there are people beyond their village who look different and dress differently. Their world has changed. It has grown larger, more exciting, but also more unstable and frightening. The trains which criss-cross India unite the far-flung villages of that vast land. Little did the British realise, when they laid the first railtrack in 1861 (for purely commercial, administrative and military purposes) that their railways would contribute to the growth of a sense of nationhood and the eventual dismemberment of their empire.[1]

These children have encountered modernity. And modernity will bring in its wake a fracturing of their world-view, throwing them into contact with people whose beliefs, customs and ways of living are fundamentally different to what they have experienced hitherto. In other words, modernity brings with it an experience of pluralism, the recognition of the social fact of human diversity—whether of language, cultures, religious systems of thought, political arrangements etc. A vast corpus of literature has arisen in recent years on the impact of modernity on traditional cultures and the psychological disorientation that is experienced as a result of that encounter.[2]

Although Christian churches in the West have had to come to terms with the institutional forces and cultural dynamic of modernity for far longer than their counterparts in Asia, the encounter with religious pluralism has only become a pervasive feature of Western life since perhaps the 1960s. Immigration of Asian peoples into Europe and North America (so that, for instance, Muslims often outnumber Christians in British inner cities), the growth of electronic communication and mass tourism, and the secularization and decline of much institutional Christianity has meant that the Christian position in many of these countries today is not dissimilar to what Asian Christians have experienced for centuries. Christian mission in Asia has a long and chequered history, and Christians have lived alongside people of other faiths in the great cities of Asia as a small, powerless and often persecuted minority.[3] In this, of course, their situation has been little different to that of the early Christian communities in the pluralistic Greco-Roman world of the mediterranean. However, if the Western experience of 'Christendom' served to shield most European Christians for many centuries from the encounter with other faiths and cultural traditions, in the East the experience of Christendom served to identify Christian mission with the hegemonic ambitions of European thought and culture.

Asia has long been noted for its pluralism of cultures and systems of thought. Professor Trevor Ling rightly reminds us that what is commonly referred to as Buddhism is an 'intellectual abstraction' and obscures its 'country-specific' nature, and that we must be careful to observe the important social and organizational differences among the various 'Buddhisms' in Asia.[4] Buddhism in Singapore, for example, has placed little emphasis on the *sangha* (the monastic order the Buddha founded) and is, thus, very different from the highly 'politicised' Buddhism encountered in, say, Sri Lanka. The same would no doubt be true of all the Asian religious traditions, including 'Asian Christianity'. Modern Asia is so complex that generalizations about what constitutes the 'Asian mind' or what is 'typical' of Asian society are dangerously superficial and often downright silly. Christian witness in India, perhaps the most complex of Asian societies, has as its context not only the great religious traditions but also modern Western culture, for Indian urban life includes the second largest middle-class population in the world. India is about caste politics *and* parliamentary government, bullock carts *and* nuclear power stations, horoscopes *and* space satellites, naked sadhus *and* a global fashion industry.

Although religious pluralism has been recognized from the earliest days of Christian mission (whether in Asia or the Greco-Roman world), and Christian theologians in Asia have long grappled with the task of communicating Christ in thought-forms appropriate to those from other faiths, the modern situation has thrown up a new phenomenon: namely, the endorsement of religious pluralism, not merely as a social fact but as a new theological understanding of the relationship between Christian faith and other faiths, by a significant number of Christian academics and Church leaders.

Thus the editors of the much-publicized symposium, *The Myth of Christian Uniqueness*, express their confidence that 'a pluralist model represents a new turn—what might be called a "paradigm shift"—in the efforts of Christian theologians, both past and present, to understand the world of other religions and Christianity's place in that world.'[5] In a book published two years previously, one of those same editors, the American Catholic Paul Knitter proposed a model of 'unitary pluralism', asserting that 'the world religions, in all their amazing differences, are more complementary than contradictory', and set a new 'goal and inspiration for missionary work' so that a process of 'mutual growth' may take place among people of all faiths and none, the success of which would be measured in terms of a Christian becoming 'a better Christian' and a Buddhist 'a better Buddhist'.[6] It is in this *normative and programmatic* sense that the word pluralism has come to function in contemporary Christian discussions. It is in this sense that I shall use the term in the remainder of the book (unless qualified).

Of course pluralism itself is pluralistic in nature. It assumes a variety of forms, some of which differ markedly from Knitter's model, and rests on different argumentative bases, in the work of different theologians. What they all tend to have in common, though, is the belief that all religious traditions (or, at least, what they tend to call the 'major' ones) have salvific value (however differently that salvific value may be identified by different writers), so that the traditional Christian concept of mission must be given up in the interests of mutual religious enrichment through dialogue and peaceful co-operation.

This book is presented as a contribution to the ongoing debate within the worldwide Church. I have written primarily for Christian pastors and those training for the pastorate (or for cross-cultural missionary service) in universities and theological seminars. But I am also concerned to reach the thoughtful 'lay' Christian man and woman who, I believe, need to listen to the writers and issues dealt with in this book. Although I write from an Asian context and address, from time to time, peculiarly Asian realities, this work is intended for a much wider audience. Western theological education is largely prochial, oblivious to the fact that the axis of the Christian Church has shifted southwards in recent times to Latin America, Africa and Asia. It is important that we all, from North and South, heed the call of the late Kenyan Anglican theologian John Mbiti, to 'embrace each other's concerns and stretch to each other's horizons'.[7] Perhaps I need to make clear that I am not attempting to develop an 'Asian theology'. I am only too conscious of the bewildering variety that is Asia today to attempt anything so grand. In any case, truly indigenous theologies can only be developed in the vernacular languages, not in a universal language such as English.

My aims are more modest. Part I explores the pluralist paradigm as it has taken shape in the work of three very different Asian writers, the Indians Stanley Samartha and Raimundo Panikkar, and the Sri Lankan Aloysius Pieris. They have all exercised a considerable influence on the older denominational churches in Asia, and they have also lived and taught in several Western countries over the past three decades. They all made significant contributions to *The Myth of Christian Uniqueness* volume mentioned above.

I have chosen these three writers, not only on account of their global stature, but because they are the best representatives of three fairly typical theological approaches that are to be encountered on the modern theological scene. I have devoted a chapter each to an exposition and critique of the main elements in the thought of each writer.

Part II comprises of two chapters. The first begins with a schematic summary of the points of similarity and dissimilarity among the three theologians considered in Part I. I then seek to locate their thought on a wider intellectual landscape, particularly in relation to some dominant trends in the Western theological heritage. I also indicate *directions* of criticism that could be culled from the work of major figures within that heritage. I may need to beg the indulgence of the Western student at this point, for what I expound here is, no doubt, a familiar feature of the standard Western theological curriculum. But I am conscious of the needs of both 'lay' readers and the non-Western theological audience.

The second chapter turns to the work of an experienced leader of the ecumenical missionary movement, Lesslie Newbigin. I have found much of his work relevant to the concerns of the present book and so I rehearse the main features of his critique of modern culture, while suggesting, briefly, ways in which his critique needs to be complemented.

Chapters Six and Seven (Part III) are essays in retrieval. Chapter Six seeks to re-focus our gaze on the person of Jesus who receives hardly any serious attention in the writings of pluralist theologians, with the possible exception of Pieris and other liberationists. I survey the synoptic testimony, drawing on recent New Testament scholarship and the insights of new hermenutical approaches, to highlight the inescapable scandal at the heart of any Christian theology that takes the early witness to Jesus with historical seriousness.

Chapter Seven, likewise, delves into the biblical and early patristic tradition to articulate an understanding of the Gospel as a message whose universality is inextricably bound up with its uniqueness. The themes of election, mission and incarnation are shown to be woven together, and that they, rightly understood, address some of the legitimate concerns of pluralist writers. Irenaeus' response to the gnostic systems of his day provides helpful lessons for Christians at the end of the second millenium.

The concluding chapter deals with missionary praxis: how should the gospel be communicated in a pluralist world? It seeks to expose some of the blind-spots of both traditional and liberal approaches to mission, and to describe some of the features of an evangelistic praxis that is truly consistent with the content of the gospel message.

Notes to Preface

1. From R.Cronin, *Imagining India* (London: Macmillan, 1989) ch.6.
2. A good introduction is P. L. Berger, B. Berger & H. Kellner, *The Homeless Mind: Modernization and Consciousness* (Harmondsworth: Penguin, 1973).
3. See S. Moffett, *A History of Christianity in Asia, vol.1* (San Francisco: HarperSan Francisco, 1992).
4. T. Ling (ed), *Buddhist Trends in Southeast Asia* (Singapore: Institute of Southeast Asian Studies, 1993) p. 3.
5. J. Hick and P. Knitter (eds), *The Myth of Christian Uniqueness* (London: SCM, 1987) p. vii.
6. P. Knitter, *No Other Name?: A Critical Survey of Christian Attitudes Towards the World Religions* (Maryknoll, NY: Orbis, 1985) pp. 220–22.
7. J. Mbiti, 'Theological Impotence and the Universality of the Church', in G.H. Anderson and T.F. Stransky, *Mission Trends No. 3: Third World Theologies* (New York: Paulist Press and Grand Rapids: Eerdmans, 1976) p. 17.

Acknowledgments

Work on this book began during a nine-month sabbatical, spent mostly in Oxford, England, in 1993–4. It was made possible by a scholarship from TEAR Fund (UK), and I am grateful to the staff and students of Wycliffe Hall who made my stay among them a pleasant one. I owe a great debt to the Rev. Dr Stephen Williams, then Assistant Director of the Whitfield Institute, for his warm encouragement and wise counsel in the early stages of the book. He also read the first draft of the completed manuscript and made several helpful suggestions. Needless to say, he bears no responsibility for any errors and shortcomings that may remain.

This is as good an opportunity as any to thank publicly many dear friends in England who have, from time to time, fed, watered and sheltered me—especially John and Celia Wyatt, David and Jean Turner, Steve and Dot Beck, and Roy and Helen McCloughry. Their long years of friendship have meant more to me that I can express.

The book was completed in the midst of a society scarred and brutalized by many years of war, inter-ethnic violence and ruthless political greed on all sides. I dedicate it to my brothers and sisters in Christ who have chosen to suffer deprivations of various kinds in order to serve the kingdom of God with courage, patience and hope.

PART I

[1]

Mystery-centred Faith:
Stanley Samartha

'In contemporary India a radical change in the Christian stance toward neighbours of other faiths is both an existential demand and a theological necessity'. So urges the Indian theologian Stanley Samartha in a contribution to the symposium *The Myth of Christian Uniqueness*.[1] Samartha has been a leading figure in ecumenical inter-faith relations since the 1960s and was the first director of the World Council of Churches Unit on Dialogue with People of Living Faiths and Ideologies. He has taught in theological seminaries both in India and abroad, and returned to India in 1981 after a long sojourn in Geneva to take up the directorship of the South Asian Theological Research Institute in Bangalore. His most recent book *One Christ-Many Religions*[2] continues to explore the theme of a Christology suitable for a religiously plural world, a theme that has engaged Samartha's mind since the publication of his first theological work, *The Hindu Response to the Unbound Christ*, some twenty years ago.

Religious Pluralism and the Secular State

Samartha is an astute and well-read observer of the Indian cultural and political landscape. He is passionately committed to the vision of a secular state under whose umbrella all the religions of the sub-continent can make their contributions to national life. He is acutely aware of how religions have become 'politicized' in the post-independence era, politicians fanning the flames of religious bigotry for short-

3

term political gain and religious communities seeking political leverage over others out of collective insecurity. The integrity of the country is in danger of being blown apart by separatist movements that are often influenced and even sanctioned by the dogmatic claims of religious traditions. The answer lies in the way of a secular political arrangement which, instead of banishing the religions to a private domain (which would be a betrayal of the religious ethos), seeks to provide space for different religions to make their specific input 'to the pool of values to undergird the life of the nation' (OCMR, p. 53). The secular character of the Indian state, in the midst of a babel of multicultural encounters, has to be 'cherished, nurtured and supported' by all communities of faith against any 'theocratic tendencies on the part of any single religion or ideology' (p. 54).

In a pluralist society, so Samartha believes, all religions must give up traditional 'exclusive' language where truth-claims are concerned, for such language, however appropriate as expressions of faith and worship within a particular religious community, becomes arrogant and divisive when used in relationships with another. Samartha sees himself as part of a 'growing number' of Christians who have rejected the 'normativeness' or 'finality' of the Christian's Christ, and who seek a revised Christology in the light of involvement in dialogue with adherents of other faiths and in collaboration with people of secular convictions struggling against the forces of death and destruction. Claims to Christian uniqueness, and especially the ontological equation of Jesus Christ with God, 'would scarcely allow any serious discussion with neighbours of other faiths or secular humanists' (CR, p. 80); for he believes that evangelical emphasis on the 'once-for-all' ness of salvation through the cross and resurrection of Jesus Christ involves 'a total rejection of the religious beliefs and convictions of neighbours of other faiths' (OCMR, p. 109).

All such claims, Samartha asserts, are 'mixed up with ideological assumptions backed up by economic affluence and political power' (p. 109). Indeed he argues that 'the roots of evangelicalism are not in Asia or Africa but in the West' and that evangelicalism assumes a ' "Christ-against-religions" attitude which goes hand-in-hand with tremendous economic power, military strength and political subjugation of nations' (p. 115). Any notion that in a pluralistic society, 'just one religion has the *only* answer to all the problems of human life at all times for all peoples and in all cultures is doubtful whatever be the vehemence with which such a notion is propagated' (p. 53, italics in text).

The quest for new ways of relating between different religious communities is not only based on pragmatic considerations but is also theologically motivated. Do not exclusive claims in a multi-religous setting contradict a theology which affirms that God is the creator, sustainer and redeemer of all humanity and that God's love and justice embrace all people at all times? Samartha believes that the Church should learn from the experience of Hindu *Vedanta* in developing a tolerant attitude towards religious dissent over long centuries of pluralistic existence. Brahmanism sought to solve the problem of the One and the Many by suggesting that while *Sat* (Truth, Being) is One, sages call it by various names.[3] By relating all such names to the One and therefore to each other, differences were not eliminated but held together in a structure of difference. The One was greater than any of the gods or even the sum total of the gods. 'Without recognizing and accepting this Mysterious Centre (the *Satyasya Satyam*—the Truth of the Truth), genuine plurality is impossible' (CR, p. 73). In this way the challenges of Buddhism and later of Christianity were met by 'co-opting' the Buddha and Jesus into the Hindu structure of the *avataras*.

The unity and noncontradictory nature of religions is taken for granted by all Hindus. The basic differences in humankind make it natural and inevitable that there should be plurality in religion. Religious differences are the different responses to the Mystery of the Infinite, so that questions of 'superiority' do not arise. Criticism of one religion based on criteria drawn from another is unwarranted. How can so great a Mystery be experienced in only one way and expressed through only one set of symbols? 'Religious plurality, therefore, is the homage which the finite mind pays to the inexhaustibility of the infinite' (OCMR, p. 5).

Transcendence and Harmony

Samartha's favourite term for the divine reality is 'Mystery'. The acceptance of a sense of Mystery and the rejection of an exclusive stance where ultimate matters are concerned are the twin factors which shape his theological method. They are the result of his espousal of the *advaita* (usually translated 'non-dualist') tradition in Hindu philosophy. The ontological basis for tolerance is provided by Mystery, the Truth of the Truth, which is 'the transcendent Centre that remains always beyond and greater than apprehensions of it or even the sum total of those apprehensions. It is beyond cognitive knowledge (*tarka*) but is open to vision (*dristi*) and intuition (*anubhava*)' (CR, p. 75). Mystery points us beyond the theistic/nontheistic debate. Samartha writes:

> Both the terms Brahman and God are culture-conditioned. One could as well use the term Mystery . . . In this case the two statements-namely, that 'Brahman is *sat-cit-ananda*' and 'God is triune, Father, Son, and Holy Spirit'—could be regarded as two responses to the same Mystery in two cultural settings . . . neither *sat-cit-ananda* nor Trinity could, in linguistic terms, adequately describe the inner ontological working of Mystery. One could ask, therefore, on what grounds can it be claimed that the trinitarian formula offers a 'truer' insight into the nature of Mystery than does *sat-cit-ananda*? At best, the two formulations can only be symbolic, pointing to the Mystery, affirming the meaning disclosed, but retaining the residual depth (CR, p. 76).

Samartha distinguishes between *faith* and *religion* in a way that seems to indicate the influence of the Islamics scholar Wilfred Cantwell Smith.[4] Faith is a response to the divine Mystery or transcendent Truth. It has to do with visions and values.

> Faith is the substance of religion and precedes it. Faith can live without religion, but religion cannot exist without faith . . . Religion seeks to enshrine and express faith in dogmas and doctrines, rituals, symbols and liturgy, in patterns of relationships, codes of conduct and structures of society. And in doing so, it may distort faith and obscure the original vision (OCMR, p. 52).

Although the criteria derived from one religious response cannot be made the norm to judge others, he asserts that faith 'has a transcendent dimension that reaches beyond human beliefs, rituals and institutions, and so provides criteria and courage to be critical of ideological distortions of religion' (p. 53). But it must be noted that there is some inconsistency in his terminology here, because he continues to refer to 'neighbours of other faiths' when, on this understanding, 'faith' seems to point to a common pre-conceptual experience of the transcendent which is subsequently embodied in different *religions*.

In multi-religious societies such as India, the human predicament is perceived differently through different religious frameworks. The contexts and expressions of 'salvation' are different. When the questions asked about the human predicament differ, the answers proffered are bound to be different. Consequently 'The nature of Mystery is such that any claim on the part of one religious community to have exclusive or unique or final knowledge becomes inadmissible. Exclusiveness puts fences around the Mystery' (CR, p. 77). Samartha argues that even within the pages of the New Testament, salvation through Jesus Christ was experienced and articulated differently by the Aramaic-speaking Jewish Christians, the Hellenic Jews of the diaspora, and the non-Jewish Christians who had no part in the Jewish 'history of salvation'. While not denying the validity of the Christian experience of salvation in Jesus Christ, 'to claim that the Judaeo-Christian-Western tradition has the *only* answer to all problems in all places and for all persons in the world is presumptuous, if not incredible.' (CR, p. 77)

Samartha's hostility is directed as much against 'inclusivist' as against 'exclusivist' approaches to the truth-claims of other faiths. They are both forms of 'theological violence' against our neighbours. Instead he urges an approach that has as its basic premise an understanding of the 'great religious traditions' as embodying different responses to the Mystery of *Sat* or God (or of Ultimate Reality) so that the distinctiveness of each response, the Christian included, should be stated in such a way as to enhance a 'mutually critical and enriching relationship' among them all (CR, p. 79).

He also rejects what he labels the 'either-or way of thinking' (which he regards as characteristic of the Western mentality) in favour of a larger 'harmony' of thought as demonstrated by the advaita or the *yin-yang* method of reconciling opposites.[5] He is impressed by recent developments in Western philosophy of language (he mentions deconstructionism as an example, but doesn't pause to explore any such developments) and the philosophy of science. He believes that these, by drawing attention to the contextual relativity of texts and theories, prepare us for more mystical and aesthetic approaches to Mystery. He asserts, with an astonishing air of self-assurance, that

> Truth is no more defined in terms of exclusion. A religion that defines itself to be true by excluding others is outmoded. In science there are no certainties, only probabilities. 'Salvation-history' is not limited to one people . . . No particular response to or formulation of Truth can claim to be unique, final or absolute. We need to *grow* into truth' (OCMR, p. 119).

Samartha has always championed *advaita Vedanta* as the best candidate for the revised conceptual framework needed for a Christian pluralist theology. Historically, 'the survival of the political unity of India is based on its cultural unity within which there persists a core of religion to which the sense of "not-twoism" and the mindset that holds together diversities by refusing to be exclusive make an enduring contribution' (p. 126). He argues that logic and dogma must be subordinated to experience in keeping with Asian sensitivities. There is an all-pervasive unity which holds together nature, humanity and truth (or *Dharma* or God) in its harmonious embrace. Consequently, there can be no 'heretics' in the Western sense of the term, nor a triumphalistic attitude to other traditions. On the contrary, there is a profound hesitation to take any exclusive stance where faith is concerned, a healthy suspicion of all rational formulations of Truth, and an emphasis on interiority, symbolism and aesthetic expression in the religious life. Moreover, 'the theory of multiple *avatars* seems to be theologically the most accommodating attitude in a pluralistic setting that permits recognizing both the Mystery of God and the freedom of the people to respond to the divine initiatives in different ways at different times' (p. 149).

Samartha believes that there are at least three areas where religions can make a significant contribution to a pluralist society such as India: namely, (i) by exercising a 'prophetico-critical' function *vis à vis* the corruption of political authority and all forms of oppression in public life; (ii) by encouraging the emergence of 'new communities of concerned individuals', cutting across visible religious boundaries, who can work for a 'fuller life' in society; (iii) by drawing attention to a transcendent centre that serves both as the source of all values and the norm to judge all human conduct, personal or public. 'Whether this is called God or *sat* or *dharma* or

Ultimate Reality is less important than for all religious communities to point to a sacred symbol that transcends loyalty to one's own religion, tribe, caste, or language. Secularism empties life of this content, faith recognizes and accepts it' (p. 63).

Is there any distinctively Christian contribution to this undertaking? Samartha is elusive at this point. Although he has often referred to the distinctiveness of each religious response, he insists that, 'If Jesus Christ is God's gift to the whole world it would be a serious mistake to insist that that the gift should be received, unwrapped and appreciated only in one particular way' (OCMR, p. 160). Christians, together with their non-Christian neighbours, are called upon to participate in God's continuing mission in the world: namely, to heal the rift between humanity, nature and God. The components of this mission are the concern for justice, service to the poor, practising charity, and 'bringing the resources of the gospel' to bear on the solution of common global problems. 'Jesus Christ points beyond himself to God and God's kingdom. In a religiously plural world the mission of the church is not to make other people Christians but to invite people to enter the kingdom of God' (p. 174).

Christology

This leads us into Samartha's christology, a topic that occupies most of the second half of *One Christ-Many Religions*. Samartha seeks what he calls a 'broader and deeper conceptual framework' than that provided by European christologies that have hitherto been imported into Asia; one that will enable the church to regard neighbours of other faiths as 'partners in the larger community which is the object of God's love and redeeming grace' (p. 108). A theocentric (or, more accurately—for the sake of nontheistic faiths such as Theravada Buddhism or Taoism—a 'Mystery-centred') christology is more helpful in establishing new relationships with people of other religious traditions.

Samartha can be a little confusing in his use of the term 'Christ'. Although he does remark that 'Christ does not belong to Christianity' (CR, p. 83) and warns against a 'Christomonism' that 'limits Christ to Jesus of Nazareth' (CR, p. 79), surprisingly he does not develop a Logos christ-ology nor does he seek to use any of the so-called 'cosmic

Christ' passages of the New Testament. Instead he argues that the biblical witness, including that of Jesus himself, is always theocentric, the ontological priority of God being taken for granted. Therefore, 'The only way to be Christ-centred is to be God-centred, but in a religiously plural world to be Christ-centred is not the only way to be God-centred' (OCMR, p. 106). He also tosses out a cryptic aside to the effect that 'The Orthodox rejection of the *filioque* clause in the description of the procession of the Holy Spirit . . . has far-reaching ecumenical significance' (CR, p. 81) and warns that 'to ignore the depth of God's being behind the Trinity to which the Trinity points symbolically is to forget that christology is not the whole of, but a part of theology' (OCMR, p. 109). Consequently one cannot help wondering whether his latest book has been wrongly titled. A more appropriate title would seem to be 'One Mystery—Many Religions'!

Be that as it may, Samartha is eager to distinguish 'between truth and truth-claims, between Jesus Christ and Christian claims about Jesus Christ, between Jesus before Christianity and Christianity after Jesus' (OCMR, p. 112). He is adamant that he is in no way diminishing the person of Jesus or diluting the substance of the Christian faith. The target of his attacks is not this faith but 'the inflated claims made for Jesus Christ, claims unsupported by New Testament evidence' (p. 152) for it is these that hinder inter-religious co-operation. His position is that 'scriptural authority becomes more important than that of the creeds' (p. 137) and that 'the whole emphasis here is that the New Testament *does* provide a basis that is historically recoverable, exegetically correct, and theologically sound for new relationships with neighbours of other faiths' (p. 152).

The situation of religious pluralism provides the hermeneutical key for Samartha's unpacking of the New Testament. A 'Christology from above makes it impossible for Christians to relate themselves, their faith in God through Jesus Christ, and the liberated and liberating life in the Kingdom of God to neighbours of other faiths' (p. 134). He quotes approvingly from those New Testament scholars (for example, Ernst Käsemann, Joseph Fitzmyer and Reginald Fuller) who argue that christology can only be done 'from below' and then proceed to deny any ontological identity between Jesus Christ and God. He is convinced that 'Jesus himself obstinately

remains a devout Jew who spoke not of himself but of God'
(p. 140), and agrees with the radical British theologian Don
Cupitt's view that 'The real Jesus is a much more interesting
and religiously relevant figure than the divine Christ of later
faith, and he has the advantage of having actually lived . . .
Christendom—Christianity does not work any more. The
historical Jesus is the real Christ for today.'[6] Yet at the same
time he makes explicit his 'assumption' that 'the being or the
truth of Jesus behind the [apostolic] testimonies is larger,
deeper and more mysterious than any portrait that may be
painted by the brushes of scholarly study. Therefore the
being or the truth of Jesus must remain the controlling factor
in interpreting the testimonies of writers.' (p. 131).

Samartha has no problem ascribing 'divinity' rather than
'deity' to Jesus, for the divine is displayed in his humanity.
'The true meaning of *kenosis* is not that he was first divine,
and then became human in order to regain divinity. He
rejected that kind of humanness which refuses to be "empty"
so that by becoming perfectly selfless he could become the
instrument of God's compassion and justice in society . . '
(p. 155). Samartha assures us that 'New Testament scholars
are generally agreed on the chronological developments of
christologies within the New Testament'; but then makes
the strangely naive assertion that this line of chronological
development 'runs through the book of Acts that provides
information about the experience of the first generation of
Christians, to the Synoptic Gospels, the epistles of Paul, and
later on, to the Fourth Gospel' (p. 137).

In Acts, 'Jesus is not regarded as a pre-existent being but a
man appointed by God and anointed by the Spirit for a
specific vocation and destiny'. The Synoptic Gospels
'strongly emphasise the humanity of Jesus, as a special
person chosen, raised up and commissioned by God for a
special purpose'. 'When one comes to . . . Paul, the historic
Jesus has receded from the scene, and Christ, crucified and
risen, has·taken over. To Paul, Jesus is Lord and the Son of
God in an exclusive sense, *the* Son, God's heavenly companion, enthroned at the right hand of God. The historical
Jesus, his words and deeds and signs, the kingdom of God
he ushered in, the vocabulary about his humanness and
temptations, his prayers in struggles, have all receded to the
background' (p. 137). But note: 'Paul is extremely careful
not to identify Jesus Christ with God.' As for the Fourth

Gospel, it has 'moved rather far from the historic human Jesus' and the portrait of Jesus is 'higher than the synoptics but lower than that affirmed in the Nicene creed' (p. 140). While admitting that Hindus have found the Fourth Gospel's portrait of Jesus highly attractive, Samartha denies that the Gospel teaches that the Son of God is himself God (p. 140).[7]

What does the cross-resurrection event mean in a religiously plural world? Samartha identifies three meanings:

(a) It symbolises the struggle of millions who have died and who are still dying as victims of unjust systems.
(b) It exposes the principalities and powers of this world in their unholy collusion against common people, and it inspires the poor and the powerless to resist public immorality in religious and political institutions.
(c) At his death Jesus was not finished and forgotten. 'The resurrection . . . is an act of remembrance on God's part of the historical Jesus of Nazareth. Jesus lives in God's memory . . . When Christians confess that Jesus, crucified and buried was raised on the third day, they affirm that the kingdom of God in the preaching of which Jesus began his ministry on earth has assumed the character and function of the crucified-and-risen One' (OCMR, pp. 159–160).

He continues, even more enigmatically,

> Because these are testimonies, the being or truth of Jesus behind them remains unknown to us . . . The residual mystery behind the testimonies is perhaps more readily recognized by people in an Eastern conceptual framework, at least in the particular strand of Hindu thought, namely, the *advaita*, because of its emphasis on the unknowability, the unthinkability and the inexhaustibility of *Sat* which is both *Truth* and *Being* (p. 160).

What place, then, for Christian tradition and the ancient creeds? Here is Samartha's answer:

> They are valid and helpful within the liturgical life and worship of the believing community. The proper place for affirmations of faith, in so far as they are expressions of commitment and not negative criticisms of neighbours of other faiths, is within the life and worship of the community as confessions of faith, and so, should not be extended beyond its boundaries (p. 152).

As for salvation, it has to be understood today as a process of 'personal healing, social healing and cosmic healing within the larger unity of nature, humanity and God to which the vision of *advaita*, for example, points . . .' (p. 158).

For Samartha, the plurality of scriptures (the Quran, Gita,etc) is not simply a historical fact to be recognized, but has implications for hermeneutical method. Any exclusive elements within each scripture are to be interpreted as expressions of self-identity and cannot be legitimately extended beyond the boundaries of particular communities of faith. In any case, the language of religion does not depend solely on texts but also on *symbols* which point to something infinitely more mysterious. 'The language of religion is a language of love and commitment. It would be most unwise to draw logical conclusions from the language of love. An exclusive claim expressed in religious language has the character of commitment, not of rejection.' (OCMR, p. 84)

Response to Samartha

One cannot but admire Samartha's passionate concern for mutual sensitivity, respect and co-operation between the adherents of different religious traditions. Moreover, his championing of more intuitive and aesthetic approaches to theological reflection is valid, and I believe he has exposed here a defect in most mainstream Christian traditions. We look forward eagerly to the fruits of such creative endeavour. However, the programme of religious pluralism that he vigorously advocates is a different matter altogether. It is a pity that Samartha does not extend the same respect that he urges *vis à vis* our non-Christian neighbours to those Christians with whom he disagrees. He is often guilty of gross caricature where his opponents' views are concerned and, more importantly, his own programme (the reason for my stressing the programmatic aspect of his theology will become apparent shortly) is seriously flawed.

(a) Samartha, like Professor John Hick who is better known in Western theological circles,[8] seeks to avoid a choice between personalist and nonpersonalist understandings of deity by using instead the language of 'Transcendence', 'Mystery', 'Sat', 'Ultimate Reality' and other highly abstract concepts. But it is clear that a choice has already been made in adopting the *advaita Vedanta* worldview as a framework for pluralism: for personal theism, whether in the form of the Semitic faiths or the *bhakti* tradition in India, has been demoted to a lower level of reality. Those believers who speak of God as personal being imply, at the very least, that God communicates with us, enters into personal relationships with us and has a purpose for the world. In asserting that Ultimate Reality/Mystery is unknowable, or that what can be known is so seriously distorted by our conceptual and cultural limitations that we cannot make any true statements about that Reality/Mystery, Samartha is imposing limits not only on our human ability but also on that Reality/Mystery. He is effectively saying that no personal God exists, or if a personal God does exist, that God does not communicate God's self to us in a way that we can know to be true. The nonpersonal 'God behind God' is clearly one who does not speak. This is a dogmatic assertion, an assumption that is necessary for Samartha's entire programme. Consequently, any faith tradition that claims that God *does* take the initiative to disclose God's self to humankind is automatically marginalized within Samartha's world-view. There is an in-built bias towards the nontheistic Indian faiths. But this makes his strictures on 'exclusivist Christian arrogance' sound extremely hollow, if not downright hypocritical.

Samartha imagines that by postulating an abstract Mystery at the centre of the religious universe he can secure a unifying religious allegiance in a fragmented world. But how could an undefinable, attributeless and undifferentiated abstraction command anyone's loyalty, leave alone worship? The *bhakti* tradition, and the *visishtadvaita* (or 'qualified non-dualism') of Ramanuja (12th century C.E) arose in India as a challenge to such an empty philosophical system which failed to engage the hearts of the people. Samartha's tendency to speak of the 'great religious traditions' also reveals his intellectual chauvinism. The primal religions of the world, followers of which comprise nearly half the population of India, are hardly mentioned in his work. Nor are new religious movements, Christian and non-Christian. Are they to be regarded as authentic manifestations of Mystery and, if so, how does he know?

(b) This leads to a further consideration. Since Samartha does not furnish us with any way of relating the various manifestations of Mystery to Mystery itself, on what grounds can we believe that the terms *Brahman* and *Yahweh* (and *Sunyata, Nirvana, Tao* etc) point to the same Mystery, but in different cultural settings? We touch here on the classic distinction made by the mathematician–philosopher Gottlob Frege (1848–1925) between the *sense* of a term and its *referent*.[9] Frege illustrated this by means of the following identity statements: (a) The Morning Star is identical with the Morning Star; and (b) The Morning Star is identical with the Evening Star. Statement (a) is necessarily true and expresses a tautology. In other words, its truth does not depend on any states of affairs in the world. It can simply be deduced from the logical form. Statement (b) is true because it expresses an astronomical discovery. Both statements refer to the planet Venus which appears on the horizon both at dawn and at dusk. 'The Morning Star' and the 'Evening Star' are thus expressions which refer to (or denote) the planet Venus. But they have different senses (in that their connotations differ); and so the two statements above, while both being true, are nevertheless significantly different.

Is Samartha inviting us to think of *Brahman, Tao*, The Triune God *et al.* in a similar way—as all having the same ultimate referent while differing in sense? Unfortunately, the plausibility of Frege's own example lies in the fact that non-controversial astronomical data is available that helps us to believe that the referents of Morning Star and Evening Star are the same. But this identity of referent is precisely what is at issue in our discussion. Given the widely differing connotations of the terms in the world's religions, surely the onus of proof that their ultimate referents are identical lies with Samartha. How does he know that one Mystery underlies all the diverse 'symbols', or even that 'The Truth is greater than the sum of all its apprehensions'? Is he laying claim to an non-symbolic, privileged access to the Transcendent: a vantage point from which he can now survey the whole world of religion and identify them as but historically and culturally conditioned responses to the same Transcendent? And how, one wonders, would such a vantage point itself escape the historical and cultural conditioning that Samartha argues is endemic to all human beliefs?

(c) Samartha's enthusiasm over *advaita Vedanta* and his attempt to develop a theology for pluralist India (and the world) within its philosophical framework plunges him into an awkward dilemma. As a Christian in the ecumenical movement, and influenced by the liberation theologies of recent years, he wants to identify with the suffering peoples of the Third World. Moreover, he wants to urge on people of all faiths and none the duty to struggle against every form of social evil in order to usher in a more egalitarian world. But this vision is at odds with mainstream, conservative Brahmanism, which is the custodian of the *advaita Vedanta* outlook. The latter has long been perceived by the tribal and 'dalit' peoples (those outside the caste system) of India as the chief ideological instrument of social and economic oppression. MM Thomas has shown that it was the promise of humanisation inherent in the gospel which led to the influx of such people into the Christian church. 'The outcastes, the poor and the orphans saw Christian faith as the source of a new humanising influence and the foundation of a human community. Where conversion was genuine, whether of individuals or of groups, the converts saw salvation in Christ not only in terms of individual salvation, of heaven after death, but also as the spiritual source of a new community on earth in which their human dignity and status were recognized.'[10]

In the light of these historical observations, Samartha needs to demonstrate more clearly than he does how an *advaita* framework for theologising can actually be socially liberating. If he rejects an 'either/or' mentality as being 'Western/Christian' (and therefore flawed!), he must demonstrate how his passionate concern for justice can be justified on a mentality that negates all particularities and refuses to make ultimate distinctions between good and evil, right and wrong. How does Samartha expect to motivate us to exercise a 'prophetico-critical' role in society when his theological framework does not permit us to make any objective, universally binding moral judgments? It is surely no accident that wherever Hinduism has become socially liberating, it was prompted either through its theistic *bhakti* traditions or, more frequently, as a result of exposure to the life and teaching of Jesus Christ through the Christian missionary movement.[11]

(d) Furthermore, the ancient Hindu tradition of religious and social tolerance that Samartha so eloquently celebrates is a far cry from what is meant by 'tolerance' in the modern world. Hindu tolerance is based on a hierarchical ordering of the world. You are born what you are, and that is right for you. If born a Muslim, remain a Muslim; if a dalit, remain a dalit. Your beliefs and behaviour, your gender and caste are appropriate to your station in the eternal round of *samsara* and karmic reincarnation. As Professor Richard Gombrich, the eminent student of Indian religion and culture, observes, 'This is a wonderful way to keep the peace in a diverse society, but at a tremendous cost to personal freedom . . . Everyone does their own thing, it is true, but 'their own thing' is not what they have chosen to do, but on the contrary what is prescribed by the category into which society puts them. The religious programme laid down for each person is a reflex of society's image of who he or she is.'[12]

Also, the Hindu—and, especially, the *advaita*—tendency to assimilate all other religious traditions and figures, thus stripping them of whatever uniqueness and innovative power they may possess, can hardly be taken as expressive of tolerance. For 'toleration' of another viewpoint implies both disagreement (even disapproval) of that viewpoint and a willingness to concede the right of the other to hold that viewpoint. My respect for another is tested only when there is a genuine clash of basic beliefs and values. A religion that *a priori* refuses to recognize fundamental disagreements, but labels every shade of opinion 'different aspects of the same thing', can hardly be called tolerant, for it simply refuses to respect the 'otherness' of the Other. This is demonstrated in Radhakrishnan's comment, footnoted approvingly by Samartha (CR, p. 190), that what the Buddha did was 'to democratise the lofty teachings of the Upanishads'. The Buddha, however, did no such thing. The Buddhist *anatta* doctrine is a denial of the Upanishadic teaching on the eternal, substantial self. The Buddha not only challenged the authority of the Brahmins and the sacrificial ritual, he also did away with Brahma as creator and undermined the entire caste-system which is at the heart of Vedic religion.[13] By reclaiming Buddhism (and later Christianity and Islam) as 'aspects' of the Hindu *Vedanta*, the adherents of the *advaita* school seem to display only arrogance, not tolerance. It is ironic to observe Samartha, who is so scornful of the 'anonymous Christian' brand of patronizing inclusivism, fawning before the Radhakrishnan–Gandhi brand of patronizing Hinduism.[14]

(e) It is obvious, then, that the kind of religious pluralism based on *advaita* and favoured by Samartha can be maintained only by radically reinterpreting the central beliefs of certain religions to mean something very different from what most adherents of those religions have believed historically and continue to believe today. Samartha evades the difficult issue of conflicting truth-claims between religious world views by employing two well-known theological moves. The first is to prohibit any judgment on one world view (or religious tradition) that is based on criteria and values drawn from another. This is assumed to be 'intolerant' and 'arrogant', hardly conducive to neighbourly relations. The second move is to reinterpret all factual claims made within a world view (or religious tradition) that appear to conflict with factual claims in other world views as non-factual, 'symbolic' expressions which point to a higher, ineffable truth. These become sources of 'values' which each tradition contributes to the common good.

The difficulty with the first proposal is that it comes dangerously close to endorsing cultural and moral relativism. Relativism moves beyond simple recognition of the obvious fact that people in different cultures and historical epochs have developed different values, viewpoints, political arrangements and so on, to assert that these can be criticized only from within their given context. In other words, what people value and believe is right for them: rightness is conformity. On this understanding, it would be improper for anyone living in Europe to condemn such practices as widow-burning and head-hunting or for a non-German to condemn the gassing of Jews by the Nazis. Likewise, we have no warrant to be critical of beliefs such as a geocentric solar system, or the controlling influence of the planets on our lives, or that women are fit only for child-bearing and motherhood, or that all illness is inflicted by malignant deities. One has only to give such examples to show how silly a thorough-going relativism can be. It also presupposes a naive view of cultures. To see cultures as sealed, self-sufficient units is to ignore the way they change over time and inter-penetrate each other. Ideas and values do meet and compete in people's heads, and somehow they make judgments among them. Thankfully not many philosophers or theologians are relativists in practice, whatever they may expound in the classroom. And Samartha is no exception. It is clear that he *does* make judgments of beliefs and practices that he does not share, and in advocating religious tolerance and socio-political justice he does so not because they happens to be values of his own culture, but because he thinks of them as universally applicable. I happen to agree. But I am inclined to think that Samartha has sacrificed consistency where his own theological position is concerned . . .

(f) Samartha's second ploy (that is, to avoid addressing the issue of conflicting truth–claims among the world faiths) is to shear off any cognitive content from the notion of 'faith' and to treat all religious doctrine as 'only symbolic' pointers (e.g. OCMR, p. 96) to the infinite depths of ultimate Mystery. It is mystical intuition and aesthetic experience that convey knowledge of Mystery.

Samartha speaks of faith reaching 'beyond human beliefs' and 'providing criteria and courage to be critical of ideological distortions of religion'. (OCMR, p. 53). But how does a faith that is conceived of as a disposition towards Mystery that lacks any informational content help human beings to identify what is true and false in the world of religion? Similarly, how does this Mystery which is not susceptible of linguistic predication become for a pluralist society 'the fountainhead of all values and the criterion to judge all human efforts in history' (p. 175)? We can recognize distortion in a particular religious (or indeed secular) perspective only if we have a reliable cognitive guide to reality. Of course all language about ultimate Mystery/Reality is subject to limitation, but how can we tell if some are more limited or distorted than others *unless we have a reliable linguistic self-disclosure of that Mystery/Reality?*

Moreover, values are not free-floating entities, but are always located in particular historical narratives which give their followers a sense of meaning and orientation in the world. Different narratives engender different sets of values, and Samartha has done little to show that the values of all the major religions are essentially the same—or, if they are not, how to deal with conflicting values. On what grounds are the religious values of the Bharatha Janatha Party in India or of the Moral Majority in the USA ruled out of court? They are both movements based on a strong 'transcendent centre' and are equally critical of corruption and materialism in society. (Indeed the irony of the BJP case is that most of the leaders subscribe to an *advaita Vedanta* worldview!)

The social anthropologist Clifford Geertz has characterized the religious way of looking at the world as 'the conviction that the values one holds are grounded in the inherent structure of reality, that between the way one ought to live and the way things really are there is an unbreakable inner connection.'[15] In other words, a religious person's 'programme for human conduct' will reflect their understanding of the world's construction. If Buddhists disengage themselves from material and personal attachments, it is because they believe that such attachments will only bind one further to the illusion that objects and persons are permanent. The world is flux and transience, and failure to perceive this is at the root of all suffering. The Buddhist ethic springs from a nexus of beliefs that comprise a Buddhist worldview. Likewise a traditional Hindu will believe that it is the nature of men born into the warrior caste to make war; therefore it is clearly their duty (*dharma*) to make war when opportunity arises. Even in modern secular societies this sense of an underlying order or 'nature' is not entirely lost. When we object to baby-bashing or the sexual abuse of children by parents as 'unnatural' we mean that it goes against our conception of the nature of parents. Differences between values are inextricably linked with different understandings of the human situation and the nature of reality.

This is why Samartha's indifference to matters of religious doctrine seems more likely to be the product of post-Enlightenment secular consciousness than of a heightened religious sensibility. Even in the Indian religious traditions, salvation/enlightenment is bound up with right belief. A correct diagnosis of the human predicament (whether, as in *advaita Vedanta*, the latter consists in forgetfulness of the soul's ontological unity with Brahman; or, as in Zen Buddhism, the discriminating and objectifying tendency of our ego-centredness; and so on) is taken to be a *sine qua non* for human salvation/enlightenment. All religions make assertions about the actual nature of reality. Evocative, even mythological, language about the Transcendent[16] derive their currency from underlying descriptive assertions—for whether or not a form of human behaviour (e.g. freeing slaves, going on pilgrimage, corporate confession of sin, killing idolators, chanting a *mantra*) is an appropriate response to the Transcendent will depend on whether or not we have been able to make true assertions about the nature of the Transcendent and our relationship to It/Him.

Samartha has always evaded the issue of the truth-value of fundamental religious beliefs out of a concern not to cause offence in inter-faith dialogue. When challenged he has replied, 'The question of truth is indeed important, but God's love is even more important . . . Love takes precedence over truth.'[17] But this is confused and confusing. Samartha's confidence in God's love would be challenged by atheists and adherents of nontheistic faiths, for it assumes *the truth* of several propositions: that a personal God exists, that God's disposition towards his creatures is one of love, and that he expects us to love one another. To wrench love out of the context of truth is to turn it into something else. Samartha has implicitly taken his stand on the very definite cognitive content of one specific, culture-conditioned 'response to Mystery': namely, Christianity. Moreover the latter has within its understanding of loving one's neighbour a sense of responsibility to share the truth of God's love, made incarnate in the life and atoning death of Jesus of Nazareth, so that he or she may participate with us in that love. It is hardly an act of love wilfully to keep others in error.

(g) Samartha appears to hold a naive view of the relation between experience and doctrine. The latter is depicted as secondary and dispensable, the cause of unnecessary divisiveness. He fails to see that religious experience does not happen 'out of the blue' but is aroused by religious expectations which are, in turn, formed by the doctrines, language and practices of a specific religious tradition embodied in a historical community. All experience, from sensory perception to the most profound mysticism, is not only interpreted but also constituted in part by the conceptual apparatus which we bring to that experience.[18]

So, for example, those who attain an awareness of oneness of *atman* with *Brahman* and experience *moksha* will have spent years meditating on the sacred vedic texts and practising yoga under the guidance of a guru who has himself been trained in the *advaita* school. If one performs *zazen*, or sitting meditation, under the tutelage of a Zen *roshi*, soaking oneself in the Zen ethos, one may succeed in suspending the ego-centred discriminating activity of the mind and 'see' the Ultimate in the flow of the world-process. As the philosopher Steven Katz argues, 'The Buddhist experience of nirvana, the Jewish of *devekuth*, and the Christian of *unio mystica*, the Sufi of *fana*, the Taoist of *Tao* are the *result*, at least in part, of specific conceptual influences, i.e the 'starting problems' of each doctrinal, theological system.'[19]

Similarly Wayne Proudfoot points out that 'Jewish and Buddhist mystics bring entirely different doctrinal commitments, expectations, and rules for identifying their mental and bodily states to their experiences, and thus *devekuth* and *nirvana* cannot be the same. It might indeed be possible to produce cross-cultural documentation of some common physiological states or mental images in the experience of mystics. But to focus on these, as some theorists have done, is not to delineate a core but to attend to something other than the experience. A decelerated heart rate may be common to some mystics and to all athletes at the height of training, and it may be a natural endowment of some individuals in contrast to others . . . But to attend to such phenomena while disregarding the content of the mystic's beliefs and the expectations he or she brings to the experience is to err in one's priorities. What others have dismissed as interpretative overlay may be the distinguishing mark of the experience.'[20]

Another difficulty concerning Samartha's model has to do with the insistence in at least one strand of the Christian tradition that doctrine serves not only to express and evoke human experience, but may, on occasion, challenge and *correct* it. Martin Luther's celebrated 'theology of the cross' provides an outstanding example.[21] For Luther, the scene of dereliction at the cross is the normative paradigm for the Christian understanding of God and the world. The immediate judgment of human experience on the scene of shame, defeat and hopelessness presented to it in the crucifixion is that God is absent. This verdict is contradicted, however, by the Word of the gospel which announces that where God appeared to be most absent, God was most fully present, but in a manner hidden to the powers of this age: *deus crucifixus et absconditus*. Experience alone cannot serve as the foundation for theological affirmations about the character and purpose of God in his dealings with us. Its inadequacy is exposed by the theology of the cross.

The Christian epistemological approach, therefore, combines the cognitive with the experiential as a response to a revelation from God that is both propositional and self-involving. The relevant biblical dichotomy to be drawn is not between experience and belief, or the real and appearances of the real, but rather between the partial and the whole: 'We know in part, then we shall know fully, even as we are fully known' (1 Cor. 13:12). Truth is always truth 'on the way', something we grow into, that beckons us forward. But it is only because we have been enabled to know *truly*, even if only partially, that we can recognize the direction in which that final vision of truth is to be found.

Pluralists such as Samartha seem to assume that we can start searching for truth wherever we are and in whatever direction we choose. But if truth is something which is discovered, rather than constructed out of our human resources, then our searching must begin with a 'clue'; otherwise we have no way of telling whether or not we are simply walking round in circles that we have fashioned ourselves. The gospel confronts head-on the religious assumption that that clue is to be found by extracting some common mystical 'core' from the 'religious experience of mankind'. It announces, instead, that that clue has been given in the contingency of historical event, namely in the life, death and resurrection of Jesus of Nazareth: given by him who is the Source and Goal of all history to guide all humanity out of its alienation and death into the fullness of life. This announcement has been scandalous and offensive, from its very inception. It is in the ongoing interaction of that message and its messengers with the various cultures of the world that the journey into truth takes shape. That journey and its destination cannot be specified in advance. To argue, as does Samartha, that the interaction between the gospel and the cultures of the world must *a priori* be non-offensive and non-scandalous is not only to turn the gospel into something unrecognizably different, but to predetermine that journey oneself. Here once again human arrogance is being presented as humility. We shall explore this epistemology in more detail in subsequent chapters.

(h) Samartha's handling of the New Testament offers an interesting insight into his agenda. On the one hand, he wants to be seen as an essentially orthodox Christian who is seeking to return to the apostolic testimonies in Scripture in order to liberate the 'historic Jesus' from centuries of credal obfuscation and pious sentimentalism. He is convinced that this historic Jesus is a simple, uncomplicated figure who can be confessed by Christians without upsetting the adherents of other religious faiths. In this he is clearly influenced by what came to be called in the 1950s & '60s 'The New Quest for the Historical Jesus', a movement associated with former students of Rudolf Bultmann who did not share their master's existentialist disdain for historical inquiry.[22] This movement has since run out of steam. On the other hand, he approaches the biblical text with the pre-understanding that 'The being or the truth of Jesus behind the testimonies is larger, deeper and more mysterious than any portrait that may be painted by the brushes of scholarly study. Therefore the being or the truth of Jesus must remain the controlling factor in interpreting the testimonies of writers.' (OCMR, p. 131). This naturally provokes our curiosity to know how Samartha enjoys access to the 'being or truth of Jesus' independently of the apostolic witness, but this is nowhere addressed. A brief aside to the effect that perhaps the *advaita* framework of Hinduism, with its emphasis on the 'unknow-ability, unthinkability and the inexhaustibility off *Sat* which is both *Truth and Being*' (OCMR, p. 160), may help, doesn't actually get us very far.

Samartha's hermeneutical method shares many of the weaknesses of Bultmann's, although the latter's concerns were, of course, very different. Bultmann embarked on his well-known programme of *de-mythologizing* the biblical material because he believed that the texts invited such *de-mythologization*. Bultmann was neither clear nor consistent in what he meant by the term 'myth', but it is generally held by commentators that what he meant was not primarily the use of imagery in describing the transcendent, but rather language that appears to portray 'objective' events, such as the atonement and the resurrection of Jesus, but is actually meant to function existentially or self-involvingly. The intention of the biblical writers, Bultmann claimed, was not to describe objective events. The form of the language disguises its function. Language about divine judgment, for instance, is simply an invitation to cultivate an attitude of human responsibility. To believe in the cross of Christ is 'not to concern ourselves with a mythical process wrought outside of us and our world, with an objective event . . . but rather to make the cross of Christ our own, to undergo crucifixion with him.'[23]

The effect on christology was disastrous. In his lecture of 1951 concerning the christological confession of the World Council of Churches Bultmann asks the question: does Jesus help me because he is the Son of God, or is he the Son of God because he helps me? For Bultmann a de-mythologized christology must be expressed purely soteriologically. The New Testament offers a christology *only* in terms of Christ's significance 'for *me*.'

In a penetrating analysis of Bultmann's hermeneutic, Anthony Thiselton[24] points out that not only was Bultmann influenced by a neo-Kantian framework which associated objective description with conceptual thought-construction (and which, therefore, in turn-of-the century Lutheran pietism came to be seen as human 'works' as opposed to 'faith'), but he was also trapped by a Kierkegaardian either/or between descriptive and self-involving utterances. He did not adequately appreciate the multi-functional nature of language. This was the age of the Vienna Circle and Logical Positivism, and of sharp polarizations in literary theory between fact-stating language and the expressive language of poetry and metaphor. Later theories of metaphor, such as that by Max Black, saw that cognitive truth could not always be disentangled from metaphor, and the 'vehicle' discarded as separable from the 'tenor'.[25] In recent theory (sometimes called post-Wittgensteinian or post-Gadamerian) language is not a husk that can be peeled off its content. For Wittgenstein, concepts are patterned *uses* of language, they reflect regularities of linguistic behaviour. 'Thinking is not an incorporeal process . . . which it would be possible to detach from speaking' as if one may detach a person's shadow from the person herself.[26]

Bultmann's positing of an either/or (rather than a both/and) when it comes to the self-involving functions of language and the language of assertion (that certain states of affairs obtain in the real world) is in some ways similar to Samartha's approach to the New Testament text. This is all the more ironic in the latter case, given Samartha's earlier scornful dismissal of either/or thinking as 'Western' and inapplicable to religious discourse. Consider, as examples, his insistence that christocentric thinking in the epistles of Paul is a contradiction of the theocentric preaching of Jesus; or that since there is no text that says explicitly that 'Jesus was God' we have to conclude that he was only a man; or that language that is intended to evoke or express devotion and commitment ('the language of love') cannot be read as asserting objective truths; or that the cross-resurrection event is to be understood *only* as 'inspiration' for the poor in the struggle against oppression.

Utilizing the 'speech-act' theory of philosophers such as JL Austin and John Searle, Thiselton points out that for certain linguistic utterances to effectively involve people and perform acts they must presuppose that certain statements are *true*. For instance, if we were to consider the earliest pre-Pauline Christian confession 'Jesus is Lord', Thiselton writes: 'To ascribe "lordship" to someone who cannot rightfully exercise it, is from the linguistic viewpoint *empty* or logically arbitrary and from the theological viewpoint *idolatrous*. The words 'Jesus is Lord' express both factual or institutional truth *and* self-involvement.'[27] At the self-involving level, the *kyrios* texts in Paul and other parts of the New Testament invite trust, obedience, surrender and devotion. They are not simply flat descriptions of abstract doctrinal truths. But at the level of their truth-claims about what is the case, the texts also speak of God instituting or exalting Christ as Lord. This aspect would remain true whether human readers acknowledged it or not; but its hermeneutical efficacy would be seen most clearly when such acknowledgement is made.

Thiselton argues persuasively that the identity of Jesus as Lord not only brings together these two distinct but related logical functions, but also provides a unifying focus within a variety of New Testament texts, especially linking the Pauline texts with material in the Synoptic Gospels: 'The basis on which Jesus invites trust and obedience arises *both* from God's exaltation and vindication of his work in the event of his resurrection *and* from his identity and character, disclosed in the words and deeds of his earthly ministry.'[28] Further discussion on the significance of the ministry of Jesus and a refutation of Samartha's claim that the reticence of the evangelists in making explicit statements about the christological status of Jesus count as evidence against Pauline, let alone Chalcedonian, Christianity, will be found in chapter six of the present book.

Finally, Samartha's hermeneutic seems to be trapped in a vicious circularity. Since he is reading with the agenda of religious harmony in mind, any textual interpretation that is likely to cause offence to the religious sensibilities of non-Christian neighbours is ruled out of court. This also leads to a highly selective use of texts when it comes to making christological assertions. Moreover, and this is where the viciousness of his hermeneutical circle becomes apparent,

there is no way the text can serve to challenge his presuppositions and call into question the legitimacy of his
agenda. The Scriptures no longer startle, disturb, expose.
They have been domesticated. Another way of putting this
would be in the form of a question: what biblical evidence
would count as an invalidation (or falsification) of Samartha's
christological assertions and general theological outlook?

(i) Samartha's assertion, presumably in defence of his own
'revised Christology' that 'within the New Testament itself
people felt free to develop different Christologies' (OCMR,
p. 131) is a half-truth, and, like others of its kind, dangerously misleading. Of course different christologies are to be
expected as the gospel interacts with different human contexts. Indeed, the variety of christologies to be found in the
New Testament is itself a consequence of the missionary
nature of the church since its inception. But the unity of the
New Testament lies in the fact that it contains, not any and
every christology, but only those recognized to be consistent
with the original testimony. For, in the absence of any
historical controls, how do we know when the Christian
tradition has ceased to be Christian, and has been turned into
something else? Samartha gives the impression that the early
church encouraged a theological free-for-all, so that any and
every christology has the right to be called Christian.

The idea that any and every christology was acceptable
within the Christian movement does not stand up to careful
scrutiny. The identity of the human person Jesus with the
resurrected and exalted Christ/Lord is presupposed throughout the New Testament, providing strict limits on the extent
of theological diversity. In his massive survey and (by no
means conservative) assessment of theological diversity in
the early church, James Dunn puts the matter thus: 'Already
within the New Testament writings themselves the limits of
acceptable Jewish Christianity and Hellenistic Christianity
were being firmly drawn . . . diversity which abandons the
unity of the faith in Jesus the man now exalted is unacceptable;
diversity which abandons the unity of love for fellow
believers is unacceptable. In other words, where the conviction
had been abandoned that worship of God was determined by
Jesus of Nazareth and his resurrection, was now 'through'
Jesus, then diversity had gone too far; or where the conviction
had been abandoned that the one encountered in worship
now was not really fully one with, continuous with, Jesus

the man, then diversity had gone too far . . . *the centre also determined the circumference.*'[29]

In a recent essay on the biblical view of human destiny, the New Testament scholar Ben Meyer has complained that what is 'conspicuously absent' from the views of scholars writing on unity and diversity in the early Christian movement is 'solid evidence supporting *not diversity, but division*'.[30] Division is incompatible with unity; diversity is not. The true opposites are unity and division, uniformity and diversity. Meyer observes that 'Every New Testament writer asserts or betrays a certain recoil from division, but unity without diversity would have been impossible and all early Christian writers seem to know this'.[31] Wherever disputes arose, none of them was left unsettled. Citing Paul's claim in 1 Cor. 15:1–11, which concludes with the words, 'So, be it I or they [other missionaries], it is in these terms that we proclaim the gospel and it was in these terms that you accepted it in faith' (v.11), Meyer argues (in the context of Jesus' resurrection and the hope arising from that belief) that 'a common confession and conviction in faith respecting human destiny was a datum of early Christianity'.[32]

Tom Wright, another renowned New Testament scholar, has warned against the subtle snare of assuming that, because the early church was by no means a uniform and 'pure' community and to be imitated as such, it was 'an early version of the ecumenical movement, and to be imitated as such'![33] Wright points out that, for a start, 'all early Christianity was Jewish Christianity. All early missionary work among Gentiles was undertaken by Jewish Christians . . . Every single document in the New Testament is in some sense 'Jewish Christian' . . . 'Gentile Christianity' is in one sense *part* of 'Jewish Christianity', since it derives its origin, its scriptures, its form of Church organization, its sacraments, even the God in whom it believed, from Jewish Christianity'.[34] What is surprising is not the various forms the Christian movement took during the first century, but how remarkably well it held together, given its rapid cross-cultural and geographical expansion. Wright quotes approvingly Martin Hengel's comment: 'For all the multiplicity brought about by the work of the Spirit, I would still see earliest Christianity as an intrinsically connected and in essentials quite amazingly coherent movement . . . Anyone who wants to reduce earliest Christianity to often quite different and indeed unconnected 'lines of development' can no longer explain why the Church in the second century remained a unity despite all the deviations . . . In their view the Church should have fallen apart into countless groups.'[35]

That the identity of the church has always hinged on the uniqueness it recognizes in Jesus was succinctly expressed over seventy years ago by Edwyn Bevan in a book entitled *Hellenism and Christianity*. Bevan wrote: 'The great dividing line is that which marks off all those who hold that the relation of Jesus to God—however they describe or formulate it—is of such a kind that it could not be repeated in any *other* individual—that to speak, in fact, of its being repeated in one other individual is a contradiction in terms, since any individual standing in that relation to God would *be* Jesus, and that Jesus, in virtue of this relation, has the same absolute claim upon all men's worship and loyalty as belongs to God. A persuasion of this sort of uniqueness attaching to Jesus seems to me the essential characteristic of what has actually in the field of human history been Christianity'.[36]

It is noteworthy that Samartha evades the central question of what it was about Jesus of Nazareth that made his *Jewish* followers come to worship him, and to refer to him in the same breath as they did the God of their fathers. Perhaps one needs to live in a monotheistic culture (e.g. Islamic) to appreciate the significance of the fact that all the earliest Christians were Jews, and that it was within the distinctively monotheistic framework of a Jewish milieu that the New Testament witness to the divinity of Jesus took place.[37] This witness is not confined to a few texts that explicitly ascribe God-language to Jesus. The evidence exists in an untidy profusion that makes systematic presentation difficult; but they include the application of Old Testament texts about God to the person and ministry of Jesus, the attribution to Jesus of divine functions and attributes, prayer and supplication addressed to Jesus, and formal worship of him. Given the monotheistic context, it is little wonder that the explicit attribution of full deity to Jesus[38] came slowly and perhaps reluctantly, not as a carefully formulated doctrine, but as the gradual awareness of the more-than-human nature of Jesus took shape in the community's life and worship. The wonder is that it happened at all.

The failure to pay attention to the social and religious context of apostolic preaching also explains Samartha's

otherwise strange remark that though the word of the cross
may have been folly to Greeks and a 'scandal' to the Jews, it
is not so in India and other Asian countries. He mentions
Gandhi as an example for whom the cross of Jesus was an
inspiration to non-violent resistance to oppression. But the
word of the cross in the early church did not present Jesus as
a mere human example of non-violent resistance. No misunderstanding, ridicule or hatred would have been provoked
if it had. It is precisely because the apostolic word of the
cross involved far more than ethical exhortation that Gandhi
objected to it and read into the cross his own private
meaning. Such a truncated cross can take its place alongside
other symbols of social protest in the Asian cultural milleu
and thus offend no one.

   (j) It is ironic that Samartha should dismiss evangelical
Christianity as a 'Western import' to Asia, yet be blissfully
unaware of how much his own reading of the New Testament and his view of religious language have been shaped by
the positivist influences on the liberal Western scholars from
whose writings he quotes. Even the idea of a secular state,
which he espouses so passionately, is foreign to Indian soil.
To hail everything that is Asian as 'contextual' and everything Western as flawed or irrelevant not only leads to
inconsistency in practice, but also shows selective blindness
and remarkable historical naivete. We shall see, in later
sections of this book, how indebted the pluralist programme
is to philosophical and theological presuppositions inherited
from post-Enlightenment Western culture.

   Neither Samartha's tolerant pluralism nor his disdain
towards either/or ways of thinking hinder him from scornful
tirades against evangelicals and 'dogmatic' Roman Catholics.
He tends to caricature all opinions other than the pluralism
he espouses. The only alternative to pluralism is to believe
that '*only* in Jesus Christ God has revealed God's self'
(OCMR, p. 135) and that 'just one religion has the only
answer to all the problems of human life at all times and for
all peoples and in all cultures' (p. 53). In a remarkable piece
of either/or thinking, he argues that stressing the once-for-
allness of salvation in Christ must lead to a 'total rejection of
the religious beliefs and convictions of neighbours of other
faiths' (p. 109)! But I know of no evangelical or Roman
Catholic theologian who has drawn this conclusion from his
or her convictions about the uniqueness of Jesus Christ and

his saving work. Sensitive listening and empathy are to be extended to the *oikoumene* of other faiths, but not, apparently, to the *oikoumene* of Christian faith!

Samartha's designation of Christianity as 'a Western religion' fails to honour the massive and significant southwards shift of the church in the second half of the twentieth century. And equally one-sided is his reading of the Western missionary enterprise as an exercise in cultural and political imperialism. It is far more refreshing to read the sober assessments of recent African theological scholarship on these issues. The Ghanian theologian Kwame Bediako, for example, points out that 'new centres of Christianity's universality' have emerged 'wherever the faith has been transmitted and assimilated', and that by bringing about the 'crumbling of the final vestiges of the notion of a territorial Christianity, namely, Western Christendom', the 'missionary movement has accomplished a feat comparable to St. Paul's, even though it may not always have used . . . the methods of St. Paul'.[39]

Bediako also observes that the phenomenon of African Christianity in the late twentieth century, far from indicating the massive Westernization of African life, may rather be 'the evidence of how much African people feel at home in the Gospel of Jesus Christ', a feeling made possible by the rendering of the Bible into the vernacular from the earliest days of Protestant missions.[40] Similarly, the eminent Gambian scholar Lamin Sanneh has cogently and persistently argued that

> In some of the most significant instances, Africans came to their sense of cultural and national self-awareness through the grammars, dictionaries, and the vernacular literacy of Christian missions. The missionary contribution of outsiders to the modern awakening of Africa has few parallels, and should stand as a monument to the scaling down of cross-cultural barriers.

He continues,

> We should give praise and honour to God that he raised in the Western church servants of his cause in Africa and elsewhere.[41]

(k) The theological programme that Samartha advocates for the church in Asia resembles the challenge of the gnostic sects in the second and third centuries CE. They argued that the great gulf between the invisible, spiritual realm of divine being and the visible, material realm of physical being could be bridged only by a series of divine 'emanations', that truth was not to be found in the contingencies of historical event but in mystical illumination vouchsafed to religious *virtuosi*, that the latter alone possessed the secret of the divine Mystery, leading them to go 'beyond' the Jesus Christ given in the New Testament so as to participate directly in the 'fullness' of divine being. The analogies with Samartha's scheme are not trivial. They will be taken up again after a fuller discussion of Gnosticism in chapter seven.

Finally, if, as Samartha holds, Jesus Christ is not God incarnate, if he is not the final and normative revelation of God and the culmination of God's saving work for humanity, if he is not the reigning Lord and coming Judge of the world, then we have to conclude that the Christian church down the centuries has completely misunderstood him, exaggerated his importance and inflated his claims. Whether through wilful distortion or ignorant fanaticism, they were wrong. And Christians who continue to put Jesus at the centre of life and worship, who give him the honour due to God alone, as indeed the church has been doing for two millenia, are simply self-deluded. If Samartha is right in his christology, then we are logically forced to admit that the Jewish and Muslim denunciation of Christians is perfectly justified. We are the greatest blasphemers the world has ever seen! For no matter how wonderful a person he may have been, and however God may have beeen actively present through him, if Jesus was not more than human, the Christian church has lived a lie. Its creeds and practices have been based on falsehood. It has elevated a mere human being to the level of God and worshipped him. We are guilty of the most monstrous idolatry.

Far from acknowledging this inescapable conclusion, Samartha affirms that it is perfectly valid and helpful for Christians to continue to recite the creeds and to use traditional liturgies that involve praying and singing hymns of praise to Jesus, provided of course that we do not bring this language into our dialogue with our neighbours! The reason he can perform what to ordinary minds appears an intellectual somersault is that, as we have seen, he works with a naive conception of the meaning of metaphor and symbolism in religious language. But the religious elitism implicit in this view is plain. Samartha and his fellow pluralists are 'in the know'. The rest of the church has been misguided for two thousand years in its central affirmations about God, Jesus and salvation. Ordinary believers can continue to be Christians provided they don't take traditional Christian language as asserting facts about reality. But this is not simply an invitation to a schizophrenic existence. It seems ultimately to enthrone hypocrisy as the most distinctive contribution that a Christian today can bring to the 'pool of values' required by the modern world.

Notes to Chapter One

1. SJ Samartha, 'The Cross and the Rainbow' in John Hick and Paul Knitter (eds.), *The Myth of Christian Uniqueness* (London: SCM, 1988) p. 72. This will be abbreviated in the text as CR.

2. SJ Samartha, *One Christ—Many Religions: toward a Revised Christology* (Maryknoll, NY: Orbis, 1991; Indian edn. Bangalore: SATHRI, 1992). All page numbers quoted in the text of this chapter refer to this book in its Indian edition. The book includes Samartha's contributions to international journals and symposia in the 1980s. It is abbreviated in the text as OCMR.

3. The classic Brahmanic text reads: 'They call it Indra, Mitra, Varuna and Agni/ And also heavenly, beautiful Garutman/ The Real is one, though sages name it variously.' (*Rig Veda*, I,164:46). In the *Bhagavad Gita*, Krishna says, 'Whatever form any devotee wishes to worship, I make that faith of his steady' (VII:21); also, 'in whatever way persons approach Me, in the same way do I accept them' (IV:11). A similar 'pluralism' is found in the 13th-century Muslim mystic, Jalalu'l-Din Rumi, 'The lamps are different, but the Light is the same.' (see RA Nicholson, *Rumi: Poet and Mystic*, 1950, London: George Allen & Unwin, 1978).

4. Cf. Cantwell Smith's well-known distinction between the external 'cumulative tradition' of religious communities and the internal faith of the religious believer (*The Meaning and End of Religion*, New York: New American Library, 1964): 'By 'cumulative tradition' I mean the entire mass of overt objective data that constitute the historical deposit, as it were, of the past religious life of the community in question' (p. 141), while faith 'is not an entity. It is rather the adjectival quantity of a person's living in terms of transcendence.' (p. 342).

5. Here again, some affinities with Cantwell Smith are to be observed: e.g. 'In all ultimate matters, truth lies not in an either–or but in a both–and', WC Smith, *The Faith of Other Men*, (New York: Mentor, 1965). Similarly the late John Robinson argued for a 'dipolar', 'two-eyed' approach which transcends the narrowness of an exclusive,

either-or perspective and embraces the visions of the religious ultimate as both nonpersonal (as in advaita Hinduism) and personal (Semitic faiths): 'Truth may come from refusing this either-or and accepting that the best working model of reality may be elliptical or bi-polar, or indeed multi-polar', JAT Robinson, *Truth is Two-Eyed* (Philadelphia: Westminster, 1979) p. 22.

6. D Cupitt, *The Debate About Christ* (London: SCM, 1979) pp. 138–9.
7. For Samartha, John 1:1 is incorrectly translated in English Bibles. Like Jehovah's Witnesses, he claims that *theos* with the article is to be translated as God, but that *theos* without the article should be translated 'divine'. It seems to have escaped Samartha's attention that there is a perfectly good Greek word for 'divine' which the evangelist could have used.
8. A brief discussion of Hick's own influential views will be found in Chapter 4. Other resemblances to Hick are seen in Samartha's occasional references to being transformed from 'self-centredness to God-centredness', his emphasis on 'theocentrism' as opposed to 'christocentrism', and the view that the historical and geographical accidents of human birth constitute a barrier to accepting any notion of 'special' revelation in history (see e.g. OCMR, p. 116).
9. See Gottlob Frege, 'On Sense and meaning', in *Collected Papers on Mathematics, Logic and Philosophy*, ed. Brian MacGuiness (Oxford, 1984) p. 157ff. Frege's term *sinn* is usually rendered in English as 'sense' and *bedeutung* as 'referent'.
10. MM Thomas, *Salvation and Humanization* (Madras: CLS, 1971) p. 14.
11. See, e.g., MM Thomas, *The Acknowledged Christ of the Indian Renaissance* (Madras: CLS, 1970).
12. R Gombrich, 'Reflections of an Indologist' in *Religious Pluralism and Unbelief: Studies Critical and Comparative*, ed. Ian Hamnett (London: Routledge, 1990) p. 256, 257.
13. For the importance of understanding early Buddhism as a reaction to and rejection of Brahmanical ideas and practices, see Steven Collins, *Selfless Persons:Imagery and Thought in Theravada Buddhism* (Cambridge: Cambridge University Press, 1982).
14. The ironies abound. The writings of both the *neo-Vedantins* (e.g. Vivekananda, Radhakrishnan) and Gandhi are replete with examples of 'theological violence' towards the fundamental concepts of other faiths. And what better example of 'dogmatism' and 'arrogance' is there than Radhakrishnan's ranking system for world religions, with advaitic mysticism as the crown: 'The worshippers of the Absolute are highest in rank, second to them are the worshippers of the personal God; then come the worshippers of incarnations like Rama, Krishna, Buddha; below them are those who worship ancestors, deities and sages; and lowest of all the worshippers of the petty forces and spirits.' (*The Hindu View of Life*, New York: Macmillan, 1969 [1927], p. 24).
15. Clifford Geertz, *Islam Observed* (Chicago:Chicago University Press, 1971) p. 97.

16. Samartha tends to be indiscriminate in his use of the adjectives 'symbolic', 'metaphorical', and 'mythological', and doesn't attempt to define anywhere what he means by them. I have assumed that his understanding of 'myth' is the same as that of Hick.
17. S Samartha, 'Reply', in *Christ's Lordship and Religious Pluralism*, ed. GH Anderson and TF Stransky (Maryknoll, NY: Orbis, 1981) pp. 54–5.
18. Here Samartha's account of faith and experience is less sophisticated, philosophically, than that of John Hick (for which see Ch.4).
19. Steven Katz, 'Language, Epistemology and Mysticism' in *Mysticism and Philosophical Analysis*, ed. S Katz (New York: Oxford University Press, 1978) p. 62 (italics in text).
20. Wayne Proudfoot, *Religious Experience* (University of California Press,1985) p. 121. Proudfoot argues, contrary to Katz, that the connection between the mystic's antecedent beliefs and his experience is not a causal one but a conceptual one. But since the relevant conceptual connection includes a judgment about causes, the difference is not perhaps significant.
    Proudfoot makes an important distinction between two different kinds of 'reduction' in philosophy of religion. *Descriptive reduction* is 'the failure to identify an emotion, practice, or experience under the description by which the subject identifies it. This is indeed unacceptable. To describe an experience in nonreligious terms when the subject himself describes it in religious terms is to misidentify the experience, or to attend to another experience altogether.' (p. 196) This kind of reductionism precludes an accurate identification of the subject's experience. On the other hand, *explanatory reduction* consists in 'offering an explanation of an experience in terms that are not those of the subject and that might not meet with his approval. This is perfectly justifiable . . . The terms of the explanation need not be familiar or acceptable to the subject.' (p. 197). This explanation stands or falls according to how well it can account for all the available evidence. An experience or an event can be explained only when it is identified under a description. For Proudfoot, the distinguishing mark of religious experience is the subject's belief that the experience can be accounted for only in religious terms: 'It is this belief, and the subject's identification of his or her experience under a particular description, which makes it religious.' (p. 223) Where Proudfoot's naturalist/secularist world-view comes to the fore is in his claim that what constitutes a valid explanation of this religious identification is a 'historical and cultural' model. Perhaps this should be included as a third—and unwarranted—form of reductionism.
21. I owe this example to Alister McGrath, *The Genesis of Doctrine* (Oxford: Blackwell, 1990) p. 72.
22. There has been much discussion, of course, regarding in what sense, if any, this represented a 'new' quest. See e.g. Stephen Neil & Tom Wright, *The Interpretation of the New Testament, 1861–1986* (Oxford: Oxford University Press, 1988²) pp. 288ff.

36   *The Recovery of Mission*

23. R Bultmann, 'New Testament and Mythology' in H–W Bartsch (ed) *Kerygma and Myth* (ET, London: SPCK, 1964) Vol.1, p. 36.

24. AC Thiselton, *The Two Horizons* (Exeter: Paternoster Press, 1980) p. 205–92.

25. 'Vehicle' and 'tenor' are technical terms coined by IA Richards in his formulation of a theory of metaphor, *Philosophy of Rhetoric*, (OUP, 1936). They correspond roughly to Bultmann's notion of linguistic 'form' or *myth* and his notion of *kerygma* respectively. Samartha tends to use 'symbolic' in a parallel way to Bultmann's form or myth. For a useful survey of theories of metaphor and an incisive critique of the view that metaphorical language is not truth-expressing see Janet Martin Soskice, *Metaphor and Religious Language* (Oxford: Clarendon Press, 1985) Chs. 3 & 5.

26. L Wittgenstein, *Philosophical Investigations* (1936–1949) (Oxford: Blackwell, 3rd ed.1967) sect.339.

27. AC Thiselton, *New Horizons in Hermeneutics* (Zondervan and HarperCollins, 1992) p. 284 (Italics in text).

28. Ibid. p. 285.

29. JDG Dunn, *Unity and Diversity in the New Testament* (SCM/Trinity Press, 2nd ed.1990) pp. 378–9 (Italics in text). Interestingly Dunn continues, '*It is not possible to hold to Jesus as the centre without also holding to the New Testament witness to the centre* . . . If we do not recognize Jesus and the character of Christian faith here, then we have no standard or definition, no criterion by which to recognize Jesus and the character of Christianity anywhere.' (pp. 382–3, italics in text).

30. BF Meyer, 'Resurrection as Humanly Intelligible Destiny', *Ex Auditu*, 1993, p. 14 (Italics in text).

31. Ibid.

32. Ibid. p. 15.

33. NT Wright, *The New Testament and the People of God* (London: SPCK, 1992) p. 452.

34. Ibid. pp. 453, 454.

35. M Hengel, *Between Jesus and Paul: Studies in the Earliest History of Christianity* (trans. J Bowden, London: SCM, 1983) p. xi, quoted in Ibid. p. 456 (note 51).

36. E Bevan, *Hellenism and Christianity* (London: George Allen & Unwin, 1921) p. 271.

37. For the monotheism of Second Temple Judaism, see e.g. Wright, op.cit., pp. 248–259. For the worship of Jesus and its significance for the development of Christology, see e.g. LW Hurtado, *One God, One Lord: Early Christian Devotion and Ancient Jewish Monotheism* (Philadelphia: Fortress, 1988), and R Bauckham, 'The Worship of Jesus in Apocalyptic Christianity', *New Testament Studies*, 1981, 27: 322–341.

38. Such as in John 1:1,18; 20:28; Heb. 1:8; Acts 20:28; Rom. 9:5; 2 Thess. 1:12; Titus 2:13; Heb. 1:8; 2 Peter 1:1; 1 John 5:20. As is well-known, most of these verses contain uncertainties of syntax and textual variations, thus making it difficult to claim in any single case that Jesus is explicitly referred to as God. But the argument is a

cumulative one. Also, early Christian praxis is as significant for our understanding of attitudes to Jesus as are specifically christological passages. As Richard Bauckham reminds us, 'In the extreme monotheism of the Jewish religious tradition, as distinct from some other kinds of monotheism, it was *worship* which was the real test of monotheistic faith in religious practice', 'The Worship of Jesus in Apocalyptic Christianity', *New Testament Studies*, 27, 1980–81, p. 322 (my italics).

39. K. Bediako, *Christianity in Africa: the Renewal of a Non-Western Religion* (Edinburgh University Press/Maryknoll: Orbis, 1995) pp. 163, 164.
40. Ibid. p. 62.
41. L. Saneh, 'Africa' in *Towards the Twenty-first Century in Christian Mission: Essays in Honor of Gerald Anderson*, eds. J.M. Phillips and R.J. Coote (Grand Rapids: Eerdmans, 1993) p. 91.

Liberating Gnosis:

Aloysius Pieris

The 'religiousness of the poor' has become a major focus of theological reflection in Asia in recent times. A key figure in this discussion has been the Sri Lankan Jesuit theologian Aloysius Pieris, whose efforts to articulate a theology of liberation in the setting of Buddhist-Christian-Marxist dialogue have earned him a reputation in ecumenical circles. In the two decades following the Second Vatican Council he became a prolific writer and a much sought-after lecturer (in Buddhism as much as in Christian theology) in Europe and North America as well as in Asian countries such as Japan, the Philippines and India. Pieris' numerous articles, many of which first appeared in a local journal, 'Dialogue', which he himself edited, have in recent years reached a global audience through the influence of his friend Paul Knitter. A compendium of his writings has appeared in two volumes, namely: *An Asian Theology of Liberation*[1] and *Love meets Wisdom: a Christian Experience of Buddhism.*[2] He was also one of the contributors to the symposium *The Myth of Christian Uniqueness.*[3]

In Pieris' writings a few themes keep recurring with stark power. He is a master of the pithy formula, the startling aphorism. In this chapter I shall identify some of these themes, allowing him to speak in his own inimitable style as far as possible, and then present a response.

Critique of Spirituality

Pieris stands in the well-established tradition of liberation theology, for which 'liberative praxis' constitutes the method

of Christian theological reflection.[4] By definition there
cannot be a non-liberational theology, for the starting point
of all theological reflection, according to Pieris, must be the
recognition of the 'irreversible antagonism between God and
Mammon' and the 'irrevocable covenant between God and
the poor'.[5] For Pieris, 'Mammon' (cf Matt. 6:24) signifies the
acquisitive, avaricious spirit of wealth-accumulation which
is at work in us psychologically and which is organized
socially into principalities and powers of domination. Hence,
Christian mission has been 'stamped from its inception with
a class option.'[6] But this liberation is more than just class
struggle, it is the culmination of the 'religious experience of
the poor.'[7] It leads to the knowledge of God, for the
liberative activity of the transcendent divine reality is imma-
nently realized within the struggle of the poor for their
liberation.

True spirituality, then, is founded on self-renunciation, in
and through the Other—not only the Other who hides in
one's own self waiting to be sought through prayer, but also
this same Other who hides in others as the 'victim-judge' of
human injustice, waiting to be served through action. Pieris
notes: 'Contemplation and action receive their authenticity
not from each other but from the cross that stands wherever
altars are built to mammon on the graves of God's poor.'[8]
Spirituality is both a struggle *to be poor* and a struggle *for the
poor*. The first aspect highlights the positive side of poverty
(what Pieris calls 'voluntary poverty'), the chosen vocation
by all disciples of Jesus as an expression of their rejection of
the enslaving tendency of mammon. The second draws
attention to the fact of 'forced poverty', which is the fruit of
sin. 'The kingdom of God can be viewed in terms of a
universal practice of the one and the *consequent* elimination
of the other.'[9] Voluntary poverty is an indispensable pre-
requisite for the elimination of the forced poverty which
reflects the rule of mammon in the unjust social order.

Economics apart, there is a christological basis for this
doctrine. For 'God's body comprises these two categories of
the poor: the poor by 'option' who are the followers of Jesus
(Matt.19:21) and the poor by 'birth' who are proxies of
Christ (Matt. 25:31–46). In other words, the struggle to be
poor cannot be recognizably Christian if it is not inspired by
each of these motives: to follow Jesus who was poor then,
and to serve Christ who *is* in the poor now.'[10] Renunciation

that does not benefit the poor who have nothing to renounce is sterile. It is not what Pieris calls 'christic spirituality'. God assumes the struggle of the poor so that it becomes God's struggle for the poor. The struggle for the poor is a mission entrusted by the victim-judge of oppression (Matt. 25) only to those who are, or have become, poor.

Pieris endorses the post-Vatican II discovery of a 'secular liturgy' (that is, socio-political commitment lived as worship), but he inverts the view of conciliar theology that 'church liturgy' is the source and summit of the liturgy of life. Consistently following a liberationist logic, Pieris argues that the liturgy of the official church should both originate and culminate in the liturgy of the life-and-death struggle for justice which is 'the primary guarantee of salvation/sanctification, and not the other way round!'[11] He continues, 'We become one with God (is this not the aim of all mysticism?) to the degree that our poverty drives us to appropriate God's concern for the poor as our own mission.'[12]

Where Pieris parts company with many liberation theologians, particularly those in Latin America, is in posing the challenge: is our vision of the kingdom of God too narrow because it is too Christian? In their attitudes towards religion most of them, he feels, have been influenced far too much by the two mighty 'Karls' of dialectical fame—Marx, with his European ethnocentrism that led him to dismiss all religion as human alienation, and the inversion of reality, and Barth, whose Christ-against-religions theology prevented him from perceiving the revelatory significance of Eastern religions (which Pieris prefers to call *Gnostic* religions, teaching redemption through intuitive knowledge, in contrast with semitic religions which are *Agapeic*, teaching redemption through love of neighbour). The occidentalism of Marx and Barth have made Latin American (and North American) forms of liberation theology quite irrelevant for Asia, because Asia is not only the locale for the largest amount of poverty in the world but is also the generator of the oldest and largest tradition of monasticism in the world. These twin features of the Asian reality, monastic non-Christian spirituality (symbolized in the voluntary poverty of the monk/nun) and the structurally-enforced poverty of the masses, are the soil out of which an Asian theology of liberation must emerge.

The 'soteriological nucleus' or 'liberative core' of all major religions, Pieris argues, carries a denunciation of a world order based on the 'mammon values' of greed, private property and the accumulation of wealth. Asian monastics teach the path of spiritual enlightenment that effects the interior liberation of humans from this acquisitive instinct. But the Asian poor also cry out for a social emancipation from the oppressive structures into which this instinct is organized today. As in the case of the church's traditional notion of spirituality, a sociological understanding of poverty has not been properly assimilated into the religious ethos of Asia. Buddhist self-analysis must be complemented by social analyis if the contemporary strategies of mammon are to be discerned. Just as in European history, the history of Asia records countless instances of individual ascetics living complacently on vast estates, being forced by a secular turn of events to practise their poverty *for the sake of* the real poverty of the peasants, so rediscovering the social and political dimensions of their religion (cf, for instance, the impact of Marxism in Mongolia and Tibet).

But Pieris also draws attention to an ancient Asian tradition of 'religious socialism', practised in tribal communities with their '*cosmic* soteriology' (a term he prefers to 'animist' or 'primal') and also in the monastic Hindu and Buddhist communities which were based on a '*metacosmic* soteriology' (an orientation towards a trans-phenomenal Beyond rather than towards immanent, cosmic powers). The 'happy symbiosis' of monastic and rural socialism in the least urbanized, least technocratized areas of Asia is what Pieris pits against Western cultural imports of capitalist 'development' and Marxist 'liberation'. He sees Gandhi as the most outstanding Asian example of the combination of voluntary poverty as both a psychological weapon and a political strategy against the citadels of mammon. Gandhi also represents what often takes place in the Christian encounter with the gnostic traditions of Asia. The latter do have their own reservoirs of agapeic religiousness, and these are re-awakened by the Christian gospel. Likewise, the 'ancient and legitimate' gnostic streams within Christian orthodoxy are replenished by being linked with the ocean of Asian mysticism. *Gnosis*, whose prototypical embodiment is Buddhism, and *Agape*, whose prototypical embodiment is Christianity, complement one another both in the individual psyche and in the Asian social arena where the battle against mammon is fiercest.[13] Pieris belives that there is a 'subliminal dialogue' between gnosis and agape that 'introspective Christians can fathom in their own hearts'.[14] Hence Christian participation in the collective traditions of Buddhism (its festivals, rites and practices)will in some ways be a *déja vu* experience. 'The Christian will recognize in the liberative nucleus of Buddhism the mirror image of Christianity's own core experience: a meeting of a gnostic agape with an agapeic gnosis.'[15]

Critique of 'Inculturation'

A liberational theology can emerge only from a church that is deeply involved in the struggle of the poor for full humanity and out of that struggle to enter into the life and culture of these people, most of whom are not Christians. It is with this insight that Pieris launches a powerful assault on the inculturationists or 'indigenizers' whose efforts to take on the *culture* of Asia have been an escape from the obligation to confront the *poverty* of Asia. He observes, 'a local church *in* Asia is usually a rich church working *for* the poor, whereas the local church *of* Asia could only be a poor church working *with* the poor . . . This church, however, is a little flock, a tiny minority in Asia and has no monopoly of this mission. The great (monastic) religions that antedate Christianity also claim to possess a message of liberation for the poor of Asia. That is why local churches *in* Asia look upon these religions as rival claimants; but in a local church *of* Asia, they will have already become collaborators in a common mission.'[16]

The process of 'becoming the local church of Asia' is a by-product of the missionary task of evangelizing the (Asian) nations. The failure of inculturation is essentially a failure of evangelism. And to evangelize Asia is to '*evoke in the poor this liberative dimension of Asian religiousness, Christian and non-Christian.* For the unevangelized poor tend to reduce religion to an opiate, to struggle without hope, and to submit too easily to the religious domination of the elite class.'[17] Expanding on this understanding of evangelism, Pieris continues, 'Jesus was the first evangelizer—poor, but fully conscious of his part in the war against mammon with all its principalities and powers.'[18]

It is in this context that Pieris makes his oft-repeated appeal to the baptismal experience of Jesus as a paradigm for the Christian mission in Asia. He draws the following four 'missiological principles' from Jesus' submission to the baptism of John (which he claims 'became a source of lasting embarrassment to the first generation of Christians'):

(i) Jesus rejected the narrow ideology of the Zealots, the sectarian puritanism of the Essenes, the Pharisaic spirituality of self-righteousness and the aristocratic spirituality of the Sadducees. He opted for the Deuteronomic tradition of prophetic asceticism represented by the baptizer. This authentic spirituality was an appropriate departure point for his mission. Christians in Asia, confronted by a variety of ideological and religious trends, have likewise to exercise discernment as to the most 'liberative religiousness' available.

(ii) The poor, too, had a 'spirituality' of their own. They were the *anawim* of the countryside, drawn by John's preaching to be receptive to the coming liberation. Where Jesus entered the Jordan, therefore, two streams of spirituality found a point of confluence. Jesus comes not to baptize others, but to be baptized, thereby identifying himself with the 'religious poor' of the countryside. Pieris draws an ecclesiological implication from this: 'Asian local churches have to be at the point of inter-section between the metacosmic spirituality of the monastic religions and the cosmic religion of the simple peasants, to be the locus where the liberative forces of both traditions combine in such a way as to exclude the aristocratic "leisure-class" mentality of the former and superstitions of the latter.'[19]

(iii) Jesus' humble submission to John was a prophetic moment because it was then that both his messianic self-understanding and his missionary credentials before the people were bestowed on him by God: 'Hear ye him'. The seeming loss of authority was the vindication of authority. Pieris draws the conclusion: 'The local church in Asia needs to be initiated into the pre-Christian traditions under the tutelage of our ancient gurus, or it will be an ecclesiastical complex full of "power" but lacking in "authority".'[20]

(iv) By plunging himself into 'the stream of an ancient spirituality' Jesus emerged with a new selfhood and mission. In similar vein, the newness of Asian Christian identity will appear only as a result of our total identification 'with monks and peasants who have conserved for us, in their religious socialism, the seeds of liberation that religion and poverty have combined to produce.'[21] Pieris appeals to the local churches *in* Asia, which still carry a Western identity, to 'enter into the stream at the point where the religiousness of the Asian poor (represented by the masses) and the poverty of religious Asians (reflected in our monks) meet to form the ideal community of total sharing.'[22] Elsewhere, he arges for what he calls a *communicatio in sacris* which is summed up by the example of 'Our Lord and Master who humbly let himself be initiated by a recognized Guru in Israel', so that we too should 'plunge into the Jordan of Buddhist spirituality in the presence of an authoritative guide.'[23]

The second 'missiological paradigm' Pieris explores is the 'trajectory of poverty that links Jordan with Calvary'.[24] The cross of Jesus is also referred to by the evangelists as his 'baptism' (e.g. Mk 10:35–40, Lk 12;50) for each was a self-effacing act that revealed his prophetic authority. The prophetic mission of Jesus was 'a mission *of* the poor and a mission *to* the poor, a mission *by* the poor and a mission *for* the poor'. He awoke the consciousness of the poor 'to their unique liberative role in the totally new order God is about to usher in'—that is the task of evangelization. This mission was consummated on the cross—a cross 'that the money-polluted religiosity of his day planted on Calvary with the aid of a colonial power . . . when true religion and politics join hands to awaken the poor, then mammon, too, makes allies with religion and politics to conspire against the evangelizer. Religion and politics must go together—whether for God or against God.'[25]

The consequences for ecclesiastical identity and inculturation are plain. A church inculturated in Asia is a church liberated from mammon, and is necessarily, therefore, composed of the poor: those who are poor by option and those who are poor by circumstance. But, unlike the *Christian* base communities of Latin America, these are *human* base communities, 'prophetic communities' that have arisen as a result of being baptized consciously or unconsciously into Asian socialism. It is they who are the 'true local churches *of* Asia, for they have been baptized in the Jordan of Asian religion and on the Calvary of Asian poverty'.[26] In other words, 'inculturation is the *ecclesiological* revolution already initiated by base human communities, with Christian and non-Christian membership, wherein mysticism and militancy meet and merge: *mysticism* based on voluntary poverty and *militancy* pitched against forced poverty.'[27]

Elsewhere Pieris brings together liberation and inculturation in a christological affirmation: 'We announce the good news in our tongues (that is, the content of inculturation)—namely, that Jesus is the new covenant or the defence pact that God and the poor have made against mammon, their common enemy (that is, the content of liberation). For liberation and inculturation are not two things anymore in Asia.'[28]

Critique of Christology

It is a fundamental conviction of Pieris that Jesus can be re-admitted to Asia today (having been born in Asia but rejected by the Asian masses as a neo-colonial Christ) only through the 'soteriological nucleus' of Asian religions. This requires a process of 'enreligionization' whereby an indigenous ecclesial identity is forged from within the soteriological perspective of Asian religions. Without succumbing to the pitfalls of trying to define religion—an enterprise which he declares is typically Western—Pieris is scornful of those indigenous theologies which develop conceptual schemes built on the study of ancient religious texts. This latter approach has often led to a 'theological vandalism' whereby concepts and practices (e.g. meditation techniques)[29] are extracted from their soteriological context and used in a way that irritates the non-Christian. The limitations of the text-centred approach are illustrated by the Weberian caricature of Buddhism as a 'world-denying asceticism', ignoring the socio-political changes brought about in the cultures of Asia over two millenia by the agapeic aspects of the Buddhist path to gnosis.

The 'core' of any metacosmic religion is the liberative experience that gave birth to it and continues to be made available to successive generations through its collective beliefs, practices and institutions. Although in Buddhism this core experience may be classified as *gnosis* and the corresponding Christian experience falls under the category of *agape*, they are 'complementary idioms that need each other to mediate the self-transcending experience called 'salvation'. Any valid spirituality, Buddhist or Christian, as the history of each religion attests, does retain both poles of religious experience . . . The movement of the spirit progresses through the dialectical interplay of wisdom and love, or, to put it in Buddhist terms, through the complementarity between *prajna* and *karuna*, and in the Hindu tradition, the sapiental spirituality known as the *jnana-marga* and the affective-active paths called the *bhakti-* and *karma-marga*.'[30] He does, however, recognize that in all the major schools of Buddhism the affective currents of mysticism must 'ultimately flow into the sapiental stream that alone reaches the ocean of nirvana.'[31] So gnostic faiths like Buddhism would nuance their agape-talk with the impersonalist idioms proper to the gnostic spirit.

It is Pieris' view that one of the major obstacles to what he calls a 'core-to-core dialogue' between Christianity and Buddhism lies in the refusal of both Christians and Buddhists to admit that *gnosis* and *agape* are both 'legitimate languages of the human spirit or (as far as the Christian partner in dialogue is concerned) that they are languages that the same divine Spirit speaks alternately in each one of us.'[32] He naturally approves of the Neoplatonism of the third and fourth centuries because its apophatic language has strong affinities with Buddhism, the Neoplatonists' 'contentless knowing' and 'knowing as such' being what a Buddhist sees in impersonalist terms as the final purpose of all love.

Pieris argues that no major religion could have travelled far from its seat of origin and become inculturated in the lives of the masses had it not put its roots deep into the popular religiousness of the latter. A metacosmic religion (whether agapeic or gnostic) cannot be firmly rooted in tribal societies except within the context of their cosmic religion. In other words, there cannot be a metacosmic religiousness having a grip on the people except on the basis of a popular religiousness. The converse, however, is not true. For there can be (and are, throughout Asia, Africa and Oceania) cosmic, non-scriptural religions independent of metacosmic, scriptural religions. A cosmic religion is an 'open-ended spirituality that awaits a transcendent orientation from a metacosmic religion. It is therefore not a question of one replacing the other, but one completing the other in such a way as to form a bidimensional soteriology that maintains a healthy tension between the cosmic *now* and the metacosmic *beyond*.'[33]

This process of popular symbiosis (for which Richard Gombrich coined the term 'accretism') has given rise to the hybrid cultures of Asia. It was also the route that the inculturation of Christianity took in Northern Europe in the early medieval period. Pieris also sees this as a missiological technique used in early Buddhist missionary expansion: the Buddha who, in the orthodox Theravada stream, was simply the discoverer and preacher of the *dhamma*, is now enthroned as cosmic saviour and metacosmic lord over all the elements of nature, gods, spirits etc. Thus the cosmic religiosity of the masses was not uprooted, but rather given a new 'metacosmic orientation—not only through the doctrine of *nirvana* but also by installing the Buddha as the sovereign lord immediately above and yet wholly beyond the local deities of each culture'.[34]

As far as Christianity in Asia is concerned, Pieris feels that it has arrived too late, for Hindu, Buddhist and Islamic cultures are already deeply entrenched in Asian soil. Christianity has 'miserably failed' outside the Philippines and some tribal societies in India and South-East Asia, despite over four centuries of aggressive propaganda. 'History shows, and sociology justifies, the phenomenon that one metacosmic religion already inculturated in a clannic society cannot be easily dislodged by another metacosmic religion except by protracted use of coercion—that is, by an irreligious resort to mass conversion'.[35]

Asian churches have no precedent to follow, since the doctrines of the early church were born of its encounter with the Semitic and Greco-Roman cultures of the Mediterranean world, not with Sino–Indian religiousness. So, 'they are called to create something new, the orthodoxy of which cannot be gauged from the available models'.[36] Asian theology must now be a process of what Pieris labels an 'explicitation' of a 'pre-existent theology implicitly contained in non-Christian soteriologies', one of 'assimilation through participation in the non-Christian ethos, a baptism in the Jordan of our precursor's religiousness . . . that alows the little flock of Christ to feed freely on the Asian pastures that it has been trampling for centuries'.[37]

Consequently, theology in the context of interreligious collaboration can no longer be 'God-talk' or 'God's talk' since the greater part of Asia religiousness is nontheistic or explicitly atheistic. But, since the common thrust remains a concern for *liberation* (variously conceptualised as *vimukti, moksha, nirvana*, and so on) rather than speculation about a hypothetical liberator, soteriology must be rediscovered as the foundation of theology. Pieris argues that all religions have a common 'triune' soteriological structure: there is a 'salvific beyond' (e.g. *Yahweh, Allah, Nirvana, Tathata, Tao, Brahman-Atman*) which is manifested in the 'salvific within' of the individual through a 'salvific mediation' (e.g. *marga, dhamma, logos, dabar*) which is also revelatory in character, and a 'saving capacity' inherent in humans (*citta, atman, Spirit*, etc) which orients us towards the Beyond. It is this that constitutes the 'basic soteriological datum in many of our religious cultures'.[38]

Pieris admits that the first dimension is not seen as the source of salvation in Buddhism but rather as the final metacosmic destiny of the individual (*nirvana*). Buddhism also differs from Christianity in having no doctrine of creation and consequently no doctrine of eschatological consummation and of divine grace. But he identifies a 'significant point of convergence' in the insistence of both that 'a positive human endeavour is a necessary condition for the arrival of final liberation', and yet that 'this final liberation (the absolute future or the further shore) is never really the automatic end-product of human causation' for both *nirvana* and the Christian *eschaton* are not susceptible of human manipulation.[39] Salvation involves the inaccessible 'beyond' becoming one's salvific 'within', and this is possible because 'the Absolute contains within its own bosom a *mediatory* and *revelatory self-expression, an accessible dimension*: the *dharma/logos*.'[40]

Thus Pieris invites us to drop the language of 'uniqueness' and 'absoluteness' as traditionally applied to Christ (or for that matter to the Buddha by traditional Buddhists). For 'Christ' (like 'Son of God' or 'Lord') is only a given title, a human categorization by which one particular culture tried to capture the 'ineffable mystery of salvation' communicated in the person and teaching of Jesus.[41] What is absolute and unique is not the title, but what all major religions have recognized for centuries as the mystery of salvation, but named differently. Pieris sees a 'striking parallelism' between the way the Buddha was elevated to cosmic lordship in animist cultures and the way Paul 'did the same with Christ in the hellenistic cultures in which he evangelized'.[42] What saves is 'the *mediating reality* itself, in whatever way it may be recognized and named'. Buddhist and Christian partners in dialogue must agree that liberation is possible only 'through what they both accept to be the "revelatory medium of salvation" and not the titles one gives to it. The real parting of ways begins when either Gautama or Jesus is identified with it by means of these titles.'[43]

For Pieris, whatever uniqueness that may be ascribed to Jesus must lie in the claim that the medium of salvation is the way of the cross, which symbolizes the 'double ascesis' of 'renunciation' (the struggle to be poor) and 'denunciation' (the struggle for the poor). Any Third World theology of religions must have a unitary perception of revolution and religion. He sums up his vision thus: 'This double ascesis is the nucleus around which an Asian theology of liberation evolves into a Christology that does not compete with Buddhology but complements it by acknowledging the *one path* of liberation on which Christians join Buddhists in their *gnostic detachment* (or the practice of 'voluntary poverty') and Buddhists join the Christian *agapeic involvement* in the struggle against 'forced poverty' as it truly happens today in the basic *human* communities in Asia'.[44]

Response to Pieris

There is much in Pieris' writings that is worthy of admiration and needs to be endorsed as salutary for the church not only in Asia but all over the world: for instance, his vigorous denunciation of the church's complicity with the forces of mammon, his scathing critique of forms of inculturation and 'leisure-class' mysticism (whether in Christian ashrams or non-Christian meditation centres) that are indifferent to the suffering of the poor, his attempt to forge a genuine Asian identity for the church, and the challenge he presents to all who are serious about dialogue with people of other faiths to go beyond the level of textual comparisons and enter into a 'core-to-core' empathy with the other.

At the same time, however, there are serious doubts I have about his major theses and, consequently, of the validity and the viability of the project he advocates. My criticisms are of both a biblical–exegetical and a theological/philosophical nature.

(a) In an examination of liberationist (including black and feminist) theologies and the alternative readings of biblical texts they offer from a particular context of experience and action, Anthony Thiselton makes a helpful distinction between what he calls a 'socio-critical' hermeneutic and a 'socio-pragmatic' one. He raises the pertinent question: 'Do the hermeneutical systems constructed or utilized by liberation thelogies or feminist approaches function *pragmatically to filter out from the biblical text* any signal which does anything other than affirm the hopes and aspirations of a given social group; or do they embody a *genuine socio-critical principle which unmasks oppression as part of a larger trans-contextual critique?*'[45]

In other words, if theology is to be truly *liberating*, texts must not be absorbed into the perspectives and social practices of the oppressed group. The latter needs to be able to distinguish its own perspective from the perspective of the text. If the horizons of text and reading community are not respected but collapsed prematurely, the community remains imprisoned within its own horizons and under the domination of the more aggressive representatives of its own unofficial ideology. As Thiselton succinctly expresses it, 'Until recently hermeneutical suspicion might duly fall on hierarchical claims for a status quo; but with egalitarian trends in socio-literary and socio-polical ideologies, suspicion needs to be exercized in a double direction about vested interests . . . Any merely selective use of texts to encourage those who are oppressed can be perceived in principle to represent precisely the same strategy of hermeneutical method as the oppressors who use texts to legitimize their own programmes. Both in this case confront each other with socio-pragmatic methods.'[46] If, on the other hand, liberation hermeneutics embodies a socio–cultural principle that transcends the interests of the community of protest, then all communities experience correction, transformation and an enlargement of horizons.

Nowhere does Pieris explain his own hermeneutical procedure. His use of Scripture is sparse, but like most liberation theologians he acknowledges that the Gospels do furnish us with a reliable account of the historical Jesus. However, it is clear from his vetoing of all theological 'God-talk' and the language of revelation on the grounds that 'the greater part of Asian religiousness is either nontheistic or explicitly atheistic'[47], from his new ecclesiology of base human communities made up of those engaged in a life-and-death struggle for justice, and from his identifying of the latter as the 'primary guarantee of salvation/ sanctification, and not the other way round',[48] that the privileged position in the hermeneutical circle belongs to the struggle against mammon as interpreted through the religiousness of the Asian poor. The only Christian 'insight' that seems to inform the dialogue is that agapeic involvement in the struggle of the poor must take the shape of the cross. But Pieris believes that this is not a radically unique or disturbing insight for it is present, but in less obvious form, in the teaching of all religions, and especially Buddhism. The Christian contribution to the religiously inspired struggle is to serve as a catalyst: drawing out the liberative streams in all faiths in the common quest towards a 'religious socialism'.

It is clear, then, that Pieris' hermeneutic falls among those socio-pragmatic versions of liberation theology that are vulnerable to Thiselton's critique. The Bible is simply not free to scrutinize and question the inadequate understandings of evil and liberation found in secular ideologies such as marxism and the ancient religious systems of Asia. Questions about the origin and nature of oppression as the Bible depicts it, and its own unique contribution to the praxis of liberation are foreclosed. Biblical texts are simply used to further goals over which the biblical message has had no decisive say. This is to use the Bible in an 'inspirational' manner rather than from a posture of humble obedience. This is the irony of such socio-pragmatic liberation theologies: the oppressed use the identical tools as their oppressors![49]

The kind of oppression suffered by the Third World poor *does* constitute a unique position from which to listen to the biblical doctrine of salvation, and theologies of liberation such as Pieris' have helped us rediscover a biblical epistemology (via Marx): namely, that knowledge of God comes, not through idle speculation, but through obedience to the truth in concrete historical situations. But right praxis ultimately depends on right theory. Marx insisted that revolutionary praxis needed to be guided by theoretical thought. Marx's famous eleventh thesis on Feuerbach ('The philosophers have only *interpreted* the world in various ways; the point is to *change* it') is often quoted in radical theologies, but severed from its context in Marx's thought as a whole. Marx's revolutionary praxis was shaped by an ethical vision as much as a theoretical analysis of human social alienation. Both the grounds of the appeal to liberate humankind and the means to be employed have to be justified by reference to a worldview which is open to question. We also need a hermeneutical method which will disclose which aspects of the world need to be changed, for otherwise our revolutionary praxis will be superficial at best and equally enslaving at worst.

We cannot use either sociological analysis or Pieris' 'religiousness of the poor' to rule out a *priori* Christian reflection on the world in the light of God's self-revelation in Jesus Christ. The former can be used in the task of setting up a critical hermeneutical circle and thus to help remove all false accretions from the Christian gospel. But if right praxis ultimately depends on right thinking, and if the gospel addresses the fundamental problem of humankind's onto-logical alienation from its Creator, then any *theology* of liberation (that also purports to be Christian) must give the Christ-event a privileged position in its hermeneutical circle.

Pieris' disposition to use the Bible, not as an alternative source of revolutionary theory and praxis for Christians in Asia but, rather, as illustrations for an understanding of praxis drawn from elsewhere, is apparent in many places. Consider, for instance, his pervasive tendency to identify sin and evil with 'mammon'. When greed and wealth-accumulation (whether individual or embodied in socio-economic structures) replace the radical biblical diagnosis of *sin*, then any understanding of liberation must be bound to disillusionment. Pieris needs to grapple more vigorously with the bibical teaching on human alienation, with the way we lose our capacity for neighbourly relations of equality precisely because we have deliberately changed the creature-Creator relationship into one in which humanity assumes the status of divinity. All those ideologies, religious or secular, which assume that we are free to throw off our shackles and

effect a fundamental transformation in our social relationships are challenged by the gospel's disclosure of the radical
nature of sin. The latter is a moral perversity and ontological
alienation whose final reality is death and which cannot be
reduced to other categories without changing the nature
of the Christian gospel to something profoundly different.
Sin undoubtedly finds expression in social oppression and
economic exploitation. But it may find more subtle—and,
therefore, perhaps more dangerous—expression in religious
quests for occult powers, self-mastery and spiritual control
over the lives of others. Inner renunciation of greed and
covetousness, coupled with outer resistance to the dehumanizing forces in society, are essential aspects of the 'obedience of
faith' (Rom 1:5). But if the gospel demands are reduced to
these, they only conceal the seriousness of the human
predicament.[50]

(b) Another example of Pieris' hermeneutical style is seen
in his frequent references to John the Baptist as an 'Asian
guru' (a term he never applies to any Old Testament
prophet, New Testament apostle or Jesus himself!) and to
Jesus' baptism at the hands of John. Pieris is quite correct to
draw attention to the importance of John's ministry for our
understanding of Jesus. In his influential study of 'the aims of
Jesus', Ben Meyer has reminded us that 'the beginning of
Jesus' public career is inextricably bound up with the public
career of John the baptist. Both careers were prophetic
appeals to the nation. Both were short, abruptly ended by
execution',[51] and, in a recent essay, RT France observes that
according to the Synoptic tradition (and Matthew in particular) not only do both Jesus and John begin their public
ministries with exactly the same proclamation (Matt. 3:2,
4:17), but 'almost every phrase of Matthew's account of
John's preaching is echoed, in content and often in phrase-
ology, in his subsequent presentation of the teaching of
Jesus'.[52] Jesus was, in more than merely a chronological
sense, John's successor. He identified himself closely with
John's mission.[53]

But the 'missiological principles' that Pieris draws from
these facts are highly suspect. The view that the early church
was embarrassed by Jesus' baptism has slender support. The
only evidence we have for any extravagant claims being
made for John as messiah or any doubts concerning the
sinlessness of Jesus on the basis of Matthew 3:14–15 come

from sectarian groups towards the end of the second century. The synoptic evangelists have no hesitation in acknowledging his ministry as a prophet (e.g. Mark 11:32, Matt. 14:5, Lk. 1:76) and in Matthew 11:9 (=Lk 7:26) Jesus endorses him as 'a prophet, indeed more than a prophet'. France points out that whatever embarrassment Matt. 3:14–15 provokes, whether in the second century or the twentieth, has do with the false assumption that John's baptism was essentially about individual sin and repentance. On the contrary, both Meyer and France point out that John's mission focused on the eschatological renewal of God's people, Israel. The movement launched by John in the wilderness was 'the assembling by baptism of an open remnant: the Israel of the converted, soon to be purified by Spirit and fire.'[54]

But it is in this preparatory and provisional character of his ministry that John's true greatness lies. All the Gospels agree that John not only warned people of impending divine judgment but also saw himself as the forerunner of 'one more powerful' who exceeded him in authority such that he (John) was unworthy to be his slave: e.g. 'The one who is more powerful than I is coming after me; I am not worthy to stoop down and untie the thong of his sandals. I have baptized you with water; but he will baptize you with the Holy Spirit' (Mark 1:7–8). In Matthew's account of the baptism of Jesus, John tries to deter Jesus, saying, 'I need to be baptized by you, and do you come to me?'(3:14)[55] In both the Synoptic and Johannine traditions the principle contrast between John and Jesus is that of water/Spirit, of anticipation and fulfilment. John's water baptism is merely an anticipation of the true eschatological purification. The real thing is still to come, and it is Jesus who will usher it in.

The obvious question, then, that must be put to Pieris is this: do you understand the religious gurus and traditions of Asia to be standing in the same unambiguous relationship of preparation for, and humble witness to, Jesus the Christ? Obviously not. Pieris is, after all, scornful of those (like Karl Rahner, for instance) who come close to saying that they are. But Pieris is anxious to co-opt John, to baptize him into the fold of ascetic Asian spirituality, and it is clear that this overriding desire has controlled his exegesis of the text.

(c) The same one-sidedness is apparent in his references to the *anawim* of the oppressed Galilean countryside who flock to John and with whom Jesus identifies himself. The evangelists record that many 'from Jerusalem and all Judea' (Matt. 3:5) went out to be baptized, among whom were tax-collectors (Lk.3:12), soldiers (Lk.3:14) and prostitutes (Matt. 21:32). Jesus was often condemned by the religious establishment for consorting with 'tax-collectors and sinners' (e.g. Mk 2:15–16); and it is clear that the 'sinners' whom Jesus embraced—and who thus experienced the kingdom of God as Good News—were all on the fringes of society, including not only the moral transgressors of the law but those ritually unclean (e.g. lepers), the physically disabled, the mentally afflicted, the demon-possessed, and women.

The literature on the Lukan emphasis on the place of poverty and wealth in the mission of Jesus is extensive.[56] Joel Green has made the interesting observation that in Luke's Gospel, Jesus, having been anointed to proclaim the good news to the poor (4:18), is found repeatedly frequenting the homes of the wealthy (e.g. 5:29, 7:36, 14:1, 19:5). Assuming that 'poor' is primarily an economic term for Luke, this 'dissonance between the announced purpose and actual ministry of Jesus is striking'.[57] Certainly there is ample instruction in the gospel about the dangers of wealth and possessions and Jesus' expectation that his disciples would be actively concerned for the economically destitute. But having examined the Lukan vocabulary of poverty and those texts which explicitly delineate the mission of Jesus, Green argues that economic or 'materialist' readings of Jesus' mission to the poor are 'too narrow' and need to be understood against a 'larger backdrop'.

Exegetes have often been misled by using concepts of 'class' and 'class struggle' anachronistically. In the Greco-Roman world poverty is better understood in terms of 'status honour' than under economically determined nomenclature such as 'class'. Status honour is a measure of social standing that embraces wealth, but also covers many other factors such as ethnicity, family heritage, vocation, gender and religious purity. Green marshalls evidence from both internal investigation of Lukan material and external data from the Mediterranean world to come up with the very plausible thesis that in Luke's gospel, the term 'the poor' has become a cipher for those of low social status: 'Although 'poor' is hardly devoid of economic significance, for Luke

this wider meaning of diminished status honour is para-
mount . . . 'good news to the poor' is preeminently a
gracious word of inclusion to the dispossessed, the
excluded.'[58]

This is an important observation for our purposes, for an
exclusive emphasis on the economically destitute may
actually rob the Good News of the kingdom of God of much
of its cutting-edge in Asian societies. Most non-Christian
religious leaders in Asia would, for example, support inter-
religious programmes of poverty alleviation, but they would
vehemently oppose the radical undermining of social identity
and status which is embodied in the gospel message. Moreover, although Pieris' exponents of an 'ascetic spirituality'
may be economically poor, their high social esteem in
traditional Asian culture often preclude them from receiving
the blessings of the 'upside-down' kingdom that Jesus
proclaims. The gospel addresses the central issues of power
and status in every society and culture, and so a too-narrow
focus on wealth (which, while often hand-in-glove with
power, is nevertheless separate) dilutes its subversive impact.[59]
We shall return to this aspect of the gospel in Chapter 6.

(d) It is also quite remarkable that though Pieris often
refers to the 'religious experience of the poor', the reader
misses any serious attempt to describe and evaluate this
popular religious consciousness. The world of the rural poor
in Asia (and, indeed, that of many 'sophisticated' urbanites)
is usually dominated by shamanism and fear of malevolent
spirits which bring ill-health, pestilence, fractured family
relationships, and other forms of oppression, including
poverty. What Gombrich writes of Sinhalese Buddhists is
also true (with the relevant contextual changes) of folk
religion in Islamic and Hindu societies: '. . . the law of *karma*
seems of remote relevance compared to the special effects
which constantly intervene, products of black and white
magic, demonic possession or the favour of a guardian deity.
In fact, though probably no Buddhist would ever deny the
supremacy of the Buddha and his Teaching, many of the
poor in this milleu have· so little contact with Buddhism as
traditionally understood that it does not affect their lives.
Their religious concerns are focused on thaumaturgy and
their relations with their personal deity.'[60] Those aspects of
New Testament teaching which speak of the reality of
malignant cosmic powers which work through (but cannot

be reduced to) socio–political structures, and of Christ's victory over all such dehumanizing elements through the cross, is surely of importance to any *Asian* theology of liberation.

(e) What is also required is a more appreciative assessment than that offered by Pieris of the contribution that modern science and technologies make to such poor societies. It is another of Pieris' ironies that while giving so much import- ance to Western social science (especially in its marxist mode), he makes disparaging remarks about the natural sciences, presumably because of the capitalist mould within which they appear. But it is a moot point whether such sciences can flourish in the climate of rural socialism that he advocates. Pieris, in any case, is heavily indebted to industrial- ism and high technology in his lifestyle as an international lecturer, and so the poor could well accuse him of double standards in seeking to deny them the benefits of modernity.

Moreover, in the histories of Asia and Africa over the past two hundred years, it is Christian medical missionaries who have frequently been the pioneers of rural health care systems, medical education for women and other under- privileged groups, and the development of special medical techniques (for instance, reconstructive surgery for lepers) which Third World conditions required.[61] In the light of all this, Pieris' glib dismissal of Christian mission as a 'miserable failure' strikes one as unduly premature. It is no longer the case that Christianity is tied to colonial or imperial power; on the contrary, the great majority of Christians in Asia, and especially in China and the Indian subcontinent, are economic- ally poor, socially marginalized and often persecuted for being Christians. Now that the gospel is no longer identified with those who wield power and wealth, the evangelization of Asia may have only just begun . . .

(f) If the baptism of Jesus by John is the commonest biblical theme in Pieris' writings, the judgement scene of Matthew 25 is his most popular text. The 'victim-judge' of the nations is served in the oppressed poor who mediate Christ to us. This view, taken for granted in many theologies of liberation, is highly questionable. Recent studies[62] have drawn attention to the fact that Matthew always uses the key phrase 'these brothers of mine' (and the attendant expressions 'the least of these', 'little ones') to refer to the disciples of Jesus (e.g. 10:42, 12:46–50, 18:10–14, 28:10). Jesus' close identification with his disciple-community is also an important aspect of his teaching in Matthew (e.g. 10:40, 18:18–20, 28:20). The 'nations' which will give account to Christ on the final day of judgment are the recipients of his disciples' mission (24:14). Some of them will hate the disciples for the testimony they bear (24:9). If these observations are combined with the historical background to Matthew's gospel (namely, that of a socially insignificant community dispersed among the nations as a persecuted minority), it follows that the discourse concerns the response of the nations to the church in their midst. It is the Matthean version of the Pauline concept of the Church as the 'body' of Christ, and it speaks of the solidarity between Christ and his redeemed, covenant people.[63]

I do not wish to be misunderstood here. That the sovereign Creator God shares, in some awesome way, in the suffering of *all* his creation, and that, in the outworking of his mercy and justice, God shows a 'bias' towards *all* who are neglected and downtrodden (a 'bias' only in contrast to our indifference or our pandering to the powerful and successful) are truths that undergird the whole biblical drama of salvation. They are, assuredly, not rejected by the above interpretation. What is rejected here is the way Matt. 25:31ff is prised out of its Matthean context to support a generalized Christ-mysticism and to justify the assertion that the 'Asian poor' (or, more generally, the 'Third World poor') are automatically the covenant people of God.

(g) Furthermore, any theology of liberation that lumps the 'poor and the oppressed' into a single, undifferentiated category serves only to perpetuate, in practice, the depersonalizing tendencies of our alienated existence. We need to distinguish among sufferings caused by disease, by environmental disaster, by civil or international war, by chronic unemployment or unjust wages, by racial discrimination, by political repression and the loss of civic freedoms, and so on. This makes for a diversity of responses to human suffering, embracing *both* the personal and the structural. By refusing to lose the suffering individual in the faceless crowd of the 'poor', we ensure that the distinctiveness of the gospel message (that the suffering are not mere statistics nor simply human victims, but creatures loved by their Creator) is not blurred. In his often justifiable tirades against global capitalism and Western technology Pieris would do well to heed the warning of the 'patriarch' of liberation theology, Gustavo Gutierrez, who, in a preface to the fifeenth anniversary edition of his classic work, *A Theology of Liberation*, writes: 'The theory of dependence which was so extensively used in the early years of our encounter with the Latin American world is now an inadequate tool, because it does not take sufficient account of the internal dynamics of each country or of the vast dimensions of the world of the poor.'[64]

A Christian liberating praxis must also take into account the fact that our human desires, motives and responses are bafflingly complex. We are all, simultaneously, both 'sinned-against' and 'sinners', desperately desirous of mercy as much as justice. The man who is intimidated by the petty government bureaucrats may at the same time be intimidating his wife and children at home; the minority ethnic group oppressed by the majority practises its own forms of oppression within its ranks . . . Most books today on the theology of suffering draw attention to Elie Wiesel's deeply moving, first-hand account of the murder of an old man by his son for the sake of a morsel of bread.[65] Both were Jewish prisoners being transferred by train from Buna to an unknown location in the middle of Germany. The son himself was then set upon by a group of other prisoners and beaten to death. It is true that such acts of savagery must be seen in the context of the unremitting terror under which they lived. But Wiesel still felt able to state the following truth about human beings in general: 'Deep down, I thought, man is not only an executioner, not only a victim, not only a spectator: he is all three at once.'[66]

If each one of us is simultaneously executioner, victim and spectator, the solidarity with victims will not *on its own* be sufficient to overcome injustice and oppression. Because we all tend to exaggerate what others owe us and to play down what we owe others, no praxis can be truly liberating as long as it focuses on only one dimension of oppression. Many among those who suffer the cruellest social and economic deprivations are also afflicted by the weight of guilt, both real and imaginary. It is here that the word of the cross, the announcement of the holy love of God reaching out to the unlovable, the gracious word that speaks of a once-for-all atonement for sin and a free and undeserved forgiveness, that promises power to overcome evil and to endure suffering, is experienced as truly life-giving.

To speak in this way is not to indulge in a form of religious 'opiate', invoking universal human corruption as an excuse for inaction in the face of human misery. There is no Christian discipleship without costly solidarity with those who suffer. But unless we reflect biblically, rather than pragmatically or ideologically, on the diverse forms of human suffering, all our praxis will simply short-circuit. We may well find ourselves replacing hopelessness with false hope, both equally cruel. We need to heed Kenneth Surin's wise reflection that 'the power which is sufficient to over-come human evil must be one which is capable of plumbing human malevolence to its uttermost depths, and, in so doing, of healing that brokenness which makes each one of us, at the same time, executioner, spectator and victim . . . our hopes for overcoming evil and suffering must accommo-date the perception that human wickedness has a depth which cannot be reached by even the most noble and heroic deeds of human solidarity.'[67]

(h) Pieris' discussions of christology are badly flawed by his assumption that christological development in the early church ran on parallel lines to buddhology in northern Buddhism. In the orthodox Theravada stream of southern Buddhism, Gautama the Buddha is never regarded as a Saviour. His soteriological role is limited to discovering and preaching the *dhamma* (the eternal salvific truth that preceded him) and founding the *sangha* (the community that realizes this truth and continues to preach and practice the path that leads to it). Pieris agrees with the Theravada Buddhist scholar DJ Kalupahana's portrait of how the human teacher grew, in the minds of his followers, into the transcendent being of the Mahayanists. Unlike the Jesus of the New Testament, 'the Gautama of the Tripitaka [the canonical Pali scriptures] did not seem to have clearly claimed that the saving truth or the liberating path was identical with his own person. He was only the path-finder and truth discoverer.'[68] Pieris sees the Mahayanist's equation of the Buddha with the preexistent *dharma* and the elevation of the Buddha in the folk-religion of southern Buddhism to a position of cosmic eminence as identical to Paul's elevation of Christ in the Hellenistic world of his day.

But this is to ignore the fact that the ascription of titles such as 'Lord' and 'Saviour' and 'Word of God' to Jesus of Nazareth were not Pauline innovations in a pagan, Hellenistic environment, but Old Testament language applied in a Palestinian setting by monotheistic Jewish Christians. Moreover the uniqueness of this development lies not so much in the titles themselves as in the *worship* that was accorded to Jesus in the early Jewish-Christian communities. As Larry Hurtado observes, ' . . . within the first two decades of Christianity, Jewish Christians gathered in Jesus' name for worship, prayed to him and sang hymns to him, regarded him as exalted to a position of heavenly rule above all angelic orders, appropriated to him titles and Old Testament passages originally referring to God, sought to bring fellow Jews as well as Gentiles to embrace him as the divinely appointed redeemer, and in general redefined their devotion to the God of their fathers so as to include the veneration of Jesus. And apparently they regarded this redefinition not only as legitimate but, indeed as something demanded of them.'[69] What Pieris calls the 'similar' process of Buddhist veneration of Gautama took over four centuries to evolve, and it did so under the influence of nontheistic or polytheistic cultures in which the Buddhist way of life took root.

A similar point is made in the striking opening words of Martin Hengel's illuminating monograph, *The Son of God: the Origin of Christology and the History of Jewish-Hellenistic Religion*:[70] 'At the feast of the Passover in the year 30, in Jerusalem, a Galilean Jew was nailed to the cross for claiming to be Messiah. About twenty five years later, the former Pharisee Paul quotes a hymn about this crucified man in a letter which he writes to one of the communities of the messianic sect which he has founded in the Roman colony of Philippi:

> . . . who, though he was in the form of God,
> did not regard equality with God as something
>   to be exploited, but emptied himself,
> taking the form of a slave, being born in human likeness.
> And found in human form, he humbled himself
>   and became obedient to the point of death—
> even death on a cross.'   (Philippians 2:6–8)[71]

Hengel continues: 'The discrepancy between the shameful death of a Jewish state criminal and the confession that depicts this executed man as a pre-existent divine figure who becomes man and humbles himself to a slave's death is, as far as I can see, without analogy in the ancient world'.[72] He goes on to note that 'Paul founded the community in Philippi in about the year AD 49, and in the letter which he wrote to the believers there about six or seven years later he will have presented the same Christ as in the preaching which brought the community into being. This means that the 'apotheosis of the crucified Jesus' must already have taken place in the forties, and one is tempted to say *that more happened in this period of less than two decades than in the whole of the next seven centuries, up to the time when the doctrine of the early church was completed.* Indeed, one might even ask whether the formation of the doctrine in the early Church was essentially more than a consistent development and completion of what had already been unfolded in the primal event of the first two decades, but in the language and thought-forms of Greek, which was its necessary setting.'[73]

Pieris' attempts to separate the person of Jesus Christ from an impersonal 'mediating reality', and to ascribe 'uniqueness' only to the latter, simply will not work. 'Christ', 'Lord', 'Son of God' etc are not 'only names' that can be dispensed with as mere 'human categorizations limited to a given culture'.[74] The affirmation 'Jesus is Lord' in historic Christian confession is a statement about a particular individual crucified under Pontius Pilate. Its self-involving efficacy, its power to motivate agapeic commitment to the poor and needy, is a *result* of its representation of (what is understood to be) an actual state-of-affairs. Concepts such as atonement, redemption and Sonship are not *merely* culturally-conditioned gropings towards a vague, unknowable reality; on the contrary, for all their cultural specificity, they are part and parcel of the self-revelation of God that Christians have identified with the election of Israel and the coming of Jesus. Certainly such metaphors and concepts need to be 'transposed' into appropriate forms in other cultures and vocabularies; but transposition is a way of *preserving* their cognitive content, not *discarding* it. To talk abstractly of a 'mediating, salvific reality' that is divorced from human language and historical specificity is to lapse into a timeless idealism that denies the heart of the gospel.

Even in the first century there were many pagans who were happy to believe in the 'uniqueness' of the Logos. What galled them, what was distinctive in the Church's proclamation, was the affirmation that the '*Logos* became *flesh* and dwelt among us'. The renowned patristics scholar Jaroslav

Pelikan has noted that all the metaphysical constructs of fourth-century Christian philosophers about the pre-existent Word/Logos found their 'religious and moral focus, and even their intellectual justification' in the historical figure of Jesus of Nazareth; and that although the sentence, 'In the beginning was the Word', could have been said, and had been said, by many who had never heard of Jesus, 'what made this portrait of the Logos as cosmic Christ special was the declaration that the Word had become flesh in Jesus and that in Jesus the incarnate Word had suffered and died on the cross.'[75] These are issues that will need to be taken up again in later parts of this book.

Before leaving this section, however, it may be worth drawing the reader's attention to some observations of RC Zaehner, who succeeded Sarvapalli Radhakrishnan (the first President of post-independence India) in the Spalding Chair in Eastern Religions at Oxford University. In his inaugural lecture, Zaehner noted that what is often held to be a point of similarity between Christianity and other religious faiths turns out to be a similarity between Christian orthodoxy and non-Christian heterodoxy.[76] Whereas the doctrine of divine incarnation and of a divine mediator between God and humankind are central to Christian belief, parallel beliefs in other religions develop in *opposition* to the dominant view of each of their sacred scriptures. Thus there is nothing in the Quran to justify the quasi-deification of Muhammed (which occurred in some Muslim circles in the third century of the Islamic era), and still less for the deification of the Buddha in popular buddhology. 'In each case the need for an incarnate God seems to have been so strongly felt that the doctrine of incarnation made its appearance in surroundings where it had no rightful place.'[77]

Zaehner continues, 'What similarity there is proves not that there is an inner unity underlying all the great world religions, but that there is in man a craving for an incarnate God strong enough to force its way into the most unpromising religious systems . . . whereas Muhammed and the Buddha achieved deification in flat contradiction to what they claimed and wished, and whereas the incarnations of Vishnu have no basis in fact, Jesus Christ both lived and died and claimed to be the Son of God.'[78] These claims will be explored at length in Chapters six and seven of the present book.

(i) Pieris, in what appears to be another ironic twist, is urging a liberationist ethic while propagating an idealist religious perspective. Jesus becomes simply an historical illustration of general truths and values established on other grounds. History is relativized by talk of a common 'soteriological nucleus' and a 'liberative essence' behind all the major religions of humankind. Pieris seems to deduce a common soteriological goal by postulating a common soteriological structure. But form and content are logically distinct. Here, too, the criticisms levelled against Samartha's religious epistemology apply. What extra–terrestrial Archimedean stance can Pieris utilize to pronounce with such splendid assurance that the referent in the terms Christ, Son of God, *Tathagata, dharma* etc are one and the same 'mediating reality' or that talk of God as Person, Creator, Redeemer etc 'do not offer us a true description of God but are only signs by which we may reach God'?[79]

Such a perception can only be reductionist for it fails to pay attention to the distinctive ethos of each religious tradition. Again there is something deeply ironic in this. For Pieris, like other religious pluralists *begins* by affirming the distinctive historical validity of each faith, defending it from Christian attempts to appropriate its unique categories of thinking in misplaced evangelistic fervour ('theological vandalism'), but *ends up* homogenizing the faiths by subsuming them under bland and unrecognizable generalizations. Thus the Christian doctrine of the Tri–unity of God, with its loving mutuality of subsistent relations, is transformed into talk of an impersonal Absolute possessing a 'triadic' soteriological structure, thereby bringing it into line with other soteriologies and robbing it—among other things—of its power to provide a radically different conception of human personhood.[80] Likewise the Holy Spirit is reduced to an innate capacity or force within each human being impelling him/her towards *nirvana*; Sin, a term which is primarily theological not moral, is now reduced to *mammon* because it chimes well with the Buddhist doctrine that *tanha* (craving) is the root of all suffering; the cross of Christ does not effect a real change in humanity's relationship with God, but is reduced merely to political confrontation with the organized forces of mammon; and the resurrection, which is a challenge to the *samsara-karma* world view of Hindu and Buddhist spirituality, is not mentioned even once.

Little wonder that Pieris prefers the abstract, impersonalist categories of Neoplatonist thought to the biblical tradition. But this can hardly be called a 'core-to-core' dialogue between the core of the Christian faith and that of Buddhism (or of any other faith). It ends up diluting, even eviscerating, the former in the interests of not causing offence to the latter. It is also strange to find Pieris calling for Western theology to return to the early medieval Neoplatonic tradition that it outgrew: strange because liberation ethics would make an uncomfortable bedfellow with the typical Neoplatonist scheme built around a hierarchy of being, celestial and ecclesiastical (as expressed, say, in the work of Denys the Areopagite[81]), its underestimation of the reality of evil and its devaluing of time and history. There is also an intellectual and spiritual elitism associated with Neoplatonism, including its Christian forms, which Pieris would find inconsistent with the privileged position he accords to the religiosity of the poor.

(j) Pieris sometimes betrays the same simplistic understanding of the connexion between religious experience and religious belief (or doctrine) that we observed in Samartha. For him, the 'core experience' of a religion is primordial and fundamental, constituting its liberative nucleus. This experience is preserved and protected not only by the basic beliefs and practices that perpetuate its memory, but also by means of the interpretations that grew around that religion.[82] He castigates Christians who are not ready to transcend the collective tradition of Buddhism and enter into an experiential encounter with the core. Now, we have seen that this would mean not merely participating in Buddhist religious festivals but also undergoing a long process of arduous discipleship, submitting to a competent Buddhist monk and so learning an extensive code of doctrine and discipline (*dhamma-vinaya*). One cannot have the experience without the beliefs and practices. And beliefs cannot be just assented to intellectually, but need to be interiorized. But Pieris admits elsewhere that, within the Buddhist worldview, the maximum that Buddhists can concede to Jesus is to call him a Bodhisattva (a being full of compassion but still on the way to Buddhahood) because to 'concede one bit more to Jesus' would be to '*cease to be Buddhists.*'[83] But how, then, can a Christian experience nirvana without first divesting herself of her basic convictions, and thus ceasing to be Christian?

(k) Pieris' choice of Gandhi as the 'outstanding Asian example' of Jesus' 'double ascesis' (via baptism and the cross) is controversial. Gandhi's genius, undoubtedly, was to bring an aesthetic religious mind to bear on political leadership, and his greatest contribution was to convince the Indian masses that possibilities for socio-economic change lay in themselves. But his 'ascesis' was very far removed from the powerlessness of the cross. On the contrary, when Gandhi fasted, the nation came to a standstill. Gandhi wielded enormous personal power over those around him, and his self-imposed austerities were a way of reasserting and reinforcing his spiritual domination. It is no exaggeration to say that they were forms of moral blackmail. Self-denial was his technique of self-assertion, and it was only his personal charm that masked this paradoxical truth from his contemporaries. Even his poverty often served a theatrical purpose.[84] Ironically, his nation-wide *ashrams* depended on the charity of wealthy industrialists, businessmen, professionals, all of whom were part of the industrial and capitalist system that Pieris, more so even than Gandhi himself, so vehemently denounces.

Gandhi's ascesis can be seen as a typical example of the quest for spiritual power that lies at the heart of Hindu spirituality. Consequently his political action was ultimately subservient to the religious quest of self-mastery and the attainment of *moksha* (liberation): hence his excessive self-absorption, the obsessive fascination with dietetics, bodily functions and sexual continence (and his demand, towards the end of his life, that his young female disciples sleep naked by his side so that he could test his vow of chastity—quite oblivious to how they themselves must have felt!). Nor was Gandhi an indigenous Asian thinker (is such a being possible, in any case, in the modern age?)—his political sensibilities were formed, negatively and positively, during a long sojourn in England and South Africa. As a law student in England he was exposed to the Protestant nonconformist tradition of radical dissent, and it was through Western eyes that he first read the Indian religious classics and reabsorbed his Indian heritage.[85] Even his philosophy of non-violence owed more to Tolstoy and the Sermon on the Mount than to any Hindu scriptural sources. Yet he spurned Western civilization, blaming it for all of India's ills. Opinion divides as to how seriously we can regard him as a model of leadership for Asia's billions, in the last decade of the twentieth century, given his apparent conviction that freedom and prosperity lay in returning to simple peasant life and the mythical conditions of medieval India.[86]

(l) Although Pieris is surely right to castigate those liberationists (Marxist and Christian) who describe the entire Hindu and Buddhist religious systems as socially reactionary, the examples he gives of significant liberation movements within the fold of these religions are less than convincing. He admits that the brahminical tradition is conservatively hidebound and so focuses instead on the tribal societies and *dalit* groups (earlier called untouchables, those outside the caste system) in India. But these are peoples outside the bounds of Hinduism, though for political purposes they are often regarded as Hindus. As for Buddhist history, the only example he gives are of medieval peasant revolts inspired by the Maithreya cult, a form of messianic Buddhism probably influenced by Christian contact, and the strange synthesis of Buddhism, Shinto nationalism and revolutionary violence embodied in the 12th-century Japanese Nichiren sect, from which the contemporary Soka Gakkai lay social organization (on the outer fringes of world Buddhism) is derived. It is odd that, while arguing for a return to the Asian tradition of rural 'religious socialism', Pieris virtually ignores recent attempts in three Theravada Buddhist countries (namely, Myanmar, Cambodia and Sri Lanka) to restore that idyllic state of affairs, all of which involved a total rejection of Western mammon and technology, and all of which led to terrible and widespread suffering.

He is on surer footing when dealing with the revolutionary potential of Islam in the Third World, but Islam hardly falls within Pieris' category of gnostic religions. But the examples he gives (Khomeini's Iran, for instance) must, surely, be embarrassing in the light of subsequent history. Also, they do highlight the naivete of supposing that the defeat of mammon (which for Pieris was embodied by Iran under the Shah) leads inevitably to the experience of freedom and community. It is the same naivete that we see embodied in the writings of other Asian theologies of liberation. The Taiwanese Choan-Seng Song, for instance, writing in 1973, hailed as 'salvation history' the efforts of the Chinese

Communist Party under Mao Zedong to 'transform man and his society', and announced prophetically that the new China was 'destined' to represent a 'future classless society in which the dictatorship of the proletariat will prevail completely.'[87]

These experiences of revolutionary history makes me more than slightly sceptical about Pieris' confident assertion that 'salvific truth dawns with the unmasking of illusion', and that 'true to our non-Christian religious traditions, we can neither describe nor define the new order but can only boldly strive towards it by the *via negativa*—namely, by negating the present order . . . in the commitment to overthrow it! The future that calls in question the present order ever remains the 'unnameable' or at least the 'unmentioned presupposition of every true revolution.'[88] There are always other gods which rush in to fill the ideological vacuum. If the Christian is forbidden to 'name' the future as the victory of the risen Christ which shapes the struggle against evil in the present, what grounds are there for supposing that negation is truly liberation, or for choosing one form of negation over another?

My unease is further increased by Pieris' suggestion that the religious instinct be defined as 'a revolutionary urge, a psycho-social impulse, to generate a new humanity. It is none other than the piercing thrust of evolution in its self-conscious state, the human version of nature's thirst for higher forms of life. The religious drive is an irresistible drive to humanize what has merely been hominized.'[89] We all clamour for justice and a new humanity but the problem is that we are torn apart by rival conceptions of what these terms mean. German Romantic thinkers in the last century identified the religious impulse with the *Volksgeist*, the distinctive 'blood and soil' ethos of a people which found its apotheosis in the Nazi programme for the liberation of German culture from foreign domination and the creation of a new race. Likewise, the Hindu mobs who destroy Muslim mosques in India and denounce capitalism and the secular technocracy of the modern state are driven by a revolutionary urge, a psycho-social impulse, to generate a new society.

It is unfortunate that, having begun with the cross as the place where God's justice shines forth, Pieris should now retreat from exploring further the particular implications of the cross and instead settle for vague generalities. There are incompatible visions in our world of what it means to be truly human, just as there are incompatible assessments of the person of Jesus. The Christian claims that the two questions are inextricably woven together, for it is in Jesus that the new humanity is made visible, and it is on the basis of *this* understanding that claims to human progress are evaluated. If it is not possible to make absolute claims for Jesus (or any particular name) anymore, then how is it possible to claim an absolute validity for the praxis of justice and liberation? Such a praxis will quickly become hijacked by the dominant impulses of the society in which it operates. To ascribe such impulses to evolution come of age is almost tantamount to a deterministic naturalism, and no project of human liberation can survive for long in such a framework (remember Marxism?). There is also a curious inconsistency in Pieris' falling back on the language of evolution: for in the evolutionary framework of thought there is no 'option for the poor', but rather the very reverse! It seems that Pieris has come dangerously close to viewing God as a *principle* grounding human emancipatory endeavour: a deity whose 'reality' is exhausted by the totality of human transformative praxis. The 'religiousness of the poor' has thus turned into Feuerbach with a vengeance . . .

(m) This leads me, finally, to suspect that, notwithstanding his vigorous denunciations of the West and his call to synthesize gnosis and agape in a new religious praxis, Pieris may still be a child of the Enlightenment belief that justice and freedom can be founded on a universal human reason. The unmasking of illusion is sufficient for liberation. Progress towards that goal is built into the nature of humanity. This may also account for the fact that, despite claiming to articulate an Asian theology of liberation, he skates over the most significant contrasts between Buddhist and Christian visions of liberation. For the Buddhist, *nirvana* is the *cessation* of the individual's history and of all that constitutes reality as we now experience it; but for the Christian, the *eschaton* is the *consummation/fufilment* of both individual history and cultural history, a 'filling out' rather than a 'dropping off'. Such fundamental divergence is no doubt embarrassing to a pluralist theology that has chosen to speak of religions as expressive of different aspects of Being rather than as different accounts of Being itself. Perhaps it is only by respecting the distinctiveness of the gospel account

of 'what is' that respect for the genuine *otherness* of the other
can be secured.

Notes to Chapter Two

1. *An Asian Theology of Liberation* (Edinburgh: T & T Clark, 1988).
   Abbreviated to ATL in the present chapter.
2. *Love Meets Wisdom: a Christian Experience of Buddhism* (Maryknoll,
   New York: Orbis, 1988). Abbreviated to LMW in the present
   chapter.
3. Pieris' essay in this symposium also appears in LMW above.
4. As expressed, for example, by the Peruvian Gustavo Gutierrez's
   celebrated definition: 'The theology of liberation offers us not so
   much a new theme for reflection as a *new way* of making theology.
   Theology as critical reflecion on historical praxis is thus a liberating
   theology, a theology of he liberating transformation of the history of
   mankind and, therefore, also of that portion of it—gathered in
   ecclesia—which openly confesses Christ . . . a theology which does
   not limit itself to think the world, but which attempts to place itself
   as a moment of the process through which the world is transformed
   . . .' (*A Theology of Liberation*, London: SCM, 1974, rev. edn 1988,
   p. 12). Socio-political transformation is the justification of all theology.
   Thus, 'If theological reflection does not vitalise the action of the
   Christian community in the world by making its commitment to
   charity fuller and more radical, if . . . it does not lead the Church to
   be on the side of the oppressed classes . . . it will have been of little
   value.' (ibid. p. 174) Likewise the Brazilian Leonardo Boff identifies
   the 'common point of departure' of all the various tendencies within
   'the one theology of liberation' as 'ethical indignation at the misery
   of social reality, and the demand for a process of liberation that will
   overcome this contradiction.' (Leonardo & Clodovis Boff, *Salvation
   and Liberation*, Maryknoll, NY: Orbis, 1984, p. 25).
5. ATL, p. 120–1.
6. Ibid. p. 36.
7. Ibid. p. 123.
8. Ibid. p. 10.
9. Ibid. p. 20 (Italics in text).
10. Ibid. p. 21 (Italics in text).
11. Ibid. p. 12.
12. Ibid. p. 23.
13. Of the 'core experience' of *gnosis* (liberative knowledge) in Budd-
    hism and of *agape* (redemptive love) in Christianity, Pieris writes
    'Each is *salvific* in that each is a *self-transcending* event that radically
    transforms the human person affected by that experience. At the
    same time there is an indefinable contrast between them that largely
    determines the major differences between the two religions . . .'
    (LMW, p. 111, italics in text).
14. LMW, p. 122–3.
15. Ibid. p. 123.
16. ATL, op.cit. p. 36 (Italics in text).

17. Ibid. p. 41 (Italics in text).
18. Ibid. p. 49.
19. Ibid. p. 46.
20. Ibid. p. 47.
21. Ibid. p. 45.
22. Ibid. p. 50.
23. LMW, op.cit. p. 123
24. Ibid. p. 48.
25. Ibid. p. 49 (Italics in text).
26. Ibid. p. 50.
27. Ibid. p. 57 (Italics in text).
28. Ibid. p. 58.
29. Thus New Age, with its syncretistic merger of Western consumer-ism with Eastern psycho-religous techniques, would be a form of 'leisure-class' spirituality that is a denial of both Semitic and Eastern faiths.
30. LMW, op.cit. p. 111.
31. Ibid. p. 118.
32. Ibid. p. 111.
33. ATL, op.cit. p. 54.
34. LMW, op.cit. p. 127.
35. ATL, op.cit. p. 55.
36. Ibid. p. 51.
37. Ibid. p. 55.
38. Ibid. p. 62.
39. LMW, op.cit. p. 132.
40. Ibid. (Italics in text).
41. ATL, op.cit. p. 62.
42. LMW, op.cit. p. 129.
43. Ibid. p. 133 (Italics in text).
44. Ibid. p. 135 (Italics in text).
45. AC Thiselton, *New Horizons in Hermeneutics* (Grand Rapids: Zondervan/HarperCollins, 1992) p. 410.
46. Ibid. p. 429.
47. ATL, op. cit. p. 62.
48. Ibid. p. 12.
49. Thiselton points out that 'Historically hermeneutics emerged as a critical discipline precisely to deliver and to free communities from being brow-beaten and placed under socio-political pressure by purely *instrumental* appeals to biblical texts *as supports for some prior interest.* Predominantly pragmatic uses of biblical texts have the status of exercises in self-justification and potential manipulation, whether we are considering a dominant social tradition or a social minority, women or men, pietists or sceptics', Thiselton, op. cit. p. 452 (italics in text).
50. Cf. Andrew Kirk's question to the liberation theologians of Latin America: 'Does not any theory of oppression that banishes from its horizon the objective reality of the 'powers' (the active presence of all demonic alternatives to the kingdom) inevitably lead to a certain romanticism concerning the possibility of structural change? It is

true that structural alienation, in Marxist terms, may be akin to the biblical concept of the 'powers', which also work against humanity, but there is also a clear distinction: whereas structural alienation as such can be concretely identified in society, the 'powers' can only be 'suspected' on the grounds that structural alienation is not an adequate way of accounting for man's resistance to liberating change', *Liberation Theology: an Evangelical View from the Third World* (London: Marshall, Morgan and Scott, 1979, p. 188).

51. BF Meyer, *The Aims of Jesus* (London: SCM, 1979) p. 115.
52. RT France, 'Jesus the Baptist?' in *Jesus of Nazareth: Lord and Christ*, eds. Joel Green and Max Turner (Eerdmans/Paternoster, 1994) p. 96. France's concern is to question the general assumption (including that of Meyer, above) that the Jesus movement was not a baptizing movement during Jesus' lifetime. He argues, quite plausibly, that there is 'good reason to believe that baptism did not fall into disuse after the imprisonment of John, only to be reintroduced suddenly after the resurrection, but that it remained for Jesus, as it had been for John, the normal means of enrolling those who joined this eschatological restoration movement. Not only at the beginning, but throughout his ministry, Jesus was a second "Baptist" ' (p. 107). If true, this would further undermine Pieris' 'missiological principles'.
53. Note how the continuity between John and Jesus is reinforced by the instinctive conjecture of the people (Mk 8:28) and of Herod Antipas (Mk 6:14) that in Jesus John the Baptist had come to life again. In Mk 9:11–13 the fate of John is a model for that of Jesus, and in Lk. 11:1–4 Jesus teaches his disciples to pray just as John had done.
54. Meyer, op.cit., p. 220. Cf. J Jeremias: 'Jesus . . . underwent John's baptism in order to take his place among the eschatological people of God that the Baptist was assembling.' New Testament Theology (London: SCM, 1971, p. 49) cited by France, op. cit., p. 104. In this context, the description of John's ministry as taking place 'in the wilderness' is significant, for it was in the wilderness that Israel had been formed into the covenant people of Yahweh (see esp.Deut. 8:2–6) and prophetic eschatological hopes centred on a new exodus and a new wilderness experience, when the eschatological renewal of Israel would be accompanied by the transformation of the wilderness (e.g. Is. 40:3;41:18–19, 44:3–5, Hos. 2;14–15; Ezek. 20 20:34–38). The Qumran community went out to the wilderness to await the restoration of Israel; and Josephus speaks of Jewish insurgents such as Theudas (*Antiquities*. 20:97–8), 'the Egyptian' (*Jewish War* 2:261–3) and Jonathan the Weaver (*Jewish War* 7:43–4) who typically took their followers into the wilderness around the Jordan valley in the hope of precipitating the kingdom of God.
55. The Fourth Gospel is even more explicit in describing the self-effacing witness of John—indeed he is referred to as 'the witness' and never as the 'baptist'! He hails Jesus as the 'Lamb of God who takes away the sin of the world' (Jn 1:29), declares that the reason he came baptizing with water was that 'he [Jesus] might be revealed to Israel' (1:31), testifies that he is 'the Son of God' (1:34) and now that the

bridegroom has arrived on the scene the bridegroom's friend must recede into the background (3:29ff).

56. See the exhaustive list of citations in Joel Green, 'Good News to Whom? Jesus and the "Poor" in the Gospel of Luke' in *Jesus of Nazareth: Lord and Christ*, eds. Joel Green and Max Turner (Grand Rapids: Eerdmans/Carlisle: Paternoster, 1994) pp. 60ff.

57. Ibid. p. 59.

58. Ibid. p. 69. Green also sums up recent investigations into the biblical semantic field of Luke's preferred term for the 'poor' by putting forward 'two widely recognized observations': namely, (1) Words of this semantic domain embrace both socio-economic and religious connotations. The poor are those who have lost their independence, are susceptible to exploitation by those with power, and who must look beyond themselves to Yahweh for help. (2) Yahweh is the deliverer of the poor, who grants mercy to the poor, judges those who pervert justice and vindicates the cause of the poor in the face of their enemies. '*That is, the emphasis falls on the relationship between God and the poor, with the former extending grace to the latter, who find themselves increasingly at the periphery of society.*' (p. 64, italics in text).

59. Although Buddhism is the most socially egalitarian of Asian faiths, in theory and in practice it has usually been an all-male affair. And, as Prof. Richard Gombrich observes, 'there is some evidence that the Buddha's message appealed especially to town-dwellers and the new social classes . . . brahmin recruits [to the Sangha] were not the traditional village priests but rather upper-class urbanites. If these figures have any foundation, they show that Buddhism, though it admitted anyone to the Sangha, was not primarily a religion of the downtrodden.' (R Gombrich, *Theravada Buddhism: a Social History from Ancient Benares to Modern Colombo* (London: Routledge & Kegan Paul, 1988, pp. 55–6). Gombrich also points out that the Buddha 'never preached against social inequality, only declared its irrelevance to salvation. He never tried to abolish the caste system nor to do away with slavery. While a famous sermon, the Samanna-phala sutta, stresses the practical benefits for a slave in leaving his servitude and joining the Order [Sangha], in fact runaway slaves were not allowed to join the Order. Moreover, though in ancient India there was no caste or other form of social ranking within the Order itself, the Order soon came to own (lay) slaves.' (p. 30).

60. Ibid. pp. 203–4.

61. See, e.g. *Heralds of Health: the Saga of Christian Medical Initiatives*, (eds.) SG Browne, F Davey & WAR Thompson (London: Christian Medical Fellowship, 1985).

62. See, e.g. Graham Stanton, *A Gospel for a New People: Studies in Matthew* (Edinburgh: T & T Clark, 1992) pp. 207–31; a survey of interpretations of this passage can be found in Sherman Gray, *The Least of my Brothers: Matt 25:31–46 A History of Interpretation* (Atlanta: Scholars Press, 1989).

63. Cf Acts 9:4–5 for the possible origins of this corporate understanding of Christ in Paul's thought.

64. Gutierrez, op.cit. p. xxiv.

65. Elie Wiesel, *Night*, trans. Stella Rodway (London: Fontana Collins, 1972) pp. 112–3. This was the only book that Wiesel wrote directly about the Holocaust. My account is taken from Kenneth Surin, *Theology and the Problem of Evil* (Oxford: Blackwell,1986) p. 121.
66. Elie Wiesel, *The Town Beyond the Wall*, trans.Stephen Barker (New York: Avon, 1970) p. 174. Cited in Surin, op.cit. p. 120.
67. Surin, op.cit. p. 121–2.
68. LMW, op.cit., p. 124.
69. L Hurtado, *One God, One Lord: Early Christian Devotion and Jewish Monotheism* (London: SCM, 1988) p. 11.
70. M Hengel, *The Son of God: the Origin of Christology and the History of Jewish-Hellenistic Religion* (Eng.trans. J Bowden, London: SCM, 1976) p. 1.
71. For the sake of consistency, I have used the (inclusive) language of the New RSV translation here rather than that found in the English translation of Hengel's book.
72. Ibid.
73. Ibid.pp. 1–2 (Italics in text).
74. e.g. LMW, op.cit. p. 133.
75. J Pelikan, *Jesus Through the Centuries* (New Haven and London: Yale University Press, 1985) p. 70.
76. RC Zaehner, 'Foolishness to the Greeks', Appendix to *Concordant Discord: Gifford Lectures on Natural Religion, 1967–69* (Oxford: Oxford University Press, 1970) p. 443.
77. Ibid. p. 442.
78. Ibid. p. 443.
79. LMW, op. cit. p. 118.
80. Neoplatonic 'triads' were part of the intellectual map of the third and fourth centuries against which Christian doctrinal formulation took place. The Church Fathers, while sharing a common language with their pagan neighbours, nevertheless gave distinctive meanings to common terms and refused to assimilate either the Trinity and Christology to Neoplatonic thought-forms. Any attempt to revert to language concerning 'triadic structures' and 'common trinitarian forms' can only be superficial and retrogressive, in effect a denial of the orthodox doctrine. See also my critique of Panikkar on this in the following chapter.
81. See e.g. A Louth, *Denys the Areopagite* (London: Geoffrey Chapman, 1989).
82. Cf. LMW. p. 121. Pieris acknowledges his debt here to Raimundo Panikkar for helping him to 'realize' that every religion operates on three levels: the primordial *experience*, the collective *memory* of that experience stored up in tradition, and the *interpretation* of that experience in philosophical and theological schools (p. 120).
83. Ibid. p. 131. (My emphasis).
84. Sarojini Naidu, one of the early followers of Gandhi and a leading political figure in post-independence India, once observed ironically, 'It takes a great deal of money to keep Bapu [as Gandhi was called] living in poverty.' Quoted in R Lannoy, *The Speaking Tree: A Study of Indian Culture and Society* (Oxford, 1971) p. 396.

85. 'We cannot read Gandhi without finding echoes of eighteenth-century Western European thinkers who first gave articulate expression to horror, pity, anger, and grief for a society in which men who work go poor', Lannoy, ibid. p. 375 (I suspect that there is an error here and that he means nineteenth-century).

86. For example: 'India's salvation consists in unlearning what she has learned during the past fifty years. The railways, telegraphs, hospitals, lawyers, doctors and such like have all to go, and the so-called upper classes have to learn to live consciously religiously and deliberately the simple peasant life, knowing it to be a life giving true happiness . . . Ideally however I would rule out all machinery, even as I would reject this very body which is not helpful to salvation, and seek the absolute liberation of the soul.' Quoted in MM Thomas, *The Acknowledged Christ of the Indian Renaissance* (Madras: C.L.S, 2nd ed, 1976, p. 224).

87. CS Song, 'New China and Salvation History—a Methodological Inquiry' in *Living Faiths and Ultimate Goals*, ed. SJ Samartha (Geneva: WCC, 1974) pp. 80, 84.

88. ATL, op. cit., p. 109.

89. Ibid. pp. 107–8.

[3]

Christic Theandrism:
Raimundo Panikkar

Raimundo Panikkar, son of an Indian Hindu father and a Spanish Catholic mother, is a unique and eminent figure in the encounter of religious faiths in this century. Born and brought up in Catalan Spain, Panikkar's studies took him to Madrid, Rome, Bonn and the Indian cities of Varanasi and Mysore. He has held Chairs in Religious Sociology, Indian Culture and Comparative Philosophy of Religion in places as diverse as Madrid, Rome, Bangalore and California.

For Panikkar the quest for inter-faith understanding has been a quest for his own selfhood as heir to two worlds. Since the 1960s, he has championed an *oikoumene* of world faiths, trying to marry the personalism of the Semitic faiths with the *advaita*, non-dual, experience of Asian faiths in such a way that diversity is not obliterated but anchored in a transcendent mystery. In an introduction to the revised edition of his influential book *The Unknown Christ of Hinduism*, Panikkar states his conviction that

> the Christian, in recognizing, believing in and loving Christ as the central symbol of Life and Ultimate Truth, is being drawn towards that selfsame Mystery that attracts all other human beings who are seeking to overcome their own present condition. The word 'mystery' though it belongs in a certain tradition, stands for that 'thing' which is called by many names and is experienced in many forms; thus it can be called neither one nor many.[1]

The reality that is 'neither one nor many' is the underlying theme of all his copious writings spanning over thirty years.

76

Panikkar offers a unique vision of religious pluralism that blends the Christian language of the Trinity with Hindu advaitin non-dualism and the ultimate silence of Buddhism.

Expounding Panikkar is a daunting task. His writings, for all their erudite eloquence, their flowing cadences and occasional bursts of passion, are often convoluted and elusive. He is an inventor of neologisms, and relishes what he loves to regard as the 'polyvalence' of words. We shall see later how frustrating this can be when he applies it to the meaning of scriptural texts. The reader is also confronted by Panikkar's own polyvalence, uncertain sometimes whether he is witnessing, even as he reads, the self-acknowledged 'historical mutation' taking place in the author[2] or simply being 'talked down to' by a mind that is already moving on to 'higher' things. Consider, for instance, Pannikar's warning that 'The only way to understand what I am saying, and shall be saying in the remainder of this book, will be to enter into the authentic silence of the mind'[3], or the enigmatic comment, at the end of his introduction to the revised edition of *The Unknown Christ of Hinduism*, 'At present, the writer would be much more radical in his approach' but has held back out of 'respect for the rhythm of the cosmos and of history.'[4] In the light of such condescension, how far is the poor reader, lagging behind in the rhythm of the cosmos yet striving to keep up with the author, expected to take seriously even the latter's most recent words? Does one regard them as tongue-in-cheek, their public meanings never disclosing the author's thoughts, or are the latter also to be regarded merely as flotsam in the samsaric flux?

Panikkar evidently wants us to see both continuity and change, not only in his own thinking but also in the social and religious map of the late twentieth century. The one reflects the other. His own pilgrimage is expressed under the imagery of the Emmaus road:

> There has been a fellow traveller on my journeys to the different lands of Man. Child of my own time and environment, I thought I knew well who that companion was in my intellectual and spiritual wonderments of over a half-century ago. There came, however, a critical moment when I reached my ancestral dwelling-place at the peak period of my life: my companion disappeared . . . And so, instead of retracing my steps to a City of Peace, to look for and perhaps find my partner again, I proceeded, alone, to a battlefield ravaged by fratricidal

warfare. Shocked and pained, I refused to take a stand and
struggle for any of the parties . . . I remained a conscientious
objector, mistrusted by both . . . Risking my life in offering
my services to everybody without accepting their respective
dialectics, I found myself suddenly in the World of Time. And
from there the sacredness of everything, even of the secular,
dawned upon me. Thus I am at the confluence (*sangam*) of the
four rivers: Hindu, Christian, Buddhist and Secular traditions.[5]

Not only does modern awareness of inter-dependence in a
global family demand the mutual fertilization of human
traditions but, Panikkar believes, so does what he sees as the
breakdown of traditional Christian concepts of divinity. His
exploration of Buddhist apophaticism, in *The Silence of God*,
takes place against the backdrop of the 'death of God'
movement and the honest-to-God debate in the Western
theological world of the 1960s.[6] He writes of modern man's
'lived experience of antagonism between God and beings'
and that if no God 'capable of guaranteeing [human] self-
affirmation' can be found, humankind would 'declare itself
favourable to atheism'.[7] Therefore, a radical purification of
the notion of 'God' is called for: the problem is how to 'save
God'—'stripped to the bone, the question comes down to
what God is good *for*, or how God is of any use to *us* . . . no
revelation, no aspect of the divine, can disregard human self-
consciousness, which is keenly aware that the question of
God is a question of something that, however sublime and
transcendent, must not only pass through human structures,
but must ultimately resolve the anthropological problem
itself.'[8]

Owing to the complexity of Panikkar's ideas and the
elusiveness of his prose, an inexperienced reader may quickly
feel overwhelmed by an uninterrupted exposition. So I have
chosen to deviate from the pattern followed in the previous
chapters, and to make my critique piecemeal at the end of
each section rather than present it entire at the end.

Christ and the Christic Principle

The disappearance of his 'companion' at the threshold of his
'ancestral dwelling-place' is an useful point of access into
Panikkar's subtle mind. Panikkar starts with 'Christ',
because that is where he says Christians start and his own
pilgrimage began, in the land of his Spanish mother. But a

major obstacle arises in the encounter with the Hindu when Christianity 'identifies, with necessary qualifications, Christ with Jesus, the Son of Mary.'[9] The historical specificities of the word 'Christ' have to fall away if communication is to take place, for the Christian concept of history is alien to the Indian mind. In any case, this idea of history, Panikkar claims, is *a posteriori* to the incarnation of Christ. 'We should not forget,' he writes, 'that the first philosophical interpretation of Christ begins with a discourse not on the "flesh" but on the "Logos" that became "flesh".'[10] But not only does this metaphysical starting-point provide a better point of contact with Indian philosophy than the historical figure of Jesus, it also gives expression to God's universal will to save humankind. It is only possible to maintain the universal embrace of Christianity if we disassociate it from its historical particularities.[11]

Christ the Saviour is not to be objectified as a 'merely historical personage'. When 'the myth of history' begins to take over Christianity, claims Panikkar, 'Jesus Christ becomes the supreme Imperium. Incarnation becomes just a little slice of history and "evangelization" consists in "civilizing" others and incorporating them into one "Christian" (and post-Christian) world-order.'[12]

In *The Unknown Christ of Hinduism*, Panikkar believes that he is preserving the substance of the traditional logos and wisdom theology of the early church and illuminating it by the inter-religious experience of today. He sees himself doing with the Hindu religious texts essentially what Aquinas did with Hellenistic wisdom in general and Aristotle in particular. For is not the discovery of Sankara and Ramanuja at least as important for Christian theology today as was the assimilation of Plato and Aristotle in the Western past? Indeed he goes back to the New Testament itself: ' . . . I venture to think that such an attempt as mine could find inspiration, illumination and justification in the famous encounter of St. Paul with the men of Athens.'[13] Christ/ Logos has always been at work everywhere, not only at the creation of the heavens and the earth, 'but also when the Indian *rishis* composed and handed down the *sruti* [the sacred scriptures].'[14] 'God is at work in all religions: the Christian kerygma does not proclaim a new God but the *mirabilia* of God, of which the Mystery of Christ hidden in God is the *alpha* and *omega*. This very expression in fact is declaring that

Christ is not yet "finished", not "discovered", until the last moment or the "end" has come.'[15] Christians should recognize that 'Christ will never be totally known on earth, as that would amount to seeing the Father whom nobody can see. It was even good that Christ disappeared and went away; otherwise Men would have made him a king or a God.'[16] Panikkar explains that by the title of the book he meant not a Christ known to Christians but unknown to Hindus, but rather the 'mysteric aspect' of Hinduism which 'Christians will find themselves obliged to call "Christ" '.[17]

At one point Panikkar echoes Karl Rahner's theology of religions (without actually quoting him) in claiming that this Christ, who always saves sacramentally, 'may be active and at work in the human being who receives any sacrament, whether Christian or any other'.[18] He continues, 'The good and *bona fide* Hindu as well as the good and *bona fide* Christian are saved by Christ—not by Hinduism or Christianity per se, but through their sacraments and, ultimately, through the *mysterion* active within the two religions'.[19] Recognizing the presence of God in other religions is equivalent to proclaiming the presence of Christ in them, for whatever God does 'ab extra' happens through Christ and 'in him all things subsist (Col 1:15)'.[20] However for Panikkar the role of *Isvara* in Hindu *Vedanta*—the personal aspect of *Brahman*/God, postulated as the connecting link between *Brahman*/God and the World, without compromising the absoluteness of the former and the relativity of the latter—'corresponds functionally to the role of Christ in Christian thought'.[21]

This ontic Christ/*Isvara* is, for Panikkar, the 'fundamental religious fact', 'a living symbol for the totality of reality: human, divine, cosmic'.[22] This totality is what he calls, in his more recent writings, the cosmotheandric reality. Christ is both symbol and substance of a dynamic, non-dualistic unity between God, humanity and the world.

> Man and God are neither two nor one . . . There are not two realities: God and man (or world); but neither is there one: God or man (or world), as outright atheists and outright theists are dialectically driven to maintain. Reality itself is theandric . . . God and man are, so to speak, in close constitutive collaboration for the building up of reality, the unfolding of history, and the continuation of creation.[23]

Theandrism is, paradoxically, 'the infinitude of man, for he is tending towards God, the infinite, and the finitude of God, for he is the end (*finis*) of man'. The Christian form of this theandrism is the mystical Body of Christ, the Buddhist form the *dharmakaya*. Either way 'God, man and the world are engaged in a unique adventure and this engagement constitutes true reality'.[24]

There is, then, only one Christ: one ontic link mediating between the one and the many, the Absolute and the relative, the infinite and the finite. Between these two poles everything that functions as mediator is 'Christ', which is the sole priest of the cosmic priesthood, both divine and human, the ground of divinity within all humanity. Thus what the Christhood of Jesus signifies is not confined there but belongs to a reality that is known there but also elsewhere. He insists, therefore, that while we may truly say as Christians that, 'Jesus is the Christ', we may not say, 'The Christ is Jesus'. Similarly for 'Lord' and other christological titles. In Jesus we make a Christian identification of an identity larger than the location given to it in Jesus. Jesus is simply one among other concrete historical names for the 'Supername'—that is, the Christ, which is always 'the name above every name' (Phil. 2:9).

It is not that this reality has many names, but that this reality *is* many names and each name is a new aspect or manifestation of it. Each authentic name enriches and qualifies it. The Way cannot be separated from the Goal. Spatial metaphors can be misleading. It is not that there are different paths to the same peak, but that the peak itself would collapse if all the paths disappeared. 'The peak is in a certain sense the result of the paths leading to it.'[25] The Hindu who has reached enlightenment, has realized *atman-Brahman*, the ultimate Mystery. Only for the Christian is the Mystery always connected with Christ; only for the Vaishnava is the Mystery connected with Vishnu or whatever has been the particular form for attaining *moksa*.

Panikkar proposes the following metaphor:

> Each religion and ultimately each human being stands within the rainbow of reality and sees it as white light-precisely because of seeing through the entire rainbow. From the outside, as an intellectual abstraction, I see you in the green area and you see me in the orange one. I call you green and you call me orange because, when we look at each other, we do not look at the totality. We do not intend to express the totality—what we

believe—but we evaluate and judge each other. And though it is true that I am in the orange strip with all the limitations of a saffron spirituality, if you ask my colour, I say 'white'![26]

Why then does Panikkar handle this Mystery within a Hindu/Christian Christology and not in terms of a general concept of God, thereby allaying the suspicions of people of other faiths that this is simply a Christian imposition? Precisely because the symbol of Christ permits neither an apersonal, undifferentiated unity nor an ultimate duality between the divine and the human. *Rama, Krishna, Purusha* or (especially) *Isvara* may be other such names, but 'most of the apparently more neutral symbols such as God, Spirit, Truth and the like truncate reality and limit the centre of life to a disincarnate principle, a non-historical epiphany, and often an abstraction'.[27]

In his contribution to the symposium *The Myth of Christian Uniqueness*,[28] Panikkar reverts to his beloved river imagery: the history of the Christian tradition in its relation to other religions is symbolized by the three sacred rivers, the Jordan, the Tiber and the Ganges. These represent 'three kairological moments of Christic self-consciousness' in historical sequence: the Jordan, the Messiah and Judaeo–Christian exclusivism; the Tiber, the imperial expansion of Christianity into an inclusivist faith; and the Ganges, the emerging pluralism of religious faiths. For Panikkar the Ganges is not Hinduism but the whole world.

Panikkar invites us to grasp what he calls the 'christic principle' neither as a universal religion nor a particular event, but as 'the centre of reality as seen by the Christian tradition'. He broadly associates the three rivers with what he distinguishes as Christianity, Christendom and Christianness respectively. Only the last is appropriate for the present *kairos* of a pluralist world. Christianness stands for 'experience of the life of Christ within ourselves', an experience 'that I and the Father are One'[29]; it is freed from monotheistic assumptions of a totally intelligible Being, holds lightly to ecclesiastical creeds and traditions, recognizes myth as 'the horizon that makes thinking possible' and that 'no single notion can comprehend the reality of Christ', regards security as of no importance, and lives by 'confidence' in the future, not by concern over truth-claims.

But what is this 'christic principle'? Panikkar characterizes it as 'the word that is in every authentic word'; the 'cross-roads of reality where all realms meet'; 'that about which one should not believe that it is here or there'. This, 'through our own synergy, is what I believe to be the Christ'. Anticipating Christian objections, he continues,

> I insist that with such a view of Christ I am not escaping the scandal of the incarnation and the process of redemption. I am not ignoring these historical facts. It is simply that I do not worship history . . . Every being is a *christophany*.[30]

In other words, each concrete moment represents, in its own particular way, the whole flow of universal interaction which is unknowable in itself but which Christians see in terms of 'christic universal vision'. Rowan Williams has paraphrased this neatly with a vivid metaphor: 'The individual reality or situation is like a single chord abstracted from a symphony: it can be looked at in itself, but only with rather boring results, since what is there and then is determined by the symphony. What it is *is* the symphony at that juncture.'[31]

. But one cannot help feeling that Panikkar has drained the word Christ of its historic significance and its continuing personal significance for Christian believers. He holds it aloft as a mere cipher, hoping that it can still evoke the same emotive response and, perhaps, the same ethical commitments, even though its very content has been transformed. If history no longer remains central to the identity and definition of Christ, how else would we recognize the 'authentic' in 'the word', or 'the reality' that is 'the crossroads', and how do we distinguish between the authentic and the inauthentic spiritualities of humankind? Panikkar proposes no criteria.

He is right to remind us that Christians do not worship history, but Christians do worship what history became the vehicle of—and with deep awe that it could have been enabled to do so. While there is a commendable desire in Panikkar's writings to stress respect for the genuine 'other-ness' of the other, he tends (especially when dealing with Christian beliefs) to dissolve particularity into universality by simple extension. His is a Christ whose Christhood is not inextricably linked with the events of Gethsemane and Golgotha. Panikkar would be justified in doing so if these events are not constitutive of the Christhood of Jesus. But the church has maintained, from its inception, that they are. It is in the wounds of Jesus that we encounter that which is ultimately real, and it is through his death and resurrection that we are not only led to affirm the value of all human history but brought into a radically new relationship with the ground and goal of that history.

It is the physical resurrection of Jesus that demonstrates the meaning of the incarnation as the taking of humanity into God. The resurrection is integral to the meaning of the incarnation in the Christian pattern of things. Not only is the divine communicated through and manifested in the human life of Jesus, but our incorporation in the divine life is through the resurrected and glorified humanity of Jesus, which remains the vehicle of our union and communion with the divine through eternity. It is in the concrete life, death and resurrection of Jesus that the universal is disclosed; *not* in a way that gives us a unifying theoretical scheme that embraces the whole history of the world, but in such a way that it becomes the *universal point of reference* for distinguishing between true and false visions of human flourishing. So in relativizing the person of Jesus, Panikkar ends up with a false 'christic' universalism. It unwittingly perpetuates the same homogenizing tendencies of the modern world against which he is, rightly, protesting.

Panikkar's scheme, with its notions of 'theandric reality' and a 'christic principle', has close affinities with GWF Hegel's (1770–1831) famous reconstruction of traditional Christian language about incarnation within the framework of an idealist philosophy.[32] Although he shared in the 'turn to the subject' characteristic of post-Enlightenment Western thought,[33] Hegel sought to transcend the dualism of an Absolute conceived as objective, static substance and a human subject caught up in the dynamic of history. He posited an essential divine-human union which came to self-recognition in a process of dialectical development through history. Christology was the culmination of this process: the doctrine of the God-Man is a sublime picture which arose in the human mind at a particular point in history and as a matter of rational necessity. This point corresponds with the birth of Christianity. The grand metaphysical truth that divinity and humanity are necessarily inseparable, that the divine and the human natures can realize themselves only through each other, this has now been taught in the pictures and parables of the Christian faith. The dialectical development of thought, from that based on sensory perception to religious representation and finally reaching its zenith in conceptual thought, is also the development of reality/God. Hegel's *Geist* (Spirit) was the unfolding and coming to consciousness in the human subject of the Absolute. The story of humankind is the history of God's becoming, the self-evolution of God as trinitarian Being.

Hegel saw himself as defender of the claims of religion in an increasingly sceptical, secular academia. The truth of the divine–human essence, fully articulate in his philosophy, has been dimly foreshadowed in the world of religion. All religions have the idea of incarnation, but Christianity makes most explicit what is only implicit elsewhere. Yet, for all his reference to history as the arena of the divine self-realization, Hegel shares in the flight from history typical both of Enlightenment rationalism and the Indian religious outlook. No one event in history is of more value than any other. No event may claim unique significance. All events are but individual instantiations of the eternal and universal patterns of rational being. The philosopher, embodied in Hegel, uncovers this pattern by pure speculative thought. He lets religion say what philosophy itself has thought and said much better.

Thus the biblical concept of the incarnation is no longer understood as a unique, once-for-all event in space and time by which the Son/Word of God embraces an alienated humanity and reconciles it to the Father through his own human obedience unto death. Historical events and the faith-claims of a historical community have been reconstructed into a timeless ontological structure. As HR Mackintosh comments, 'The general trend of Hegel's argument is sufficiently indicated by the fact that the name of Christ is not mentioned until the speculative treatment of reconciliation between God and man has been given in full, while the name of Jesus is never used at all.'[34] It is one thing to draw out the ontological implications of a historical fact; it is quite another to let contingent events be swallowed up by neccessary truths in an abstract philosophical synthesis. It is this that provoked Soren Kierkegaard (1813–1855) to his famous anti-Hegelian jibe: 'That the human race is or should be akin to God is ancient paganism; but that an individual man is God is Christianity'.[35]

Panikkar, of course, unlike Hegel, will not give any central place to Christianity among the religions. But, like Hegel, his link between the philosophical 'principle' of incarnation and the concrete history of Jesus of Nazareth is so tenuous as to be non-existent. He lays himself open to the charge levelled at Hegel by contemporary critics such as Kierkegaard that he had actually redefined fundamental gospel beliefs so that they were transmuted into something totally unrecognizable as Christian. For all his concerns to find a place for religion in an age of unbelief (a concern that we saw is shared by Panikkar), Hegel's heritage was deeply ambiguous. His left-wing followers, beginning with Feuerbach and Marx, had little trouble in developing his system in a thoroughly secularist direction. It is likely that the same fate awaits the development of Panikkar's thought.[36]

To revert to Panikkar's terminology, expressions such as 'christic' and the formula 'Christ is not the only Christ' are very close to being mere vacuous slogans. When Panikkar points to Paul's words in Phil. 2:9 to identify his Christ with the 'Supername' that is above all other concrete historical names, he overlooks the fact the apostle states explicitly that it is the name of *Jesus* that God has exalted 'above every name'! As for the Logos christology of the Fourth Gospel, Panikkar is right to draw attention to the truth that the Logos is 'the true light that gives light to every man' (John 1:9), but that claim is made in the context of the larger claim that that same Logos was now coming in to the world in a radically new way (namely, 'in flesh', v14). Panikkar also overlooks the indictment of the human race, including the world of human religion, implicit in the text: it is in the darkness that the light shines (v.5), the world fails to recognize the Word that is its life and rejects the Word (v.10), the Word brings the fullness of grace and truth over against law (v.16,17), incorporation into the family of God is not a human right but a gift that comes through receiving the incarnate Word (v.12,13), and so on.

As for Panikkar's claim that he is essentially doing what Paul was doing in Athens, while one admires his mastery of and sensitivity to the Hindu and Buddhist scriptures and philosphical systems, one has also to conclude that his reluctance to draw distinctions and his eagerness to synthesize too quickly are at variance with Paul's own example. For while Paul did build bridges into the Stoic and Epicurean thought-worlds by using their own philosophical texts and identifying common ground, he nevertheless did not flinch from declaring the resurrection of Jesus from the dead and the latter's appontment by God as the eschatological Judge of the whole world. One cannot imagine a message more at odds with the religious presuppositions of his audience.[37] Panikkar insists that he is not escaping 'the scandal of the incarnation', but why should his non-historical theandrism constitute a 'scandal' to anyone-then or now? It is clear that the Ganges of pluralism needs to be fed by the waters of the Jordan if it is not to evade the real 'scandal' of the Incarnation.

I respect Panikkar's concern that Christians should not have a 'monopoly' over Christ. A Christ who is only 'for Christians' would not be the Christ of the New Testament gospel with its eschatological promise of human and cosmic reconciliation. The intent of the truth disclosed in Jesus Christ is universal; and surely it is important to distinguish this universality of intent from a kind of universality which is actually the relinquishment of its content. Far from history being opposed to universality, in the perspective of the gospel, it is the very historicity of the cross and resurrection that furnishes the basis for a universal hope. Panikkar would be hard pressed to extract anything that would be Good News for the world from his universal 'christic principle'. For news that is simply entailed in what has always been so (and has been known already) can hardly be news. This is a theme to which we shall return in Chapters six and seven of the present book.

Cosmotheandrism and Trinity

Within the Christian tradition, Jesus Christ is incomprehensible without the Trinity. A non-Trinitarian God cannot become incarnate. A non-Trinitarian Christ cannot be fully divine and fully human. Panikkar acknowledges and shares the theological 'personalism' of the Semitic faiths provided it can be fused with a fully Indian view of non-duality in which God, man and the world constitute a single being, thereby holding and surmounting the familiar distinction beween immanence and transcendence. Being is 'cosmotheandric' being, wherein man and the world are as necessary to God as God is to man and the world. There is no longer 'encounter' between God and man, but 'union'. In *The Trinity and the Religious Experience of Mankind* (a book which Rowan Williams acknowledges as 'one of the best and least read meditations on the Trinity in our century'[38]), he asks, 'Can one conceive an authentic spirituality in which God is not a 'thou' for man nor his commandment the 'ultimate' of all perfection?' and looks to *advaitic* Hinduism for an answer. The *Upanishads* point to a religious attitude 'that is not founded upon faith in a God-Thou, or a God-will sovereignty, but in the supra-rational experience of a 'Reality' which in some way 'inhales' us into himself. The God of the Upanishads does not speak: he is not Word. He 'inspires', he is *Spirit*. In the personalist schema, God . . . is Someone, he is a Person who calls to himself another person, is met, so to speak, face to face and is capable of either responding by love to another's love, or refusing to do so. In the schema of the Upanishads the main place is not given to call/response nor to acceptance/refusal. The basic categories here are know-ledge and ignorance. The Absolute is discovered in its own realisation, i.e in the experience in which it is attained. This meeting is not situated in the level of dialogue. Dialogue is itself transcended.'[39] Here, too, the similarities with the Hegelian scheme in Western philosophical theology are strong.

Is there a faculty in humans by which we can grasp the theandric reality? Panikkar points to *anubhava*, mystic in-tuition, the authentic advaita experience 'when one has seen, felt, experienced that God is in all, that all is in God, that nevertheless God is nothing of that which is . . .'[40] Panikkar, as a Christian-Hindu, wants to insist that that *advaita* is not monism. In *Myth, Faith and Hermeneutics*,[41] he considers the question of how the *advaitin*, the self in union with the Absolute, can also be in a relation of *bhakti* devotion to the Lord. Can love be another name for experience of the Absolute? Even to pose the question is problematic, for interrogation presupposes objectivity. For the *advaitin*, it is idolatrous to apply the language of personality to the Absolute. Yet Panikkar must preserve the legitimacy of *bhakti*. He does so by arguing that 'if the structure of the ultimate is love' then *bhakti* devotion is 'love loving love' and 'love of love is like an eye that sees itself, or a will that loves itself'.[42] Yet, one wonders, is this not to slip back into monism? If 'the *advaitin* has realised the absolute non-duality of Being', the 'he' who is thus aware is no longer necessary to the awareness. Panikkar's escape route from monism is to assert that the *advaitin* is 'full of personality but devoid of individuality'.[43]

It seems that Panikkar fears that understanding God as 'beyond', 'other', in relation to man is to be left with a God who arbitrarily intrudes *ab extra* into human affairs. He warns against 'objectifying' God/Christ outside the manwardness in which his reality consists. Nor must we 'subjectify' man outside his Godwardness. Faith is the intuitive awareness of our theandric being. It is a consequence of 'fasting from thought'. Knowledge of God is not cognitive in the traditional sense: 'To say: "I believe in God" is cognitive only in the sense of the act of believing: it is not cognitive as to its content. For the belief is only real that does not know *what* God is [i.e does not externalise him as a 'fact'] . . . The God of belief is a symbol but not a concept. In a way we believe only [what we believe to be] the unquestionable'.[44]

This raises profound questions about human freedom and the tragedy of evil, questions which Panikkar evades as a result of his fascination with the Absolute at the expense of the historical. Theandrism may be right to refuse to think of God and humanity (and the world) other than in mutual relationship. But within that mutuality there must be room for that about God which is more than the mutual relation, and also room for that about man capable of denying and seeking to distance himself from that mutuality. Panikkar has no room in his schema for unbelief, and hence no acknowledgement of the sincerity of doubt (and of doubters) and the anguished, Job-like questioning of reality. There is no sense of human perversity, no place for crises of repentance and conversion. So 'grace' and 'freedom' become mere ciphers, devoid of any real content, relics perhaps of his Christian inheritance. For grace, a theistic notion, presupposes an undeservedness in the recipient; and it calls forth a freely willed human response. Also given the vast diversity of religious myths and ideologies which have claimed to house the theandric experience, Panikkar provides no criteria by which they might be sifted and evaluated.

This is surely where Panikkar's distaste for history leaves him vulnerable. Nowhere in his copious writings does he engage in any serious wrestling with the reality of human wickedness. There is no attempt to relate his cosmotheandric

vision to the moral struggles of humanity. What spiritual
and moral resources does his vision provide, one wonders,
for resisting other versions of theandrism: say, for instance,
the *Volk* cult of the Nazis? Panikkar envisages a 'continuous
incarnation, not only in the flesh, but also in the acts and
events of all creatures. Every being is a christophany'.[45]
But are there no distinctions to be drawn, no degrees of
'christophany' to be recognized? If there is no qualitative
difference, historically, between 'incarnation' in Jesus and
'incarnation' in you or me (let alone Hitler or Pol Pot!), then
there is no possibility of self-correction or social criticism. If
there is, then in what does it consist and how does it become
universally normative? We shall have cause to return to this
theme when we consider Panikkar's hermeneutic.

The question is especially important when Panikkar proposes a new 'Copernican revolution' in which reality is itself
multiple: 'Each solar system has its own centre, and every
galaxy turns reciprocally around the other. There is no
absolute centre . . . each being (each tradition) is the centre
of the universe—of its own universe to begin with . . . a sort
of trinitarian dynamism in which all is implied in all.'[46] But
this is actually a reversal of the Copernican model in
astronomy: for in the latter the centre of the solar system was
not located in the human astronomer's laboratory, leave
alone in his human self. But Panikkar's flight from an
absolute beyond the human self only creates a void which
can now be filled by any definition of reality. It is ultimately
the enthronement of the human self (and the myriad products
of the human imagination) at the centre of reality.

Trinity and Religious Experience

Panikkar believes that only a trinitarian concept of Reality
can reconcile different understandings of the Absolute and
the three forms of spirituality found in all religious traditions
(viz. in Hindu terminology, *jnana-marga, bhakti-marga and
karma-marga*). The Trinity is 'the junction where the authentic
spiritual dimensions of all religions meet'.[47] (But once again
we are constrained to ask: how do we distinguish the
'authentic' from the, presumably, 'inauthentic' spiritualities?).
The mystery of the Trinity is 'existent in all religions but
differently expressed'. But Panikkar prefers 'theandric' to
'trinitarian' when speaking of 'the end towards which the

religious consciousness of humanity tends', which is also 'the most adequate interpretation of mystical experience (which is itself the culmination of all religious experience) . . . It would destroy the whole mystery to envisage in separation from one another—even more so live—the apophatism[48] and transcendence of the mystery of the Father, the immanence and fullness of the mystery of the Spirit and the homogeneity to man of the personal mystery of Christ.'[49]

For Panikkar, any attempt to speak about the Father involves a contradiction in terms, for every word about the Father can only refer to the one of whom the Father is Father, that is, to the Word or Son. 'In begetting the Son he gives up everything, even, if we may dare to say so, the possibility of being experienced in a name that would speak of him and him alone . . .'[50] Panikkar sees this '*kenosis* of Being at its very source' as the location of the Buddhist experience of *nirvana* and *sunyata*.[51] God is total Silence. This is affirmed by all the world religions. One is led towards the Absolute and in the end one finds nothing, because there *is* nothing, not even Being. The Father *has* no being; the Son/ Logos is *his* being. The source of being is itself not being, for otherwise how can it be its source? No-one can go to the Father except through the Son. Properly speaking, the spirituality appropriate to the Father is not a way of spirituality. 'It is like the invisible bedrock, the gentle inspirer, the unnoticed force whih sustains, draws and pushes us. God is truly transcendent, infinite. The moment that one stops, takes a stand, objectivises and "manipulates" religion, faith and God, one destroys, so to speak, this ultimate ground of all things, which in itself is quite "ungraspable" '.[52]

Therefore, there is no God except the Father who *is* his Son through his Spirit—'but without three "whos" or "whats" of any sort'.[53] Only the Son is Person; there is no real analogous factor common to the Father, Son and Spirit. 'Correctly speaking, then, it is only with the Son that man can have a personal relationship. The God of theism, thus, is the Son; the God with whom one can speak, establish a dialogue, enter into communication, is the divine Person who is in-relation-with, or rather, is the relationship with man and one of the poles of total existence.'[54]

Panikkar's most distinctive, and perhaps most contro-versial, contribution concerns his understanding of the Spirit. Already in the *Unknown Christ of Hinduism* he had

identified the Holy Spirit of the New Testament with
Hinduism's 'Divine *Sakti* penetrating everything and mani-
festing God, disclosing him in his immanence and being
present in all his manifestations'[55], and as the place where
religious encounter and communication occurred. In *Trinity
and the Religious Experience of Man*, he sees the 'signs of
the times' expressing what he calls the 'thrust' of the
Spirit 'pushing the Christian forward beyond what we call
"christianity", beyond, I am tempted to add, even the
institutional and visible Church. His ever more vivid awareness of the irresistable movement of all things towards the
apokatastasis, the restoration, of all in Christ . . . impels him
in the Spirit to immerse himself at the deepest level in all
endeavours related to man and this universe . . .'[56]

The revelation of the Spirit is the revelation of God
immanent. But 'revelation' for Panikkar is strictly inappropriate, for just as transcendence once revealed ceases to be
transcendent (for it has entered Being) so immanence which
also needs to manifest itself is no longer immanent. What
one finds at the deepest level of Divinity is the Spirit; the
Spirit is the 'non-exhaustion of the source in the generation
of the Logos . . . For the Father the Spirit is, at it were, the
return to the source that he is himself'.[57] Just as the Father
has no name because he is beyond every name, even the
name of Being, likewise with the Spirit. 'Being and
beings—and hence all existence—belongs to the kingdom
and sphere of the Son'.[58] One can only have a non-relational
union with the Spirit, the foundation of Being who is itself
not Being.

It is again to *advaitic* Hinduism, rather than the New
Testament, that Panikkar turns in expounding his theology
of the Spirit. He is of the view that most of the *Upanishadic*
assertions about the Absolute point to the Spirit. 'Indeed
what is the Spirit but the *atman* of the *Upanishads*, which is
said to be identical with *brahman*, although this identity can
only be existentially recognized and affirmed once 'realisation'
has been attained?'[59] One attains the Spirit neither by word
nor action. The Spirit is not Someone to be discovered or to
be worshipped. The 'spirituality of the Spirit' for Panikkar
consists rather 'in the "consciousness" that one is not found
outside reality, in the "realisation" that one is, so to speak,
included in it, that one is already *there* . . . that one is as

though enveloped, submerged in knowledge and love, in the beauty that one has with joy penetrated. It is a kind of total passivity . . .'[60] Arguing from 'the teaching and example of the One who came to the world solely to witness to the Father' and who later explained to his disciples that it was well for them if he went away, because otherwise the Holy Spirit, the teacher of all truth, would not come, Panikkar makes the bold assertion that 'If we remain attached exclusively to the "Saviour", to his humanity and his historicity, we block . . . the coming of the Spirit and thus revert to a stage of exclusive iconolatry'.[61]

Thus, for Panikkar, the Christian belief in God as Trinity furnishes us with a way of accounting for the divergent spiritualities that we encounter in the world of religions. Belief in an ineffable ultimate ground, some acknowledgment of a dialogical human relationship with the ultimate, and a sense of the limitless depth of our own being—these can all be found, without much difficulty, in the major religious traditions. Since the Christian doctrine has the *form* of a transcendent principle, a personal principle and an immanent principle, such a doctrine could be extended to serve as an explanation for how the various spiritualities are possible and to assert that they are all grounded in the silence of the ultimate.

It is here that a challenge posed by the philosopher Michael Durrant to all trinitarian theologies is pertinent.[62] Durrant raised the important question of criteria: how does one judge whether a given formulation put forward as 'trinitarian' is a formulation of the doctrine of the Trinity or a formulation of something quite different? Both Panikkar and Pieris (Chapter 2) use trinitarian vocabulary, and construct ontologies and soteriologies that express triadic patterns, but they nowhere address the criteriological issue: what are these new formulations exactly formulations of? can the proposers identify what constitutes the essence of Christian belief in God as Trinity apart from its formulation?

There are several reasons why this is important. Firstly, because the doctrine of God as Trinity was not a speculative philosophy about God in the abstract but emerged out of a specific historical claim about Jesus of Nazareth.[63] Trinitarian theology, as Leonard Hodgson observed, is 'the product of rational reflection on those particular manifestations of the divine activity which centre in the birth, ministry, crucifixion, resurrection and ascension of Jesus Christ and the gift of the Holy Spirit to the Church . . . It could not have been discovered without the occurrence of those events, which drove human reason to see that they required a trinitarian God for their cause.'[64] Similarly the Dutch Roman Catholic scholar E Schillebeeckx notes that the way is from Jesus to the Trinity, not from the Trinity to Jesus: 'Only in the light of Jesus' life, death and resurrection can we know that the Trinity is the divine mode of God's perfect unity of being. Only on the basis of Jesus of Nazareth, his Abba experience —source and soul of his message, ministry and death—and his resurrection, is it possible to say anything meaningful about Father, Son and Spirit.'[65]

Brian Hebblethwaite puts it like this: 'It was because the early Christians in the light of the resurrection of Jesus from the dead, came to recognize his divinity and to experience him as the self-expression of God that they perceived the necessity of believing that God himself, in his own being, exists in an internal relationship of love given and love received. That love, they saw, was mirrored in the relationship of Jesus to the Father. That same love they experienced in their own lives as poured out upon them and as a relationship in which they too were caught up and could come to share. But they also came to realise that the very notion of a God who is love requires us to think in terms of an internally differentiated and relational deity.'[66]

What this implies is that a trinitarian model like Panikkar's, which prohibits us from speaking any more of the *Father's* love for us his creatures or of the personhood of the Holy Spirit and of the Spirit's witness to the Son, and which distinguishes sharply between the order of reality of the Son and that of the Father,[67] and which not only refuses to acknowledge the uniqueness and normativeness of the Son's incarnation in Jesus but despises any attempt to do so, must be deeply suspect as an adequate reformulation of the classical doctrine.

Secondly, to assert that it is only with the Son that man can have a personal relationship and that the 'God of theism is the Son' and that there is 'no real analogous factor common to the Father, Son and Spirit'[68] is to stand the historic trinitarian doctrine on its head. It is to use traditional Christian language in an idiosyncratic way. It also requires that Christian practice be radically transformed. The essence of Christian prayer, for example, has been understood as communion with the Father in the name of the Son and by the Holy Spirit. As it stands Panikkar's assertion would be deeply offensive also to non-Christian theists. What Panikkar's apophaticism does is to effectively undermine any religious faith that sees the initiative in knowledge of the Ultimate as lying with the latter and not in the believer.

From a Christian perspective—and Panikkar is writing primarily for Christians—the use of traditional trinitarian language to construct a general religious metaphysic must be regarded as a sleight of hand. When patristic theologians used language about the 'relational' and 'non-relational' aspects of divine life it was to refer to the particular *hypostases* or *personae* in their consubstantial unity. It was never intended as an abstract framework for a metaphysics of being and non-being. Such concrete relations, as expressed eventually in the Niceno–Constantinopolitan Creed of the fourth century or the so-called Athanasian Creed of the fifth, simply expressed the biblical data in the light of Christian experience and discipleship: namely, (1) The Father is God (2) The Son is God (3) The Holy Spirit is God (4) The Father is not the Son or the Spirit (5) The Son is not the Father or the Spirit (6) The Spirit is not the Father or the Son (7) There is one God, not three.[69]

I see no objection, in principle, to the use of ideas drawn from Indian religious philosophies in Christian theology. Panikkar quite rightly points out that if concepts drawn from Platonic and Aristotelian systems of thought shaped the articulation of Christian doctrine in the Western Church, use of Shankara, Nagarjuna or Ramanuja by Asian theologians should be perfectly feasible. But it is evident that the best of the Western theologians did make a determined effort to be faithful to the biblical revelation and not to go beyond the tradition of the catholic church. And where they failed to do so, it was more in the nature of an unconscious presupposition than a self-conscious attempt to supplant the tradition with philosophical innovation. And in such instances (the notion of divine *apatheia* being a notorious example) the church has suffered in her witness as a result of the defect, and we have sought to return to more biblical concepts of God in recent times.[70]

The reserve with which the Church Fathers approached the task of relating the biblical revelation to non-Christian philosophy has been recognized by twentieth-century church historians. Contrasting the Augustinian doctrine of God with the superficially similar Neoplatonic metaphysic of the One, the Mind and the World-Soul (which did historically influence Augustine's own formulation), Henry Chadwick writes of Augustine's 'tenacious hold on the Christian presupposition that the untidy flux of history is the stage of divine self-disclosure: God's saving word to man was embodied, at its nodal and focal point, in a personal historical life, and is witnessed through and in a historical visible community'. Chadwick continues, 'Platonist though Augustine was, he did not think salvation lay in timeless abstractions.'[71]

Another eminent patristics scholar, Jaroslav Pelikan, observes that the defence of the doctrine of the Trinity did not rely primarily on metaphysical identifications such as the divine ousia, or 'being'/'nature', as a Platonic universal. 'Even Gregory of Nyssa, philosophically the most brilliant and bold of the three Cappadocians, stopped short of providing a speculative solution for the relation of the One and the Three or of the distinction between the properties of the One and those of the Three. Despite his great debt to Middle Platonism, Gregory did not assign to the Platonic doctrine of universals a determinative place in his dogmatics, which was finally shaped by what the Church believed, taught, and confessed.'[72] And, as a final illustration of my point, that renowned scholar of medieval philosophy, Etienne Gilson, writing of Thomas Aquinas' indebtedness to the thought of Aristotle, nevertheless urges that 'One should not forget that even the elementary notions of physical substance, of matter and of form, above all of potency and act have not the same sense in Aristotle and in Thomas Aquinas, because his own notion of being is other than that of Aristotle.'[73]

Thirdly, the danger of not attending to the criteriological question posed by Durrant is that one runs the risk not only of confusing *form* for *content*, but also of confusing form with goal. For, even if we grant that there are similar triadic, and even incarnational, 'patterns' or 'structures' running through the different religio-philosophical systems we encounter, it does not follow that the experience of *nirvana* or *satori* is an experience of Christian salvation. We have seen how all human experience is concept-dependent. Even an experience of 'ultimate silence' will not be entirely devoid of all beliefs, and thus cannot furnish a grounding for the diversity of human spiritualities.

Panikkar's triadic first principle seems more akin to the 'One' of Plotinus (c.205–270) than the biblical 'Father of our Lord Jesus Christ'; for Plotinus too denies that being or thought pertains to the One, even denying that they can be called one or good. Panikkar welcomes the statement by Gregory of Nyssa (c.330–395) that God has 'but one name that can represent his proper nature, the single name of being "above every name" ' as an invitation to ground modern spirituality in the ineffable silence of mystery and not in the Logos. But Gregory's words only need to be quoted in full for us to see that Panikkar's way of distinguishing Mystery, Logos and Pneuma actually turns Gregory's apophaticism upside down! For Gregory writes:

> The simplicity of the True Faith assumes God to be that which he is, viz. incapable of being grasped by any term, or any idea, or any other device of our apprehension, remaining beyond the reach not only of the human but of the angelic and of all supramundane intelligence, unthinkable, unutterable, above all expression in words, having but one name that can represent his proper nature, the single name of being 'above every name', *which is granted to the Only-begotten also, because 'all that the Father hath is the Son's'.*[74]

As we noted earlier, Gregory shares the patristic theologians' desire to be faithful to the biblical revelation. In the Cappadocian formulation, the only difference between the Father and the Son lies in the word 'ungenerate' (Gk. *agennetos*) as applied to the Father. It is only in their concrete relations that the persons are to be distinguished. Whether Panikkar similarly misreads the apophaticism of the later Christian tradition is an issue we will explore in the following chapter.

Hermeneutics and History

In the epilogue to *The Unknown Christ of Hinduism*, having just exegeted a text from the *Brahma-Sutras* to show the near-equivalence of Isvara and Christ and that the statement 'God and the world are neither two nor one' is the central affirmation of the *advaita Vedanta*, Panikkar goes on to warn his readers: 'We must refrain from rejecting a religious text or tradition . . . simply because it does not accord with our already crystallized ideas or formulations.'[75] However,

Panikkar's own hermeneutical approach is not to reject any text that may be embarrassing to his theological position, but rather to rewrite the text with what might be called a disingenuous ingenuity! I give below a few representative samples of his style of textual exegesis.

The fly-leaf of the above book brings together the *Kath Upanishad* V:3 ('The Spirit whom all the gods worship is seated in the middle') with John 1:26 (translated as 'In-between you stands whom you know not') which is further elucidated by means of a bizarre translation of Luke 17:21: 'The Kingdom of God is (neither among you nor within but) *between* you' (emphasis in the text). Panikkar goes on to 'explain' that the in-between is the 'radical relativity of all things' held in creative intra-relation by the unknown mediator, the *madhyamaka* . . .

Likewise, introducing the chapter on Hindu-Christian encounter, he cites the *Kena Upanishad* II:3 ('It is not understood by those who understand it; it is understood by those who do not understand it') and blends it with Rom 10:20 ('I have been found by those who did not seek me; I have shown myself to those who did not ask for me'). 'I' becomes 'it', the Jew/Gentile context is ignored; the only link between the texts (one of which speaks of a historical covenant which is now opened to others, the other of rational limitation) being the feature of paradox . . .

Elsewhere, the Buddhist theme of ultimate silence is linked with Jesus' giving Pilate no answer at his trial, on the ground that to 'question' ultimate Reality can have no meaning.[76] Paul's celebrated statement in Phil. 3:13 of his apostolic ambition ('to press on toward the goal to win the prize for which God has called me heavenward in Christ Jesus') now becomes, under Panikkar's exegetical dexterity, 'I let fall everything that in any way weighs me down: all substantiality, every possession, every spiritual, or even ontological, acquisition—in a word, all that I am—and I strive, I stretch, I tend towards something ever before me, ever beyond, something ever unreachable and unseizable not only in this world but in the definitive life as well . . .'[77]

Panikkar's intention is evidently to de-historicize the New Testament, to read it through ahistorical Hindu/Buddhist spectacles, just as he began by reading the *Brahma-Sutras* in the light of the Thomist tradition. The 'possibly new Christian awareness'[78] that he is seeking is not to be circumscribed or disciplined by Scripture. By invoking the principle of a *sensus semper plenior,* an ever fuller meaning to the sacred texts, he can envisage an expansion of human consciousness, new 'divine revelation' and a 'mutual fecundation' between religious traditions.[79] For the ever-changing experiences of the reader form new horizons for the Scriptural text, and these have epistemological priority in the act of reading.

Panikkar's hermeneutic is grounded in the radical disjunction he makes between Logos and Spirit or the second and third term in his trinitarian structure. Only the Spirit is capable of being universal. Logos presupposes the rationality which mystery must transcend. 'Being as such . . . does not need to be reduced to consciousness . . . The Spirit is freedom, the freedom of Being to be what accompanies Being; it does not precede it; it does not predict what Being is. It tells only what Being is. But the *is* of Being is free'.[80] Logos, or intelligibility, does not exhaust Being. Logos is there for the sake of life, he says, not vice versa. So no unified theory of religion is possible. Theology progresses from myth to Logos, while worship lives by both. But both must eventually reach beyond them into pure life in the Spirit. So, just as all religious communication is 'in the Spirit', the scriptures of all the religions have to be subject 'to the Spirit'. Hermeneutics gets beyond the texts and their historical contexts to the universal realm to which their particularities relate. This universal context is (in his river imagery) the Ganges, the challenge posed by the existence of world religions to the 'Christian economy of salvation'.

We have already seen how Panikkar prefers concepts to narrative, and that his 'christic principle' and 'trinity' are very loosely related to the historical event of Jesus Christ. The latter simply becomes a launching pad, as it were, to project into universal orbit a trinitarian way of speaking about reality. But this is where both lack of coherence and of consistency appear in his approach. He is committed to an ontology in which differences are real and do matter, and in this he parts company with the ordinary variety of liberal pluralism. But he cannot be content with a freewheeling plurality either. If the relation between Logos and Spirit were purely arbitrary, the whole quest to understand the movement in which our situation is a moment would be doomed from the start.

In the biblical and traditional Christian perpective, Jesus is the unifying point of reference for all the creative acts of God. The *eschaton* towards which our human life-stories are moving has a recognizable pattern only because of the life-story of Jesus. Human possibilities are defined with reference to Jesus who, as the Logos made flesh, not only becomes the authoritative form of human flourishing and response to God, but also brings the present disorder of reality into a new intelligiblity and unity. So, while this intelligibility can never be captured in a theoretical scheme or by a single mind, and the fullness of Christ is still to be discovered in the unpredictable diversity of human histories, the divine action as Spirit is grounded in the divine act in Jesus the incarnate Logos.

Panikkar is quite right to remind us of the freedom of Spirit: it is the Spirit who makes a genuine 'hermeneutical spiral' possible, helping us to be critical of the church's language and practice and of our recurring temptation to seek conceptual neatness and theoretical closure. It is a historical fact that the Roman Catholic and mainstream Protestant churches have tended to restrict the operation of the Spirit to official ecclesiastical channels; and so Panikkar is right to stress that the Spirit must not be identified with either Christendom or (empirical) Christianity. However, if we are to think biblically, we must recognize that there is a necessary and reciprocal relation between Jesus, as the Logos made flesh, and Spirit. Jesus is both the gift of the Spirit and the giver of the Spirit. According to Jesus, the world neither knows nor sees the Spirit (John 14:17). It is the coming of Jesus that makes the gift of the Spirit universal and accessible to all; and the work of the Spirit is to bear witness to the Logos made flesh, to convict the world of guilt, sin, righteousness and judgment, and to lead people to truth by 'taking what is mine and making it known to you' (John 15:26, 16:7ff). Since the Spirit is the source of Jesus' authentic humanity, he is the means by which the benefits of Jesus's life, death and resurrection are made available to us.

Thus it is a mistake to conceive the Spirit in terms of divine immanence. The biblical Spirit is not identified with our human spirits or with any part of the world, for this would be to deny the freedom of the creature before the Creator. As Spirit God is present as *other*, as the transcendent one who mediates to the creation God's immanence as

Logos. He is the liberating Spirit, liberating *because* he is transcendent. 'When we cry "Abba!" "Father!" it is the Spirit himself bearing witness with our spirit that we are the children of God' (Rom 8:15ff). The Spirit is not only universal, but the one who establishes concrete, particular relations—both within the divine life and the created life of the world (e.g. 1 Cor. 12). He is God bringing human and cosmic history to their eschatological goal, giving it the liberty to respond creatively to the future which is antici-pated in the resurrection of Christ.

Much nineteenth century theology in the West can be seen as an attempt to liberate the divine Spirit from ecclesiastical control; but it succeeded only in replacing immanence within an institution by immanence within 'nature'—whether human or nonhuman. Spirit ceased to be transcendent, eschatological, liberating. This is why Kierkegaard saw Hegel's near indentification of the Spirit with the human spirit (or self-consciousness) as simply a return to paganism, as enslaving rather than liberating. Panikkar, like Hegel, has only exchanged one form of slavery for another. To sunder Spirit from Logos and to locate the former in a 'cosmotheandric' immanence is, paradoxically, the route to the demonic.

There is, then, a movement of self-correction as well as critical witness already built into our theologies and inter-religious dialogue by the Logos–Spirit relationship as given in the New Testament. Lacking this revelational reference point, and using the form of Christian langage but without its historical content, Panikkar's project of a genuinely interactive pluralism falters between the two poles of a reductionist pluralism and an uncritical relativism. He approaches the former pole when he states, in his recent essay 'The Jordan, the Tiber and the Ganges', that the contemporary Christianness which has moved beyond Christianity and Christendom has discovered that 'Christianity simply incarnates the primordial and original traditions of humankind'.[81] Here he seems to be denying his own warnings and simply collapsing distinctive traditions into a universal form of natural religion. On the other hand, he claims that 'the incommensurability of ultimate systems is unbridgeable. This incompatibility is not a lesser evil (that would be to judge only by the Logos) but a revelation itself of the nature of reality.'[82] But if the ultimate coherence of all things is now abandoned, then is not the desire to unify humanity itself misguided? All that is left is the will to power of several human projects.

This suspicion is strengthened by the claim that 'different theologies can be recognized as Christian by their own self-affirmation . . . We cannot prescribe from one single perspective what the other Christian views should be.'[83] But on this basis, what becomes of Panikkar's own curt rejection of other theologies which do not work within his idiosyncratic paradigm? And what does Panikkar's celebration of the 'tensile co-existence of ultimate human attitudes, cosmologies and religions' amount to, if not perpetual resignation to conflict? It is at this point that Panikkar's ontological pluralism, which was built more on neo-Vedantist lines than Christian Trinitarianism, shows its affinity with some nihilistic forms of postmodernism.

The criteriological question we raised earlier regarding Panikkar's trinitarian and christological formulations also needs to be raised with reference to his reworking of traditional Christian terminology. In his desire to de-historicize theology in general and christology in particular, Panikkar ends up identifying 'sin' as a purely ontological category, so that creatureliness itself becomes an expression of 'sin' and 'forgiveness' is to de-subtantialize being:

> When God 'gives us' being, that which God 'gives' us is not nothing; God simply pardons us for not not-being, pardons us for not being God. God cannot *give* being; God can only give divine self to divine self (in the Trinity) or God can forgive not having given divinity *ad extram* (in creation) . . . Creation, the making of something that is not God, is God's 'sin', God's 'sacrifice'. Non-God is sin, and we ourselves are to be the extent that we are not God. And this is sin.[84]

Panikkar's defective understanding of creation robs his theology of any sense of tragedy and, consequently, of the capacity for profound engagement with social evil.[85] By discounting the uniqueness of the biblical account of evil as historical, not metaphysical,[86] the 'mutual fecundation' of religious traditions that he aimed for has become a purely one-way street.

Thus it is not surprising to find Panikkar reducing faith, too, to a vague 'act of sheer openness'. In his overriding concern to eliminate all 'reification' and 'objectification' of religious faith, Panikkar makes the startling claim (startling, at least, to Christian or Muslim ears) that 'The very presence of God is detrimental to the constitutive openness of faith. Neither the Buddha, nor the Prophet, nor the Christ can remain at the believer's side without representing a dangerous obstacle to that believer's leap of faith.'[87] I doubt if even a Kierkegaardian existentialist would go thus far! Panikkar appears to have wandered so far away from basic Christian understandings that the possibility of genuine dialogue must seem remote, for want of a shared language.

In conclusion, Panikkar does issue a healthy corrective to any notion of Christian witness as involving a claim to possess all authentic insight into the human story and which fails to see that the fullness of Christ remains a process of human discovery. But the saddest experience in any Christian reading of Panikkar must surely lie in the almost total absence (in a considerable corpus of writings) of attention to the ministry, teaching, death and resurrection of Jesus.[88] The further lack of any theology of atonement is of a piece with the lack of any serious treatment of sin, guilt and the reality of evil.

In view of Panikkar's preoccupation with the 'hidden' Mystery, shrouded in the 'beyond' of unknowing, the most serious defects of his entire approach may ultimately stem from a failure to heed Paul's description of the gospel as 'the revelation of the Mystery that was kept secret for long ages but is now disclosed, and through the prophetic writings is made known to all . . . to bring about the obedience of faith' (Rom. 16:25, 26), and John's assertion that 'No one has ever seen God. It is God the only Son, who is close to the Father's heart, who has made him known' (John 1:18). The failure means that the only basis for affirming an authentic human pluralism has been eroded. It ends up turning Christ into a cipher, revelation into obscurity, and inverting the wise counsel of the Deuteronomist: 'The secret things belong to YHWH our God, but the *revealed* things belong to us and to our children forever . . .' (Deut 29:29). Revelation does not take away mystery. But it tells us that our knowledge of Ultimate Reality does not begin with ourselves, not even with our culturally-mediated 'religious experiences'. We are not left to our own speculative ingenuity, and it undermines our intellectual pride.

At the end of the last century, the great German dogmatic theologian Martin Kähler (1835–1912) posed a crucially important question to the christologies of his liberal contemporaries. Surveying the different ways the biblical doctrine of atonement had been interpreted since the days of the so-called European Enlightenment, Kähler asked: 'Has Christ merely provided us with insights concerning an existing state of affairs, or has he *actually brought about a new state of affairs?*'[89] There is all the difference in the world between seeing Christ as, for instance, an 'icon of God's grace' or a 'symbol of humanity's transcendence', and seeing Christ as establishing, in some way, a fundamentally *new* relationship between God and humanity.

Notes to Chapter Three

1. R Panikkar, *The Unknown Christ of Hinduism* (London: Darton, Longman & Todd, Revised edition, 1981) p. 23. This will be abbreviated to UCH in subsequent notes.
2. Ibid. p. x.
3. R Panikkar, *The Silence of God: the Answer of the Buddha* (Madrid 1970; Eng. trans. Maryknoll, NY: Orbis, 1989) p 155. This is abbreviated to SG in the subsequent notes.
4. UCH, op. cit. p. 30.
5. Ibid., pp. ix–x.
6. The book was written in Spanish in 1970, but its English edition, via the Italian, appeared only in 1989. The text was not revised or expanded in any way, and carries a brief preface by the author.
7. SG, op. cit. pp. 144–5.
8. Ibid. p. 145.
9. UCH, op. cit. pp. 56–7.
10. Ibid. p. 165.
11. He writes, 'Today we are critically aware that the Christian a priori of Christ being the unique Mediator and Christianity the true religion is embedded in time, space, culture, and a particular human understanding . . . Any Christian reflection today must reconsider its starting-point and, at the least, justify it in the human arena', UCH, p. 167.
12. Ibid. p. 83.
13. Ibid. pp. 167–8.
14. Ibid. p. 165.
15. Ibid. p. 168.
16. Ibid. pp. 8–9.
17. Ibid. p. 26. Elsewhere he writes, 'I speak . . . of that unknown *reality*, which Christians call Christ, discovered in the heart of Hinduism, not as a stranger to it, but as its very *principle of Life*, as the light which illumines every Man who comes into the World', pp. 19–20 (Italics in text).
18. Ibid. p. 85.
19. Ibid. pp. 85–6.

20. Ibid. p. 169.
21. Ibid. p. 164.
22. Ibid. p. 27.
23. R Panikkar, *The Trinity and the Religious Experience of Man* (London: Darton, Longman & Todd, 1973) pp. 74–5. Abbreviated to TREM in the subsequent notes.
24. Ibid. p. 75.
25. UCH, op. cit., p. 24.
26. Ibid. pp. 29–30.
27. Ibid. p. 27.
28. R Panikkar, 'The Jordan, the Tiber and the Ganges: Three Kairological Moments of Christic Self-Awareness' in *The Myth of Christian Uniqueness*, ed. J Hick & P Knitter (London:SCM, 1988). This paper is abbreviated to JTG in the following notes.
29. Ibid. p. 113.
30. Ibid. p. 114.
31. R Williams, 'Trinity and Pluralism' in G.D'Costa (ed), *Christian Uniqueness Reconsidered* (London: SCM, 1990) p. 5.
32. Studies of Hegel still constitute a flourishing academic industry. For recent introductions to his Christology see P.C.Hodgson, 'Hegel' in Ninian Smart et al. (eds), *Nineteenth-Century Religious Thought in the West*, 3 vols (Cambridge: Cambridge University Press, 1985), vol 1, pp. 81–121; J Yerkes, *The Christology of Hegel* (Albany,NY: State University of New York Press, 1983).
33. See Chapter 4.
34. HR Mackintosh, *Types of Modern Theology: Schleiermacher to Barth* (London: Collins, 1964 [1937]), p. 109. In a footnote on the same page Mackintosh cites Emil Brunner's pungent comment (in *The Mediator*) on Hegel: 'To him history is merely a picture-book, whose text he knows without the aid of the pictures; to him it means the Idea made concrete, hence there is nothing decisive about it. In its absolute and serious sense, there is no room here for the category of uniqueness.'
35. S Kierkegaard, *Training in Christianity* (Eng. trans. Walter Lowrie, Princeton University Press, 1941) p. 84.
36. The affinities with Panikkar are not, of course, to be pressed. Panikkar's pluralism diverges strongly from Hegel's rationalism. The latter tends to identify mystical contemplation with metaphysical speculation: while religious understanding (*Vorstellung*) cannot penetrate the higest reaches of reality, there is no mystery that cannot be grasped by the speculative philosopher's conceptual thought (*Begriff*).
37. Paul's insistence on the unity of humankind would also have been offensive to proud Athenian ears!
38. Williams, op. cit. p. 3.
39. TREM, op. cit. p. 29.
40. Ibid. p. 37.
41. R Panikkar, *Myth, Faith and Hermeneutics* (London:Darton, Longman & Todd, 1970). This is abbreviated to MFH in the following notes.

42. Ibid. p. 281.
43. Ibid. p. 286.
44. Ibid. pp. 5–6.
45. JTG, op. cit. p. 114.
46. Ibid. p. 109.
47. TREM, op. cit. p. 42.
48. Apophaticism refers to the essential incomprehensibility of God (or the religious ultimate), beyond the reach of human description and finite human apprehension. It is an important strand in all the world's religious faiths, including Christian theology, and is a major focus of the *advaita Vedanta* of Shankara and Nagarjuna's *Madhyamika* philosophy in Buddhism. *Advaita* distinguishes between *nirguna* Brahman, Brahman without attributes, exceeding the reach of thought, and saguna Brahman, Brahman with attributes, known in human religious experience as *Ishvara*, the personal Lord of the universe. The Taoist classic *Tao Te Ching* begins with the statement, 'The Tao that can be expressed is not the eternal Tao' (*Tao Te Ching*, trans. Ch'u Ta-Kao, London and Boston: Mandala Books, 1982, p. 17).
49. TREM, op. cit. p. 72.
50. Ibid. p. 46.
51. *Sunyata*, one of the most important terms in the Mahayana, is usually translated into English as 'emptiness' or the 'void'. This can be misleading. The negative force of *sunya* excludes all positive determinations. It is sometimes translated by Buddhists as 'formless'. TRV Murti, expounding the Madhyamika doctrine which he believes to be the 'central philosophy of Buddhism' writes: 'The Absolute is very aptly termed Sunya, as it is devoid of all predicates. Even existence, unity, selfhood and goodness cannot be affirmed of it.' (*The Central Philosophy of Buddhism*, London: George Allen & Unwin, 1955, p. 229). The Japanese Zen scholar, DT Suzuki, writes: 'A field without an inch of grass in it symbolizes *sunyata*, the ultimate reality of Buddhist philosophy. *Sunyata* is literally 'emptiness'. To say that reality is 'empty' means that it goes beyond definability, and cannot be qualified as this or that. It is above categories of universal and particular. But it must not therefore be regarded as free of all content, as a void in the relative sense would be' ('The Buddhist Conception of Reality', in *The Buddha Eye*, ed. F Franck, New York: Crossroad, 1982, p. 104).
52. TREM, op. cit. p. 50.
53. Ibid. p. 52.
54. Ibid.
55. UCH, op. cit. p. 57.
56. TREM, op. cit. p. 57.
57. Ibid. p. 60.
58. Ibid. p. 63.
59. Ibid. pp. 63–4.
60. Ibid. p. 64.
61. Ibid. p. 58.

62. I owe this reference to Dr. Stephen Williams. Michael Durrant, *Theology and Intelligibility* (London: Routledge & Kegan Paul, 1973), esp. pp. 186–91.

63. Williams too observes that Panikkar is inclined 'to take for granted the developed structure of Trinitarian theology, without too much direct consideration of how this pattern of speaking about God actually came to be', and that his treatment of it in TREM is 'quite heavily marked by Augustinian and scholastic formultions, and sketchy on origins', op.cit.pp. 6–7.

64. L Hodgson, *The Doctrine of the Trinity* (Nisbet, 1943) p. 32.

65. E Schillebeeckx, *Jesus: An Experiment in Christology* (New York: Crossroad, 1979) p. 658.

66. B Hebblethwaite, *The Incarnation: Collected Essays in Christology* (Cambridge: Cambridge University Press, 1987) pp. 21–2.

67. E.g. On the ineffability at the heart of ultimate reality itself: '. . . inasmuch as its *logos* (its expression and communication) . . . no longer pertains to the order of ultimate reality but precisely to the manifestation of that order', SG, op. cit. p. 14.

68. TREM, op. cit. p. 52.

69. Or, as Augustine put it: 'Father and Son and Holy Spirit in the inseparable equality of one substance presents a divine unity; and therefore there are not three Gods but one God; although indeed the Father has begotten the Son, and therefore he who is the Father is not the Son; and the Son is begotten by the Father, and therefore he who is the Son is not the Father; and the Holy Spirit is neither the Father nor the Son, but only the Spirit of the Father and of the Son, himself co-equal to the Father and the Son, and belonging to the threefold unity.' *De Trinitate*, Book I, 4.7.

70. Far from seeing the complete Hellenization of the New Testament gospel, the period from 325 to 451 CE witnessed the destruction of some of the most cherished presuppositions of Greek philosophy and the formation of an alternative philosophical tradition. Timothy Gorringe notes, for example, how the 'bi-polar' *homoousion* formula as used by Athanasius (which expressed the necessity of a twofold solidarity if God's redemption of creation was to be achieved in a manner that showed respect for his creation), played a crucial role in this process, 'replacing the metaphysic of Being and beyond Being with that of the interaction of the Creator and creature in complete identity and complete difference'. (TJ Gorringe, ' "Not Assumed is Not Healed": the *Homoousion* and Liberation Theology', *Scottish Journal of Theology*, vol. 38, 1985, p. 488).

71. H Chadwick, *Augustine* (Oxford: Oxford University Press, 1986) pp. 94–5.

72. J Pelikan, *The Christian Tradition, vol.1: The Emergence of the Catholic Tradition (100–600)* (University of Chicago Press, 1971) p. 222. It is a well-known fact that while Gregory refused to accept that even terms like 'Godhead' were more than simply descriptions of human comprehensions of God, he ascribed ontological reality to the concrete relations within the Trinity. 'In opposition to the danger that the distinctiveness of the three hypostases would dissolve in a

Platonically defined ousia, the Cappadocians, with varying degrees of emphasis, found the guarantee of the unity of the Godhead in the Father.' (Ibid.).

73. E Gilson, *History of Christian Philosophy in the Middle Ages* (London: Sheed and Ward, 1955) p. 709.

74. Gregory of Nyssa, *Against Eunomius*, Bk 1, sec. 42, in *A Select Library of Nicene and Post-Nicene Fathers of the Christian Church*, vol 5, eds. P Schaff and H Wace, 2nd series (Grand Rapids: Eerdmans, 1976) (My emphasis).

75. UCH, op. cit. p. 163.

76. MFH, op. cit. pp. 258–70.

77. SG, op. cit. p. 142.

78. JTG, op. cit. p. 111.

79. UCH, op. cit. p. 163.

80. JTG, op. cit. pp. 109–10.

81. Ibid. p. 102.

82. Ibid. p. 110.

83. Ibid. p. 111.

84. SG, op. cit., p. 132. (Italics in text) He continues, 'To have consciousness of being is to discover ourselves debtors. Sin occurs when being . . . ceases to be a transitive verb gliding directly to its terminus and is instead converted into *esse*, into substance . . . God can be beyond being only if the experience of being is not that of a positivity but simply that of a lack. And we are once more very near Buddhism.' (p. 133).

85. Panikkar, in contrast to Pieris, also tends to rob Asian religious traditions of their socio-critical dimensions. E.g 'The Buddha's reaction against sacrifice and the caste system is perhaps due more to the need to tear up by the roots the creative act and the status of the preservation of creation than to motives of nonviolence (*ahimsa*) or social justice.' SG, Ibid. p. 188, note 55. (Italics in text).

86. Cf. Paul Ricoeur on the uniqueness of the biblical picture of evil: 'Creation is good from the first; it proceeds from a Word and not from a Drama; it is complete. Evil, then, can no longer be identical with a prior and resurgent chaos; a diferent myth will be needed to account for its appearance, its 'entrance in to the world'. History, too, then, is an original dimension and not a 're-enactment' of the drama of creation. It is History, not Creation, that is a Drama. Thus Evil and History are contemporaneous . . . Evil becomes scandalous at the same time as it becomes historical', P Ricoeur, *The Symbolism of Evil*, Eng. trans. E.Buchanan (Boston: Beacon, 1967) p. 203.

87. SG, op. cit., p. 154.

88. We have seen earlier that this is a feature of Panikkar that he shares with Hegel.

89. M. Kähler, *Doctrine of Reconciliation* (1898), cited in A. McGrath, *The Making of Modern German Christology*, 1750–1900 (Leicester, Apollos, second edn. 1994) p. 136 (my emphasis).

PART II

[4]

Interweavings

Ideas, no less than persons or nations, are shaped by the past. And the ideas of the writers we have been exploring are no exception. The pluralist paradigm in the theology of religions may be of recent origin, prompted by the peculiar circumstances of the late twentieth century world; but some of the assumptions it embodies can be traced to earlier phases of European intellectual history. The story is complex, the threads difficult to unravel. But just as the road to modern paganism was paved (partially, at least, and unwittingly) by speculative theologies of an earlier age, so the theologies of the late modern world seem to have been sculpted out of (again, often unwittingly) the pagan thought of an earlier age.[1]

So, in this chapter and the next, we propose to stroll through a few of the important thoroughfares of the post-Enlightenment intellectual landscape, viewing in particular its seeming influence on the thought-patterns of contemporary religious pluralism. This will serve the purpose of locating our discussion on a wider philosophical and theological canvas; and of indicating—in an admittedly cursory and preliminary way —some general directions in which our critique can be strengthened from within the Western theological tradition itself.

But first we begin with a brief review of the three Asian theologians we have been studying. It may be useful to identify, schematically, the more important similarities and divergences among them, before proceeding with our critique.

Comparisons: Samartha, Pieris & Panikkar

As an introductory observation, none of these writers discusses the views of any of the others considered here, although Samartha and Pieris cite Panikkar (but without discussion) in their footnotes. Samartha does the same with Pieris.

(a) Differences

1. While both Samartha and Panikkar are deeply influenced by non-dualist *advaita vedanta* thought, both seeing this (albeit in different ways) as providing a satisfactory framework for religious pluralism, Pieris is more sceptical of the major religious traditions because of their historical resistance to social change. He emphasises the 'cosmic religiousness' of the poor and argues that it is this liberative stream of religiosity that must invigorate the church's theological awareness. Consequently, he is more sympathetic to the *dalit, minjung* and goddess theologies of Asia while endorsing the themes of self-renunciation and intuition in Buddhism and *advaita vedanta*.

2. Samartha regards the Trinity as a model of divine being appropriate for Christian discourse, but falling short of the ultimate Mystery. This ineffable Mystery is disclosed differently in other cultures and religious traditions. Pieris sees a common trinitarian or triadic structure underlying all the 'metacosmic' faiths, expressed in a salvific Beyond, a salvific mediation Within, and a salvific compulsion towards the Beyond. For Panikkar the Trinity is at the heart of his pluralism: Myth/Mystery, Logos and Spirit undergird and pervade all things. Unlike Samartha, and even more than in Pieris, his trinitarianism is the *sine qua non* of his pluralist vision.

3. Panikkar, especially in his later writings, argues for a radical pluralism on the level of intelligibility or 'Logos': the incommensurability of ultimate systems is unbridgeable. No unified theory of religion is possible. The universe has many centres; each tradition forms its own centre. All theology must leave the realm of Logos and go beyond to the pure life of the Spirit in which 'Christianness' is realized. Samartha too argues against the legitimacy of evaluating other religious traditions by means of criteria drawn from one's own; but he does believe that all religions express a common salvific experience and refer to the same transcendent reality. Pieris, however, is more willing to criticize the beliefs and practices of all religious

systems and ideologies in the light of 'God's covenant with the poor'.

4. Pieris' criticism of text-centred approaches to other religious faiths by Christian scholars and missionaries could be used against Panikkar's approach, which pays scant attention to either the history of textual development and interpretation or to popular religious consciousness.

(b) Different concerns

1. Samartha stresses the urgency of inter-religious harmony in a world disintegrating under communal conflict, ecological disaster and sectarian politics. He sees as the only hope for the pluralist societies of Asia a secular political arrangement which enables all religious communities to contribute their distinctive values in building a common future. Pieris, on the other hand, is motivated not so much by a desire for religious harmony as by the global struggle to resist the imperialism of 'mammon', drawing on the spiritual resources of all religions to do so. He has no discussion of the secular state in his writings. His utopian vision is of an agrarian society organized as a 'religious socialism'. Panikkar's dialogue with Hinduism and Buddhism arises from his own biculturalism and the way the modern world has drawn together people in what he sees as an *oikoumene* of faiths.

2. In reading the Bible, Samartha tends to employ as his hermeneutical key the following question: 'what texts (or interpretation of a given text) would be conducive to peaceful co-existence with neighbours of other faiths in a pluralist society?' Pieris uses a liberation hermeneutic, focusing on the gospels and parts of the Old Testament. Panikkar's hermeneutic is more idiosyncratic. He dehistoricizes the biblical text, with the experience of other religions and their sacred texts forming the horizon of his reading. His hermeneutics goes beyond the text and its historical context—the world of Logos—to the universal realm of Spirit to which all particularities relate.

3. Both Samartha and Pieris see Jesus as embodying the ideals of self-renunciation and compassionate struggle for social justice. The crucifixion is a focal point of solidarity

with suffering humanity, and it motivates us likewise to become poor for the sake of the poor. Panikkar, however, rarely mentions the historical Jesus, and even less the cross. His concerns centre on the theandric principle of mutual inter-penetration by the divine and the human, and the mutual inter-penetration of traditions, religious and secular.

(c) Different arguments for similar concerns

1. All are concerned to put an end to a confrontational posture between Christians and people of other faiths. They assume this posture is implicit in any attempt to seek the 'conversion' of other people to faith in Jesus Christ. The only legitimate form of conversion is from the anti–God forces of death and oppression to the values of the kingdom of God. Pieris uses sociological arguments for his belief that the church itself must be 'converted' by the non-Christian milieu: since no metacosmic religion can displace another except by anti-religious methods, we need to accept a 'first come, first served' basis in Asia where other metacosmic religions are concerned. Samartha argues that all major faiths are different, but equally valid, historico–cultural embodiments of the same transcendent Mystery and so conversion is as unnecessary as it is intolerant. Panikkar sees religious plurality as intrinsic to reality, each tradition expressing the theandric experience. We are enriched by indwelling the religious traditions of others, which in turn are enriched by our own participation in them.

2. All stress that though Jesus is the 'Christ', the 'Christ' is more than Jesus; and draw from this the conclusion that the 'Christ' is present salvifically everywhere, although under different names. Samartha argues this by explicitly denying the deity of Jesus (he prefers to speak of Jesus as divine in the way all of us are, in varying degrees). The high christological affirmations of the New Testament and the later creeds are to be read mythologically. Pieris argues that what is unique and absolute about Jesus is the salvific reality that is mediated through him. He sees a parallel development between christology and buddhology. Panikkar accepts the deity of Jesus, but only because the theandric union of which the Incarnation speaks is a

general pattern disclosed in all reality. Jesus is one cultural instantiation of this general 'christic' principle, but is by no means normative or final in authority for all peoples.

(d) Agreements of a relatively minor kind

1. All emphasize intuitive, mystical and 'gnostic' approaches to the Transcendent over and above rational, scriptural or doctrinal articulation. Samartha also encourages aesthetic perception as a bridge to deeper inter-religious understanding.
2. All invoke, from time to time, apophatic theology and the *via negativa* of traditional Western theology to justify a pluralistic treatment of religious propositions, and to point to the Mystery that lies beyond all our limited perspectives. Christian Neoplatonism is often mentioned (though never elaborated) as a theological current, now long buried, but which needs to be rediscovered in Western Christianity and injected into the bloodstream of Christian theology in Asia.
3. All regard inter-religious dialogue not as an end in itself but as indispensable for securing justice and social well-being.
4. All see Western science, technology and capitalist models of economic development as perpetuating structures of domination and dependence in the Third World.

(e) Major agreements

1. All regard attempts to preach the gospel to people of Asian religious traditions (with a view to their conversion) as obsolete, in addition to being intolerant and arrogant, in the modern situation. The latter has made not only co-existence but active collaboration among people of all faiths (and none) imperative. Christians must take their place alongside others in making their own contribution to the values necessary for the making of a better world.
2. All identify traditional Christian notions of evangelism with Western imperialism and the colonial past. Evangelical Christianity is dismissed as a Western cultural imposition, and unable to take root in Asian cultural and ideological soil.

3. All regard any ascription of uniqueness, normativity and historical finality to Jesus as neither intellectually tenable nor morally desirable. All are concerned to obviate any scandal of particularity attaching to Christian claims about Jesus. There is no 'monopoly' of Christ by Christians.

4. All are agreed that the church, understood as the professing Christian community, is not to be identified with the people of God. For Pieris it is the Third World poor who are the new people of God. The 'basic human communities', comprising the poor and those who struggle with them and on their behalf, are God's means of evangelizing the church. For both Samartha and Panikkar, too, the church has no special standing in relation to God and the expansion of this church is actually a hindrance to the true mission of spreading the kingdom of God.

5. All emphasize the mutual inter-penetration of religious faith traditions as a way of enhancing human consciousness at the end of the twentieth century. It is the only way one can provide spiritual roots for tolerance and active collaboration in working towards a more just and peaceful world.

These, then, are some of the important issues to which we have made a preliminary response in previous chapters and which will be addressed repeatedly during the course of this book.

The Wider Landscape

We now turn to explore some of the common ground between the Asian Christian writers whose work we have been examining and significant trends in the European theological tradition, especially developments in the latter which have taken place in the past two hundred years as the church in Europe has interacted with the dominant culture of modernity. We have already noted several affinities with Hegel in Panikkar's christology and doctrine of Spirit, the indebtedness of Pieris to the relatively recent tradition of liberation theologies (which, in turn, took their cue from the political theologies of post-War Europe) and the influence on Samartha of some of John Hick's and Wilfred Cantwell Smith's work on religious pluralism. Indeed the ideological agenda of religious pluralism in much contemporary theological discussion has been nurtured by older, subterranean streams that have long fed into the main arteries of academic theology.

(1) The Turn to the Subject

Alongside Hegel, probably the greatest influence on the Western theological tradition in the last hundred years has been Immanuel Kant (1724–1804). Kant was the giant of the German Enlightenment which let loose intellectual currents that significantly (and, many would say, disastrously) re-wrote the legacy of the Protestant Reformation. In Kant's programme, the Protestant principle of individual con-science before ecclesiastical authority and the reformers' rediscovery of the biblical concept of the 'priesthood of all believers' was transformed into the proclamation of the 'autonomy' of the individual human subject, in all acts of knowledge and morality. The Frenchman René Descartes (1596–1650) had embarked on a similar intellectual project over a century earlier, but the centering of human know-ledge on the human self came to fullest bloom in Kant.

For Kant, the principle of unity that holds all life together was the concept of God. But Kant's God was remote, unknowable, beyond human conceptual categories. How-ever the existence of this God could be inferred from the human experience of moral obligation. At the beginning of Book IV of *Religion within the Limits of Reason Alone*, Kant defines genuine religion as 'the recognition of all duties as divine commands'. Human beliefs about God, free-will, the soul and immortality are not within the scope of demon-strable reason, but they are practical presuppositions of the moral life. God's existence is presupposed in following the dictates of conscience, as God is the beneficent and powerful being that ensures the just proportioning of happiness to virtue.

Kant often comes dangerously close to reducing Christian faith to moral duty. Thus, for instance, he writes,

> Faith needs merely the idea of God, to which all morally earnest (and therefore confident) endeavour for the good must in-evitably lead; it need not presume that it can certify the objective reality of this idea through theoretical apprehension. Indeed, the minimum of knowledge (it is possible that there may be a God) must suffice, subjectively, for whatever can be made the duty of every man.[2]

Consequently the Kantian legacy in modern theology was a shifting of theological interest from God's revelation of himself in Christ and the Scriptures to a preoccupation with human religious states and their communal expressions.

What Kant was seeking was a synthesis of the rationalism of philosophers such as Descartes with the empiricism of John Locke (1632–1704) and David Hume (1711–1776). He was deeply impressed by Hume's biting critique of 'the clear and distinct ideas' that rationalists such as Descartes had held to be the indubitable foundations of knowledge. But he also wanted to avoid the sceptical conclusions to which Hume's argument led. Kant's solution moved along the following path: things appear as they do to us, not because that is how they are irrespective of human observers, but rather because that is how our minds process the data received by the senses. Our basic categories such as substance and causation, in terms of which we identify things and persons and the way they interact, are *a priori* concepts which *the mind brings to experience*. Kant referred to space and time as 'forms of intuition', in terms of which the whole world is spatially extended and our human consciousness temporally structured. Things and events in the world appears to us as temporally related or spatially extended only because our faculties process them that way. If we wear blue-tinted spectacles all the time, then naturally everything in the world appears blue (this, I should make clear, is not an illustration that Kant himself gave).

This view radically restricts our knowledge and experience. It is not only that factual knowledge has been restricted to the data of our senses, but also the most basic forms of sense experience are now due to the filtering activity of the human mind. Kant does not say that we invent the world by pure thought. The data of sense impinge upon us from beyond ourselves; but the manner of their appearing is determined by the forms of intuition and the categories of understanding that structure the human mind. This implies that we can never know things in *themselves* (what Kant called the 'noumenal' world), but only as they appear in our consciousness (what he called the 'phenomenal' world). Thus, in the post-Kantian world, each one of us is trapped within our own conceptual framework.

Kant believed himself to be articulating the one basic conceptual scheme which all humans are constrained to use in processing the data of their senses. But subsequent Western philosophy has lost this confidence that there is only one categorial framework, common to all humankind. Kant listed twelve basic categories of understanding which he organized in groups of four: quantity, quality, relation and modality. These, along with his spatio-temporal frame-work, were heavily dependent on Euclidean geomery and the reigning Newtonian world-picture. With the develop-ment of non-Euclidean geometries in the nineteenth century and the change from a Newtonian to an Einsteinian cosmology in the twentieth, the cultural imprisonment of Kant's schema has become evident. Social anthropologists and cognitive psychologists believe that whatever Kantian categories there may be, they surely change over time and vary from culture to culture across the globe. Thus, the Kantian world-view can easily slide into a position known as 'cognitive relativism': the way the world appears to me is entirely the result of my own culture's way of processing information, so I have no way of seeing things differently, leave alone any basis for questioning the perceptions of others in other cultures or historical epochs.[3]

This conclusion would have shocked and disturbed Kant, but it is hard to see how it can be avoided once the notion of a *given* world with an intelligible structure of its own has been abandoned. Complete subjectivism is usually avoided by recognition of the social constraints upon the way in which any one individual represents things to herself. We cannot live together with others unless some, perhaps most, of our perceptions and representations refer to a shared reality. At best we are left with an inter-subjective concep-tion of the nature of the phenomenal world.

It was in the sphere of moral agency that Kant himself claimed to find an antidote to the poison of scepticism distilled by Hume and marketed by his own theoretical philosophy. In Kant's view, the universal experience of moral obligation, the conviction that I stand inexorably under the categorical claims of the moral law. is not a law imposed from outside but a law of my own nature as a rational being. It is not grounded in any of the deliverances of the human mind regarding the world 'out there'. But the very fact that, as a free moral agent, I am unconditionally bound by the claims of duty shows that I transcend the limits of sense experience and theoretical understanding. In other words, moral experience alone penetrates through the screen of appearance to the noumenal world of things as they are in themselves. At this point, according to Kant, the unknowableness of noumenal reality, including God, finds a necessary exception.

Other thinkers in the Kantian tradition, but contrary to Kant's own argument and aim, have found in religious experience itself a clue to the transcendent reality that grounds the whole world process. Rudolf Otto (1869–1937) is perhaps the most famous for his conception of the 'holy' as an *a priori* category, a predisposition of the human spirit to experience the world religiously—that is, to respond to specific occasions, places and entities as both awesome and fascinating. Otto calls this response the experience of the 'numinous'. He argued that it is possible only because human beings are endowed with this *a priori* disposition. It is a matter both of felt experience and of morality. Otto uses Kantian terminology in speaking of the rational, moral elements in the world religions serving to 'schematize' the nonrational apprehension of the *mysterium tremendum et fascinans*.[4]

John Hick stands squarely within the Neo-Kantian perspective in the philosophy of religion. Thus, for Hick, using language resembling that of Samartha, 'Allah and Brahman are two ways in which limitless divine reality has been thought and experienced by different human mentalities formed by different intellectual frameworks and devotional techniques.'[5] In his most recent book he has stated this general outlook quite succinctly: 'I am suggesting, then, that religious experience in all its forms is a mode of consciousness that occurs when someone is freely (though not necessarily by conscious volition) open and responsive to the universal presence of the transcendent Reality. The impact of this presence comes to consciousness as a mode of experience whose specific forms are provided by the experiencer's religious concepts and symbols. This of course could explain how it can be that Christians have distinctively Christian forms of religious experience, Muslims distinctively Islamic forms, Hindus distinctively Hindu forms, and so on.'[6]

The familiar Indian story of the blind men and the elephant has been employed by Hick and others to illustrate this diversity of forms. A group of blind men were brought before an elephant. One felt a leg and reported that the object before him was a great living pillar. Another felt the trunk and reported that he was feeling a great snake. A third felt a tusk and reported that it was a sharp plough-share. A fourth felt the tail and reported that it was a coil of rope. And so on . . . The conclusion is drawn that all were true in their own partial ways, each referring to one aspect of the total reality and expressing that aspect in imperfect analogies drawn from individual experience. There is no ultimate perspective which transcends our culture-bound concepts.

Hick, however, argues that to admit the anthropomorphic projection of religious concepts on the divine is not damaging to religion. For these are imperfect attempts to respond to the activity of the Ultimate (or The Real, Hick's equivalent to Samartha's 'ineffable Mystery') in our lives. In his hitherto most comprehensive exposition of the 'pluralist hypothesis', *An Interpretation of Religion* (based on the 1986–7 Gifford Lectures), Hick explains his extension of Kantian epistemology to the realm of religious experience:

> For Kant, God is postulated, not experienced. In partial agreement but also partial disagreement with him, I want to say that the Real *an sich* [in itself] is postulated by us as a presupposition, not of the moral life, but of religious experience and the religious life, whilst the gods, as also the mystically known Brahman, Sunyata and so on, are phenomenal manifestations of the Real occurring within the realm of religious experience. Conflating these two theses one can say that the Real is experienced by human beings, but experienced in a manner analoguous to that in which, according to Kant, we experience the world: namely by informational input from external reality being interpreted by the mind in terms of its own categorial scheme and thus coming to consciousness as meaningful phenomenal experience. All that we are entitled to say about the noumenal source of this information is that it is the reality whose influence produces, in collaboration with the human mind, the phenomenal world of experience.[7]

Using this distinction between the Real-in-itself and the Real-as-humanly-thought-and-experienced, Hick elaborates his well-known thesis that 'the great world faiths embody different perceptions and conceptions of, and correspondingly different responses to, the Real from within the major variant ways of being human; and that within each of them the transformation of human existence from self-centredness to Reality-centredness is taking place'.[8]

But the 'different perceptions and conceptions' are often incompatible, so that even 'self-centredness' and 'Reality-centredness' would be understood in radically conflicting ways among the major world faiths. How does Hick deal with the problem of such conflicting truth-claims? Basically by classifying all descriptive statements about the religious Ultimate under the category of *Myth*: 'I define a myth as a story or statement which is not literally true but which tends to evoke an appropriate dispositional attitude to its subject matter. Thus the truth of a myth is a practical truthfulness: a true myth is one which rightly relates us to a reality about which we cannot speak in non-mythological terms.'[9] So, it is a mistake to inquire if the central affirmations of the world's religions are true or false in the way that, say, scientific beliefs are asserted to be true of false. It is equally mistaken to set one set of religious concepts against another. It is not doctrine but personal transformation that constitutes the core of religious faith. Religious doctrines, such as the incarnation of the Son of God or the inerrancy of the Quran, should not be unduly emphasized. Historical claims are attempts to answer personal existential questions. Consequently, their truth lies in how far they succeed in effecting a change in our present attitudes and lifestyles.

In our discussions of Samartha and Pieris we exposed some of the inadequacies of this type of approach to religious truth-claims. Some further brief comments with respect to Hick's pluralist hypothesis seem in order.

Firstly, it leads inescapably to religious *scepticism*. If we are all truly in the position of the blind men not only can we never know anything about the real elephant, but we can never even conclude that an elephant exists. The story shows not that all the blind men were correct, even in a partial way, but rather that all of them were profoundly mistaken. The object before them was *not* a snake, pillar, rope or any combination of all these things. Hick responds that we must *postulate* the existence of an elephant—of a transcendent, noumenal Reality that encompasses us all. But unless we can say something about the nature of that Reality itself, what have we postulated? It is thus hardly surprising that this whole neo-Kantian scheme in Western philosophy has come home to roost in the radical scepticism that denies any trans-linguistic reference to our texts, thoughts and images.

Hick's scheme is a sophisticated attempt to avoid the pitfalls of non-realism and relativism where religious belief is concerned. By speaking in a pseudo-scientific way of 'informational input' being transmitted by the divine Reality to human minds he thinks he has succeeded in defending religious realism. But the concept of information pre-supposes a cognitive content; yet Hick is at pains to deny that any cognitive content is transmitted by the divine Reality. No 'substantial' concepts or properties (whether being a person or process, good or evil, one or many) can be applied to the Real in itself; at most, only purely formal concepts (such as 'being the referent of a term') apply.[10] It seems that Hick has failed to observe not only that 'being capable of transmitting information' is a substantial property but that all *information* (in contrast to mere noise) is structured, and herein lies the dilemma. Moreover, unless that informational content can be specified in some way as the common denominator behind the various 'mythological' statements about the Real, the sceptic is perfectly justified in dismissing all religious language as empty, merely human illusion.[11]

Hick also invokes the principle of 'complementarity' from modern physics to assert that the different ways of conceiving and experiencing the Real, as personal and as non-personal, are in fact 'complementary'. Thus, he writes that

> the purely physical structure of light is not directly observable; but under different sets of experimental conditions it is found to have wave-like and particle-like properties respectively . . . The reality itself is such that it is able to be validly conceived and observed in both of these ways. Analogously the divine Reality is not directly known *an sich*. But when human beings relate themselves to it in the mode of I-Thou encounter they experience it as personal. Indeed in the context of that relationship it *is* personal, not It but He or She. When human beings relate themselves to the Real in the mode of non-personal awareness they experience it as non-personal, and in the context of this relationship it *is* non-personal . . .[12]

But this analogy will not work. For in quantum physics we know that however invalid any single physical model is to 'picture' the subatomic system with which we are dealing, yet there is an objective mathematical description of the physical state of the system, *valid for all observers*, so that we can confidently assert that all our models, for all their limitations, refer to the same reality. This is what allows us to use the language of 'complementarity' in physics. We are dealing with a single state–of–affairs, but lending itself to description through several models. Moreover, in any realist understanding of science (and Hick is a defender of realism), progress in scientific discovery does not depend on an arbitrary choice of model by the human investigator, but rather on the adequacy of any proposed model to do justice to the way reality actually behaves. I suggest that the world of conflicting religious truth–claims is far more complex than the world of subatomic physics, and that the language of complementarity needs to be justified by those who use it, and not simply taken for granted.

Secondly, if no substantial properties can be applied to the Real in–itself, how does Hick distinguish 'authentic' from 'inauthentic' manifestations of the Real? Surely not all propositions referring to experiences of the Real can be true. There must be some distinction between true and false religious reports. Hick, after all, speaks repeatedly of 'authentic manifestations of the Real', so presumably inauthentic manifestations are possible. But this entails that we have some true information concerning what the Real is like, and therefore that some beliefs must be wrong. The concept of 'mythological truth' does not get Hick out of this dilemma. For to say that a true myth is one that 'rightly relates us' to the Real and tends to evoke 'an appropriate dispositional attitude' to the Real, is simply to beg the question! What one considers an appropriate dispositional attitude to X will obviously depend on what one takes X to be. Moreover, Hick's last-ditch attempt to identify 'soteriological efficacy' with the attainment of moral virtue runs into the same dilemma: if the Real is neither good nor evil, how can a moral criterion serve to distinguish between appropriate and inappropriate responses to the Real?[13]

Thirdly, Hick's hypothesis, for all its hospitable accommodation of the world's religions, is ultimately biased against the Semitic traditions. It simply rules out, *a priori*, the possibility that God/Reality is ultimately, and not simply in its manifestations, personal. For to entertain this possibility one must then also be willing to acknowledge the other possibility that this God wills to reveal God's self and enter into personal relationship with us. Hick has effectively excluded any meaningful concept of divine revelation from his 'meta-religion' of religions, and so it is doubtful whether any orthodox Jew, Christian or Muslim can subscribe to it. It is not accidental that Hick should choose as an illustration of his epistemology a story from Hindu culture. There is, in fact, a cunning sleight-of-hand in the telling of the story. For any of the blind men to have postulated that what he really felt was an elephant, he must have known what an elephant was. It is the narrator (or, as in some versions of the story, the King who brought the blind men before the elephant) who alone is 'in the know'. He alone has access to the true nature of Reality. From his lofty vantage point he can see that the reports of the blind men are clumsy images that need to be complemented by other reports. So, what passes for a posture of intellectual humility before the variety of religious truth-claims is, in fact, a posture of intellectual imperialism.

This imperialism is also prominent in Hick's attempts to rewrite the reports of individual traditions in such a way that they can be accommodated within a Neo-Kantian world-view. Among the candidates suggested for mythological reinterpretation are the following: within Buddhism, the doctrine of rebirth and the Mahayana discourse about the heavenly Buddhas; within Judaism, the notion of Israel as a chosen people of Yahweh and Jewish history as a record of Yahweh's providence and judgments; within the Christian tradition, Jesus' virgin birth, bodily resurrection and ascension, the idea of divine incarnation, penal concepts of atonement, the ontological nature of the Holy Trinity, the image of the church as the body of Christ . . . The finished product, in each case, is unrecognizable to most adherents of the respective traditions.

The price for resolving the problem of conflicting truth-claims in this manner is considerable. It calls into question Hick's entire project of constructing a 'meta-religion' of religions: for it simply refuses to respect both the ontological intention and the integrity of the major doctrines of these historic faiths. It seems that what was advanced initially as a humble attempt to account for the rich diversity of human religious traditions has quickly turned into a reductionist onslaught on the factual affirmations of those traditions, with the Semitic traditions taking the brunt of the assault. What we are left with are a series of Procrustean beds on which a new elite of 'progressive' theologians dismember the religions of the world.

(2) The Flight from History

Both the ancient religions of the Indian subcontinent and much of twentieth-century European theology share a disdain for the epistemic value of historical events. Religious knowledge is taken to be knowledge of a timeless, universal realm. Religious truth must be accessible to all rational human beings through the exercise of reason, direct personal encounter or mystical experience of the divine. History, subject to the flux of change and uncertainty, cannot be the source of ultimate truth. Moreover, the traditional Jewish-Christian notion of divine revelation being mediated through specific events at specific times and places is morally repugnant, because it seems to deny to people at other times and places that direct, immediate access to God which any global religion must entail. We have seen how Asian theologians such as Samartha and Panikkar share this particular outlook, so that religious faith is cut loose from any mooring in empirical, and especially historical, events.[14]

These assumptions have their philosophical roots both in Hindu *vedanta* and classical Greek (especially Plato and Stoic) sources. They were resuscitated in Europe during the 17th and 18th century by the English Deists who championed a 'natural religion' based on an universal reason and enlightened moral sensibility; and they received their classic articulation in the German Enlightenment under thinkers such as Kant and, especially, GE Lessing (1729–1781). Rigid dichotomies were drawn, in different but related ways, between 'faith' and 'knowledge', and between 'reason' and 'history'. Post-Enlightenment European culture came, for the most part, to view history as little more than an useful source-book for illustrations of truth. It displayed universal principles and recurrent patterns discovered through either introspective contemplation or metaphysical speculation.

In his famous essay, *On the Proof of the Spirit and of Power*, Lessing begins with the vexing problem of chronological distance. For our knowledge of Jesus Christ we are obliged to depend on the eyewitness accounts which underlie the gospel narratives. But how do we know that these are reliable? Can faith depend on the deliverances of historical enquiry? 'If I had lived at the time of Christ', says Lessing,' then of course the prophecies fulfilled in his person would have made me pay great attention to him. If I had actually seen him do miracles. I would have believed him in all things in which equally indisputable experiences did not tell against him.'[15] In other words, to those fortunate enough to have experienced at firsthand the reported miracles of Jesus, above all his resurrection from the dead, they would have had the 'strongest inducements' to believe. But for Lessing himself, living in the eighteenth century when miracles no longer occur, he is forced to rely on the 'infinitely less inducements' of the historians of his day.[16] And, true to the spirit of the Enlightenment, Lessing insists that truth cannot be received through any external authority. It can only be recognized by the autonomous individual as being congruent with those truths derived from his own thought and experience.

The contingent character of historical knowledge, then, is a poor basis for religious knowledge, for the latter must be of truths accessible to universal human reason. So, Lessing, who began his essay by raising doubts about the historical reliablity of the gospel accounts, goes on to assert that, even if the historical evidence for their reliability were compelling, nevertheless: 'Accidental truths of history can never become the proof of necessary truths of reason . . . That, then, is the ugly broad ditch which I cannot get across, however often and however earnestly I have tried to make the leap.'[17] It is important to note that the 'ugly broad ditch' is now a metaphysical one.[18] Anxiety over the uncertainties of historical evidence is not the main issue, for even if Lessing experienced the resurrection of Jesus in his own bedroom, that would still count as a 'particular' event, just another of the 'accidental truths of history', and so fall short of what Lessing takes to be the epistemological standard for religious knowledge. It is, after all, simply not the case that historical beliefs are always less certain than beliefs which I have acquired through firsthand experience. I suppose I can imagine that the Holocaust never occurred by doubting the testimony of living survivors and all the archival documentation on which its historicity rests. But I cannot detect any less certainty in my belief about this event than in my beliefs about what is happening now in my body as I write this page. All empirical beliefs, and not just historical judgments, are subject to uncertainty. Lessing's objection has to do with an unspoken assumption that religious truths are grounded in the deliverances of a universal reason that is exempt from such uncertainty.

The concern that 'faith' should not simply be another name for 'assent to empirical evidence' has often led to the claim that faith has *no* empirical content at all. Since religion concerns ultimate reality, it is insulated from the risks attached to the pursuit of knowledge in lesser disciplines that are concerned with the empirical world of human beings and natural events. Thus, Paul Tillich (1886–1965) expresses a view that has been prevalent among twentieth-century Protestant philosophers of religion:

> Faith does not affirm or deny what belongs to the pre-scientific or scientific knowledge of the world . . . The knowledge of our world (including ourselves as part of our world) is a matter of inquiry by ourselves or by those in whom we trust. It is not a matter of faith. The dimension of faith is not the dimension of science, history or psychology. The acceptance of a probable hypothesis in these realms is not faith, but preliminary belief, to be tested by scholarly methods, and to be changed by every new discovery.[19]

Faith, on this understanding, involves no commitments on any matters pertaining to the 'dimension of science, history or psychology', that is the empirical realm altogether; it is thus immune to criticism by scholarship in any of these areas. For Tillich all human cultural activity, such as historical inquiry, is so restricted by human finitude that it cannot tell us about matters of 'ultimate concern'. Since faith is not anchored in the facticity of any historical events, Tillich reaches a conclusion that is more in accord with existentialism or mainstream Indian religious thought than the orthodox Judaeo-Christian position: 'Faith cannot be shaken by historical research even if its results are critical of the traditions in which the event is recorded.'[20]

The price paid for such immunity has been immense. Western Christianity in the late twentieth century has been relegated to a position of cultural marginality. The churches most infuenced by the forces of modernity and their intellectual baggage have ended up as private religious clubs, the gospel reduced to existential categories having no bearing on the public domain.

The claim that ultimate religious truths must be either self-authenticating or necessarily true is itself neither self-authenticating nor necessarily true. Nor is there any reason why as Christians we should assume that epistemological immunity is a desirable, let alone attainable, goal. The

[handwritten note at top: True — our faith is historical and we must claim that]

Christian message is radically historical in its orientation. The doctrine of creation states that we are not godlike, timeless beings but profoundly contingent creatures. We are rooted in social and cultural existence. The choices we make and the actions we perform shape both our personal future and that of the world we inhabit. Sin and evil too are historical in character, and so it is not surprising that our redemption should pivot on real events in history. Since Christian faith has this historically-mediated cognitive content, it naturally shares in the uncertainty that besets all empirical, and especially historical, beliefs. To empty the faith of this pivotal historical content, or to marginalize it in favour of timeless 'religious values' or 'principles', is to turn it into something other than Christianity.[21] We shall return to this theme in the next chapter.

The mind-set that seems to underlie the view that ultimate religious truths must be equally available to all human beings does have a certain psychological appeal. For if the knowledge of ultimate reality is tied to historical events, that is to particular events at a particular space-time location, it seems to exclude those people who by accident of birth were not able to share in those events. This is one aspect of the well-known *scandal of particularity*. Is not the claim that Israel was vouchsafed a special disclosure of God's purposes tantamount to contempt for all other nations and cultures? How can the life, death and resurrection of Jesus of Nazareth carry such momentous significance for the life of the whole world, as Christians have claimed down the ages? Does this not impugn the goodness of God?

I shall venture to deal with these questions at length later. Here all that needs to be done is to clarify, in a preliminary way, some of the assumptions that lie behind these objections.

First, the problem of particularity seems to be a problem that is framed within a largely rationalist conception of religious knowledge and an optimistic view of human nature. It is assumed that human beings have a natural predisposition towards truth. Also, however arduous may be the process of acquiring that truth (whether through disciplined mysticism, sustained philosophical reflection on human experience or the natural world, etc) that truth can eventually be grasped without any need to be dependent on another in the process. The 'truth that saves' is essentially an individual cognitive process. By contrast, the biblical notion that truth is something that breaks in on us from 'outside' our individual consciousness and catches us by surprise, and in that very act forges relationships of inter-dependence among us, is subversive of this particular mind-set and is naturally offensive to it.

Second, the problem of particularity should not be confused with the problem of the ultimate status of those who are not Christians. The claim that God has revealed his truth in historical events does not entail, at least without further premises, that those who lack this revelation are excluded from the benefits of that revelation. It is perfectly possible for someone to argue *both* that Jesus' life, death and resurrection are the normative and ultimate revelation of God to humankind *and* that all human beings will eventually come to that knowledge of God in Jesus. Someone else may reject this universalism but still maintain that, even as the Old Testament saints looked forward to God's gracious redemption and trusted in the Christ in whom redemption took shape without clearly understanding how that redemption would come about, so there are many who are saved by Christ and serve him without realizing who it is they trust. It is not my intention here to debate these theories but simply to point out that there is no logical connexion between the claim that specific historical events uniquely reveal God's saving purpose and the further claim that this is to condemn all who for reasons of history or geography have been denied the chance to respond to that revelation.

(3) Ultimate Silence

We have seen that both Pieris and Panikkar suggest that we draw on the (Neoplatonic) apophatic tradition in Western theology[22] in order to proceed beyond personal theism to a transcendent, ineffable Beyond in which to ground the complex plurality of religious beliefs and experience. Since God is utterly unique and categorically distinct, clearly any attempt to think of God in terms of images or concepts drawn from the world with which we are familiar can only be idolatrous. No comprehensive knowledge of God can be possible, and no coherent descriptions of God can be captured in language. The thunderous challenge of the prophet Isaiah reverberates through the world of human religion: 'To whom then will you liken God, or what likeness compare with him?' (Is 40:18). As ultimate Mystery, God can only be spoken of by a *via negativa*: we cannot speak positively of what God is, only of what he is *not*. Only negative predication applies to ultimate Mystery.

Panikkar develops this in the most radical way through dialogue with Buddhism. As is well known, Gautama the Buddha refused to answer what we might call 'the ultimate questions of life'—the existence or non-existence of God, the eternity or non-eternity of the world, mind–body identity, and so on. When questioned he replied in terms of the parable of a man pierced by a poisoned arrow. If, before receiving medical treatment, he were to insist on knowing who shot him, what kind of bow he used, of what the bowstring and the arrow-shaft were made and so on, he would die before his demand for knowledge could be satisfied. Likewise the Buddha set aside disputed cosmological questons because they are not conducive to the supreme goal of liberation from *dukka*. 'Wrongly, basely, falsely, and without foundation do certain ascetics and Brahmins accuse me, saying that Gautama the ascetic is a nihilist, and that he preaches annihilation, destruction, and nonexistence. Such I am not, such I do not assert. Today, monks, as before, I proclaim one thing alone: sorrow, sorrow's destruction . . .'[23]

There have, of course, been a variety of interpretations by both Asian and Western scholars of the Buddha's silence. He has been called everything from an agnostic to a pragmatist to an early deconstructionist. The orthodox answer in later developments of the tradition was to emphasize the omniscience of the Buddha and the inherent cognitive limitations of his audience. The pragmatic approach is clearly unsatisfactory, for in teaching the path to liberation the Buddha has also enunciated a particular world-view. Answers to metaphysical and cosmological issues have been given, implicitly as well as explicitly, in the identification of the human condition as one of *dukka* and in its sophisticated psychological analysis. To live as if the question of 'God' was irrelevant or superfluous is, of course, to have already assumed a certain view of 'God'.

For Panikkar, the ultimate reason for the Buddha's silence is rooted in what he calls an 'ontic apophaticism'.[24] He points out that the Buddha never denied *existentially* what conventionally we call ultimate reality, but rather what he did reject was any name for it, any determination (including that of 'ultimate' or of 'reality'), any personification of it because personification was tantamount to anthropomorphism. The Buddha resists any attempt 'to penetrate God by the force of our volitive and intellective formulas'.[25] Panikkar sums it up neatly: 'Not only did the Buddha proscribe every idle word—he proclaims every word idle that purports to bear on the ultimate mystery of reality.'[26] Just as the third-century Platonist Plotinus recognized the possibility of knowing *that* a thing exists without knowing *what* it is,[27] so the Buddha realized that if the target can be known when we are still short of it, the target would share in our contingency. If the target is really 'beyond', how can we know when we are still short of it? The Buddha has realized the fact that the ultimate end, by definition, cannot be known before it is reached.

Panikkar sees in this attitude of the Buddha an 'indispensable element for the spirituality of modern humankind'.[28] Both traditional Buddhist culture and modern Western culture have an apophatic attitude towards ultimate questions about reality. The religion of the Buddha can be described as atheistic religion, and it corresponds to the religious atheism of our own day which is 'a new stage along the journey of humanity, a new degree of awareness . . . that there 'is' no God, not only because neither 'is' there humankind . . . The world, humankind, and God are as it were incompatible as three separate, independent entities.'[29]

The silence of the Buddha is not simply the silence of body and of voice, but the silence of thought itself. Since God is beyond the attribute of existence and non-existence, and every human affirmation implies an attribution of nonbeing, Panikkar turns Anselm's famous ontological argument ('God is that than which nothing greater can be thought') into an 'apophatic argument': namely, 'God is that which cannot be thought'. Citing Aquinas, Augustine, Denys the Areopagite, and biblical texts such as Habakkuk 2:20 ('The Lord is in his holy temple, let all the earth be silent before him'), Panikkar writes, 'Silence is the hallmark of God's most important characteristic: mystery. A God who would not be "mysterious" would *eo ipso* cease to be God . . . Those who have "understood" God have acknowledged that silence alone describes and expresses God. Silence alone is God's finest praise.'[30] Indeed, Panikkar is even bolder: 'The very claim to "know" God—in any way—is in and of itself idolatry. "If someone seeing God, knew what he saw, he did not see God" said Denys the Areopagite and, with him, the greatest part of the Christian tradition.'[31]

That Panikkar has seriously misread the Western theological tradition should be evident from the examples he gives in the defence of his own argument. Certainly Gregory of Nyssa reminds his readers that God is 'incapable of being grasped by any term or any idea, or any other device of our apprehension'[32] but, as we saw in the previous chapter, Gregory's entire theological position is founded on the conviction that a true knowledge of the Father is communicated through the Son and the Spirit, and that the relations within the divine Trinity are ontologically real.

In fact the *via negativa* (negative predication of God) can be viable only if there is presupposed some identifiable positive knowledge of God. If we have absolutely no positive knowledge of God, on what basis could we say that no properties can be ascribed to God? A radical apophaticism is caught in its own circularity. If no truths about God can be known, we could never *know* this to be true. If no thoughts about God are possible, that thought itself would be unthinkable. We need not be bothered by the fact that exhaustive knowledge of God is impossible; after all, exhaustive knowledge of even the simplest material objects in the world eludes us! The theological problem has been how to understand the transcendence and uniqueness of God in such a way that his 'mystery' (or 'otherness') is truly acknowledged and the possibility of genuine knowledge maintained.

Thomas Aquinas (1224–1274), who was himself deeply influenced by the apophatic tradition transmitted through Denys the Areopagite and others, did not wholly share the view that our talk about God should be construed as chiefly or primarily negative.[33] We do not know what God *is*, he wrote. But talk of God is not always saying what something is *not*. For example, he observes: 'When a man speaks of the "living God" he does not simply want to say that God . . . differs from a lifeless body.'[34] One of Aquinas' leading modern commentators, Brian Davies, points out that even Denys the Areopagite wanted to say that God can and should be described as his creatures can be described. For, in believing that God is the cause of his creatures, he also held that a *cause* of something shows itself in its *effects*, so that these reflect it in some manner. Since all creatures are God's effects, Denys the Areopagite affirmed, it can be said that they are all somehow like him, and that things which can be said of them can also be said of God. 'What has actually to be said about the Cause of everything', he writes, 'is [that] since it is the Cause of all beings, we should posit and ascribe to it all the affirmations we make in regard to beings.'[35] (By way of comparison, it is important to note that *nirvana* in Buddhism is not the *cause* of anything, but is simply the uncaused, unconditioned goal of existence).

In this area, Aquinas was probably influenced by Denys the Areopagite. He contends that, since creatures are caused to be by God, 'We speak of God as we know him, and since we know him from creatures we can only speak of him as they represent him. Any creature, in so far as it possesses any perfection, represents God and is like him, for he, being simply and universally perfect, has pre-existing in himself the perfections of all his creatures.'[36] Aquinas' position is that, though God is above naming, our statements about him *can*, nevertheless, signify the divine nature. 'God is said to have no name, or to be beyond naming because his essence is beyond what we understand of him and the meaning of the names we use.'[37] So the language we use to speak of God is at one level inadequate and we do not know what God is. But in speaking of God we can, says Aquinas, speak *truly. And we can know that we are doing so.* In other words, his view is that what we say of God can be literally true, though the full reality signified by our words defies our comprehension. We can speak of God and mean what we say, but we cannot comprehend the reality which makes our statements true. 'God is good' and 'God is wise' are true statements, literally true, but also understatements. They are, as Brian Davies expresses it delightfully, like saying 'Mozart is musical'—inadequate and understated, but not necessarily false.

Aquinas held that words used *analogously* of God and creatures apply primarily to God and secondarily to creatures. Since he believed that we name God from creatures, we might have expected him to say that terms applied to God and creatures apply primarily to creatures and secondarily to God. Yet his view is the very opposite. For Aquinas, the 'goodness' of creatures is a pale reflection of the goodness derived from and exemplified in God: 'Because we come to a knowledge of God from other things, the reality in the names of God and other things belongs by priority in God according to his mode of being, but the meaning of the name belongs to God by posteriority. And so he is said to be named from his effects.'[38]

Once again the idea which Aquinas is presenting can be found (in a less developed form) in Denys the Areopagite. According to the latter, the negations concerning God must themselves, in a sense, be negated. For, as we have seen, he holds that God can be 'named' from everything because he is the Creator of everything. This, in turn, leads him to be inordinately fond of the prefix 'hyper' ('above'). We may deny that God is good, but not in order to assert baldly, 'It is not the case that God is good', for we must say rather that 'God is hyper-good', meaning that his goodness transcends the goodness of created things while at the same time being reflected in them.[39]

To summarize Aquinas' *analogia entis* ('analogy of being') as simply as possible, he held that: (1) We do not know what God is in himself, for he is beyond definition and differs quite radically from anything to which we may compare him; (2) As the Creator of his creatures, however, God may be said to resemble them in certain ways, though he lacks all creaturely limitations. (3) There is room for arguing that certain specific predicates can be ascribed to him. The Anglican theologian Eric Mascall reminds us that 'The function of the doctrine of analogy is not to make it possible for us to talk about God in the future but to explain how it is that we have been able to talk about him all along.'[40]

Powerful as Thomas Aquinas' theological reshaping of Aristotle's analogical language was in his own day, equally powerful in modern times has been Karl Barth's (1886–1968) epoch-making rediscovery of Anselm of Canterbury's (c.1033–1109) theological method, *fides quaerens intellectum* ('faith seeking understanding'. This was the original title of Anselm's *Proslogion*, which Barth took over as the title for his own study of Anselm in the summer of 1930).[41] Barth was confronted with a liberal Protestantism for which the object of religious knowledge was not rational in its own right; but, rather, it came to symbolic expression as theology penetrated its essence and interpreted it through the use of concepts drawn from philosophy and ethics.[42] Against this prevailing notion of the theological task Barth, following Anselm, pitted the biblical witness to a divine revelation. Faith is not something vague and formless but specific, arising from an encounter with God through the preaching of the Word of God 'made flesh'. God is unique and incomparable, so that we cannot conceive of him except on the basis of the Word which we hear about him, the Word of Christ which comes from him. Hence the act of faith is never irrational but essentially cognitive and conceptual.[43]

Barth follows Anselm's route of *fides quaerens intellectum*. God is the Author of all true knowledge of him on our part. God gives himself to us in his Word to be the object of our trust and knowledge. The faith which his Word evokes is a movement of understanding, not a wordless mysticism that seeks to grasp the divine. Therefore theological inquiry is now feasible, because it involves not a movement from the unknown to the known, but a movement from what is *given* to our knowledge into a clearer and deeper knowledge of it. The rationality of faith and theology is grounded in the *prior rationality* of the object of faith. Theology is an act of reverent obedience, a humble response to a disclosure of the divine object whose being is Truth. It is a dynamic rationality springing from the active self-communication of God.

Barth points out that Anselm's designation of God as 'That than which nothing greater can be conceived' is not just a logical abstraction but a form of thinking imposed on us by the self-revelation of God which will not allow us to imagine anything greater than God, for any conception of a 'God' we could form on our own in this way would thereby cease to be a conception of the true God. In standing before God, we do not stand as one being before another being, but as a creature before its Creator. Not only our existence, but even our thinking about our existence, depends on the Creator. Thinking can be true only in so far as its truth is in the Creator himself. Expounding Anselm, Barth writes, 'The conception of a "better" beyond the Creator would imply for the creature an ascent to a point where by nature he cannot stand, a judgment by a standard of truth or value which by nature he cannot possess. Conceiving a greater than the Creator would therefore mean absurdity.'[44] Understanding God as greater than anything we can conceive is inseparable from a knowledge of the object of faith, and therefore that object would disappear for our knowledge if we displace this 'God' by one of our own imagination, even if that 'God' were reached by a *via negativa*.

It follows from this that to acknowledge that all our theological propositions about God fall short of who he is, is actually *a consequence of faith in his revelation*. In their essential nature they point beyond themselves to the God who transcends them. Barth writes: 'Every theological statement is an inadequate expression of its object. The actual Word of Christ spoken to us is not an inadequate expression of its object, though of course every effort on our part, even the highest and the best, to reproduce that Word in thought or in speech is inadequate. Strictly speaking it is only God himself who has a conception of God.'[45] Yet, at the same time, he continues, 'just as everything which is not God could not exist apart from God and is something only because of God . . . so it is possible for expressions which are not identical with God, to be true expressions . . . even when these expressions are applied to the God who can never be expressed.'[46]

True theological thinking, then, is thinking that allows God to be God, by allowing our thoughts to be subdued by his objective truth. True thinking is thinking that proceeds by humble, prayerful meditation on the Word of Christ in Scripture, and we rejoice in the fact that God himself makes our thoughts and expressions of him which we undertake in obedience to his Word, capable and adequate beyond any capacity of their own. For it is he himself who validates them by supplying himself as their object and thereby conferring upon them their truth.

So, for Barth, the peculiarity of biblical faith is that it is directed towards an objective basis in a manner that is totally self-involving. According to Barth, it is the activity of God which creates a correspondence between human speech and divine revelation. He thus sets up a doctrine of analogy which he later described as an analogy of faith (*analogia fidei*). So, Barth and Aquinas, in their very different ways, show how it is possible for the creature to speak truly of its Creator even while acknowledging its inability to capture the glory and mystery of the Creator in any human confession.

Thus, over and against the ultimate silence of Buddhist *nirvana*, the Neoplatonic One and the Kantian *noumenon*, the gospel announces a divine speech–act: a Word that brought into being a creation now bring into being a new creation. The divine initiative in creation, redemption and revelation are what make language about God at all possible. We can speak, only because we have first been spoke to, and summoned by, another. All Christian language is a response to the divine initiative: at the soteriological level this initiative is expressed as 'grace'; at the epistemological level, in the notion of 'revelation'. The events that centre in Jesus of Nazareth force the redrawing of intellectual and spiritual horizons, inviting us to enter into a conceptual world which we ourselves did not fashion. The initiative has been taken from us. 'The mode of speaking of the Christian tradition,' writes the contemporary German systematic theologian Eberhard Jüngel, 'insists that we must be told what we are to think of the word God.'[47]

Conclusion

We have seen that Samartha, Pieris and Panikkar are united by a common vision of a pluralist world in which Christian claims to uniqueness and finality are rejected as false and obsolete. They argue this in a variety of ways and from different perspectives. But, at several points in their writings, we have found common ground with the assumptions, concerns and overall world view of the liberal, post-Kantian theological tradition in Western Christianity. This in itself would not be a matter worthy of much attention, if not for the fact that they are strident in their scorn for Western theology and the Asian church's alleged dependence on the West. (I have also indicated, in a necessarily sketchy and preliminary way, that there *are* rich resources within the Western tradition itself which can be explored and used to correct some of the shortcomings of their own theological methods.)

In the case of Samartha, the anti-Western scorn borders on a xenophobic inversion of reality. What, for instance, are we to make of the following comment: 'Even as there is an *economic* injustice in the relationship between the rich nations of the North and the poor countries of the South there is also a *theological* injustice in the relationship between Christianity as the religion of the rich and powerful North and the religions of the poor and weak in the South'?[48] This betrays a remarkably myopic view of present global realities. Christianity is no longer a religion of the 'rich and powerful North'. Over half of the world's Christians live in the poor countries of the South. It is estimated that by the year 2010, there will be more cross-cultural Protestant missionaries sent from or within the South than from the countries of the affluent North.[49] Most evangelical Christians who live in Asia are economically poor or are from the lower middle-class, they are politically powerless and often victimized by state-sponsored discrimination and persecution (e.g. in many Islamic states, in Nepal prior to 1991, in China to the present day). As for the so-called 'religions of the poor and the weak', Samartha ignores the facts that Japan, India and China are superpowers on the world stage and that the imperialist experience in Asia has not been exclusively Western!

Although it is difficult to demonstrate direct lines of intellectual influence, and not simply affinities, the fact that all of them have spent a considerable period of their life in the West, especially in academic theological environments, must count as evidence of their moulding by the preconceptions of liberal Western culture. Once again, I repeat: this is not in itself a negative criticism, least of all a matter for censure. But it does expose the hypocrisy of their disdain towards both the Western Church and evangelical Christians elsewhere.

The British political theologian John Milbank has drawn attention to what he terms a 'stark paradox' lying at the heart of the pluralist project: 'The terms of discourse which provide both the favoured categories for encounter with other religions—dialogue, pluralism, and the like—together with the criteria for the acceptable limits of the pluralist embrace—social justice, liberation, and so forth—are themselves embedded in a wider Western discourse become globally dominant'.[50] This provides the cue for the following chapter.

Notes to Chapter Four

1. For a fascinating account of the former development see M. Buckley, *At the Origins of Modern Atheism* (New Haven and London: Yale University Press, 1987). See also the discussion in Ch. 5 of this book.

2. Immanuel Kant, *Religion within the Limits of Reason Alone*, trans. Theodore Greene & Hoyt Hudson (New York: Harper and Row, 1960) p. 142.

3. In the debate surrounding religious pluralism, one example of such cognitive relativism is found in the writings of the American, Gordon Kaufman: e.g. 'A universal frame of orientation for human understanding and life is no more available to us than is a universal language . . . If we understand human historicity in the sense that I am urging here, Christian faith (like every other faith) will be seen as one perspective, one worldview, which has developed in and through a long history alongside other traditions . . . We now see the great theologians of Christian history, for example, not simply as setting out the truth that is ultimately salvific for all humanity (as they have often been understood in the past), but rather as essentially engaged in discerning and articulating one particular perspective on life among many others.' (Kaufman, 'Religious Diversity, Historical Consciosuness, and Christian Theology' in *The Myth of Christian Uniqueness*, ed. J Hick & P Knitter, London: SCM, 1988, pp. 5, 9). Presumably, Kaufman's thesis is itself simply one particular, historically-conditioned, perspective among others; for, if not, his thesis would be falsified by his own example. Why then should others accept it?

4. R Otto, *The Idea of the Holy* (Oxford: Oxford University Press, 1958).

5. J Hick, *Problems of Religious Pluralism* (London: Macmillan, 1985) p. 96.

6. J Hick, *Disputed Questions in Theology and the Philosophy of Religion* (London: Macmillan, 1993) p. 28.

7. J Hick, *An Interpretation of Religion* (London: Macmillan, 1989) p. 243. He adds: 'In terms of information theory, we are speaking of the transmission from a transcendent source to the human mind/brain and its transmission by the mind/brain into conscious experience.' (p. 244).

8. Ibid. p. 240.

9. Ibid. p. 248.

10. Ibid. p. 239.

11. The spectre of non-realism haunts all Neo-Kantian forms of religious pluralism. Thus Ninian Smart writes that 'If we do not postulate the ultimate Focus, the subject, the inaccessible X lying beyond the contents of belief and experience, we might consider the real Focus as it enters into lives itself to be a projection' (Ninian Smart, *Beyond Ideology: Religion and the Future of Western Civilization*, San Francisco: Harper & Row, 1981, p. 187).

12. Hick, *An Interpretation of Religion*, op. cit. p. 245.

13. Note: 'The Real *an sich* . . . cannot be said to be one or many, person or thing, conscious or unconscious, purposive or non-purposive, substance or process, good or evil, loving or hating.' Ibid. p. 350.

14. Panikkar's attitude to temporality is well summed up by his comment, 'Everything is equidistant from eternity' (*The Silence of*

God: the Answer of the Buddha, Maryknoll, NY: Orbis, 1989, p. 171).

15. GE Lessing, 'On the Proof of the Spirit and of Power', in *Lessing's Theological Writings*, ed.Henry Chadwick (Stanford: Stanford University Press, and London: A& C Black, 1957) p. 51–2.

16. Ibid. p. 53.

17. Ibid. pp. 53–5.

18. Gordon Michalson, Jr, has distinguished a temporal ditch, a metaphysical ditch and a ditch of appropriation in Lessing's writings, each of which in turn takes different forms. See GE Michalson, Jr., *Lessing's 'Ugly Ditch': A Study of Theology and History* (Pennsylvania State University Press, 1985).

19. P Tillich, *The Dynamics of Faith* (New York: Harper and Row, 1957) p. 33. Note, especially, his comments: 'It is a disastrous distortion of the meaning of faith to identify it with the belief in the historical validity of the biblical stories' (p. 87), and 'Faith does not include historical knowledge about the way in which [significant religious events] took place.' (p. 89).

20. Ibid. p. 89.

21. As, for example, when Don Cupitt asserts dogmatically that the timeless moral possibilities embodied in the life of Jesus constitute the essence of Christian faith: 'The core of a religion does not lie in the biography or personality of the founder, but in the specifically religious values to which, according to tradition, he bore witness. By these values I mean possible determinations of the human spirit whereby it relates itself to the ultimate goal of existence . . . How can we depend upon the uncertainties of historical tradition for knowledge of, and our power to attain, a history-transcending truth?' (D Cupitt, 'A Final Comment' in *The Myth of God Incarnate*, ed. John Hick, London: SCM, 1977, p. 205).

22. Christian forms of Neoplatonism are usually associated with the unknown author of the 6th century known as Dionysius (or Pseudo-Dionysius or simply Denys) the Areopagite, his Celtic translator (into Latin) John Scotus Erigena (c.810–877), the German mystic Meister Eckhart (1260–1329) and Nicholas of Cusa (1401–1464). While exerting a profound influence on medieval Christian thought (e.g. on Albert Magnus, Thomas Aquinas and Dante) through the works of Denys and Erigena, as well as on earlier thinkers such as Augustine and the Cappadocian Fathers, Neoplatonism was always in tension with orthodox Christianity. Those influenced by the more radical tendencies within Neoplatonism, as, for example, Erigena and Eckhart, have frequently been regarded as heretical.

23. *Majjhima-Nikaya*, 1:139.

24. R Panikkar, *The Silence of God: the Answer of the Buddha* (Madrid, 1970; Eng. trans. Maryknoll, NY: Orbis, 1989) p. 14.

25. Ibid. p. 23.

26. Ibid. p. 14.

27. Plotinus, *Enneads*, V, 5, 6.

28. *The Silence of God*, op. cit. p. 102

29. Ibid. p. 97.

30. Ibid. p. 165.
31. Ibid. p. 205, note 74.
32. *Against Eunomius*, Book 1, sec. 42 in *A Select Library of Nicene and Post-Nicene Fathers of the Christian Church*, ed. P Schaff, 2nd series, vol.5 (Grand Rapids: Eerdmans, 1976). As we noted in the preceding chapter, the full quotation continues: '. . . remaining beyond the reach not only of the human but of the angelic and of all supramundane intelligence, unthinkable, unutterable, above all expression in words, having but the name that can represent his proper nature, the single name of being "above every name"; which is granted to the Only-begotten also, because "all that the Father hath is the Son's".'
33. I follow the discussion in *Brian Davies, The Thought of Thomas Aquinas* (Oxford: Clarendon Press, 1992 esp. Ch 4).
34. *Summa* Theologiae, Part 1, Q 13. art. 2.
35. Denys the Areopagite, *The Mystical Theology*, ch.1, cited in Davies, ibid. p. 62.
36. *Summa*, Part 1 Q.13. art. 2.
37. Ibid. Part 1 Q13. art.1 ad.1.
38. *Summa Contra Gentiles*, 1:34, cited in Davies, op. cit. p. 72.
39. 'What has actually to be said about the Cause of everything is this. Since it is the Cause of all beings, we should posit and ascribe to it all the affirmations we make in regard to beings, and, more appropriately, we should negate all these affirmations. Now we should not conclude that the negations are simply the opposites of the affirmations, but rather that the cause of all is considerably prior to this, beyond privations, beyond every denial, beyond every assertion', *The Mystical Theology*, ch.1, cited in Davies, op. cit., p.72.
40. E Mascall, *Existence and Analogy* (London, 1949, p. 94), cited in Davies, op. cit. p. 73.
41. Karl Barth, *Anselm: Fides Quaerens Intellectum* (Eng. trans. London: SCM, 1960). See also TF Torrance, *Karl Barth: an Introduction to his Early Theology, 1910–31* (London: SCM, 1962) pp 180ff.
42. This was, for instance, also Tillich's view as expressed in *The Dynamics of Faith*, op. cit.
43. Torrance points out that this does not mean that faith is simply intellectual, for it involves trust and operates through love (for Anselm and Barth no less than Augustine), op. cit. p. 183.
44. Barth, op. cit. pp. 152–3.
45. Ibid. p. 29.
46. Ibid. pp. 29–30.
47. Eberhard Jüngel, *God as the Mystery of the World* (Edinburgh: T & T Clarke, 1983) p. 13.
48. SJ Samartha, *One Christ-Many Religions: Towards a Revised Christology* (Indian ed. Bangalore: SATHRI, 1992) p. 154 (italics in text).
49. Cf. Bryant Myers, *The Changing Shape of World Mission* (Monrovia, CA: MARC Publications, 1993).
50. J Milbank, 'The End of Dialogue' in GD 'Costa (ed), *Christian Uniqueness Reconsidered* (London: SCM, 1990) p. 175.

[5]

Engaging Modernity

Modernity is the first truly global civilization to emerge in human history. It traces its historical and geographical roots to modes of social life and organization which developed in the countries of northern Europe from about the seventeenth century onwards and which have subsequently extended their reach worldwide.[1] Its impact is felt even in the more remote villages of the world as much as in the universities, commercial centres and government offices of major cities. It is full of paradoxes and ambiguities, bringing in its wake both enormous blessings and terrible sufferings. It unites the world while fragmenting it; dispels ancient, local fears only to replace them with fears on an unimaginable scale; reduces ignorance while destroying meanings; advocates rationality while subverting reason; creates wealth while impoverishing the earth . . .

Modernity, according to the British academic sociologist Anthony Giddens, is 'inherently globalising', and he uses a telling image to describe its state today: 'living in the modern world is more like being aboard a careering juggernaut . . . rather than being in a carefully controlled and well-driven motor car.'[2] The English word 'juggernaut' comes from the Hindi *Jagannath*, one of the titles for the god Krishna. A huge chariot was used to take an idol of the deity out of its temple in Orissa once a year, and as it trundled through the streets devotees would throw themselves under its wheels and be crushed to death. Riding on the juggernaut of modernity is often exhilarating and rewarding, but there are times it veers away violently in directions one cannot foresee or control. It crushes both its devotees and its opponents. Giddens identifies the following as the major 'institutional dimensions' of

143

modernity: capitalism (capital accumulation in the context of competitive labour and product markets); industrialism (the transformation of nature into 'created environments' through science and technology); the apparatuses of surveillance (the control of information and supervision of the population, especially in the modern nation-state); and the control (monopoly) of the means of violence by the nation-state.[3]

It would take us well beyond the scope of the present book to discuss the huge challenges that these institutional dimensions of modernity have posed, and continue to pose, for Christian identity and witness. What concerns us in the present chapter is the dominant worldview of modernity, especially in the way it impinges on how men and women in the modern world have come to regard religious truth-claims. We shall do so through the recent writings of a Christian missionary leader who has spanned the divide of East and West in his own life as a communicator of the gospel, and who has mounted one of the most vigorous theological critiques of modern secular culture. His name is Lesslie Newbigin.

Newbigin: Gospel as Public Truth

Newbigin brings to his analysis and critique of modern culture not only an acute mind but a wealth of experience as both a cross-cultural missionary (in South India) and an ecumenical pioneer (through the International Missionary Council and, later, the World Council of Churches). His galvanizing summons to a slumbering, divided and tragically compromised church in the West invites comparison with the challenge of the early Barth.

Newbigin recognizes the eighteenth-century movement in Europe, popularly called the Enlightenment, was one which contributed much to the distinctive self-consciousness of contemporary Western culture. Complex as it was, one of its best-known features was the rejection of tradition and its authority. Kant summed up the central theme of the Enlightenment in his famous phrase 'Dare to Know'. It was a summons to have the courage to think for oneself, to test everything in the light of reason and conscience, to dare to question even the most hallowed traditions. That robust determination remains operative as perhaps the central thrust of modern culture.

Newbigin identifies four distinctive intellectual features of modernity, all stemming from the influence of the Enlightenment:

(a) A sharp dichotomy between a world of 'facts' and a world of 'values'. 'Facts' are what we have to reckon with, whether we like them or not. 'Values' are what we choose because we want them, either for ourselves or for someone else. 'Middle-class parents,' observes Newbigin,

> want values to be taught to children in schools because life will be more pleasant if these values are adhered to. But they do not ask whether these values have any relation to the 'facts' as taught in school. They do not ask whether it is possible to believe that concern for minorities, for the poor, for the disabled is important if the fact is that human life is a result of the success of the strong in eliminating the weak. If it is a 'fact' that human life is the accidental result of the ruthless supression of the weak by the strong, and it is not a fact that 'Man's chief end is to glorify God and enjoy him for ever' [as stated in the Westminster Confession], then 'values' have no factual basis. They can only be the expression of what some people choose, and—inevitably—it will be the strong who prevail. The language of 'values' is simply the will to power wrapped up in cotton wool. And we cannot use the language of right and wrong because it has no basis in the 'facts' as we understand them.[4]

In the world of 'values' we are all pluralists, values being a matter of private choice. In the world of 'facts' we are not; facts are facts, whether you like them or not. In such an intellectual environment, the church and its preaching are assigned to the world of 'values'. The church is simply one among the many 'good causes' which must be supported by good people, and without this support it will collapse. The church is not generally perceived as concerned with facts, with the realities which finally govern the world and which we shall in the end have to acknowledge whether we like them or not. 'In this cultural milieu, the confident announcement of the Christian faith sounds like an arrogant attempt of some people to impose their values on others. As long as the church is content to offer its beliefs modestly as simply one of the many brands available in the ideological supermarket, no offence is taken. But the affirmation that the truth revealed in the gospel ought to govern public life is offensive.'[5]

(b) Closely intertwined with this is another distinction, that drawn between 'knowing' and 'believing'. Ever since Descartes' (1596–1650) quest for clear and distinct ideas which could not be doubted, knowledge has come to be identified with that which is secure from error. The ideal is taken to be an 'objective' knowledge of the 'facts' of a matter, involving no personal commitment, no risk of being wrong, and which is universally binding. This is contrasted with a range of beliefs, purely subjective, which may express 'what I feel' or 'what is true for me', but fall short of universal applicability. To suggest that these latter beliefs ought to be accepted as true for all is to be guilty of the unforgivable sin of 'dogmatism'.

This is demonstrated by the differing approaches to learning which are currently used in science and religion. The statement 'All physicists are agreed that . . .' is normally enough to settle an argument, and the teacher expects that the pupils will submit to the authority of the text and come to believe what he believes. This 'believing' must mean, of course, that the pupil has really understood it, believes it to be true because he sees that it is true; it will not be enough that the pupil learns to repeat what the teacher says. And that means that the pupil will have to be encouraged to ask critical questions. But the teacher will certainly not be satisfied, if, at the end, the pupil chooses to keep an open mind on the truth or otherwise of what is taught. Nor will the teacher at any stage give the pupils the impression that the truth or otherwise of what is taught is a matter of private opinion.

(c) All claims to truth are to be scrutinized by reason and universal experience. Post-Enlightenment culture prides itself on its willingness and ability to subject all sources of authority and all claims to truth to fearless criticism. The notion of 'honest doubt' has been elevated to a supreme epistemological status. No area of thought or conduct can escape the acid of critical doubt. All demands based on revelation and authority (whether divine or human) must be justified before the bar of a reason that is, in principle at least, available to all human beings.

(d) Historical contingency and particularity are played down in the interests of truths that are universally recognizable. If Christian faith is true, it can be true only as a system of timeless metaphysical truths about God, nature, and man. The Bible is, at best, a source of information about such of these eternal truths that could not be discovered by observation, contemplation or reflection on innate human ideas.

(i) Critique of Modernity: Epistemology

The recent history of Western thought reveals how the quest for certainty through universal doubt has led to a blind alley. The Cartesian programme of universal doubt, the proposal that every belief should be doubted until it could be validated by evidence and arguments not open to doubt, can in the end lead only to universal scepticism and nihilism. To doubt all one's beliefs at the same time is impossible. One can be doubtful of some beliefs only if one is holding firmly on to others at the same time. Newbigin notes: 'You cannot criticize a statement of what claims to be the truth except on the basis of some other truth-claim which—at that moment —you accept without criticism. But that truth-claim on which your critique is based must in turn be criticized. The critical principle must ultimately destroy itself.'[6]

Newbigin is deeply indebted to the work of the Hungarian-born physical chemist and philosopher Michael Polanyi (1891–1976) in developing an alternative epistemology for our times. Polanyi expresses in a more sophisticated idiom the Augustinian dictum *credo ut intelligam*: I believe that I may know.[7] There is no knowing without believing, and believing is the way to knowing. In a series of deeply insightful works on the philosophy of science, written from the perspective of a practising scientist rather than a professional philosopher, Polanyi showed that the authority of science, as in all areas of knowledge, rests on tradition, and that the scientific tradition is passed on through *personal* contact between teachers and learners.[8] This is true from the elementary level through to the highest levels of original research. We rely on the authority of teachers until we are in a position to come to see for ourselves that what is taught is true. In other words, doubt can never be the first step on the road to knowledge. It is a secondary intellectual activity. It comes into play only after we have thoroughly assimilated the scientific tradition as embodied in textbooks, scientific journals and the personal authority of a skilled practitioner who is certified by the scientific community to be a competent teacher.

Polanyi emphasized the importance of the personal relationship of master and pupil in every aspect of scientific learning. After a long period in which a student has been soaked in the tradition of his subject, and submitted to its authority, he is then considered competent enough to work alongside a scientist who is doing original research on problems which are not only unsolved, but perhaps not even recognized except by this scientist. It is only through watching this scientist at work, seeing how he tackles problems, chooses lines of inquiry, evaluates ambiguous evidence, and projects fresh and original ideas that the student will learn the skill of research. There are no impersonal and mechanically applicable rules by which such original research can be guided. There are no objective criteria by which the work of the scientist can be judged; he, along with his peers, is the one who sets the standards and determines the criteria, and, in doing so, accepts the risks of failure as well as the possibility of success.

Polanyi draws our attention to the importance of *tacit* knowledge in human living. Consider a surgeon using a probe to explore a cavity which cannot be observed directly. He doesn't pay attention to the pressure of the probe on his hand because his focus is on the patient's body. His awareness of the instrument in his hand is tacit. The probe is an extension of himself, he *indwells* the probe. But when he was a student and first introduced to this instrument, no doubt he did give his central attention to it. But with experience he comes to rely on it. A time may come when he feels it is no longer adequate for the task at hand and needs to be replaced. But as long as he is using it, he must continue to trust it. He uses it non-critically. He cannot simultaneously rely on it and doubt it. Likewise, every working scientist indwells the scientific tradition as a whole, as well as the reigning paradigm in his or her field of inquiry. Without such a commitment to the tradition, science would collapse. At any moment in history some part of the tradition may be under critical scrutiny, but this scrutiny is possible only if the tradition as a whole is accepted tacitly. The authority of this tradition is maintained by the scientific community. It is held together by the free assent of its members, and exercised in practice by those who determine which article will be accepted for publication in research journals and which rejected, and by those in charge of appointments to research and teaching posts in universities and other institutions.

In his writings Polanyi gives examples of many theories which were rejected without discussion simply because they fell outside the accepted tradition. Unless the tradition was protected from every maverick idea, science could not develop. At the same time, if the tradition did not make room for questioning and radical innovation, science would stagnate. Innovation, however, can be responsibly accepted only from those who are already skilled 'indwellers' of the tradition. And one new fact, or even several new facts, do not suffice to displace an established paradigm. This can happen only when a new paradigm is offered in its place, one that conveys an alternative vision of reality that commends itself by its beauty, rationality and comprehensiveness.

The acceptance of such a vision is a personal act in which I commit myself in the knowledge that I am in a cognitive minority and could be proved wrong. It involves personal commitment to the new paradigm (or theory) and the willingness to risk one's scientific reputation. But it is not on that account merely subjective. 'The scientist who commits himself to the new vision does so—as Polanyi puts it—with universal intent. He believes it to be objectively true, and he therefore causes it to be widely published, invites discussion, and seeks to persuade his fellow scientist that it is a true account of reality . . . he may have to wait several years before there is convincing experimental verification of his vision . . . But at no stage is it merely a subjective opinion. It is held with "universal intent" as being a true account of reality which all people ought to accept and which will prove itself true both by experimental verification and also by opening the way to fresh discovery. It is offered not as private opinion but as public truth.'[9]

In the light of Polanyi's emphasis on the character of scientific knowledge as 'personal knowledge', Newbigin questions the validity of the Cartesian project which has held European culture in its thrall for the past three hundred years: namely, the mythical notion of indubitable knowledge which does not involve the knower personally. He draws attention to the similarity between the Christian believer and the scientist. The Christian tradition, embodied in the Scriptures and the history of their interpretation in different ages and places, expresses and carries forward—like the scientific tradition—certain ways of looking at things, certain models for interpreting experience. Unlike science it involves us in questions about the ultimate meaning and purpose of things and human life.

> The models, concepts, and paradigms through which the Christian tradition seeks to understand the world embrace these larger questions. They have the same presuppositions about the rationality of the cosmos as the natural sciences do, but it is a more comprehensive rationality based on the faith that the author and sustainer of the cosmos has personally revealed his purpose.[10]

Like the scientist doing research, the Christian believer has to learn to indwell the tradition. Its models and concepts are things which she does not simply examine from the perspective of another set of models, but have to become the models through which she makes sense of the world. She internalizes them and 'indwells' them. And, as in the case of the pupil learning physics or mathematics, this has to be in the beginning an exercise of personal faith. But, Newbigin points out repeatedly, being personal does not mean that it is subjective. 'The faith is held with universal intent. It is held not as "my personal opinion" but as the truth which is true for all. It must therefore be publicly affirmed, and opened to public interrogation and debate. Specifically, as the command of Jesus tells us, it is to be made known to all nations, to all human communities of whatever race or creed or culture. It is public truth.'[11]

Thus, the 'integrity and fruitfulness of this continuing process of learning and sharing the gospel will require, as in the case of the science, the honouring of the authority of the tradition'. As in the development of science, there will be theological proposals from time to time which are considered too implausible to deserve serious consideration. But, on the other hand, Newbigin notes, 'Those who have learned to indwell the tradition and to become skilled interpreters of it will also be called from time to time to propose modifications in the tradition, modifications which must be submitted to the judgment of the Christian community as a whole, and which may be the subject of debate and dispute for many years.' Moreover the purpose of

Missions! Living in hermeneutical Community

such modifications, Newbigin argues, should always be that
'the community as a whole should advance toward a more
complete understanding of and living by the truth.'[12]

   This parallel, however, is not complete. In the case of the
scientific community, the tradition is one of human learning,
writing, and speaking. In the case of the Christian community
the tradition is that of witness to the action of God in history,
action which reveals and effects the purpose of the Creator.
'These actions are themselves the reality which faith seeks to
understand. Thus the Christian understanding of the world
is not only a matter of "dwelling in" a tradition of understanding; it is a matter of dwelling in a story of God's
activity, activity which is still continuing. The knowledge
which Christian faith seeks is knowledge of God who has
acted and is acting.'[13]   *Reason and Revelation in tension with each other during modernity*

(ii) Critique of Modernity: Reason and Relativism

Christian writers influenced by the presuppositions of the
Enlightenment tried to show that their faith was acceptable
within the limits of reason and without recourse to revelation.
But to pit reason in this way against revelation, as if it were a
rival source of information, is absurd. Reason is a faculty
with which we seek to grasp the different elements in our
experience in an ordered way. It is not a separate source of
information about what is the case. It can only function
within a linguistic and cultural tradition. Newbigin points
out, for instance, that the word 'reason' in the theological
apologetic of the eighteenth century denoted a set of assumptions about what is the case, assumptions derived from the
science and philosophy of the time. 'The sociology of
knowledge', he writes 'has taught us to recognize the fact,
which is obvious once it is stated, that in every human
society there is what Peter Berger calls a "plausibility
structure", a structure of assumptions and practices which
determine what beliefs are plausible and what are not. It is
easier to see the working of the plausibility structure in a
culture of a different time or place than it is to recognize it in
one's own.'[14]

   All reasoning is dependent on, and embodied in, a
tradition. The 'development of this tradition of rationality is
never unrelated to the social, political, economic, military,
and cultural changes which the society in question is going

Key: 'Community looks together → community advancing together'

through. The tradition is never merely cerebral. The rationality which is accepted is part of the total life of a community. It responds to the new experiences which that community is having–whether these come from outside or from within. The tradition of thought is not a disembodied ghost which has a life apart from the total life of the society which carries this tradition. The rationality is embodied in *this* society, with all its elements of contingency, particularity and sheer happenedness.'[15] The idea, therefore, that a disembodied 'reason' can act as impartial umpire between rival claims is a myth. Every exercise of reason depends on a social and linguistic tradition which has the contingent character of all historical happenings. Lessing's great gulf between 'the accidental events of history' and 'the universal truths of reason' disappears.

It might be objected that this plunges us into a cognitive relativism. Newbigin faces the question: 'If all rationality is the exercise of the reasoning powers of a particular community, responding to particular historical happenings and using a particular language . . . do we then have to surrender the quest for truth? Is there no truth which is true for us all, but only "truth–as–it–appears–to–us–in–our–culture"?'[16]

He responds by noting that all traditions of rational discourse are continually changing, old formulations and concepts are called into question as not being adequate to the realities which the community faces. Traditions go through crises, when a growing number of experiences accumulate which cannot be understood in terms of existing patterns of thought. If at this point another tradition of rationality appears on the scene, it confronts the reigning tradition with a challenge. It offers another way of seeing things, another vision of the shape of things and of the human story. The fact that some adherents of the older view are attracted to the new paradigm and experience a 'conversion' to it shows that, although all discourses of rationality are embodied in a social tradition, the latter is not ultimate: truth can only be grasped within a tradition, but traditions *can* be compared and *are* judged in respect of their perceived adequacy to lead their adherents to a better grasp of the realities with which all human beings have to deal.

He goes on to argue that the relativist conclusion that no truth–claim can therefore be sustained rests on a false basis. It is a claim to know something about reality, namely, that reality is unknowable. This claim itself is formulated within a social context of a rootless world in which individuals live without a stable social tradition. One element in this cosmopolitan culture is the availability of an international language like English into which, it is supposed, all forms of human thought can be translated. 'A person shaped by this culture will thus have the illusion of having an overview of all these different traditions without having had the actual experience of seeing the world through any of them.[17] Relativism itself is the product of a false universalism: the cosmopolitan modern world, shaped by the dichotomy between 'facts' and 'beliefs', tends to relativize all the different belief systems.

Newbigin's conclusion is that when, in this culture, an autonomous 'reason' is set against the historically shaped tradition of Christian belief, the reigning 'plausibility structure' is at work. The Christian task is to relativize that plausibility structure in the light of the gospel. The tradition of rationality of the Christian community has its point of departure not in any alleged self-evident truths, but in what was disclosed to those who were witneses of the events which are described in the Bible. These are all happenings within the world of secular events, the world which is investigated by the natural and human sciences. The resurrection of Christ cannot be fitted into a secular plausibility structure; for it generates its own plausibility structure, inviting people to look at their world and human life in the light of that event. These disclosures were addressed to men and women in specific contexts and called for specific responses within those contexts. The specificity, the contingency of those events, and the consequent particularity of the Christian community as one community among many does not invalidate the universality of the claims that its rationality makes and must make.

How do we avoid withdrawing into a relativist ghetto in a consumer-orientated society? The Christian calling is to live within both traditions, secular and Christian, in such a way that the debate between them is internalized:

> Insofar as my own participation in the Christian tradition is healthy and vigorous, both in thought and in practice, I shall be equipped for the external dialogue with the other tradition. There is no external criterion above us both to which I and my opposite number can appeal for a decision. The immediate

outcome is a matter of the comparative vigor and integrity of the two traditions; the ultimate outcome is at the end when the one who alone is judge sums up and gives the verdict.[18]

(iii) Critique of Modernity: Church and Society

The rejection of the dichotomy between a false objectivity and an equally false subjectivity, both of which are based on an abdication of personal responsibility in the search for truth, leads in the public domain to a rejection of the extremes of a return to theocracy, on the one hand, and an agnostic pluralism, on the other. The church is called to enter vigorously into the struggle for truth in the public domain. Western Christians must neither seek the security of a restored Christendom nor accept the security of a pluralism where they are free to have their own opinions provided they are held only as private opinions. 'We are called, I think, to bring our faith into the public arena, to publish it, to put it at risk in the encounter with other faiths and ideologies in open debate and argument, and in the risky business of discovering what Christian obedience means in radically new circumstances and in radically different human cultures.'[19]

Following Polanyi's model of what he called the 'Republic of Science', Newbigin argues for a 'committed pluralism' based on a vision of knowledge that is available to anyone willing to take personal responsibility for pursuing truth and making it known. A committed pluralism 'values freedom as the necessary (though not sufficient) condition for grasping the truth about the real world, and the fundamental relation between truth and freedom is that enunciated by Jesus when he said, "The truth shall make you free." '[20] The church must affirm that freedom is not the natural endowment of every human being but something to be won by the acknowledgment of the truth, and that ultimately truth is something received in faith through the grace of God.

How is the church to speak the word of the gospel to the public life of our societies? There is, Newbigin admits, a long and sad history of alliances between the church and various political programmes. The church has been committed to the defence of the divine right of kings, of oligarchy against democracy and of free market capitalism against communism. The Church cannot be totally identified with

Missions

Christian faith shapes how we partic in public life

these causes. And yet it cannot be indifferent to them. thinks the Barmen Declaration gives us a good model of how to exercise a prophetic role in society: 'Perhaps the most important thing to say, and it is important even if it is negative, is this. The affirmations of the Barmen Declaration would have made no impact without the anathemas. The Declaration names and rejects a false ideology. It does not tell the German people what to do in the area of politics. It affirms the truth of the gospel and, in its light, condemns the reigning falsehood. I think that perhaps that is the first thing to say about the duty of the Church in relation to political issues. The Church has to unmask ideologies.'[21]

One ideology Newbigin challenges is the language of the 'rights' of the individual. These rights are part of public doctrine enshrined in legislation. But he points out that 'rights are totally void of meaning unless there are parties who acknowledge the responsibility to meet the claim of right. Since there is no corresponding public doctrine about human responsibility, the multiple and contrary claims to right can only destroy society.'[22]

Newbigin also challenges the contemporary church to equip its members for active and informed participation in public life in such a way that their Christian faith shapes their participation. We are to be 'undercover agents' subverting the Enemy's strongholds. If such training were available, 'We could look for a time', he writes, 'when many of those holding responsible positions of leadership in public life were committed Christians equipped to raise the questions and make the innovations in these areas which the gospel requires.'[23] But the most important contribution that the church can make to a new social order is to be itself a new social order, and in this the local churches are strategic: '. . . the local Christian congregation, where the word of the gospel is preached, where in the sacrament of the Eucharist we are united with Christ in his dying for the sin of the world and in his risen life for the sake of the world, is the place where we are enabled to develop a shared life in which sin can both be recognized and forgiven. If this congregation understands its true character as a holy priesthood for the sake of the world, and if its members are equipped for the exercise of that priesthood in their secular employments, then there is a point of growth for a new social order.'[24]

this is how we bring about change in the world

Church must be a New social Order True distinctively christian

Response to Newbigin

Newbigin's analysis and critique of modernity is often profound and always exhilarating. He writes with an enviable combination of biblical commitment, intellectual acumen, and missionary passion. I share many of his concerns, not least for the public relevance of the gospel and for the healing of the rifts between conservatives and liberals in the Christian Church. I fully endorse his central argument: namely, that the gospel carries its own plausibility structure which confronts many of the assumptions of modern intellectual thought and popular culture.

(i) 'Enlightenment' and Secularism

Anyone who writes sweepingly of the 'Enlightenment' and of 'Post-Enlightenment culture' is liable to generalizations and one-sided distortions. Newbigin, unfortunately, is no exception. Although it has been fashionable among Christian writers to regard the eighteenth-century Enlightenment as the most significant point of rupture between the old order of Christendom and the secularized culture of modernity, this view needs to be supplemented by other historical perspectives.

Newbigin's reading of Western intellectual history in the seventeenth and eighteenth centuries seems to resemble the view of Barth that the modern period involved a radical break of epochs and was characterized by the rebellious assertion of intellectual autonomy from the God of the biblical revelation.[25] In contrast to this, others have traced the origin of modern secular culture to the Reformation distinction between the spiritual and secular realms and Luther's doctrine of the two swords (itself a legacy of late medieval political theory).[26] It formed an important aspect of Luther's quarrel with the radical wing of the Reformation. This distinction has been an important aspect of the Christian understanding of the Kingdom of God and the socio-political order, thus distinguishing it from, say, Islam. The distinction has not always been well expressed; with the result that the 'secular' has often come to be seen as standing outside the sovereignty of God and hence outside the church's concern. Hence the confusion, which still reigns today, between 'secularization' and 'secularism'. The Reformation spearheaded an emancipation of public life ('secularization'), including the practice of science and civil government, from the control of clerical authority, though not from divine authority. In the sixteenth and seventeenth centuries, many in England and the Netherlands referred back to the Reformation idea of freedom to legitimate their quest for civic liberties.

The political philosopher Charles Taylor has identified as 'one of the central features' of the modern world the 'affirmation of ordinary life' that lay at the heart of the Reformation's rediscovery of human vocation. According to the traditional Aristotelian ethics of the West (and, one may add, Hindu or Buddhist ethics in Asia) the 'secular' or 'lay life' of production and reproduction was important as the necessary background and support to 'the good life' of contemplation and action as a citizen. But with the Reformation in sixteenth-century Europe, Taylor writes, 'We find a modern, Christian-inspired sense that ordinary life was on the contrary the very centre of the good life. The crucial issue was how it was led, whether worshipfully and in the fear of God or not. But the life of the God-fearing was lived out in marriage and their calling. The previous "higher" forms of life were dethroned, as it were. And along with this went frequently an attack, covert or overt, on the elites which had made these forms their province. I believe that this affirmation of ordinary life, although not uncontested and frequently appearing in secularized form, has become one of the most powerful ideas in modern civilization.'[27]

Whatever elements of truth there may be in such readings, the connexions between the Reformation and the rise of modern secular culture may be seen more clearly in the unintended historical consequences of the former. During the bitter confessional wars that followed the Reformation, an attempt was made to impose political unity in terms of adherence to one or other of the contesting confessions. The conviction that religious unity is the presupposition for social peace was widespread, and it is in this light that we should understand these attempts to enforce faith allegiance, which extended down to the middle of the seventeenth century and, in some countries, well beyond. The ideas of tolerance and freedom of religious loyalty found little place in political theory and action. Although Luther valued the freedom of individual conscience so highly, he did not— any more than did other Reformers—envisage confessional pluralism in social life. He did not want heretics burnt, but nor did he espouse political tolerance for those of other beliefs. Rather, all the Reformers believed that for the sake of public order and the unity of religious confession which they stood for, those who believed otherwise should leave the country and go to a territory of their own confession.

Over the decades an increasing number of people came to feel that religious passion destroys social peace. In any case, no side was in a position to impose confessional unity, and such attempts only had the opposite effect. This insight originated in the Netherlands where in 1572 the circle around William of Orange formulated the idea of religious tolerance for the first time and proclaimed it publicly. These ideas spread to England and gained support during the Puritan revolution (though the Puritans themselves for the most part sought a theocratic unity of faith in society along the lines of Calvin's Geneva). Finally, with the revolution of 1688 and the Act of Toleration in the following year, the principle of religious freedom was also established in England under the influence of the Netherlands.[28] But, even here, such stout defenders of tolerance such as John Locke refused to extend religious freedom to Roman Catholics whose loyalty to the English crown was always doubted.

The impact of the 'wars of religion' on the continent of Europe, culminating in the Peace of Westphalia in 1648, led to increasing questioning of the assumption that social peace must rest on confessional unity. Christian thinkers such as Hugo Grotius and Lord Herbert of Cherbury sought the basis of public order and peace between states in the concept of 'natural law' and, in connection with that, in a natural religion common to all human beings. The mutually conflicting positions of belief among various Christian confessional parties were bracketed off, and in the place of religion based on traditional authority, human 'nature' became the basis of public order. The basic concepts of law, morals, politics and religion were reconstructed on the basis of what was considered to be universally human. This became the starting point for a secular culture in Europe. The doctrine of political sovereignty, with natural law, came to be based on anthropology. Even in those countries which continued to have a confessional unity there was a shift towards basing social order and public culture on the concept of the human rather than on God. This is still true of modern secular democracies: in spite of the influence of various forms of so-called postmodernist doctrine, the abstract notion of human rights based on the concept of a universal human nature continues to occupy the central place which once was given over to a religious vision of human well-being.

The significance of the religious wars for the rise of the new secular culture of Europe in the seventeenth century is neglected in Newbigin's thesis. The reorientation of thought on universal human nature which took place in the middle years of that century, complex as its origins were, was surely nourished by the division of the churches and the destructive intolerance of religious passions. Philosophers such as Locke were motivated largely by practical concerns that related to the intellectual and political confusion of Europe. Newbigin is fond of quoting Locke's comment (in *A Third Letter on Toleration*) that 'Faith is a persuasion of our own minds short of knowledge', and he sees in this a typical example of the dualistic epistemology that shaped the rise of modern culture.[29]

But this reading of Locke is open to question.[30] The context in which Locke is writing is political rather than epistemological. In distinguishing between matters of faith and matters of demonstrable knowledge, his intention is to make the justification and enforcement of law a function of the epistemic status of beliefs. Where a conviction does not amount to public demonstrability, magisterial coercion is illegitimate. We know from his other works that Locke did not identify faith with 'subjective opinion' nor confine reason to the objectively demonstrable.[31] He saw faith in divine revelation as apprehending cognitively what reason could not apprehend, and he sought secure epistemological principles by which religious beliefs could be commended as rationally unimpeachable. To assess whether he was always consistent, let alone successful, in this venture is another issue altogether and outside the scope of the present book and the competence of its author. All I want to point out is that Locke was wrestling with a problem that has become increasingly acute in our modern, pluralist societies, and is not confined to Christians alone: namely, how to commend a moral conviction on the widest possible social grounds.

In all his writings, Newbigin quite rightly draws attention to the central importance of Descartes in any understanding of the temper of the modern age. Although not himself a figure of the eighteenth-century Enlightenment, Descartes' methodology was enormously influential on the thought of the Enlightenment *philosophes*, and the spirit of the age was essentially the spirit of Descartes.[32] In his *Discourse On Method*, Descartes expresses his bewilderment at the multiplicity of different thought-systems he had encountered in his education and the lack of any coordination between them. He was particularly concerned to find a place for the new science of his day, physics, and to put human knowledge on a secure and unshakeable foundation. Newbigin stresses Descartes' search for certitude and his belief that he had found a basis for it in his own existence as a critical thinker. Newbigin sees this new Cartesian starting point for knowledge as being foundational for all that followed in the Enlightenment and beyond, and as being a small-scale repetition of the Fall: 'Adam is not content to trust God. He wants to have his own certitude, based on an experimental test of the validity of God's promise. He is the first inductive theologian. We are all Adam's heirs, and we in our particular culture are all heirs of Descartes.'[33]

A closer reading of Descartes' work and background, however, casts his enterprise in a still more fascinating light. Regarding background, Taylor and others[34] have drawn our attention to the enormous importance of the mode of thinking roughly designated 'neo-Stoic' in the late sixteenth and early seventeeth centuries in Europe. This was bound up with a broad movement among political and military elites towards more rigorous application of discipline and mastery in a host of fields: military organization, the 'absolutist' state and civil administration, institutions such as hospitals, schools and workhouses. The ideal of the human agent who remakes himself by methodical and disciplined action begins to emerge. What this trend demanded was the ability to take an instrumental stance to one's given desires, inclinations, habits of thought and feeling, so that they could be *worked on*. Taylor suggests that 'Descartes' picture of the disengaged subject articulates the understanding of agency which is most congenial to this whole movement, and that is part of the grounds for its great impact in his century and beyond.'[35]

In his book *Descartes and the Enlightenment*, Peter Schouls points out that although Descartes' theoretical system was founded on the autonomous reason, central to his position was the autonomous *will*. The will is unfettered, and engagement in rational construction arises out of that conviction. All of Descartes' works are pervaded by the desire for mastery, over self and nature. The human desire for mastery expresses the human 'essence'. In Descartes' system the passion for mastery dominates. Apart from this master passion, reason is held to be of no use to man. Reason itself is instrumental in the satisfaction of the master passion. That alone is its value. In a letter to Queen Christina of Sweden after the publication of his last work *The Passions of the Soul*, Descartes wrote: 'Now free will is in itself the noblest thing we can have because it makes us in a certain manner equal to God and exempts us from being his subjects; and so its rightful use is the greatest of all the goods we possess, and further there is nothing that is more our own or that matters more to us.'[36] Here is expressed the Enlightenment project of self-creation, to carve out a territory that is exclusively one's own possession.[37]

If modernity rejects Christianity, then, it often does so because it perceives the Christian doctrines of creation and redemption as inimical to human self-definition and self-mastery. Divine creation implies a given moral order and consequent limits to human endeavour; redemption implies human guilt and alienation within the created order and the necessity of divine action on behalf of humankind. Modernity sees divine and human freedom, divine and human creativity, divine and human action, as antithetical to each other. Grace is seen as supplanting rather than establishing human dignity.

Thus what is involved here goes deeper than epistemology. On the one hand, human beings will see no need for revelation if they see no need for redemption. How does this shape our reading of the various phases of the Enlightenment in seventeenth and eighteenth century Europe? Behind the various epistemological critiques of revelation and divergent forms of 'natural religion', can we glimpse an underlying moral repugnance to the biblical emphases on sin, grace and reconciliation—a repugnance that would link the birth of the modern age with the spirit of Stoicism that the early church had to counter in the Roman world and which Christians in Asia confront today in the philosophies of Theravada Buddhism, Confucianism and advaita Vedanta? One wonders: is it only a historical accident that the most influential movements proclaiming self-salvation in East and West should have 'enlightenment' as their identifying label?[38]

If revelation were merely the conveying of information about God to the human creature, then it could coexist alongside systems of human moral and religious self-sufficiency. No offence would be caused. But revelation in Christian terms is intertwined with reconciliation, of an act of atonement by which we are rescued from our alienated self-will and brought to a response of loving obedience to the will of God as exercised through human history. Newbigin is right to see a connexion between the Cartesian project and the story of Genesis 3; but the connection runs deeper than he envisages. Doubt is shot through with self-will. More seems to be at stake than an intellectual certitude independent of divine revelation.

On the other hand, the perversity of the human will has often been fuelled by negative and distorting presentations of biblical truth by Christian theologians. Taylor points out, with some justification, that Enlightenment naturalism 'is in part motivated by the sense that in rejecting religion it is for the first time doing justice to the innocence of natural desire, that it is countering the calumny implicit in ascetic codes'.[39] The challenge to Christians is to articulate the doctrines of creation, redemption and revelation in such a way that they are experienced as liberating truths, issuing in creative lifestyles, but without pandering to human pride. Is our human dignity established by the human will seeking total mastery of itself, or is it grounded in our relationship with, and accountability before, our Creator?

On the opening page of *The Gospel in a Pluralist Society* Newbigin refers briefly to the celebrated work of Henning Graf Reventlow, *The Authority of the Bible and the Rise of the Modern World*. Reventlow demonstrates how the attack on the Christian world view in European society had its origins, far earlier than the rise of modern science and the subsequent Enlightenment, in the strong humanist tradition inherited from Stoic sources which surfaced powerfully in the late medieval age and in the period of the Reformation. Reventlow's study shows how, during the latter part of the seventeenth and through the eighteenth centuries, all intellectual life, whether in discussions of political constitutions or of natural science, continued to be dominated by the Bible, but by a reading of the Bible increasingly controlled by the dictates of a 'natural reason' and a 'universal conscience'. Those who sought to defend the Christian faith did so on the basis that it was 'reasonable', that is to say, that it did not contradict the fundamental assumptions of a naturalist humanism. As the eighteenth century rolls on, we find that reason and conscience come to constitute a 'natural religion' that eventually dispenses with the need for 'revealed religion'. Christian apologetics centred on the idea that the existence of God as the Governor of the universe and the knowledge that moral action accords with his will can be an additional and stronger motive to moral action than the fact that moral action is simply in accord with the ordering of things. Religion is now identical with moral agency, and the advantage of religion based on revelation over natural religion lies only in the fact that it provides us with more arguments for such action than we would have otherwise.

An apologetic working with such weak arguments could not defend its position for very long. The Deists had already launched influential attacks on traditional Christian arguments from prophecy and miracle. The fact that the debate took this turn is grounded in the attitude of contemporary apologetic: the Deists had to remove these supports if they were to carry their battle for the sole validity of natural religion to a victorious conclusion. Reventlow comments, 'In their efforts to rescue at least a basic element of the Christian tradition, even if this was only a cloak for the natural religion which was all that they advocated, to some degree they even remained apologists themselves. Thus in the last resort they represented no more than a transitional situation. David Hume's acute criticisms of the possibilities of reason arriving at a certain knowledge in the sphere of religion meant the end of Deism as well as of its opponents.'[40]

Reventlow draws a connecting thread from English Deism in the first half of the eighteenth century to the German Enlightenment of the second half, which represented a relatively late phase in the general development of ethical rationalism.[41] In Reventlow's own words, 'We cannot overestimate the influence exercised by Deistic thought, and by the principles of the Humanist world-view which the Deists made the criterion of their biblical criticism, on the historical-critical exegesis of the nineteenth century; the consequences extend right down to the present.'[42] Foremost among those consequences, notable, as we have seen, from

Kant to the present day, has been the way Christianity has
come to be '*largely understood as a system of moral action*'.[43]

In the light of Reventlow's picture of how patterns of
thought deriving from the ancient Greek world experienced
a fresh flowering in the late Middle Ages and found their
way into the general awareness of modern times, it is rather
strange that Newbigin does not make more of this thesis, but
continues from time to time to invoke scientific 'objectivity'
as the villain of the piece. If he had expanded on the insights
he recognizes in Reventlow's work, he would perhaps have
been led to a more nuanced critique of post-Enlightenment
society. It is clear that the eighteenth century Enlightenment
movements in France and Germany were simply new phases
in the development of a re-pagan culture in Europe that had
been going on for some considerable time (aided by both
Christian scholasticism and bitter confessional rivalries).

In his more recent essays Newbigin does refer to the work
of the American Jesuit historian Michael Buckley and draws
out warnings for Christian witness today. Buckley finds the
cultured roots of the atheism of Enlightenment figures such
as Diderot and D'Holbach in the self-alienation of late
medieval Christianity itself. 'In an effort to secure its basis,
religion unknowingly fathered its own estrangement . . .
Religion abandoned the justification intrinsic to its own
nature and experience, and insisted that its vindication would
be found in philosophy . . .'[44]

Buckley's contention is that much of the responsibility for
the modern displacement of God must be attributed to the
way 'God' became increasingly abstract and impersonal in
the Western theological tradition. The great medieval synthesis of faith and philosophy involved a downplaying of the
work of Christ and of the Holy Spirit, so that Christians in
seventeenth-century Europe tended to defend Christianity
without appealing to anything distinctively Christian: 'The
absence of any consideration of Christology is so pervasive
throughout serious discussion that it becomes taken for
granted, yet it is so stunningly curious that it raises a
fundamental issue of the modes of thought: How did the
issue of Christianity vs atheism become purely philosophical?
To paraphrase Tertullian: How was it that the only arms to
defend the temple were to be found in the Stoa?'[45]

By turning away from the person and work of Jesus Christ
and the experience of the Christian Church, and turning

instead to philosophical apologetics in order to demonstrate
its inherent 'reasonableness', Christian theology at the beginning of the modern era had already surrendered its own
competence. Attempts to develop so-called physico-
theologies (deductions of God's existence and nature from
the world view of Newtonian science) backfired on biblical
theology. As philosophy developed into natural philosophy
and then into mechanics, the latter 'established its own
nature by denying that its evidence possessed any theological
significance and by negating any theological interest'.[46] Over
the centuries that followed, physics, medicine, mathematics
and other disciplines could assert their own autonomy from
physico-theologies only by denying their own theological
character. If they moved into atheism, Buckley argues, they
did so because theology had made them the primary area of
its evidence and of its argument. Thus the theologians who
had deposited their entire inheritance with them gradually
found themselves bankrupt.[47]

Similarly the Christian historian of science, Christopher
Kaiser, in his survey of the complex and dramatic shifts that
took place in eighteenth-century French natural philosophy
away from the creationist tradition that had hitherto shaped
European science, highlights (among other factors) several
longer range trends which had been running in Western
thought since the twelfth century: for instance, the tendency
to define the self-sufficiency of nature and the direct operation of God as mutually exclusive alternatives; and the
tendency to treat the gifts of healing and reform in secular
terms in contrast to the 'spiritual' ministry of the clergy.[48]

Kaiser's comments on the French mathematician d'Alembert's programmatic elimination of theology from the work
of the scientist are worth pondering: 'The context was one in
which the principal proponents of French theology were
incessantly in conflict with social and scientific progressives.
Of course, d'Alembert particularly despised the Jesuits who
worked to suppress the *Encyclopedia*, of which he was the
scientific editor. But to d'Alembert, all varieties of priests and
theologians—Jesuits, Jansenists, Doctors of the Sorbonne, and
ministers of Calvinist Geneva alike—were characterized by
bigotry and intolerance. They were more concerned with the
maintenance of their own authority and privileges, he felt,
than with the welfare of the people. For centuries they had
made open war on natural philosophy. All spiritual authority,

it appeared, was corrupted when exercized in a secular context. If the Church would not reform itself (as it did in the eleventh and sixteenth centuries) then it was up to less religious people to take the initiative in ridding secular affairs (e.g. the administration of the universities) from ecclesiastical control and scientific research of theological presuppositions.'[49]

In restrospect it appears that any Christian imbued with the Christian ideal of public service could be faithful to that aspect of his calling only by attempting to eliminate the influence of the church and its theology in matters of public concern. 'One might say that the creationist tradition was rejected by d'Alembert. D'Alembert, on the other hand, might have argued that it was merely rescued (in a secularized form) from the power of its previous guardians.'[50]

In fairness to Newbigin it must be said that he does acknowledge our abiding debt to the Enlightenment. 'It would be utter folly,' he has noted, 'to try to play down the immense achievements of the past 300 years of Western culture.'[51] Although, following the eminent classicist, Charles Norris Cochrane,[52] he draws a parallel between the present situation in the West and that of Augustine living amid the disintegration of Greco-Roman culture, he also emphasizes the fact that the best of the classical inheritance was preserved for future generations because the Christian church in the first four centuries had developed new patterns of thought which gave to it a new foundation:

> To those who fear that a fresh and unambiguous affirmation that the Gospel of Jesus Christ must be the starting point and the criterion of all human thought and action will threaten the achievement of the Enlightenment and of those who have shaped our society on its principles, we can say with confidence that, on the contrary, we are offering the only basis on which the true fruits of the last 300 years can be saved from the new barbarians.[53]

But how is this to be done? Newbigin is critical of the discourse of human 'rights', and from a Christian perspective I agree that the language is defective and often abused. But how does one safeguard what this language seeks to preserve, namely an understanding of justice that would be acceptable within a world which contains multiple doctrines of what constitutes human flourishing? The attractions of a secular, liberal state are especially strong in many of our non-Western societies. For they are often ravaged by repressive governments and/or religious fundamentalisms which, far from 'privatizing' faith, openly aim to establish their particular religious faith at the centre of public life in a way that denies elemental civic freedoms to others. What viable alternative is there to a secular, liberal state that is founded on a minimalist ethic common to all cultural and religious communities? Any Christian vision of the social and political order (on this side of the consummation of the kingdom of God) must include a place for all those, perhaps the majority, who do not share values that are consistent with the gospel.[54]

Newbigin is right to expose the double standards that operate in secular society, the universal validity claimed on behalf of science and the restricted agenda decreed for religion. But the universal appeal of science does not lie in its claim to universal rationality. Its appeal is a pragmatic one. Its successes are evident to all. Despite its abuses and the suffering it has left in its wake, most societies are still desperately eager to avail themselves of its benefits. One of the paradoxes of the modern age is that pragmatic arguments are offered in support of the absolutist pretensions of science, and of the rationalist mentality linked with it. (This is where the critique of Polanyi is relevant, though, because it does show science's continuing indebtedness to tradition and to a specifically Christian worldview. But in a pragmatic age, the credibility of Christianity to be an alternative to the secular scientific outlook will be assessed not only by the intelligibility of its truth-claims but also by the cogency of its advocates' social practice. This is the challenge that Christian witness faces, in the modernizing countries of Asia and Africa no less than in the supposedly 'postmodern' West).

So, while Newbigin's description of the features of modernity and of the reigning plausibility structure can hardly be faulted, his analysis of the historical development of these in the intellectual and social millieu of the West needs perhaps to be augmented and enriched by other historical perspectives.

(ii) Faith and Rationality

Newbigin has been taken to task by the American evangelical philosopher Harold Netland[55] for his view that, since all human reasoning involves prior acts of faith commitment and occurs within a given 'plausibility structure', the gospel cannot be demonstrated to be true or false by any allegedly neutral norms of rationality. Newbigin's argument, as we have seen, is that the gospel offers the world a new starting point for thought, centred in the resurrection of Jesus as God's act of new creation. We cannot validate this claim by enlisting for its support philosophical ideas drawn from other worldviews. Nothing can be more ultimate and fundamental than the church's conviction that Jesus Christ is Lord. As Newbigin writes in *Truth to Tell*,

> That means that he is Lord not only of the Church but of the world, not only in the religious life but in all life, not merely over some peoples but over all peoples. He is just not my saviour, but the saviour of the world. We have no way in which we can demonstrate the truth of that claim by reference to some supposedly more ultimate realities.[56]

Netland, who, like Newbigin, has served as a missionary in Asia (Japan), is deeply concerned to establish 'objective, non–arbitrary criteria' by which to evaluate the truth-claims of religious worldviews. He is disturbed by the fact that Newbigin appears to be opening the door to 'theological fideism' by rejecting the possibility of a rational, context-independent adjudication between conflicting cognitive claims. For Netland, such an adjudication is both necessary and possible. The truth of the Christian faith can be demonstrated by means of criteria which are 'neutral' in the sense that they are 'logically independent of one's religious commitment' and which are 'applicable for all persons regardless of religious orientation.'[57]

What criteria does Netland propose for appraising the diversity of world-views? He begins with a set of definitions.[58] First, p is a 'defining belief' of a religion R if and only if being an active participant in good standing within the religious community of R entails acceptance of p (as an example from within Christianity, he contrasts belief in an eternal creator God, which is a defining belief p, with peripheral beliefs such as the appropriate mode of baptism). Secondly, a religion R is true 'if and only if all of its defining beliefs are true; if any of its defining beliefs are false, then R is false.'[59] He then suggests ten principles for evaluating any worldview. These include logical principles such as noncontradiction, coherence and internal consistency, which Netland argues are universally valid—although the fact that certain schools of Hinduism and Buddhism (e.g. Madhyamika, Zen) accept such logical rules only to expose their inadequacy when it comes to ultimate experience makes the 'neutrality' of his argument somewhat dubious.

Netland is on much weaker ground with his other principles because they are question-begging, and all clearly pre-suppose his particular orientation. For instance, 'If one or more defining beliefs of R are incompatible with widely accepted and well-established moral values and principles' or R entails 'the denial of the objectivity of basic moral values and principles', these constitute good reasons for rejecting R as false'. It is hardly surprising that Netland draws the conclusion that 'the Christian faith is the only worldview that satisfies the requirements of all the above criteria.'[60] The dice seem to have been loaded, and it doesn't take a non-Christian to see how tradition-specific his proposals are.

Consequently, Netland's confident claim that the ten basic principles he has enunciated are part of the 'stuff of reality' and are 'independent of the mental states and psychological processes of any human being'[61] is extremely naive. His strictures against Newbigin are also rather unfair. He tends to run together the adjectives 'objective', 'universal' and 'nonarbitrary', thereby implying that anyone who highlights the subjective, human pole in the act of knowing is left with totally arbitrary and non-universal judgements. But Newbigin has consistently stressed the objective, universal intention of faith-commitments as much as their situatedness within a contextual 'plausibility structure'. All reasoning operates within a specific tradition of rationality which is carried by a specific human community. This does not lead to either fideism or relativism because all human reasoning is subject to the test of adequacy. There are more and less adequate ways of making sense of human experience, and the fact that these cannot be articulated in a precise, formal system hardly constitutes grounds for a charge of arbitrariness.

Netland's desire for a formal scheme for adjudication between world views smacks of rationalism; and Newbigin is quite right to protest[62] that 'neither the disciples, nor any of their successors, became believers by attending to the "logically prior question of the grounds upon which one is to choose a worldview in the first place" (Netland)', and that 'there is all the difference in the world between a certainty

which rests wholly on the faithfulness of God, and a
certainty which rests on a chain of human reasoning.'
Netland's concern that the irrationalism which is widespread
in the late twentieth century should be resisted by the
Christian apologist is perfectly laudable. But he fails to see
that this calls for a more exacting use of reason than the
construction of formal principles. To 'indwell' the Christian
gospel and to seek to show in every new generation its
ability to account for all human experience, and its power to
make sense of new situations, will be a fully rational
enterprise.

Where Newbigin *is* vulnerable is in his rejection of any
form of natural theology and his insufficiently critical stance
towards George Lindbeck's 'cultural-linguistic' model of
Christian doctrine.[63] For Lindbeck, doctrine serves as the
regulatory grammar of the Christian language, ensuring the
internal consistency of the narrative. But he sits far too
lightly on the issue of the extra-linguistic referents of the
narrative and so reduces all questions of truth to purely
'intrasystemic' (or 'intratextual') cohesion. His model, for all
its illuminating insights into the pervasive undergirding of
life and thought by the theological framework we hold,
tends to sever Christian language from its historical anchor-
ing. The Christian narrative, however—which he identifies
Christian doctrine as regulating—cannot simply be taken as
given. For, after all, it may be based on a huge historical
misunderstanding of the significance of Jesus Christ, or a
deliberate fabrication or a gigantic exercise in wish-
fulfilment. Lindbeck is unable and even unwilling to consider
such possibilities. Yet the very fact that the Christian story
emerges out of allegedly historical events makes it susceptible of historical investigation.

Newbigin is attracted to Lindbeck's approach because
Lindbeck is at pains to emphasize that the Bible is not
something we look *at* so much as look *through* in order to
understand the world. He does, however, vigorously reject
the view that the historical truth of the story is not important,
that such a narrative which 'structures human experience and
understanding' (Lindbeck's language) has no ontological
status beyond the believing community's imagination.
The story is *the* true story, of human life and the cosmos.
But what may, legitimately, cause Netland and others
consternation are remarks such as 'the Christian tradition of

Holy Spirits illumination
and sold reason from receivi...
Engaging Modernity 171 *...*
Christian
narrative
as truth

rationality rests upon alleged revelations which cannot be experimentally checked but have to be accepted in faith.'[64] Here is a tendency to speak in either/or categories which simply do not ring true to the way in which most people come to believe from a position of total scepticism. It is undoubtedly true that no experimental 'proof' can be given of any alleged revelation; and it is also true that anything that would count as historical evidence can only do so if it presupposes certain beliefs about the existence and nature of God. But it simply does not follow that such evidence is unimportant. It is true that believing in the resurrection of Jesus requires an assumption about God. But examining the historical evidence may impel one in the direction of that very assumption. We shall consider the subject of the resurrection in the following chapter.

Perhaps greater care is needed in distinguishing between *grounds* for belief and psychological *certainty*. The former are matters for logical argument and persuasion. But they alone can never impel conviction. And this has to do with the nature of the object of faith, for if ultimate reality is personal then only a personal mode of knowing (involving a humble disposition and fully responsible engagement) is appropriate. If God *is*, then there can be no higher authority than God, and what we apprehend when God communicates God's self to us has every entitlement to be called 'knowledge', even though it cannot be demonstrated by canons drawn from alien modes of knowing. This is the truth that Newbigin defends with much skill and passion. Certainty or assurance is the work of the Holy Spirit. It is a matter of gift rather than logic. But it is equally important to note that the Holy Spirit is not a substitute for evidence.[65] We can articulate grounds for belief in God's self-disclosure in Jesus at the same time as we acknowledge our indebtedness to the Holy Spirit's illumination.

Conclusion

Newbigin has given us a perceptive critique of the global culture of modernity and set an exciting but daunting agenda before the global Church. It is an agenda that I fully endorse, though his historical judgments need to be augmented by other perspectives, and the political dimensions of the

declare Christian narrative as truth without
being arrogant nor apologetic and neither
authoritarian nor
individualistic

172   *The Recovery of Mission*

'tradition of rationality' created by the gospel require further exploration. He has, however, shown how it is possible to recapture intellectual confidence in the truth and relevance of the gospel of the crucified, risen and reigning Lord Jesus, without being intimidated by the dominant mind-set of modern secular culture. By drawing on the insights of Michael Polanyi, among others, he has also shown how that gospel may be proclaimed as universal truth in a spirit that is neither arrogant nor apologetic, neither authoritarian nor individualistic. He has also shown how the painful and unnecessary divide between conservatives and liberals in the church may—and indeed must be—bridged if the church is to have any credibility in a fragmented world.

Notes to Chapter Five

1. A Giddens, *The Consequences of Modernity* (Cambridge: Polity Press, 1991) Ch. 1.
2. Ibid. p. 53.
3. Ibid. pp. 55ff.
4. L Newbigin, *The Gospel in a Pluralist Society* (Grand Rapids: Eerdmans and Geneva: WCC, 1989) p. 17.
5. Ibid. p. 7.
6. L Newbigin, *Truth to Tell: the Gospel as Public Truth* (Grand Rapids: Eerdmans, 1991) p. 29.
7. On faith as the indispensable starting-point for knowledge, see Augustine, *On the Trinity*, XIII, 9, 12.
8. Polanyi's best-known work is also his first, *Personal Knowledge: Towards a Post-Critical Philosophy* (Chicago: University of Chicago Press, 1958). He refines his epistemology in *The Tacit Dimension* (Garden City, NY: Doubleday & Co., 1966). See also the collection of essays in M Polanyi and H Prosch, *Meaning* (Chicago: University of Chicago Press, 1975). For the appication of Polanyi's thought to theology, see, for example, TF Torrance (ed), *Belief in Science and in Christian Life* (Edinburgh: Academic Press, 1980).
9. *The Gospel in a Pluralist Society*, op. cit. pp. 47–8.
10. Ibid. p. 49.
11. Ibid. p. 50.
12. Ibid.
13. Ibid. pp. 50–1.
14. Ibid. p. 53.
15. Ibid. p. 54.
16. Ibid. p. 55.
17. Ibid. p. 57.
18. Ibid. p. 65.
19. *Truth to Tell*, op. cit. p. 59–60.
20. Ibid. p. 60.

21. Ibid. p. 74.
22. Ibid. p. 78.
23. Ibid. p. 84.
24. Ibid. pp. 86–7.
25. K Barth, *Protestant Theology in the Nineteenth Century* (Eng. trans. London: SCM, 1972).
26. See the discussion in Ch.1 of W Pannenberg's *Christianity in a Secularized World* (Eng. trans. J Bowden, London: SCM, 1989).
27. Charles Taylor, *Sources of the Self: the Making of the Modern Identity* (Cambridge: Cambridge University Press, 1989) pp. 13–14. Taylor sees the modern concept of respect, embodied in the notion of human rights, as deriving from the New Testament concern for human welfare (of which modern utilitarianism is a 'secularized variant') coupled with the post-Reformational affirmation of the dignity of ordinary life and the Lockean (and later Romantic) notion of individual autonomy. The influence of the Reformation, he says, 'underlies our contemporary "bourgeois" politics, so much concerned with issues of welfare, and at the same time powers the most influential revolutionary ideology of our century, Marxism, with its apotheosis of man the producer. This sense of the importance of the everyday in human life, along with its corollary about the importance of suffering, colours our whole understanding of what it is truly to respect human life and integrity. Along with the central place given to autonomy, it defines a version of this demand which is peculiar to our civilization, the modern West.' (p. 14).
28. See Pannenberg, op. cit.
29. See, e.g. *Truth to Tell*, op. cit. p. 30; 'Truth and Authority in Modernity' in P Sampson, V Samuel & C Sugden (eds) *Faith and Modernity* (Oxford: Regnum Lynx, 1994) p. 61.
30. See S Williams, 'John Locke on the Status of Faith', *Scottish Journal of Theology*, vol 40:4, 1987; and the same author's *Revelation and Reconciliation: a Window on Modernity* (Cambridge: CUP, 1995) ch. 2.
31. See Book IV of *Essay Concerning Human Understanding*, (ed) P Nidditch (Oxford: Clarendon Press, 1975).
32. The case is argued persuasively by, for example, Peter Schouls, *Descartes and the Enlightenment* (Edinburgh University Press, 1989).
33. *Truth to Tell*, op. cit. p. 27
34. See, in addition to Taylor (op. cit), Henning Graf Reventlow, *The Bible and the Rise of the Modern World* (eng. trans. J Bowden, London: SCM, 1984); Gerhard Oestreich, *Neo-Stoicism and the Early Modern State* (Cambridge: Cambridge University Press, 1983)
35. Taylor, op. cit. p. 159–60
36. Anthony Kenny, *Descartes, Philosophical Letters* (Oxford, 1970, p. 228), cited in Schouls, op. cit. p. 172. Schouls observes that *The Passions of the Soul* is 'the only work in which [Descartes] deals with an area of life in which he believes each individual can walk the road of progress to the end. Once that journey has been completed, the highest level of autonomy which is possible in that area of life has been reached: man then has exempted himself from being subject to

God and has achieved complete mastery in that area of life. In this declaration of independence, *The Passions of the Soul* present what is perhaps Descartes' clearest articulation of the spirit which pervades the Enlightenment.' (p. 172)

37. There is, therefore, much to justify the observation attributed to Pascal: 'I cannot forgive Descartes. In all his philosophy he would have been quite willing to do without God. But he could not help allowing him a flick of the fingers to start the world in motion; after that he has no further use for God', *Pensees* (trans. A Krailsheimer, Penguin, 1966, p. 355).

38. I hasten to add that this tendency of the Enlightenment (to relegate God to the periphery of life through human moral self-sufficiency rather than systematic doubt) is not limited to Buddhist philosophy or secularism, but is there in all of us. It is the outworking of sin in all cultures. But these two philosophical systems (Buddhism in its Theravada form and secularism in its various offshoots of the political left and right) have understood human salvation/liberation in a way that makes God redundant, if not the biggest hindrance to its achievement.

39. *Sources of the Self*, op. cit., p. 516

40. HG Reventlow, op. cit. p. 410

41. An alternative interpretation is given by Klaus Fischer. He argues that the influence of English thinkers on the Enlightenment has been greatly exaggerated (as, for instance, by Peter Gay in his famous work, *The Enlightenment: an Interpretation*, 2 vols (1966–9)), and that what kept British empiricist and deist influences in Germany to a minimum were the mystical–idealist strain in German thought, the legacy of French intellectual and institutional traditions from the seventeenth century(including Cartesianism), and, above all, the towering influence of Leibniz' philosophical system. See, KP Fischer, 'John Locke in the German Enlightenment: an Interpretation', in *Journal of the History of Ideas*, vol 36:3 (1975). The only argument that Reventlow gives in support of his claim is to point to the numerous translations of English Deistic literature which appeared on the German market after the publication of Johann Lorenz Schmidt's translation of Matthew Tindal's *Christianity as Old as The Creation* (1741).

42. Ibid. p. 412

43. Ibid. Preface to the English edition, p. x (my emphasis).

44. M Buckley, *At the Origins of Modern Atheism* (New Haven and London: Yale University Press, 1987) p. 359.

45. Ibid. p. 33.

46. Ibid. p. 358

47. See also Ibid. p.349: 'God was the ultimate condition for the possibility of knowing nature in Descartes, and mechanical nature was the ultimate condition for the possibility of knowing God in Newton. Both moved inexorably to a final dualism that posited the difference between God and nature as between members of a coordinate duality that made up a larger whole . . . Individual things

needed explanation—ideas or individual facts—and God provided that explanation.'

48. C Kaiser, *Creation and the History of Science* (Basingstoke: Marshall Pickering and Grand Rapids: Eerdmans, 1987) pp. 243–4
49. Ibid. p. 262.
50. Ibid. p. 263. Note also Kaiser's summary, p. 269: 'The secular ideals of d'Alembert and Laplace are important because they have become the motivating ideal of many physical scientists of the nineteenth and twentieth centuries. We are suggesting that they are the product of a particular history and theology, not a necessary concomitant of progressive science . . . in the seventeenth and eighteenth centuries, a long-range tendency to view the active role of God and the innate properties of matter as alternative modes of explanation gained credence to the extent that the ideals needed for the furtherance of science could no longer so readily be sustained by positive Christian commitment.'
51. Ibid. p. 18.
52. C.N. Cochrane, *Christianity and Classical Culture* (Oxford: Clarendon Press, 1940), esp. p. 450ff. Newbigin's debt to Cochrane is stated explicitly in *Truth To Tell*, op. cit. p. 15, and also in *The Other Side of 1984*, op. cit. p. 24.
53. *Truth to Tell*, op. cit. p. 38–9.
54. See too Wesley Ariarajah's postscript to Newbigin's *The Other Side of 1984* (Geneva: WCC, 1984) pp. 64ff.
55. See H Netland, *Dissonant Voices: Religious Pluralism and the Question of Truth* (Grand Rapids: Eerdmans, 1992), pp. 178–79. Also, 'Truth, Authority and Modernity' in *Faith and Modernity*, op. cit. p. 106ff.
56. *Truth to Tell*, op. cit. p. 34.
57. *Dissonant Voices*, op. cit. p. 194.
58. Ibid. p. 180ff.
59. Netland seems unaware that this proposal conceals an underlying assumption deriving from a particular world view, viz. that truth is propositional and refers to real states of affairs, that others may not accept. His account of 'defining beliefs' also pays insufficient attention to the way defining beliefs also function as social demarcators for a religious group and so may change in times of crisis. There are periods when what counted as a peripheral belief may assume the status of a defining belief, and vice versa. For examples from the history of Christian doctrine, see A McGrath, *The Genesis of Doctrine: a Study in the Foundations of Doctrinal Criticism* (Oxford: Blackwell, 1990) pp. 37–52 & pp. 103–151.
60. *Dissonant Voices*, op. cit. p. 193.
61. In 'Truth, Authority and Modernity', *Faith and Modernity*, op. cit. p. 114 (footnote 22).
62. In a footnote to his most recent paper, 'Truth and Authority in Modernity' in *Faith and Modernity*, op. cit. p. 86–7.
63. George Lindbeck, *The Nature of Doctrine: Religion and Theology in a Post-Liberal Age* (London: SPCK, 1984). Newbigin refers to Lindbeck's model in *Gospel in a Pluralist Society* (p. 24) and in his essay, 'Truth and Authority in Modernity', op. cit., p. 73ff.

64. 'Truth and Authority in Modernity' in *Faith and Modernity*, op. cit. p. 81.
65. Cf. the interplay of 'tradition' and 'facts' in 1 Cor. 15:3ff. The people Paul mentions are still alive and can corroborate the tradition embodied in the Gospel preaching.

PART III

[6]

The Scandal of Jesus

In his book *Many Mansions*, the American theologian Harvey Cox recalls his surprise on discovering that non-Christian people actually *want* to talk about Jesus! Cox had long been embarrassed to speak 'too quickly about Jesus' in his dialogue with people from other religious traditions because he feared stirring up painful controversy and giving the appearance of 'insensitivity'. But he soon discovered that his interlocutors 'wanted me to, and their bearing sometimes suggested that they did not believe they were really engaged in a brass-tacks conversation with a Christian until that happened.'[1] Cox notes that when reference to Jesus is postponed or down-played, 'conversations between Christians and people of other traditions tend to become arid, but when the figure of Jesus is brought to the fore, either by the Christians or—as sometimes happens—by the others, the dialogue comes alive. . .'[2]

Cox's observations are significant, especially in the light of what he wrote about inter-faith dialogue only a few years previously. In his earlier work *Religion in the Secular Society: Towards a Postmodern Theology* Cox argued for a 'kingdom-centred' approach to dialogue that makes the latter neither an end in itself nor a 'strictly religious quest', but rather 'a step in the anticipation of God's justice. It becomes praxis. Similarities and differences which once seemed important fade away as the real differences—between those whose sacred stories are used to perpetuate domination and those whose religion strengthen them for the fight against domination —emerge more clearly.'[3] Cox admits in *Many Mansions* that any approach that ignores or seeks to set aside the question of Jesus is both dishonest to Christian experience and also

179

Jesus not a background figure but
central — needs to be central in our
services

180   *The Recovery of Mission*

contrary to the facts of personal encounter: 'For the vast majority of Christians, including those most energetically engaged in dialogue, Jesus is not merely a background figure. He is central to Christian faith . . . I confess that I find all these approaches, all of which hold the Jesus-fact in abeyance, not wholly satisfactory . . . any honest dialogue between Christians and others will sooner or later—and in my experience it is usually sooner—have to deal with the figure of Jesus.'[4]

While not wishing to ignore the importance of Cox's earlier concerns in dialogue, I would strongly endorse Cox's observations regarding the abiding significance of Jesus even in our modern pluralist societies. Jesus of Nazareth continues to attract men and women of all cultures today. Many are drawn by the moral sublimity of his teaching, others by the way he ruthlessly exposed the barrenness and hypocrisy of the religious and political establishment. His witty aphorisms and devastating parables are continuing sources of delight and admiration to professional communicators and literary critics. Many women see in him a man who was liberated from the pervasive chauvinism of his society, at ease in the company of women. He showed them respect not only by teaching them and inviting them to minister to him, but by often associating with the most despised among them, so risking his reputation as a prophet-rabbi. Many social reformers and political revolutionaries find in Jesus an inspiring model in the struggle for social justice. He was not reluctant to trample upon social conventions and taboos. More books, plays and films have been made of him—and more music and art inspired by him—than of any other figure in human history. And a good deal of this by people who would not consider themselves Christians.

Jesus of Nazareth is a controversial as well as an attractive figure. But the controversy that surrounds him is not like the controversy that surrounds other famous men and women. In the latter case, the controversy rages over the content and relevance of their teaching. So, today, the debate over Darwin in modern biology concerns whether or not the neo-Darwinian paradigm, with its exclusive emphasis on random gene mutations and natural selection, is sufficient to explain the origins and behaviour of all living organisms. Marx and Freud have fallen into some disrepute in recent years, even as their theories have lost their persuasive hold on individuals and whole societies. Gandhi is still a figure of controversy in India today: Brahmins and dalits argue over whether Gandhi himself sanctioned the caste system, and political activists disagree among themselves as to how far the Gandhian principles of non-violent resistance are applicable under regimes more brutal and repressive than the British raj. Note that these are all debates that hinge on the assessment of a person's message or teaching for the world. They apply to anyone we care to mention, whether Confucius, Mohammed, Calvin or Nietzsche.

Not so with Jesus. The controversy that he attracts has relatively little to do with his moral teaching. (The best-known exceptions to this in recent times in the West have been Nietzsche and Bertrand Russell). No prominent non-Western thinker, past or present, has offered any serious objection to the ethical content of Jesus' message. Their assessments of what constitutes the content of that teaching may sometimes appear seriously defective (cf the notion, popular in the West as much as in Asia, that Jesus simply taught us to 'help other people in need'); but no one has taken exception to him on moral grounds.

The controversy over Jesus concerns *who he is*. For the historic Christian claim regarding Jesus of Nazareth is that no human category, whether that of 'charismatic prophet', 'religious genius', 'moral exemplar' or 'apocalyptic vision-ary' can do adequate justice to the evidence of his words and actions. No category short of deity itself is sufficient. It is this traditional claim—that in the human person of Jesus, God himself has come amongst us in a decisive and unrepeat-able way—that constitutes an offence to a pluralist society. It is this that invites the scorn of the secular humanist, the puzzlement of the Hindu and the indignant hostility of the Muslim. The same range of responses were encountered in the Greco-Roman world that the earliest followers of Jesus inhabited.

Stephen Neill, himself a missionary statesman and church historian, argued that the old adage 'Christianity is Christ' is exactly true in the context of other faiths. 'We shall encounter other religions which have historical founders; but in none of them is the relation between the adherents of that religion and its founder in the least like that which the Christian believer supposes to exist between himself and Christ.' Indeed, he continued, 'The historical figure of Jesus of Nazareth is the criterion by which every Christian affirmation has to be judged, and in the light of which it stands or falls.'[5]

In a different but related context, the German systematic theologian Wolfhart Pannenberg has warned against the tendency in post-Kantian theological thought to subordinate the question of truth to questions of personal meaning ('what he means for me') and so reduce Christ to no more than the sum of benefits that are conceived to derive from him: 'Christology, the question about Jesus himself, about his person, as he lived in the time of the Emperor Tiberius, must remain prior to any questions about his significance, to all soteriology. Soteriology must follow from Christology, not vice versa. Othrwise, faith in salvation loses any real foundation.'[6]

Which Jesus?

It is often taken for granted in modern theological discussion that the high view of Jesus that is characteristic of traditional Christianity (and which reached its classic expression in the credal formulations of the fourth and fifth centuries C.E) was a product of the church's interaction with Hellenistic culture and philosophy. Jesus himself, it is assumed, had no pretensions about himself, and the earliest followers of Jesus did not think of him as anything more than a prophet and/or Israel's Messiah. The 'high' christologies developed as the church lost its Jewish roots and absorbed the language and concepts of the numerous mystery cults that sprouted all over the ancient Mediterranean world. There is no connexion, at least no intellectually credible connexion, between the Jesus of early Christian testimony and the God–Man figure of Nicean and Chalcedonian orthodoxy.

This position is often assumed and loudly asserted, but with very little accompanying argument, in the writings of religious pluralists today. I shall not critique this assumption at any length, for that would require a detailed exploration not only of all New Testament material but also of the Palestinian and Hellenistic milieu of the early Christian communities.[7] That the Christian church came to a fuller understanding of the significance of Jesus of Nazareth in the course of its mission to the Gentile world is indisputable; but that this was a development of an understanding already given *in embryo* in the gospel events themselves, not least in Jesus' own self-understanding as communicated to his disciples, and not a completely alien framework imposed on the primitive Christian message, has been persuasively demonstrated by several scholars in recent times.[8]

Here I propose simply to examine some of the evidence from the Gospel narratives themselves which bear on our assessment of who Jesus was and the significance of that for our life-orientation in the midst of a secular and pluralist world. Unless we are prepared to be totally sceptical about the historical value of these narratives (in which case the only logically consistent position would be to have nothing at all to do with Jesus of Nazareth, since no claim concerning his worth as a leader, moral guide, visionary etc. would have any historical credibility), these remain the principal source of testimony concerning Jesus of Nazareth. Even the most sceptical of scholars would accept that the four Gospels were complete by the end of the first century, while a great many would bring that date forward to a little over one generation after the crucifixion. This comparatively brief interval between the events reported and the writing down of the tradition (parts of which were, of course, circulating well before their final redactions) is itself unique in the history of religious movements.

The well-known attempt of much nineteenth and mid-twentieth century New Testament scholarship, under the influence of the 'history of religion' school, to drive a rigid wedge between a so-called 'historical Jesus' and a 'kerygmatic Christ' is now of little more than archaeological interest.[9] The whole enterprise (along with what was dubbed the New Quest for the Historical Jesus following on the heels of Bultmann's historical scepticism) shared the assumptions of post-Enlightenment thought which, as we have seen in earlier chapters of this book, tended to work with a positivist view of history and untenably sharp distinctions between 'faith' and 'knowledge', 'facts' and 'interpretation' and so on.[10] Biblical scholars who professed to be Christians but operated within such a paradigm either tended to separate their investigations into a 'historical Jesus' (who could be fitted into a category befitting a rationalist methodology) from the 'Christ' figure (found in the tradition of the church) who still inspired their private acts of piety; alternatively, they completely jettisoned the Christ of Christian worship and turned instead to a unitarian God and a Jesus who inspired not adoration but simply admiration as a 'religious genius' or a 'prophetic example'. We have observed the influence of such approaches, based on the secularist world-view of modernity, on the thought of many contemporary Asian theologians. Some, following Panikkar, work with an immanent Christ-principle over and above the life and events turning around Jesus of Nazareth; others, including Samartha and Pieris, locate Jesus in the wider context of an all-embracing kingdom of God which does not depend, in any fundamental way, on what he was or did.

As we noted in our critique of Samartha and Pieris, the fact is often overlooked that the time-scale involved in christological development is much briefer than that involved in any comparable claims made for any other historical figure, so that facile talk of 'creative innovation' must be treated with healthy scepticism. Theological creativity there was, and no one reading through the books of the New Testament can fail to be impressed by the extraordinarily rich variety of graphic expressions, metaphors and pictorial representations used by the writers to express the signifi-cance of Jesus within God's purpose for the world. The eminent New Testament scholar Martin Hengel reminds us that this christological creativity progressed in *'a very short time'*: *'more happened'* in the first two decades of Christianity than *'in the whole of the next seven centuries, up to the time when the doctrine of the early Church was completed.'*[11]

This is well illustrated by even a cursory examination of 1 Thessalonians, widely held to be the earliest of the New Testament writings. It is often dated to the early 50s C.E, though a date as early as 41 C.E has been proposed[12]—thus roughly between ten and twenty-five years years after the crucifixion. Yet already, Paul is describing Jesus as the one who died and rose again (4:14; 1:10; 2:15), and who as God's Son (1:10) will usher in God's final judgment on human history (1:10; 3:13; 4:14–16), so that the Old Testament Day of Yahweh now becomes the 'Day of the Lord Jesus' (5:2). Moreover, in this same early letter Paul speaks of Jesus as the one through whom we are rescued from God's wrath and receive his salvation (1:10; 5:9); as the one who 'died for us' so that we may 'live with him' (5:10); as, at least, the source of grace (5:28) and of Paul's authority to give moral instruction (4:2; 1:6); as the one who will punish those who offend against such teaching (4:6); and, most amazingly, as one whose name is uttered in the same breath as God the Father and the Holy Spirit (1:3–5). Moreover, Paul can assume that his readers in Thessalonica already hold at least the tradition that 'Jesus died and rose again' (4:14) . . . We search in vain for parallels for such rapid developments among followers of other religious leaders; and it is difficult to imagine say such a range and depth of expressions of faith being attached, at the date of publication of the present book, to someone who had died around 1970 at the earliest.

That all the Gospel narratives were written in the light of the resurrection faith of the early Christian communities has become a truism in New Testament scholarship. The Gospel writers are not biographers but evangelists: the events surrounding the death and public ministry of Jesus of Nazareth are seen now, in the faith-perspective of the resurrection, as conveying a divine purpose. Much that was incomprehensible to the first disciples now fell into place. The Gospel writers select from and shape the received oral tradition to highlight those aspects of Jesus that speak to the situation of their audience. So far the scenario is very plausible, perhaps even obvious when spelled out clearly. Where it becomes highly implausible is when the assumption is made that the enthusiasm of the evangelists so over-whelmed the Gospel tradition that fresh interpretations, embellishments and elaborations of the original sayings and deeds of Jesus were so extensive, especially in the Gentile churches and the Hellenistic diaspora, that in due time the original picture of the Jesus movement disappeared under an overlay of devotion focused in the risen Christ. Highly subjective criteria of authenticity are then employed to remove the 'accretions' of faith from the Gospel narrative, leaving behind a 'kernel' of fact. Some recent popular accounts of Jesus have taken such assumptions to ludicrous lengths.[13]

These assumptions are implausible not only because of the time-scale involved, but also because of the curious act of 'double-think' that readers of the Gospels are asked to perform. On the one hand we are invited to believe that the Big Bang of christological creativity was an overwhelming Easter experience of the 'risen Christ'; at the same time the fruits of meticulous and painstaking 'historical reconstruction' leave us with a figure of Jesus so ordinary and uninspiring that the Easter 'experience' itself becomes utterly inexplicable! Christian 'faith', the source of so much innovative brilliance, is itself irrational, a surd in an intellectual vacuum. What was it about Jesus, compared to other similar figures in both contemporary Judaism and non-semitic religions, that he should become the object of extraordinary truth-claims and personal allegiance within a generation after his death? If we invoke a 'faith-experience' of a 'risen Christ', why was such an experience and such a 'Christ' associated exclusively with Jesus of Nazareth and not with the other prophets, revolutionaries, miracle-workers, itinerant cynics, charismatic healers and exorcists who dotted the Palestinian landscape? Also, unless it was Jesus who was raised from the dead, the very existence of the Jesus movement and its growth beyond the confines of Judaism becomes hugely problematical. We shall return to these issues.

What is even more paradoxical is that some theologians who assume that the resurrection narratives refer to a real historical event yet baulk at instances of the miraculous in the Gospel narratives. This, as CS Lewis pointed out, is to strain out gnats while swallowing camels. And, if it is accepted that Jesus is in some way an expression of God's purpose for humanity, is it unreasonable to suppose that God should himself ensure that a trustworthy account of his life and teaching should be provided for humanity? The Gospel narratives combine theological faithfulness with theological creativity. To suppose otherwise implies that throughout the first Christian generation there were no eyewitnesses to the original events who could act as a control on fertile imaginations, nothing about Jesus' sayings or actions that stuck in his hearers' memories. When a saying of Jesus is dismissed as 'inauthentic' without adequate reasons, or simply because it 'fits' the 'post-resurrection situation' of the early Christian communities, the assumption seems to be that the disciples' experience of the presence of the risen Lord not only transformed their recollection of Jesus' teaching but *inevitably* led to deep-seated changes in the content of that teaching.

The Gospel narratives themselves falsify this conjecture. Given that they were mostly written in the context of vigorous Gentile evangelism, it is very surprising (in the light of the above assumption) to find relatively scanty evidence in the words and actions of Jesus for any Gentile mission, and no teaching at all on the most pressing issue of all, namely, circumcision for Gentile converts. All the disciples, and especially those who were highly respected leaders of the early church, are depicted in a less than flattering light as cowardly, ambitious and slow to understand what Jesus was saying. Jesus often rebukes their behaviour. Moreover, even John, customarily regarded as the last and most 'theological' of the four evangelists, does respect historical distance (distinguishing, for instance, between what the disciples thought 'then' and what they understand 'now'). Because of the continuing bias in some academic circles against the historicity of the Fourth Evangelist's portrayal of Jesus, I shall draw more on the synoptic tradition than on the Fourth Gospel in my presentation of Jesus below. But it needs to be said that the only reasonable way to evade the testimony of the Fourth Evangelist is to dismiss him as a hypocrite: for no other New Testament writer lays such emphasis as he on 'truth', and especially on 'truth-telling', 'bearing witness to truth' etc.

That the resurrection experience of the disciples should be seen as *illuminating* the unique proclamation of the kingdom of God by Jesus, rather than as retroactive *projection*, is well expressed by Jurgen Moltmann. While emphasizing the importance of the resurrection for the church's christological reflection on the mission of Jesus, Moltmann also argues that we have no grounds for simply assuming that it led to a significant modification in the presentation of Jesus: 'Historically speaking, it is inadmissible to assume that on the basis of its experience with the risen and present Christ the Christian community projected anything into the history of Jesus which was inconsistent with the remembrance of him as he was during his lifetime. Historically it is more plausible to assume that the experience of the present Christ and the remembrance of the Christ of the past corresponded, and complemented one another; for the fundamental assertions "Jesus is the Christ" and "Christ is Jesus" identify remembrance and experience, experience and remembrance.'[14]

Jesus: lifestyle

Jesus saw his life's mission as an invitation to sinners to share in the banquet of God's kingdom. His habit of associating not merely with the poor but, especially, with the outcasts of

Palestinian society drew hostile criticism from the religious authorities.[15] The Jewish scholar Geza Vermes sees this aspect of the lifestyle of Jesus as what served to differentiate him 'more than any other' from 'both his contemporaries and even his prophetic predecessors'. He writes, 'The prophets spoke on behalf of the honest poor, and defended the widows and the fatherless, those oppressed and exploited by the wicked, the rich and powerful. Jesus went further. In addition to proclaiming these blessed, he actually took his stand among the pariahs of his world, those despised by the respectable. Sinners were his table companions and the ostracized tax collectors and prostitutes his friends.'[16] How Jesus spoke and acted within the social structures and religious assumptions of his day will serve as some kind of definitive paradigm for his followers today.

Jewish society in the time of Jesus was characterized by internal divisions as well as external occupation. In Jewish understanding the law marked out the covenant people of God. Loyalty to God was expressed by loyalty to the law, and the latter defined the boundaries of the people of God. Sin was the breach of the law, and so a sinner by definition was one who put himself or herself outside the people of God by transgressing the boundary marked by the law. Apart from the wicked, the term also became a synonym for Gentile (e.g. Ps. 9:17; Jub. 23:23–4; Pss. Sol. 2:1–2; Luke 6:33, Mark 14:41; Mark 15:1,10; Gal. 2:15). In such passages the unifying idea is not that the Gentiles are by definition murderers or robbers, but that their conduct lay outside the boundary of the law. They did not belong to the covenant people because they did not possess the Torah. And so, not knowing the Torah, they did not keep it.

But boundaries could also be drawn *within* the people of Israel. Indeed, as James Dunn observes, 'no period of ancient Judaism was so riven with factional dispute as the time of Jesus'.[17] The Torah itself provided atonement by ritual animal sacrifices for less serious transgressions of the law. But what of those members of the covenant people who by their actions lived in disregard of the Torah and so effectually disowned their covenant status? This became an issue especially during the Maccabean crisis. The Maccabeans were in no doubt that those Jews who began to live like the Hellenistic Syrians had abandoned the covenant and so were also 'sinners' (1 Macc. 1:34; 2:44, 48; 7:5; 11:25). Such apostate Jews had put themselves beyond the divine favour by departing too far from the Torah. This was also the popular attitude in the time of Jesus towards the tax-collectors whose collaboration with the occupying Roman enemy went beyond the boundaries of conduct appropriate to the covenant people of God. Hence the natural synoptic formula, 'tax collectors and sinners', and the equation of sinners, Gentiles and tax-collectors (cf. Matt. 5:46–7 & Lk. 6:32–4).

In the aftermath of the Maccabean crisis the covenantal heritage of Israel became the subject of heated dispute. Different groups came into being, each denouncing other Jews for disloyalty to Yahweh and each laying claim to be the true custodians of the Torah and thus the true members of the covenant. The best known of such groups are the Pharisees and the Essenes. The term Pharisees is probably a nickname, meaning 'separated ones'. Out of their zeal for God they separated themselves by their lifesyle from their fellow Jews in order to observe more scrupulously the religious traditions of their forebears. They themselves were laymen, scholars rather than priests, but they tried to live at the level of holiness and purity required of priests in the Jerusalem temple. From early rabbinic traditions we learn that they desired to treat the whole land as sacred, as sharing in the holiness of the temple where God had put his Name, and so sought to maintain at the level of everyday life the purity laws designed for the temple worship.[18]

The Essenes, such as the famous community at Qumran, took such separation even further. They physically withdrew into the Judaean wilderness, there to await God's imminent judgment on apostate Israel. They attacked their political and religious opponents, particularly the Pharisees, as the wicked, the men of Belial, who had departed from the paths of righteousness and transgressed the covenant.[19] Likewise, those Jews who composed the *Psalms of Solomon*, written less than a century before Jesus' ministry, regard themselves as the 'righteous', 'the devout',[20] and often using the term 'sinners' of their fellow Jewish opponents, probably the Hasmonean Sadducees who had usurped the monarchy and defiled the sanctuary.[21] The sin of the 'sinners', as understood by Pharisee, Essene or any other sectarian group, is that they stand outside the boundaries of righteousness as defined by the 'righteous'. The term itself came to express a factional viewpoint. It could be regarded as a sectarian expletive, used to stigmatize those considered beyond the pale. The Pharisees were not as rigid on this matter as the Essenes—they did not necessarily regard all non-Pharisees as sinners, but those who disregarded their concerns and ridiculed their fastidiousness.[22]

The question at issue here is what behaviour is appropriate to the covenant and who has the authority to determine it. Jesus' mission to sinners embraced those traditionally identified as outside the fold of the religiously orthodox: Samaritans, lepers, women and children, tax-collectors. By cutting across social conventions he incurred the enmity of those who saw themselves as the defenders of covenant loyalty. Along with sabbath observance, the issue of table-fellowship had become a particularly sensitive test case of covenant loyalty since the Maccabean period. During the Maccabean crisis itself, the attempt to maintain the Jewish food laws and ritual purity had resulted in martyrdom (e.g. 1 Macc. 1:62–3). In the Middle East, as in most Asian societies, the sharing of a meal takes on a quasi-religious character: it is an act of hospitality, a mark of acceptance and fellowship. When the head of a Jewish housefold breaks the bread and distributes it to those with him at table, he invites them to share in the blessing spoken over the bread. Eating is an act of covenant solidarity. Naturally the scope of table-fellowship has to be restricted to those considered acceptable. Sinners are, by definition, disbarred.

For the Pharisees, the meal table was the point at which their zeal to maintain in everyday life the purity of the temple was most at risk. It was not simply a matter of abstaining from the flesh of unclean animals, or of ensuring that the animal had been slaughtered in the religiously prescribed manner. It was more the problem of whether food bought in the marketplace had been properly tithed, whether the utensils used in cooking and serving the meal had been properly washed, and whether someone 'unclean' had been sitting in the vicinity of the meal table. The 'unclean' included people with various bodily discharges and those involved in certain occupations which led to their being treated as non-Jews.[23]

Jesus not only disregarded such ritual observations when eating with his disciples (cf. Mk. 7:1ff, Lk. 11:37ff), but angered many of the Pharisees by his festal sharing of food and drink with 'sinners' (e.g. Mk. 2:6; Matt. 11:19; Lk. 9:16; 14:1–24). Sometimes he was their guest, but more often he invited himself (e.g. Lk. 19:1–11), thus demonstrating the good news of the kingdom of God. In striking contrast to the Pharisaic drawing of boundaries, Jesus broke down social barriers, forming around himself an alternative community drawn from the marginalized elements in Palestinian society. What the Pharisees saw as a sinful disregard of covenant ideals, Jesus saw as the birth of a new covenant, the visible expression of God's liberating reign. In the table-fellowship that he and his disciples celebrated, and to which the 'tax-collectors and sinners' were invited unconditionally, Jesus was enacting a parable. Here was a foretaste of the messianic banquet, when 'many will come from the east and the west, and will take their places at the feast with Abraham, Isaac and Jacob in the kingdom of heaven' (Matt. 8:11; cf.Lk. 13:21).

Indeed, one could see the festal meals of Jesus and his disciples as the social context for many of his teaching parables. Three of his best known parables—the Lost Coin, the Lost Sheep, and the Lost Son—are said by Luke to have been Jesus' rejoinder to the charge that he ate with sinners (Lk. 15:1–32). Other parables also defend, implicitly or explicitly, his friendship with outcasts: the Unmerciful Servant (Matt. 18:23–35), the Two Sons (Matt. 21:28–32), and the Wedding Banquet (Matt. 22:1–10 = Lk. 14:15–24).

Jesus' teaching and lifestyle would also have provoked the Qumran community. Their ideal of the purity of the covenant assembly is given in a document listed as the Annex to the Community Rule: 'No one who is afflicted with any human impurity may come into the assembly of God . . . Anyone who is afflicted in his flesh, maimed in hand or foot, lame or blind, or deaf or dumb, or with a visible mark in his flesh, or who is a helpless old man who cannot stand upright in the assembly of the community— these may not enter to take their place in the midst of the community of the men of the name, for the holy angels are in their community' (1QSa. 2:3–9). In (most probably) a deliberate antithesis to this, Jesus encouraged his host on one occasion, 'When you give a luncheon or dinner, do not invite your friends, or your rich neighbours . . . But when you give a banquet, invite the poor, the crippled, the lame, the blind, and you will be blessed.' (Lk. 14:12ff). In the parable that follows, in which the coming of the kingdom of God is likened to a man throwing a party and sending his servant out to invite the guests, it is exactly the same groups whom the servant is urged to bring to the feast—'the poor, the crippled, the blind and the lame' (Lk. 14:21).[24]

Thus it is sinners, not the righteous, who are the recipients of God's kingdom. The righteous, like the rich and power-ful, are secure in the confidence of their status and accept-ability, have little sense of need, and their pride thus blinds them to what God is doing in their midst through Jesus of Nazareth. The outcasts whom Jesus befriended and to whom he gave a new identity as members of his disciple-community were caught completely unawares by the shatter-ing generosity of God's acceptance, experienced through Jesus. Many of these people were virtually 'untouchables', not very different from the lowest castes of the Hindu social system, though the status of outcaste was not hereditary in the Judaisms of Jesus' day.

The distinction between pure and impure lies at the base of all religious cultures and is probably the greatest single source of *fear*. This is especially true of the Brahminical tradition in Indian religion. An ethos of fear permeates every aspect of Indian society: the fear of ritual defilement by things, persons and events. Men fear women as sources of moral impurity and spiritual debilitation. Women fear the sexual violence and social dominance of men, the latter often sanctioned by religious decree. Eating, drinking, sleeping, travelling, working, copulating, touching, all become potential sources of pollution.[25]

Moreover, extending beyond the system of caste to embrace tribal people and the popular Buddhism and folk Islam of the subcontinent, there lurks the all-pervading fear of evil spirits, threatening illness, misfortune and death. As Richard Gombrich, Boden Professor of Sanskrit at Oxford, and well-known as a student of South Asian Buddhism, has observed: '. . . what strikes the observer is the widespread flight from the rational and interest in every form of the occult: palmistry, table-tapping, hypnotism, astrology. Astrology is a pseudo-science traditionally of great importance in Indian culture, traditionally not unknown in Sinhalese culture and considered compatible with Buddhist cosmology. But like all forms of divination it has greatly increased, a product no doubt of the widespread anxiety which there seem to be few rational means to allay.'[26]

To such cultures of fear Jesus' lifestyle, particularly his repudiation of the religious–social distinctions between pure and impure, his authoritative offer of divine forgiveness, and the demonstration of his absolute power over the spirit realm, are perceived as joyfully liberating. But, as in the Judaea of Jesus' day, it is also perceived as threatening by the defenders of the *status quo*. In religious cultures, such as the traditional villages and towns of Asia, the monk or holy man wields considerable social power while living a life of economic poverty. And, as the Bengali writer Nirad Chaudhuri has acutely observed, even the most 'world-denying' tradition of Hindu spirituality is, in reality, 'a pursuit, not of beatitude, but of power'.[27] A quest not only for mastery of body and mind, but also mastery of the spirit world through the magic arts, 'This kind of power has as its complement or rather fulfilment, the power to dominate other men. Actually, an appearance of indifference to things that the world has to offer, even without occult powers, has by itself created a moral authority for those who have shown it.'[28] The self-giving lifestyle of Jesus, reflected in his disciples who, for instance, are found cleaning the sores of leprous beggars, providing free nursing care for terminal AIDS victims or building half-way homes for 'degraded' heroin-addicts, offers a radically different conception of spiritual power for cultures where fear and spirituality are often but twin sides of the same coin.

Jesus: self-understanding

Thus the good news announced by Jesus and embodied in his actions was addressed not to a religious elite but to the non-religious, the outcast or the 'outsider'. In his presence, men and women find forgiveness for their sins and a new social identity. Jesus reconstitutes the People of God around himself. It is no longer the Torah *per se* that defines the covenantal response of the People of God, but the Torah as interpreted and elaborated by him.[29] In choosing and commissioning *twelve* of his disciples to be his apostles, he deliberately posits an alternative community to the twelve tribes of Israel (we note in passing that he does not include himself among the twelve but stands above them).[30] In declaring, unconditionally, the forgiveness of sin he bypasses the Temple cultus with its divinely-instituted priesthood and sacrificial system.

There are profound christological implications here which can profitably be explored through the work on 'speech-acts' of linguistic philosophers such as JL Austin and JR Searle.[31] Speech-act theories draw attention to an important contrast between the 'causal' force and the 'institutional' authority of an utterance. I may be persuaded (causal force) to work harder in the office by the anxious warnings of a friend; but this is different from a formal warning by my employer which carries real consequences if ignored (institutional authority). I may give up smoking because my wife disapproves of the smell; but her disapproval does not carry the same authority as that of a warning from my doctor who has just examined the state of my lungs. Institutional status carries with it rights, obligations, a representational character and a delegated authority. Whether the utterances 'You are fired!' or 'You have two weeks to live' or 'I acquit you' have extra-linguistic consequences depends on the institutional status and role of the speaker. If the speakers in the above instances were, respectively, my employer, my doctor and a judge, then in each case the operative effectiveness of their words would be enormous.

The aspect of John Searle's speech-act theory which is relevant to our discussion is his careful distinction between two 'directions of fit' between a speaker's words and the world. In what he terms the *logic of assertion*, the 'direction of fit' which is entailed is that of words reflecting a state-of-affairs in the world. Here it is the world that exercises 'control', and the words that report states of affairs perform their function insofar as they 'fit' the world they purport to describe. On the other hand, in the *logic of promise*, states-of-affairs in the world must be changed in order to 'fit' the word of promise. In the first case, reality shapes the words. Here descriptive report is the appropriate model. In the second case, directive speech-acts shape reality to the speaker's intention.

Anthony Thiselton invokes Searle's speech-act theory to draw attention to the importance of the biblical language of *promise*. Such language, he points out, operates in both directions. 'The important direction of fit in terms of *cash*

value for the process of salvation is that the promissory language of
Jesus can transform states of affairs to fit the messianic word of
promise. Here the promissory word is primary and life-changing. But this can be so . . . only because certain *truths*
about the status, authority, and role of Jesus can in principle be
asserted—that is, that the word fits the state of affairs which
it portrays.'[32]

In the light of these considerations, the sharp wedge that is
often driven between 'functional' and 'titular' christologies
must be seen as artificial and naive. The primary data for
christology in the pre–Easter period arises not so much from
the *explicit* claims of Jesus concerning his identity and
authority, but more from what is *presupposed* about his
identity and authority on the basis of his speech–acts. The
relation of presupposition entails more than formal logical
inference. The speech–acts rest on a transcendental role and
status, and point to God and the relation between God and
Jesus. In the language of speech–act theory, this status and
role may be described analogically as an institutional status
and role which is established by the authorization of God. As
we shall see, it also reflects a certain *sharing* of divine status
and function, even if this remains hidden, not being directly
stated, in the Synoptic Gospels. The latter make the language
of promise explicit, leaving the christological assertions
which give efficacy to the overt speech–acts of Jesus *implicit*.
The Fourth Gospel, partly because of its more reflective
perspective, allows equal prominence to be given to both
directions of fit. An adequate christology must involve an
interplay between assertions which 'fit' reality and extra-linguistic transformations which make reality 'fit' the word
of promise.

While all the Gospel narratives testify to the extraordinary
character and behaviour of Jesus, they also depict another
side, what we may call the 'unobtrusiveness' of his life,
namely his relative social obscurity and the initial sense of
puzzlement he generated among his hearers ('Isn't this the
carpenter? Isn't this Mary's son and the brother of James,
Joseph, Judas and Simon?', Mk 6:3). This is significant when
we read the Gospels from the perspective of the myths and
folk-tales of the Asian religious traditions. Here is no
superhuman *avatar*, no handsome prince nor ascetic recluse
in total mastery of his bodily reactions, but a man who sheds
tears, feels hunger and pain, experiences anger at the evil he

encounters, and overflows with humour and the joy of life. This also stands in contrast to some nineteenth and twentieth century christologies that tended to depict Jesus, usually in rather sentimental ways, as one whose force of personality alone was sufficient to launch what later became the Christian movement. Whatever 'uniqueness' is ascribed to Jesus is then understood in terms of some human quality developed to a superlative degree (for example, 'self-transcendence' or 'piety').

However, along with the unassuming and meek posture Jesus demonstrates in his relationships with other people, there are also the extraordinary and startling claims he makes, both implicitly and explicitly, concerning his person and vocation. It is these that eventually prompt the progression from puzzlement to hostility and to outright rage.

In the earlier parts of the triple tradition common to Mark, Matthew and Luke, we find a number of 'performative utterances' of Jesus which well illustrate Austin's famous definition of *illocutionary* speech-acts: the performance of an act *in* the saying of something.[33] Jesus says to the paralytic, 'My son, your sins are [hereby] forgiven' (Mk 2:5; Matt. 9:2; Lk. 5:20).[34] The similarly authoritative utterance, 'Peace! Be still' (Mk 4:35–41; Matt. 8:23–27; Lk. 8:22–25) subjugates the winds and the waves in the act of being uttered. Jesus' effective words of exorcism ('Be silent! Come out of him', Mk 1:25) are seen in the triple tradition not simply as a miracle as such, but as a Messianic word-deed which in its utterance constitutes the binding of the 'strong man' and the plundering of his kingdom (Mk 3:23–27; Matt 12:22–30; Lk 11:14–23).[35] On all such occasions, the response of the crowds and the disciples is one of shock and amazement: who then is this? . . . what sort of person is this? . . . with what authority does he do these things? . . . why does this fellow talk like this? He is blaspheming! . . .[36]

Mark, Matthew and Luke make room for the reader to reflect on the presuppositions which allow such illocutionary speech-acts to function effectively. To use language that is associated with the later Wittgenstein, these speech-acts 'show' rather than 'say' the christological dimensions of status and role that Jesus enjoys in the purposes of God for the world. Liberationist and existentialist christologies that rightly focus on the self-transforming dimension of disciple-ship to Jesus, nevertheless tend to ignore the presuppositional basis (beyond the textual) which makes the promissory language of Jesus effective. The transformation of discipleship is not self-generated. Even Bultmann recognized that for the very earliest Christians 'Jesus' call to decision implies a christology.'[37] 'Something greater than Solomon . . . greater than Jonah is here' (Lk. 11:31, 32) . . . 'Follow me, and leave the dead to bury their dead' (Matt. 8:22).

How high a christology is involved can be seen when such words are read in their monotheistic, Jewish context.[38] The words of Jesus reinterpret the Old Testament traditions which shaped the pattern of Jewish national and individual life for centuries, and his word is set above the law of Moses and the tradition of the Elders as the means to life (e.g. Matt. 5:21–37; Matt. 8:24ff). He calls people to put himself before every other relationship in life and to be willing even to give their lives away for his sake (e.g. Matt. 10:34ff, Mk 8:34ff, Lk. 14:25ff). All this in a culture imbued with the passionate conviction that God the Creator was the source, owner and Judge of the whole world and that allegiance to this God came before everything and everybody else. We have already seen how Jesus assumed authority to declare to men and women the forgiveness of sins in anticipation of the eschatological judgment of God, and thereby circumvented the God-given Temple cultus (e.g. Mk 2:1–12). He is not only Israel's Judge but also the one to whom *all nations* will give account at the end of history (e.g. Matt. 25:31ff). Moreover, the basis of judgment will be the nations' response to him—and expressed in their response to those with whom he has identified himself. He proclaims the arrival of God's reign, inaugurating the New Age of Old Testament promise. We need to bear in mind that, within the background of Jewish apocalyptic and eschatological hope, this in-breaking of the kingdom of God in the coming of Jesus constitutes a cosmic, and not simply a national, turning-point (e.g. Mk 1:15, 2:21, 22).[39] The matter-of-fact way in which Jesus assumes the rights and prerogatives of Yahweh startled his contemporaries and often provoked the indignation of the scribal authorities.

Certainly, christology cannot be reduced to description and titles alone. But what I am seeking to show here, in the light of the emphasis on 'following Jesus' to the *exclusion* of 'proclaiming Jesus' that we find in the particular theologies described in earlier chapters, is that the self-involving aspects of Jesus' pronouncements imply christological presuppositions of a profound kind. If the implicit christology is false, then the entire performative dimension collapses. In that case the whole series of illocutionary acts depicted in the Gospels (the language of forgiveness, the rebuking of the storm and the casting out of demons, the invitation of outcasts to the banquet of the kingdom, the call to discipleship and the commissioning to mission etc) have no proper institutional basis. They must be dismissed as nothing more than pious constructs of a fertile imagination.

In his study of Matthean christology, the Roman Catholic scholar John Meir has noted how Matthew, while leaving his most explicit christological declaration to the post-resurrection commissioning of Matt. 28:18–20, interweaves his account of Jesus' teaching with an emphasis on the uniqueness of his person. The two are inextricable: 'What Jesus teaches depends on his own person for its truth, validity, and permanence. Teacher and teaching become inextricably tied together. You do not fully understand what the teaching is unless you understand who the teacher is. You cannot accept the teaching as true unless you accept the teacher as your Lord . . .'[40]

Likewise recent research on the parables of Jesus, drawing on speech-act theory and the understanding of language as communicative action, has overturned older liberal views that saw them as simply homely illustrations of general religious truths. Johannes du Plessis summarizes the results of an exhaustive study of parabolic language as follows: 'The parables' main aim is to *let the recipients recognize Jesus' authority as the sole source of a salvific relationship with God.*'[41] A semi-popular study of the parables by Craig Blomberg comes to a similar conclusion: 'Without denying that God the Father is the primary referent behind all of the master figures in Jesus' narratives, we may argue that Jesus frequently intended his audiences to associate him with the Father in some respect.'[42] The parables, by both concealing and revealing the truth of Jesus, invite the reader to participate in an extra-linguistic relationship with Jesus that transforms his or her way of seeing both God and the world.

It has long been observed that the synoptic tradition, and Mark in particular, shows a relative reticence in the words of Jesus to make explicit statements about the basis on which his own illocutionary utterances and the disciples' personal commitments to him were valid. Part of the reason for this has already been intimated above. Also, christology prior to the resurrection remained incomplete, awaiting divine corroboration. But, as Thiselton points out, a further consideration aises from the very *uniqueness* of Jesus. He writes, 'It was important that *an understanding of Jesus*, seen in his words and in his *completed work, should govern interpretations of conventional 'messianic' language, rather than that ready-made assumptions about the meaning of such language should govern an understanding of Jesus.*'[43]

If we turn (briefly) to more explicit claims on the part of Jesus, we could classify these under the following separate, albeit overlapping, headings:

(a) *A claim to enjoy a unique filial relationship to God.* We find the title 'Father' for God some fifty-one times on the lips of Jesus in the Synoptic Gospels (excluding parallels), of which on seven occasions it is in the direct address of prayer. Perhaps there was nothing very startling in a Jew's referring to God as Father, but the way Jesus used that term was extraordinary. There is no suggestion that all human beings are sons of God by virtue of the fact that God is their Creator. Rather, the relationship of which Jesus spoke was was not one shared by all men, or even by all Jews. God was always 'my Father' and he himself was never 'a son' but always 'the son' of God. Jesus never linked the disciples with himself so that together they could say 'our Father'. The prayer of Matt. 6:9 is for the disciple community to use, and it is privilege made possible through their faith in Jesus. Every use of 'Father' in Jesus' teaching is found in sayings addressed specifically to his disciples. If the evidence of John 20:17 be allowed, Jesus distinguishes between 'my Father' and 'your Father', making explicit what is implicit elsewhere.[44]

In the provocative parable of the Wicked Tenants, aimed squarely at the Jerusalem priestly establishment, Jesus regards himself as the uniquely loved son of the vineyard owner, unlike other messengers (prophets) who are simply his 'servants' (Mark 12:1–12). And, in the most startling passage of all, he announces that the Father has entrusted 'all things' to him and that 'no one knows the Father except the Son and those to whom the Son chooses to reveal him' (Matt. 11:27 = Lk. 10:22).[45] Thus Jesus claims a unique

intimacy with God and a unique authority, born of that
intimacy, to reveal the heart of God to humankind. It is on
the basis of this authority to make known the Father that he
invites all the 'weary and burdened' to come to him for rest
(Matt. 11:28). The promise of rest echoes the Hebrew text of
Jeremiah 6:16 where it is the offer of God to those who
follow his way. Here it is contingent on a disciple-
relationship ('learn from me') with Jesus: a relationship that
frees men and women from the oppressive 'yoke' of
religious legalism. In what might be perceived as a casual
manner these claims to a unique relationship with God and a
unique offer of freedom/rest are accompanied, in almost the
same breath, by a claim to be 'gentle and humble in heart'
(v.29)!⁴⁶

In the Jewish context, sonship entailed not only privilege
but obedience to one's father. For Jesus, therefore, the
consciousness of a unique God–relatedness was accompanied
by a sense of a unique vocation. On the one hand this is seen
in Matthew 11:27 (above) where the unique authority
delegated to the Son by the Father is bound up with the Son's
vocation to make him known. On the other it is seen in his
undertaking of the tasks variously (and confusingly) assigned
to the Messiah, the Son of Man and the suffering Servant of
Yahweh. Thus, even the words quoted above (11:29) echo
the description of the Servant of Yahweh in Isaiah 42:2–3,
53:1–2, and also the words of Zechariah 9:9 which Matthew
picks up again at 21:4–5.⁴⁷

(b) *A claim to be the unique fulfilment of Scripture.* We have
seen how another prominent feature of Jesus' teaching is the
manner in which he understands his life and ministry as
bringing into focus various strands of Old Testament hope.
He not only proclaims the approach of God's kingdom but is
the one through whom that kingdom takes shape (e.g. Mk
1:14–15, Matt. 12:28). His disciples are blessed because they,
unlike the prophets of old, are actually able to taste the
powers of God's kingdom through their association with
him. 'Blessed are the eyes that see what you see. For I tell
you that many prophets and kings wanted to see what you
see but did not see it, and to hear what you hear but did not
hear it.' (Lk. 10:23). The cities of Nineveh, Tyre and Sidon,
Sodom and Gomorrah, all by-words of pagan idolatry in the
Old Testament prophetic writings, now become witnesses
against the unbelief of Israel, for now one greater than Jonah

and Solomon is here (Lk. 11:29ff, Matt. 11:20ff). He is the one of whom Moses wrote, the one whose day Abraham rejoiced to see, the one who is David's Lord (Mk 12:35–7, Jn. 5:46, 8:56). In other words, he is not so much a prophet as *the object of all prophecy*. On him converge the Old Testament imagery of the Isaianic Servant of Yahweh, bearing the wrath of God for the healing of the nations, and Daniel's Son of Man, receiving an everlasting kingdom which embraces all peoples. He sets his face to Jerusalem, convinced that what is written of him *must* be fulfilled.[48]

(c) *A claim to be in a different category from others.* Even while identifying himself with the 'sinners' of Palestinian society, Jesus frequently put himself in a different category from the rest of his fellows. They were like lost sheep, he was the shepherd sent to seek and to save the lost. They were in darkness, he was the light that would dispel the darkness. They were in the thrall of death, he was the resurrection and the life. We have noted how he saw himself as not just another subject of God's kingdom but the one who had the authority to decide who would be included and who would be excluded from the benefits of that kingdom. We have already noted how, in appointing twelve disciples to represent the true Israel of God, he did not include themself in their number. He occupied a position above them, though he interpreted that position in terms of lowly servanthood.[49] He presents himself as the ultimate arbiter of a human being's destiny.[50]

Although Jesus anticipated the suffering and death that befell other prophets and righteous men in Jerusalem, unlike them his death was the climax of his God-given vocation, having redemptive significance for Israel: it was a 'ransom for many' (Mk 10:45, Matt. 20:28),[51] the inauguration of a new covenant between God and his people through the forgiveness of their sins (Matt. 26:27–8, cf.Is. 53:12 and Jer. 31:31–4). Whether or not the Last Supper was the regular Passover meal, the sacrifical language and the Old Testament allusions are unmistakable, and Jesus uses the traditional Passover 'this is that' language ('this is my body', 'this is my blood of the covenant') to announce the redemptive character of his impending death.[52] Under the old covenant he bears the judgment of God on sinful Israel so that the true Israel, constituted by the vicarious sacrifice of Jesus, may emerge as a new people of God.[53]

It is thus, in the public world of historical action and transformation, and not in some interior mystical world of 'religiosity', that Jesus of Nazareth stakes his claims. His many utterances concerning what he has come to do pre-suppose an authority to put into operative effect the promises of God concerning his world. Jesus claims to do what prophets, sages and others failed to do.

What, then, are we to make of Jesus Christ? The one thing we cannot say is that he was no more than a great religious teacher, for we have already seen that it is impossible to separate the content of his moral instruction from the self-conscious authority that is *presupposed* by that instruction —an authority surpassing that of any Jewish prophet or ancient sage. If what he believed about himself was not true then he can hardly be a religious examplar for the rest of us. If one hesitates to acknowledge the truth of his claims, then logically one is compelled to dismiss him either as a liar/ charlatan, thus implying that the whole edifice of Christianity is built on a gigantic hoax, or as a megalomaniac, a self-deceived fool. (We have already seen that attributing all such truth-claims to the pious imagination of the Christian faith-community does not get us very far. This assumption overlooks a vital question: what was it about Jesus of Nazareth, compared to other messianic claimants and charis-matic figures in Palestine and elsewhere, that led to such outrageous claims about him being made—and believed —within a generation of his death? We are also faced with the same choice—true, false, or deluded—but this time with regard to the Christian church. *Someone* said the things attributed to Jesus, and that someone was true, false or deluded.)

Why is the charge of megalomania so difficult to stick on Jesus? Simply because his lifestyle and the values he em-bodied strike even the most hardened sceptic as eminently sane, indeed deeply attractive. Here is a man who describes himself as 'gentle and humble of heart' and stoops to wash the feet of his disciples in act of menial service. No contemporary of Jesus, nor any serious thinker since, has accused Jesus of being insincere or hypocritical in his relationships with either friend or enemy. Gandhi and Martin Luther King both drew their inspiration for how to deal with those who opposed them from the example and teaching of Jesus. And, as mentioned above (pp. 179f), Jesus' lifestyle of lowly, compassionate service towards the sick, the vulnerable and the oppressed of his day continues to attract many people to him from diverse cultural backgrounds. I believe that this combination of an *other-oriented lifestyle with self-directed claims* is what makes Jesus of Nazareth utterly unique.

When we explore the great religious traditions of the world, we come across many great figures who impressed their contemporaries with the other-centredness of their way of life. They lived lives of exemplary courage, compassion and sacrifice. Gautama, the Buddha, would be an outstanding example from the Asian context. But such people make no grand claims for themselves, other than to be pointers to the truth. One noted authority on Buddhism observes that the Buddha 'saw himself as simply preaching the Dharma'[54] (that account of the world which presents the possibility of liberation from the world). In the Mahayana tradition, Buddhahood is an ideal state open, in principle, to all life-forms. Likewise, in Islam, Mohammed is simply a prophet, albeit the final prophet, in a long tradition of prophets and messengers commissioned by God to turn people away from idols. In all these cases there is no call to personal allegiance, no claim to be communicating anything other than a word from God or an insight into ultimate reality.

On the other hand are individuals who do make self-centred claims, but these claims do not impress for very long. The Caesars, Hitlers and Idi Amins of the world have not only disappeared into the mists of history, but their megalomania led them into forms of brutality and self-aggrandizement which seemed to fit quite naturally with the claims they made for themselves. But it is here that Jesus stands out as unique. One can search all the religious traditions—indeed all the great literature—of humankind, and you will not come across one like Jesus, who makes seemingly the most arrogant claims concerning himself yet lives in the most humble and selfless manner conceivable. Jesus of Nazareth simply confounds our imagination.

Resurrection: language

Jesus was not *remembered* by the early disciples in the way that martyrs and sages from the past live on in the collective memory of a people. They did not make pilgrimages to the hill on which he was crucified or the tomb in which his corpse was laid. Something happened soon after Jesus' death that transformed a situation of defeat and desolation into one in which a new movement came into being, a movement characterized not by nostalgia but by 'hope'. At the heart of New Testament faith and preaching lies the claim that Jesus was *resurrected* by God: that over a period of forty days after his crucifixion he encountered his followers in a physical body that was recognizable as that of the man they knew before, and that after that period he continued to communicate with them, 'indwell' them and empower them in a new mode of Spirit. All the earliest accounts of Christian origins are agreed that what distinguished the new 'Jesus movement' in its Jewish and Greco-Roman environment was not that it proclaimed a new religion or ethic; but rather a new *event*, namely the resurrection by God of the crucified Jesus, and the implications of that event for the world.

That this formed the indispensable substance of apostolic preaching is indicated by the earliest Pauline letters (which are also the earliest Christian literature). In 1 Cor. 15 Paul refers to the earliest tradition concerning Jesus that he himself had received and passed on to them: namely, 'that Christ did for our sins according to the Scriptures, that he was buried, that he was raised on the third day according to the Scriptures . . .' (v.3). Here, as always, fact and interpretation are intertwined. Christ's death was a death 'for our sins' and 'according to the Scriptures'. But this interpretation was not plucked from thin air. As we shall see, it is *given* in the event of the *resurrection*. The latter event interprets the cross; and that it is an event within history, while at the same time reaching beyond history, is shown by Paul's insistence, in the second half of the sentence quoted above, that the presence of contemporary eye-witnesses is itself part of the Gospel tradition (vv.5–8). However interpretative the language of resurrection is (and the implications of such language will be explored in what follows), it nevertheless rests on the objectivity of specific historical truth-claims, notably the empty tomb and the post-mortem physical appearances of Jesus to his disciples. Little wonder, then, that Paul, in stark contrast to Kant, Lessing and some of their modern followers, can draw the obvious conclusion: 'If Christ has not been raised, our preaching is useless and so is your faith' (v.14, cf.v.17). The proclamation of the Gospel is not the recitation of timeless truths. 'Whether, then, it was I or they [other apostles and missionaries], it is in these terms that we preached the Gospel and it was in these terms that you accepted it in faith' (v.11).

We need not rehearse the traditional arguments in support of the empty tomb tradition and the reality of the post-Easter appearances of Jesus. However, the evidence, though circumstantial, is quite impressive and, in my opinion, often under-estimated in contemporary theological discussion no less than in secular historiography. For example, although we have much evidence of anti-Christian polemic from Jewish and Roman sources in the early years of the Jesus movement, no one disputes the claim that the tomb was empty. What reasonable hypothesis, other than the early Christian kerygma, can account for this? It is *prima facie* unlikely that a story concocted in a Jewish milieu should have as its principal eye-witnesses a group of women (and some of dubious moral character at that!) whose testimony would not have been permissible in a Jewish court of law. As fabrications, these accounts lack historical plausibility. *Something* happened to compel the early disciples of Jesus to break with a centuries-old tradition and to meet to worship God on the first day of the week. *Something* happened to make these Jews, within a few years of the death of Jesus, ascribe to him titles and honorifics that they traditionally ascribed to Yahweh, the covenant God of Israel, and to address prayers and worship to him as they did to Yahweh.

However much one might seek to sidestep these awkward historical questions, the New Testament demands that we do not attempt to evade their disturbing challenge by resorting to language about 'a present experience of the risen Christ'. It simply will not do to say, as many in the liberal Western theological tradition (including Asian writers influenced by this tradition) have said, that the disciples had such a wonderful inner experience of the love and grace of God mediated through Jesus that the 'mythical' language of 'resurrection' was the only way they could express the abiding significance of this experience. The Jewish people had experienced God's love and grace in many fresh and illuminating ways after catastrophic experiences of humiliation and suffering. They had several ways of describing this experience, but the language of 'resurrection'—least of all applied to an individual leader, however inspirational—was never one of them. The more natural way of highlighting the importance of Jesus would have been to continue the traditional language Jews used of their great heroes Moses (whose body was never found) or of Enoch and Elijah, that God 'received them' by way of direct translation into his presence. Or they could have done what the followers of John the Baptist did with their dead master who had been beheaded by Herod Antipas. They could have revered him as a dead and martyred prophet lying in his grave. This would have been considered normal by the Jewish establishment. But by choosing to speak of Jesus' 'resurrection' they incurred the fury and persecution of the Sadducean hierarchy.[55]

Nor does it make any historical sense to assume that the disciples of Jesus were so crushed by his death and the failure of their dreams that they projected the latter into a fantasy about Jesus' being raised from death as a way of coping with their painful situation. The Jewish world of the first century was awash with revolutionaries with messianic pretensions, most of whom were put to death in a violent way by the authorities. Never do we hear of their disappointed and dispersed followers projecting their broken dreams into claims that their hero had been raised from the dead. That option was not available to them. For Jewish language about 'resurrection' was not about a private experience: it was physical and public. The followers of the failed revolutionary had either to give up the revolution or else find another leader. The question that cannot be evaded, therefore, is simply this: *why did the earliest disciples use the language of 'resurrection' in relation to Jesus?*

The discussion of chapter 5 has shown that, philosophically speaking, there are two opposite perils to be avoided. The first, against which the liberal theological tradition is in justifiable revolt, is to reduce the resurrection language of early Christianity to 'rational proofs' of an empty tomb and the reality of the post-mortem appearances of Jesus to his disciples. The second, under the influence of the Cartesian and post-Kantian 'turn to the subject' in modern secular culture, is a tendency to talk of resurrection in a way totally alien to the outlook of the biblical tradition.[56] In both cases the objective and the subjective poles of faith–claims have been wrenched apart.[57] In both cases the tendency is to speak of the resurrection of Jesus as something that can be fitted into a secular or traditionally religious world view. But the past two decades of New Testament scholarship, which has sought to rediscover the distinctively Jewish environment of Jesus and the Gospel tradition, has drawn attention to the remarkable uniqueness of early Christian language about the resurrection. And, as Newbigin and other have maintained, such language provides an alternative 'plausibility structure' that challenges both modern Western secularism and the traditional Indian religious outlook.

It cannot be stressed too strongly that contemporary Jewish belief in resurrection had nothing to do with the resuscitation of a body nor the immortality of a disembodied soul or spirit. It was about the conquest of death, of going through death into a new world of *physically embodied* existence, and the birth of a new creation. It is expressed in the desire of the Maccabean martyrs of the second century BC that the God of Israel would vindicate their cause by restoring the limbs and bodies they would lose through horrible torture and death.[58] It was a late development of Israelite faith, and is clearly evidenced in only a handful of Old Testament texts (such as Isaiah 26:19, Psalm 49:15 and Daniel 12:2). Resurrection, for all first-century Jews, was bound up with the hope of the Kingdom of God, of God's vindication of his people Israel before their pagan enemies and the renewal of his disfigured world. Resurrection was corporate, as well as public and physical. It was not something that happened to isolated individuals, here and there. The age to come would be a renewed space-time world in which the righteous dead would be given new bodies in order to inhabit a renewed earth. Thus, the resurrection of the dead—the righteous to eternal life and the wicked to destruction—marked the consummation of the human drama. It spelt the triumph of Israel's God who was also the universal Creator and Judge of all humanity. Resurrection marked the dawn of a new world order, the final and supreme manifestation of God's justice, mercy and power in history.[59]

Although resurrection was a relatively late belief in Old Testament times and comes to the fore only during the Maccabean period, it was made possible because of what was foundational to faith in the God of Israel. As Richard Bauckham has shown in a recent essay, the hope of resurrection was a necessary consequence of a 'radical faith in God the Creator' who was also the God of the covenant with Israel.[60] To trust in a God on whom everything depends for its existence is to rely, not on the immanent possibilities of human life, but on the transcendent possibilities of the Creator. 'Even when all immanent possibilities of life run out—in death—he who is the source of all life can create new possibilites of life—in resurrection.'[61] Paul's characterization of Abraham's faith as faith in the God 'who makes the dead live and calls that which is not into being' (Rom. 4:17) comes close to providing a definition of Yahweh and is probably borrowed from Jewish liturgical language.[62] When Jesus is questioned by the Sadducees about the reasonableness of belief in the resurrection, he responds by pointing to the revealed name of God as the 'God of Abraham, Isaac and Jacob' who is 'not the God of the dead but the living' (Matt. 22:23–32 = Mk 12:18–27 = Lk. 20:27–40). In other words, the God who is the source of life and who freely enters into personal relationship with his creatures can be trusted to continue that relationship with them on the other side of the grave. Radical faith in this God issues in radical hope for his creation.

In the Old Testament God's power over life is typically displayed in situations of human hopelessness. In such situations life is experienced as a gift which God bestows and which, when virtually lost, can be restored by God.[63] To know the living God is to know that one's life can be absolutely entrusted to him (e.g. Ps. 73:24–26). He is the righteous God who can be expected to vindicate the righteous who trust in him against their mocking oppressors. Thus hope of life with God beyond death did not strictly originate in connexion with the Maccabean martyrs, but, as Bauckham points out, the martyrs 'remain paradigmatic for the hope of resurrection because the martyrs are those who so trust God with their lives that they can give them up for him'.[64] Herein lies the basic difference between theories of the immortality of the soul and the biblical hope of resurrection: it is the difference between believing in some immanent power within oneself to survive death, and recognizing oneself to be given by God and so entrusting oneself to him even in death. There is no natural orientation of human life to resurrection; the latter becomes a possibility only through radical faith in a trustworthy Creator who graciously gives life to us as his gift.

Early Christian faith in resurrection shares this Old Testament and first-century Pharisaic perspective (Acts 23:6). But with a *revolutionary and decisive difference*: the early Christians proclaimed that the resurrection had occurred in Jesus *before* the day of resurrection for all. Here was a proleptic anticipation of the end of history. In the resurrection of Jesus, God not only gives a glimpse and pledge of the new creation, but he announces the dawn of that new creation before its promised fulfilment. Here is a foretaste of the future age in the present age. This is how the early Christians proclaimed the resurrection: not only as the vindication and legitimation by God of Jesus as universal Lord and Saviour (e.g., Matt. 28:18; Acts 2:24ff; 4:11; 5:30ff; 17:31; Rom. 1:2–4) but as the 'firstfruits' of the new humanity which is created through him (e.g. 1 Cor. 15:20ff; Acts 26:23; 1 Pet. 1:3). He was raised uniquely before all others *because* he died and was raised uniquely *for* all others.

The first followers of Jesus had come to discipleship in the midst of fervent Messianic expectations. We have also seen that the language of 'resurrection' was used deliberately; it was very far from being the only option available for expressing whatever they had experienced of God through his life and ministry. What made them claim, in a totally unique way, that Jesus had experienced 'resurrection' as a single individual within history? After all, nothing had happened on the social and political stage that could have convinced anyone that Israel was being exalted before its pagan oppressors and that Israel's God was now becoming King over his enemies. Apart from the resurrection itself, the only event that had occurred recently was that yet another messianic pretender had been executed by the Romans. That was a common enough occurrence, and all it communicated to the Jewish community in general was not that the kingdom had come but instead the very reverse!

In the ancient Jewish world, as in our modern one, for someone who had been certifiably dead to become visibly alive again would not at all justify a claim that the person to whom this odd event had happened was therefore the saviour of the world, the Son of God, or anything else in particular. David Hume pointed out three hundred years ago that, faced with an anomaly in our experience, we are more likely to explain it away than label it a miracle. If, say, one of the two thieves/brigands crucified along with Jesus had appeared to his friends a few days later, we may suppose it very unlikely that he would have been hailed in any such way, or that anyone would deduce from that event that Israel's salvation had dawned. This forces us to ask: could the belief that someone had been raised from the dead, whatever precisely was understood by that, have produced the results it did unless it was also known that the one who had been crucified and raised had lived in such a manner and made such extraordinary claims concerning himself that resurrection was actually remarkably consistent with all that had occurred before?

The cross and resurrection are central to virtually all forms of early Christianity. But, as Tom Wright argues plausibly, 'The rise of that early Christian understanding is only comprehensible on the basis that certain things continued to be known, as history, about the one who (among so many others) was crucified outside Jerusalem and who (unlike any others before or since—a fact of some significance) was declared by his followers to be alive shortly afterwards . . . More particularly, if the resurrection was believed to be part of that complex of events through which the covenant God would restore the fortunes of his people, any telling of a 'resurrection' story about Jesus could only make sense in a context of *telling Israel's story in the form of Jesus' story*'.[65] Wright points out that it could not do simply to announce that there was a man who had died, even who had died a particularly brutal death, and who had been found to be alive. That is not the point: 'The gospel of the early church, of Paul, of the evangelists, is that the promises of the Jewish scriptures had come true in the resurrection. That is why Paul and others keep insisting that Jesus' death and resurrection happened 'according to the scriptures', or in fulfilment of them.'[66]

Resurrection: implications

What are the implications of the resurrection of Jesus for the issues we have been discussing in this book? I suggest the following, rooted in the New Testament witness:

(a) ESCHATOLOGICAL HOPE is now *christologically* focused. The New Testament writers establish a strong connection between life for the world and the historically specific life of Jesus (e.g. 1 Jn. 1:1; 1 Cor. 15; Rom. 8). Faith in the resurrection sends us back to the words and works of Jesus and his proclamation of the reign of God. The resurrection of Jesus is now *the* sign of the imminence of God's reign and the pledge of what is to come. The powers of the age to come are already tasted by the followers of Jesus in the midst of the old order (Heb. 6:4–5;cf. Rom. 8:23; 2 Cor. 1:22). In the resurrection of Jesus the Creator has affirmed his commitment to his creation; so that, far from devaluing the creation, hope in resurrection and new creation proclaims a God who remains faithful to his creation.

In the glorious apocalyptic[67] vision with which the Book of Revelation ends (Rev. 21–22), God's throne is set right in the midst of the New Jerusalem where the living waters stream from the throne, the leaves of the tree of life are for the healing of the nations, and God's servants, sealed with the mark of God, will see God face to face. In contrast to chapter 4, where God's dwelling is in heaven, here he tabernacles with humanity on earth. The division between heaven and earth has disappeared in the new creation. Fractured human existence is now healed. But God's un-mediated presence can be enjoyed only after evil has been rooted out of his kingdom. God and humanity cannot dwell in harmony as long as an unrepentant world persists in rejecting divine truth and justice. And so, central to the apocalyptic picture is *the Lamb who shares the throne of God* in the New Jerusalem. There are no more temples (religions?) in the city, for the Lord God Almighty and the Lamb are its temple (21:22). The cultural and material wealth of the nations will embellish the city, but there is no more sun nor moon (rival powers?) for the Lamb himself is its lamp, conveying the light of the glory of God by which the nations of the earth will walk (21:23–4). The tabernacling of God with humanity has begun with the Lamb's exaltation (chapter 5). His is a hidden dominion, only to be fully manifested on the day of final resurrection. Then the world will realise the ultimate significance of what has already happened in Jesus as they look on him 'whom they have pierced' (1:7).

(b) FAITH IN GOD is now *christologically* focused. In the light of the resurrection, Jesus' proclamation of the coming kingdom of God was translated into the early church's proclamation of Jesus as the Messiah who both embodies and ushers in that kingdom. Jesus' understanding of God as uniquely his Father was translated into the early church's preaching of Jesus' sonship to God and into a new understanding of God as 'the Father of the Lord Jesus Christ'. Radical faith in the Creator God 'who raises the dead' is now focused on the risen Christ. The Jewish hope of resurrection now becomes faith in Jesus who *is* the resurrection and the life (e.g. Jn. 11:25). It is in Jesus' resurrection that God gives those who believe in him their resurrection. The New Testament writers go even further: in raising Jesus God has given him his own life-giving power to raise the dead. He is the 'author of life' (e.g. Acts 3:15), 'the living one' (e.g. Rev. 1:18; cf. its use as a divine title in Deut. 5:26; Josh. 3:10; Ps. 42:2 etc), the 'life-giving spirit' (e.g. 1 Cor. 15:45), the one to whom the Father has granted 'life in himself' so that he may give life to others (Jn. 5:21–26). Behind the variety of symbols and expressions, there lies an impressive convergence of belief. The Jewish understanding of God as the source of all life is retained, but given a christological orientation. The power of Jesus' risen life is God's power to give life to the dead.

Within the pages of the New Testament we see this christological reorientation taking place at the most fundamental level, in the transformation of language and symbolism. GB Caird observed that it was 'the contention [of the New Testament writers] that with the coming of Jesus the whole situation of mankind has so altered as to change the semantic content of the word "God".'[68] Caird lists among his examples the Day of Yahweh becoming 'the Day of our Lord Jesus' (2 Cor. 1:14); and, against a schismatic group claiming to know God and to love him in some esoteric fashion (1 Jn. 1:6; 2:4; 4:20), the John of the First Epistle insisting that we do not even know the meaning of the word 'love' and fill it with its true ethical content until we believe that the love of God took human form in his 'Son' Jesus who was 'sent' as an atoning sacrifice for human sin (1 Jn. 4:9).

The unique claim of Judaism, namely that the Creator God, actively present everywhere, had acted specifically within the history of Israel, was taken over by the early Christians and given a new focal point: this Creator God had brought the story of Israel to its climax by acting specifically in Jesus, and was now acting by his Spirit in a new way that Jesus' death and resurrection had inaugurated. By speaking of Jesus, Spirit and God in the same breath, they not only make remarkable claims about Jesus within the monotheistic framework of Jewish thought, but, at the same time, make stupendous claims about God.

(c) ETHICS, understood as the way of being truly human, is now *christologically* focused. The crucifixion can be seen as a point of convergence for two fundamentally opposed visions of human being. The first is seen in the self-righteousness of the Pharisees, the calculating self-protectiveness and self-seeking of the priestly establishment, the callous pragmatism of their political overlords, and the fickleness of the 'masses' whose lust for power and revenge have been fuelled by disillusionment. The second is embodied in Jesus himself: a radical surrender to, and dependence on, the One he knew as Father, which issues in the willingness to lay down one's life in self-forgetful love for others. Two ways of defining humanness clash: *self-assertion* (or 'survival' as the highest value) and *self-giving* (or the way of the cross). The resurrection of Jesus is then God's vindication, within history and in anticipation of the eschaton, of the way of the cross.

The radical faith in God that Jesus taught his disciples and lived himself is based on a vision of life as a sheer gift from a faithful God. What has been freely received must be freely given (Matt. 10:8). Since God alone can be trusted with one's life and one's future, the self-centred clinging to life is ultimately futile and self-destructive. Jesus lives out the paradox that 'He who saves his life will lose it, and he who loses his life will save it'(Lk. 7:33, cf. Jn. 12:24,25).[69] Only in the abandoning of the attempt to secure (or establish) one's own good and in the forgetting of oneself in the love of God and neighbour (who, in Jesus' definition, included one's national and personal enemies) can one's true self be realised and one's true good be received as a gift from God. The resurrection, in vindicating the trustworthiness and power of God, simultaneously vindicates Jesus' unique sonship and the way of self-denying love that he embodies.

Finally, we should take account of two ways in which the resurrection hope has been distorted and 'hijacked' in the interests of some dominant ideology. Both entail severing the tradition from its grounding in Jewish eschatological hope. The first (always a temptation in Hellenistic, Indian and secularist environments) is to turn it into a belief in personal survival or an interior 'religious experience' rather than an affirmation about the transformation of the universe.

Heaven becomes a haven for the beleaguered soul. As the church accommodates itself to the existing order and becomes preoccupied with its own internal life, theology becomes an academic pastime rather than missionary reflection, and the expectation of a coming reign of the Messiah on earth recedes from view. It is not surprising that, in the history of the church, the biblical hope of resurrection has always been recovered by and maintained among those Christian groups which were marginalized by the official ideology.

The second distortion is exemplified in the writings of those theologians who, while continuing to use 'resurrection' and 'kingdom' language, understand hope in terms of either a general anthropological characteristic such as self-transcendence or as an evolutionary unfolding of the immanent possibilities of a world-process. We have observed this Hegelian strand in the writings of Panikkar, and the evolutionary paradigm (coupled with socialism) in the case of Pieris. But God's promise of a 'new heaven and a new earth in which righteousness dwells' has no necessary connexion with cosmic or human progress. What God desires for the world and will accomplish for it is set forth in the description of the eschaton. Even if the world were to decline further and further into nuclear madness, it does not follow that God's promise to turn the spears of nations into plough-shares has failed or that our peace-making is futile. The kingdom/resurrection is a staggering and undeserved *gift*, not an achievement, and all our works of faith and love are 'signs' that point beyond our practice to the new creation that will come about by the transforming power of God in history.

In summary, we have seen that the Jewish hope of resurrection expressed, at one and the same moment, hope in the creator God's reaffirmation of his covenant with Israel and the reaffirmation of his whole creation. We shall look a little more closely at the former aspect in the next chapter, especially at the way this hope was fulfilled and also transformed by early Christian praxis. But here it is worth emphasing again that resurrection is a fresh creative act of God in which he displays his faithfulness to his creation by raising it to new life in his presence beyond death and decay. Resurrection appears as an unacceptable breach of the created order only if the creation is viewed deistically. But, as Bauckham wisely notes, resurrection is anticipated in every experience of finding life through losing it—'life rescued from the jaws of death, hope raised out of despair, freedom experienced in the face of oppression, forgiveness found beyond the vicious spiral of guilt and retribution, love given improbably to the unlovable, one's true self received through self-denial and self-giving. All such possibilities of this moral life are given by the Creator, who thus sustains, redeems and renews his creation in the face of evil and death.'[70]

Resurrection, then, is the Creator's final act of faithfulness to his creation, and the uniqueness of the resurrection of Jesus *within* history is consistent with Jesus' *self-consciously unique role* in God's saving purpose for his world.

Conclusion

It is extremely important to bear in mind such continuities and consistency when we reflect on the significance of Jesus. We have seen how the language of 'resurrection' applied to Jesus arose because his appearance on the other side of the cross, far from being a mere historical anomaly, gave coherence to his words and works before the crucifixion. Much damage has been done, both in liberal and conservative theological circles, by wrenching Jesus and early Christian preaching from their background in Old Testament and first-century Jewish belief and practice. Jesus is then turned into another itinerant Asian guru, Cynic philosopher or political revolutionary, depending on the ideological slant of the modern reader. I have argued that the much-admired lifestyle of Jesus goes hand in hand with his teaching, and that the latter is inextricably interwoven with the authoritative claims he makes about his own person and ministry. Indeed we have seen that the particular combination of lifestyle and claims that is embodied in Jesus marks him out as singularly different from Moses, the Buddha, Mohammed, Confucius or any other historical—or even fictional—character we meet in the world's cultures.

To say, as some do, that this is irrelevant, as every religious community claims uniqueness for its 'soteriological agents', is to sidestep the awkwardness of the *unique nature of the uniqueness* that is claimed by Jesus (or, if one prefers, claimed for Jesus by the early church). To say, as some do, that stressing the uniqueness of Jesus is divisive in societies where there are multiple world views, is perfectly true; but if this is taken further to imply that divisiveness must be avoided *at all cost*, then that is itself part of a particular world view that Jesus and his early disciples call into question. To say, as some do, that concepts such as 'resurrection' and 'justification' are culturally-conditioned concepts that can be detached from the Christian message without loss to its 'core experience' is to presuppose certain (also culturally con-ditioned) views of culture, experience and revelation that the biblical writers challenge.[71] The gospel of the resurrection carries its own epistemology and world view as well as its own revolutionary praxis.

The normativeness and ultimacy of Jesus Christ in God's salvific dealings with his world (which is what the language of uniqueness, I suppose, really seeks to convey), far from being an arbitrary and repressive doctrine, is *intrinsic to Christian praxis and self-understanding*, then and now, and also safeguards some of the legitimate concerns of contemporary Asian theologians. This will be the argument of our final chapters.

Notes to Chapter Six

1. H Cox, *Many Mansions: A Christian's Encounter With Other Faiths* (Boston: 1988, British edition, London: Collins, 1989) pp. 8–9.
2. Ibid. p. 6.
3. H Cox, *Religion in the Secular City: Towards a Postmodern Theology* (New York: Simon and Schuster, 1984) p. 238.
4. *Many Mansions*, op. cit. pp. 7–8.
5. S Neill, *Christian Faith and Other Faiths* (Oxford: Oxford University Press, 1970) p. 9.
6. W Pannenberg, Jesus–God and Man (London: SCM, 1968) p. 48.
7. That 'Palestinian' and 'Hellenistic' are not mutually exclusive desig-nations has been vigorously argued by Martin Hengel. See, e.g. M Hengel, *The 'Hellenization' of Judaea in the First Century After Christ* (London: SCM & Philadelphia:Trinity Press International, 1989).
8. See e.g. CFD Moule, *The Origin of Christology* (Cambridge Univer-sity Press, 1977); A Grillmeier, *Christ in Christian Tradition, vol 1: From the Apostolic Age to Chalcedon* (Eng. trans. J Bowden, Mow-brays, 1975); IH Marshall, *The Origins of New Testament Christology* (Leicester:InterVarsity, 1976); JDG Dunn, *Christology in the Making* (London:SCM, 1980); C Gunton, *Yesterday and Today: a Study of Continuities in Christology* (London: Darton, Longman & Todd, 1983).
9. The influential works have been W Bousset, *Kyrios Christos* (1913, Eng, trans, Nashville: Abingdon, 1970); and R Bultmann, *Theology of the New Testament*, vol.1 (Eng. trans. London: SCM, 1952).

10. Recent surveys and critiques of these approaches to biblical criticism can be found in S Neill and NT Wright, *The Interpretation of the New Testament, 1861–1986*, (Oxford: Oxford University, 1986[2]); AE Harvey, *Jesus and the Constraints of History* (London: SPCK, 1982); BF Meyer, *The Aims of Jesus* (London: SCM, 1979).

11. Hengel, op. cit. p. 77, 2 (Italics in text).

12. E.g. I Howard Marshall, *1 and 2 Thessalonians*, (Grand Rapids: Eerdmans, 1983) pp. 20–23.

13. E.g. the works of writers John Spong, Barbara Thiering and AN Wilson discussed and criticized by a New Testament scholar, Tom Wright, in *Who Was Jesus?* (London: Hodder, 1992). These assumptions also pervade more scholarly writings, leading to bizarre reinterpretations such as, for instance, John Crossan's attempt to portray Jesus as a 'peasant Jewish Cynic', a Galilean peasant whose understanding of the kingdom of God aligned him with itinerant Cynic philosophers rather than with Old Testament prophets or Jewish apocalyptic preachers. (*The Historical Jesus: The life of a Mediterranean Jewish Peasant*, San Francisco: Harper, 1991).

14. Jurgen Moltmann, *The Way of Jesus Christ: Christology in Messianic Dimensions* (San Fransisco: Harper, 1990) p. 137.

15. Some have seen this as the primary cause for Jesus' being handed over by some of the Jewish leaders to the Romans for crucifixion. See, e.g., N Perrin, *Rediscovering the Teaching of Jesus* (NY: Harper and Row, 1967) p. 103.

16. G Vermes, *Jesus the Jew* (London:Collins, 1973) p. 224.

17. JDG Dunn, 'Pharisees, Sinners,and Jesus' in *Jesus, Paul and the Law* (London: SPCK, 1990) p. 76. The discussion that follows is indebted to Dunn.

18. Cf. The Jewish scholar Jacob Neusner's massive 3-volume study, *The Rabbinic Traditions about the Pharisees before 70* (Leiden: EJ Brill, 1971) and the more popular *From Politics to Piety: the Emergence of Pharisaic Judaism* (Englewood Cliffs, NJ: Prentice-Hall, 1973) This general view has been disputed by EP Sanders (in *Jesus and Judaism*, Philadelphia: Fortress, 1985 and, more recently, *Jewish Law From Jesus to the Mishnah*, SCM/TPI, 1990) who believes that it is distorted by post-70 C.E anti-Jewish Christian polemic, and that there was no substantive point of disagreement between the Pharisees and Jesus. Sanders' arguments have been countered by James Dunn (in Ch.3 of *Jesus, Paul and the Law*, London: SPCK, 1990) and by Neusner himself in a review of Sanders's book ('Mr. Sanders' Pharisees and Mine', *Scottish Journal of Theology*, vol. 44, no.1, 1991). Note Neusner's scathing conclusion: 'In the end Sanders wants to defend Judaism by his re-presentation of Pharisaism in a form that, in his view, Christianity can have affirmed then and should appreciate today—and therefore now cease to denigrate. That approved Judaism turns out to be a Judaism in the model of Christianity (in Sanders's pattern) . . . his "Judaism" represented as *kosher* to Liberal Protestantism is only a caricature and an offence. With friends like Sanders, Judaism needs no enemies.' (p. 95).

19. E.g. 1QS 2:4–5;1 QS 5:7–11, CD 1:13–21; 1QH 2:8–19; 1QH 7:12.

20. E.g. 3:3–7; 4:1, 8; 9:3; 13:6–12; 15:6–7.
21. E.g. 1:8; 2:3; 8:12–13; 17:5–8.
22. Cf. E Schurer, *The History of the Jewish People in the Age of Jesus Christ*, rev. and ed. G Vermes et al., vol.2 (Edinburgh: T & T Clark, 1979): 'The Pharisees must have obtained their name from a separation in which the main body of the people did not participate, in other words, from having set themselves apart, by virtue of their stricter understanding of the concept of purity, not only from the uncleanness of the Gentiles and half-Jews but also from that uncleanness which, in their opinion, adhered to a great part of the people itself.' (pp. 396–7).
23. Occupations included in the list of 'most-despised' were: usurers, organizers of games of chance, dealers in the produce of the sabbatical year, shepherds, tax-collectors, and revenue farmers (that is, 'supervisory' tax collectors who purchased the rights to collect the taxes for a given area). Deprived *de jure* of all Jewish civic and religious rights, they were viewed as 'Jews who had made themselves Gentiles'. Another list of occupations only slightly less despised includes workers in the transport trades, herdsmen of all kinds, shopkeepers, physicians, launderers, bath attendants, and tanners. These groups were deprived de facto of Jewish rights. For full lists and commentary, see J Jeremias, *Jerusalem in the Time of Jesus* (Philadelphia: Fortress, 1969) p. 303–312.
24. Cf. J Fitzmeyer's observation: 'Three of the four ('the lame, the blind, the crippled') are mentioned (along with 'one who has a permanent blemish in his flesh') as those to be excluded . . . from the community meal in 1QSa 2:5–6', in *The Gospel According to Luke (X–XXIV)* (The Anchor Bible, NY: Doubleday, 1985) p. 1047; and also I Howard Marshall, 'It is clear that on this point Jesus was opposed to the Qumran viewpoint' in *The Gospel of Luke: a Commentary on the Greek Text* (Exeter: Paternoster, 1978) p. 584.
25. RF Gombrich, *Theravada Buddhism: a Social History from Ancient Benares to Modern Colombo* (Routledge and Kegan Paul, 1988): 'The language in which brahmanism expresses the hierarchic ranking of society is that of purity: the higher group is 'purer' than the lower. Purity and pollution are ideological constructs; but by a metaphor which still speaks to us they did have connections with cleanliness. Excreta are polluting, and purity is commonly regained by bathing. Personal purity, which is a way of conceiving how to deal with ineluctable biological facts, was not the same as the social purity of a descent group, but the two were related. Thus a menstruating woman and a corpse were both impure, so those who professionally handle garments stained by menstrual blood or dispose of corpses are permanently impure, and their children inherit that impurity even before they begin to exercise their professions.' (pp. 39–40).
26. Ibid. p. 205.
27. N Chaudhuri, *Hinduism* (London: Chatto and Windus, 1979) p. 315.
28. Ibid. p. 325.
29. E.g Matt 5–7.

30. The link between the appointing of the twelve and the twelve tribes of Israel is indicated by Matt 19:28, Lk 22:30.

31. See, e.g., JL Austin, *How to do Things with Words* (Oxford: Clarendon Press, 1962); JR Searle, *Expression and Meaning: Studies in the Theory of Speech Acts* (Cambridge: Cambridge University Press, 1979); AC Thiselton provides an excellent survey of speech-act theories and their application to biblical studies in *New Horizons in Hermeneutics* (HarperCollins, 1992) pp. 272–307. He explores further the implications for christology in a paper entitled 'Christology in Luke, Speech-Act Theory and the Problem of Dualism After Kant' 'in *Jesus of Nazareth: Lord and Christ*, eds. J Green and M Turner (Grand Rapids: Eerdmans and Carlisle: Paternoster, 1994). I follow Thiselton in his application of Austin and Searle to the christological context.

32. Thiselton, 'Christology in Luke . . .', op. cit. p. 466 (Italics in text).

33. Cf. JL Austin, op. cit. pp. 94–119.

34. For the view that by forgiving sins in his own name (that is, as the Son of Man) Jesus implicitly claims a divine prerogative and thus provokes the theologians of his day, see S Kim, *The Son of Man as the Son of God*, WUNT 30 (Tubingen: JCB Mohr [Paul Siebeck], 1983); IH Marshall, *The Gospel of Luke: a Commentary on the Greek Text* (Grand Rapids: Eerdmans, 1978, p. 213). Note that there is no Jewish tradition that the Messiah has the right to forgive sins. The Messiah would exterminate the godless in Israel, crush demonic power and protect his people from the rule of sin, but the forgiveness of sin was never attributed to him. Jesus does not speak (either here or in Luke 7:48) as an agent, priestly or prophetic or angelic, assuring the other of God's forgiveness on the day of final judgment, nor does he offer a provisional pardon to be later ratified by a higher court.

35. Many commentators draw attention to the contrast with Jewish and pagan charismatic exorcists. E.g. William Lane, *The Gospel of Mark* (London: Marshall, Morgan and Scott, 1974) pp. 74–5: 'In contrast to contemporary exorcists, who identified themselves by name or by relationship to some deity or power, who pronounced some spell or performed some magical action, Jesus utters only a few direct words, through which his absolute authority over the demonic power that held the man captive was demonstrated.' More recently, Grant Osborne, in an essay 'Structure and Christology in Mark 1:21–45' (in *Jesus of Nazareth: Lord and Christ*, eds. Green and Turner, op. cit) writes: 'The startling aspect of these stories (indeed of the exorcism miracles) is that there is never any actual battle. Jesus expels the demons wih hardly a conflict, and the battle is over before it can begin . . . In one sense the silencing of demons is emblematic of Jesus' total victory in the cosmic war (v.25); in another sense the silencing is to keep them from making his true identity known ('Because they knew him', v.34). Jesus refuses to identify with the people's fascination with him as a wonder worker. This is connected with Mark's theme on the hiddenness of Jesus, who cannot be understood apart from the events of the cross and resurrection. It is

also connected with Jesus' desire to avoid the sensational, which
leads him to go to the remote places rather than the densely
populated areas.' (p. 163).

36. RT France draws out the implications of Jesus' rebuking of the
    storm: 'In the Old Testament it was a mark of the sovereignty of
    God himself that the sea obeyed his orders (Job 38:8–11; Ps 65:5–8;
    89:8, 9 etc); a passage like Psalm 107:23–32 must have been in
    Matthew's mind as he narrated this story and recorded the response
    of amazed recognition. He does not draw out the implication
    explicitly, but in the light of the Old Testament passages above it is
    clearly revolutionary. Jesus is being progressively revealed as the
    Messiah-and more', *The Gospel According to Matthew: an Introduction
    and Commentary* (Leicester: Inter-Varsity Press and Grand Rapids:
    Eerdmans, 1985) p. 162.

37. R Bultmann, *Theology of the New Testament, II*, p. 43, quoted in
    Thiselton, *New Horizons*, op. cit. p. 285.

38. For summaries of the monotheism of Second Temple Judaism, see
    e.g. AE Harvey, *Jesus and the Constraints of History* (Philadelphia:
    Westminster, 1982) pp. 154–73; NT Wright, *The New Testament and
    the People of God* (London: SPCK, 1992) pp. 248–259.

39. Cf. Thiselton's observation that 'Language about the Kingdom of
    God . . . does include the dual dimensions of the ontological and the
    existential. The Kingdom of God in the apocalyptic tradition
    represents God's cosmic reign; 'taking upon oneself the yoke of
    the Kingdom' in rabbinic traditions entails human obedience and
    response.' (*New Horizons in Hermeneutics*, op. cit. pp. 287–8).

40. JP Meier, *The Vision of Matthew: Christ, Church and Morality in the
    First Gospel* (New York: Paulist Press, 1979) p. 43.

41. JG du Plessis, *Clarity and Obscurity: A Study in Textual Communication
    of the Relation Between Sender,Parable,and Receiver in the Synoptic
    Gospels* (University of Stellenbosch D Theol Dissertation, 1985),
    quoted in A Thiselton, *New Horizons*, op. cit. p. 289 (my italics).

42. CL Blomberg, *Interpreting the Parables* (Downers Grove, Ill: IVP,
    1990) p. 319. He argues further that the 'implicit Christology' of the
    parables 'stands as strong a chance as any of representing what the
    historical Jesus actually intended to communicate. For, on the one
    hand, it remains sufficiently muted and ambiguous that it would not
    likely have arisen in the early church. A post-Easter desire to exalt
    Jesus would have almost certainly done so more explicitly.' (p. 322).

43. *New Horizons in Hermeneutics*, op. cit. p. 287 (Italics in text).

44. The Aramaic word *Abba* that Jesus used was preserved in the early
    Church and used by Christians (Rom 8:15; Gal 4:6). The most
    exhaustive study of the word and the authenticity of the sayings in
    which it occurs remains that of J Jeremias, *Abba* (Gottingen, 1966)
    and *The Prayers of Jesus* (ET, London: SCM, 1967) pp. 11–65. The
    significance Jeremias attaches to the word Abba has been challenged
    by J Barr, ' "Abba" isn't "Daddy" ', *Journal of Theological Studies*,
    1988, 39, pp. 28–47. Although Barr is correct to question the use of
    term as a child's word for 'Daddy', this does not affect the

fundamental issue that Jesus spoke of God as his Father in a way that was unique (or, at least, extremely rare) in Palestinian Judaism.

45. For the Semitic character of this saying, see Jeremias, *Abba*, op. cit., pp. 47–51. A full discussion of its authenticity can be found in JDG Dunn, *Jesus and the Spirit* (London: SCM, 1975) pp. 27–34. See also RJ Bauckham, 'The Sonship of the Historical Jesus in Christology', *Scottish Journal of Theology*, 1978, 31, pp. 245–60.

46. As is well known, the theme of Sonship is specially prominent in the Fourth Gospel. In the fifth chapter, the Jews perceive that the manner in which Jesus keeps referring to God as his Father is virtually tantamount to a rival claim to deity and so take steps to get rid of him (Jn 5:18). Jesus replies that his relationship to God is not one of rivalry but rather of humble submission. He is in a position of total dependence on his Father for all his words and works (v.19, 36; cf 14:24). He models his life on his heavenly Father even as a boy in a typical Jewish home would apprentice himself to his father and so learn the latter's craft. Yet, in the same breath, he goes on to claim that 'whatever the Father does the Son does' (v.19) and that 'the Father loves the Son and shows him all that he does' (v.20). While other prophets and sages may have received a glimpse into the heart of God and been 'mouthpieces' of his will to humankind, Jesus claims that the knowledge he enjoys of God is total and exhaustive, the fruit of a unique intimacy. The Father has entrusted all judgment to the Son, so that 'all may honour the Son as they honour the Father' (v.22, 23). So closely is Jesus bound up with his Father, both in his person and in his words and deeds, that every attitude directed towards him is no less directed towards God. Failure to honour him is failure to honour the Father (v.23), to perceive who he is is to perceive the Father (14:8ff), and so on.

47. See RT France, *The Gospel According to Matthew* (Leicester: IVP and Grand Rapids: Eerdmans, 1985) p. 201.

48. See e.g. RT France, *Jesus and the Old Testament* (London: Tyndale, 1971) pp. 125–32, 148–50.

49. See Mk 10:42–45; Lk 22:24–7.

50. E.g. Matt 7:21–23, 10:28.

51. For the authenticity of this saying and its basis in Is. 52:13–53:12, see e.g. France, *Jesus and the Old Testament*, op. cit. pp. 116–121.

52. For the idea of redemptive covenant blood see especially Exodus 24:8 and Zech. 9:11. It is interesting that the latter appears immediately after the prophecy of the humble king riding into Zion on a donkey. Note also how the fourth Servant Song of Isaiah (52:13–53:12) with its theme of substitutionary atonement follows 52:7 which announces Yahweh's return to Zion and the inauguration of his universal reign. For the understanding, in some circles, of the second-century BC Maccabean martyrdoms as atoning sacrifices for the sins of the nation (under the influence, no doubt, of Is. 53 and Gen. 22) see 4 Macc. 6:29, 17:21ff (cf. 2 Macc 6–7).

53. Even EP Sanders, *Jesus and Judaism*, op. cit. p. 324, admits that 'The Christian interpretation of Jesus' death as atoning was so immediate

and so thorough that one could argue that even here Jesus prepared his followers'.

54. R Gombrich, 'Introduction: The Buddhist Way', in *The World of Buddhism: Buddhist Monks and Nuns in Society and Culture,* Heinz Bechert and Richard Gombrich (London, 1984) p. 13. In a famous simile, the Buddha compared his doctrine to a raft (*Majjhima Nikaya,* 1, 134–5). Just as one uses a raft to cross a river, but only a fool would carry the raft on the further shore, so his teaching was intended to help men across the ocean of samsara; once they were across, they could go their way without depending on his words.

55. The chief priests in Jerusalem and most of the lay aristocratic familes belonged to the party we know as the Sadducees. We know little about them except for their political conservatism, perpetual dog-fights with the Pharisees, and their denial of the hope of resurrection. The latter had nothing to do with 'rationalist' scepticism regarding its physical possibility, but was an offshoot of their privileged status. A hope that centred on an overturning of Israel's status quo (as we shall see below) would not have been congenial to the guardians of that status quo. See.e.g. NT Wright, *The New Testament and the People of God* (London: SPCK, 1992) pp. 209–213; EP Sanders, *Judaism: Practice and Belief,* 63 BCE–66CE (London: SCM & Philadelphia: Trinity Press International, 1992) ch.10.

56. A typical example of the important shift that has taken place is seen in this excerpt from P Perkins who, though she does not deny the validity of the empty tomb tradition, can write: 'Nor . . can one insist that if a tomb containing the body of Jesus were to be found by archaeologists, the Christian proclamation of Jesus as the one who has been raised and exalted by God would be destroyed and with it the Christian claims about Jesus' place in salvation', *Resurrection: NT Witness and Contemporary Reflection,* (New York: Doubleday, 1984) p. 84. Indifference towards empirical claims/evidence indicates an understanding of resurrection and salvation very different from that proclaimed by the apostles.

57. According to the biblical witness, the actual resurrection of Jesus, unlike the empty tomb and the post-resurrection appearances, had no witnesses but remained a divine mystery, the truth of which can only be confessed in faith. It cannot be established by any historical method that works with secular presuppositions. Acts 10:41 also states that Jesus 'was not seen by all people, but by witnesses whom God had already chosen'. But it is a fallacy to conclude from this that it is, therefore, 'merely subjective'. It claims to be a real event with real consequences for both the human and non-human world. The empty tomb tradition, the post-resurrection appearances and the beginnings of the Christian movement are valid, and important, subjects for historical enquiry.

58. 2 Maccabees 7:9, 14, 21–29. See also 12:43–45; 14:45ff.

59. See e.g. Wright, op. cit. pp. 320–334.

60. R Bauckham, 'God Who Raises the Dead: the Resurrection of Jesus and Early Christian Faith in God' in *The Resurrection of Jesus Christ,* ed. Paul Avis (London: Darton,Longman & Todd, 1993).

61. Ibid. p. 136.
62. Echoed again in 2 Cor 1:9 and John 5:21.
63. For God's gift of life in desperate situations, see, for instance, such passages as Gen 25:21, 29:31, 30:22–23; Ps 30:3, 86:13; Is 38:10; Jonah 2:6; 1 Samuel 1, 2:4–8; Daniel 3:28, 6:23.
64. Ibid. p. 143. Wright also draws attention to the fact that 'the eschatological expectation of most Jews of this period was for a renewal, not an abandonment, of the present space-time order as a whole, and themselves within it. Since this was based on the justice and mercy of the creator god, the god of Israel, it was inconceivable that those who had died in the struggle to bring the new world into being should be left out of the blessing when it eventually broke upon the nation and thence on the world', op. cit. pp. 331–2.
65. Wright, op. cit. p. 400 (emphasis in text).
66. Ibid.
67. Jewish 'apocalyptic' language uses cosmic imagery to express the theological significance of dramatic, *this-worldly* events.
68. GB Caird, *The Language and Imagery of the Bible* (London: Duckworth, 1980) p. 51.
69. In the equivalent sayings of Lk 9:24, Mk 8:35 and Matt 16:25, this losing of life is 'for my sake'. We have noted the implications of this for the authority of Jesus in an earlier section.
70. Op. cit. p. 153.
71. See the discussion of Ch. 5.

[7]

A Gospel for the World

Perhaps the best-known feature of the early Christians was their sense of world mission. The impetus to mission sprang from the very heart of the gospel itself. Missionary outreach, both to Jews and to pagans, was not an activity tagged on later to a faith that was basically 'about' something else (e.g. a new metaphysical system); rather, it flowed from the very logic of the death and resurrection of Jesus. The truth that the early Christians believed had been disclosed in Jesus was *for* the world because it was *about* the world. It revealed both the tragic alienation of the world from its Creator and the glorious hope of its reconciliation and recreation. Consequently, as Ben Meyer observes, 'Christianity was never more *itself* than in the launching of the world mission.'[1]

The missionary thrust of the early Christians was a force for cultural awakening and integration. Bethlehem, Nazareth and even Jerusalem swiftly recede from view, and the new Christian communities that sprang up, eastwards and westwards, recognized no fixed geographical centre. The church did not sacralize the place of its origins. What is even more remarkable, especially in comparison with the great world religions of Semitic and Asian origin, is that the original language that Jesus used in his preaching was quickly abandoned in favour of country (*koine*) Greek and 'vulgar' Latin as the uniting media of communication. The entire New Testament was written in a language other than the one in which Jesus preached. That the eternal counsels of God belonged to the commonplace, everyday speech of ordinary men and women was a view that was, and remains, revolutionary. It resisted the tendency in some parts of the early church to cast the gospel into an elitist gnostic-type discourse. Unlike the widespread 'mystery religions' (and the dominant ethos of traditional Vedic, Tantric and Buddhist religious thought and practice), no attempt was made to develop a professional cultic language or make a virtue out of elitist secrecy.[2]

A Mission Movement

Tom Wright has vividly captured the striking speed of growth of the early Christian movement: 'In AD 25 there is no such thing as Christianity: merely a young hermit in the Judean wilderness, and his somewhat younger cousin who dreams dreams and sees visions. By AD 125 the Roman emperor has established an official policy in relation to the punishment of Christians; Polycarp has already been a Christian in Smyrna for half a century; Aristides (if we accept the earlier date) is confronting the emperor Hadrian with the news that there are four races in the world, Barbarians, Greeks, Jews and Christians; and a young pagan called Justin . . . tells of his meeting with an old man who talked to him about Jesus. Pliny speaks of the poison of Christianity spreading into villages and countryside. Ignatius finds churches wherever he goes throughout Asia Minor. Tacitus, in the tone of voice of one who has come across a dead rat in his water-tank, comments that all the worst features of world culture find their way to Rome sooner or later.'[3] Evidently not only the apostles but many 'ordinary' (unknown) Christian men and women saw it as entirely natural to their faith to travel about the known world and to tell those they met, irrespective of culture and religious adherence, that there was 'another King', namely Jesus.

Such a message was deeply offensive for more than one reason. The Jesus of whom the Christians spoke had been crucified, not too long ago, by the Roman authorities. Crucifixion, though widespread and frequent in the Roman world, was viewed with horror and disgust. The great senator and orator Cicero declared that 'the very word "cross" should be far removed not only from the presence of a Roman citizen but from his thoughts, his eyes and his ears'.[4] Crucifixion was a way of obliterating not only the victim but also the very memory of him. A crucified man had never existed. It is in a world such as this that we meet a movement of people proclaiming that among those forgotten 'nobodies', those degraded criminals of the Roman empire, there had been one who was no less than the Son of God, the Lord of Caesar himself!

Morever, the earliest Christian profession, 'Jesus is Lord', was never merely a statement of personal devotion but a claim to universal validity. Christian mission made sense only on the premise that the crucified Jesus had been enthroned as the true Lord of the whole world, and thus claiming the allegiance of the whole world. The Roman pantheon was most hospitable and could readily accommodate any new deity in a manner somewhat similar to that of Hindu *Vedanta*. The public cultus of the emperor was a way of preserving the cultural and religious pluralism of the empire. The new Christian movement would have been accorded a ready welcome if it took its place as simply another private cultus among the myriad that the empire boasted. The early Christians refused the offer. For them Jesus was not a deified man, like the emperors the senate decreed to be divine; nor was he a mythological hero, like Hercules. His labours had been real: the humiliating agony of a cross in the reign of Tiberias.

It was not only the message that proved subversive but the lifestyle in which it was expressed. The Christians behaved as a new social grouping in the ancient world, a non-racial fellowship comprising both Jews and pagans.[5] They affirmed, again and again, their loyalty to Jewish monotheism, but parted company from mainstream Judaism in using the language of divinity in worship to Jesus and in refusing to define the people of God in the traditional Jewish sense of ethnic identity. They perceived themselves to be a 'third race', neither Jewish nor Gentile but drawing men and women from both.[6] The gospel constituted a new category of human being, a new way of being human. Their primary identity was found in a new familial community whose social inclusiveness was unparalleled. Despite their marginal social status, their vision embraced the whole empire and beyond. They believed they were the means by which God was bringing to fulfilment the Jewish hope of a global peace, while they themselves were *paroikoi* (1 Pet. 2:11)—resident aliens—at home everywhere, but settled nowhere.

At the cross-cultural frontiers of mission much creative innovation occurred. The complex plurality of cultural forms was upheld as linguistic and other cultural resources were rummaged for tools through which the message of Jesus could be conveyed. No cultures were inherently unclean, and none was absolutized in its particularity. All cultures in their distinctiveness could serve the one God's unfolding purpose for human life. Tribal self-awareness became a frontier in the course of the gospel, but tribalism itself was sabotaged.

So, while showing loyalty to the Roman state, they held loosely to local custom. They were accused by their pagan neighbours of 'atheism', which, in the ancient world, meant not so much the denial of the existence of gods or of a supreme deity, but the failure to pay proper honour to the gods (or god) in public religious rituals. Not only did they refuse to burn incense before the statue of Caesar, they set up no statues of their own god. They did not consult oracles, make pilgrimages to sacred sites, erect temples or offer animal sacrifices. They did not organize themselves into a political grouping or a military force. Indeed they scorned the traditional Roman values of honour and glory as mere vanity. They incurred popular suspicion, resentment or outrage by boycotting gladiatorial shows and other brutal forms of mass entertainment which provided a focal point of popular identity; by saving female infants who were left exposed in the open to die; by teaching a stern ethic of sexual morality, and by standing aloof to both the incessant glorying in military achievements and the competitive struggle for civic 'honour' that pagan political life took for granted. The social and political pluralism of Greco-Roman paganism could make room for the Christian God within its expansive pantheon. But what it could not tolerate was its social order being called into question by Christian values.

It is sometimes suggested that the first- and second-century Mediterranean world, in contrast, say, to the worlds of India and China, was easy to evangelize as the gospel entered a spiritual/ideological vaccuum. Stoicism was too dry and remote from the masses, popular religion was morally lax and invited the scorn of the philosophers, the mystery cults were complex, esoteric and forbidding. Judaism, while it attracted many monotheistic pagans, was too tied to strange customs to win their full adherence (and, in any case, after 70 C.E it became introverted and law-bound). While there is some truth in this overall picture, it hardly does justice to historical reality. The Christian gospel

summoned proud pagans to be willing to face torture and
death out of loyalty to a crucified Jewish peasant. We have
seen how Christians advocated a love which cuts across
racial boundaries, and provoked widespread hatred by challenging many practices in the pagan world which were taken
for granted, even by the most sophisticated intellectuals. If
one wanted a comfortable life or to move ahead in respectable social circles, the last thing one did was to become a
Christian.

As Wright observes,

> Choosing to become a Christian was not an easy or natural
> thing for the average pagan. A Jew who converted might well
> be regarded as a national traitor. Even slaves, who might be
> supposed to have less to lose than others, and hence to
> appreciate an elevation of status through conversion, might face
> a cost . . . Pliny thought it normal to interrogate, with torture,
> slave-girls who happened to be part of the early Christian
> movement. We have no reason to suppose that interrogation
> under torture was any easier for a young woman in the second
> century that it is in the twentieth.[7]

Likewise, in most parts of Asia today, Christians live as
politically marginalized communities. Until very recently a
Nepali Hindu who chose to become a Christian was punish-
able by imprisonment under the national constitution; in
Malaysia and Pakistan, Muslims who become Christians lose
many of their civic rights; Christians in China are denied
access to high academic and other public office; and all over
the continent, Christian converts are subject to intimidation,
ostracism and frequent violence at the hands of family and
neighbours.

Why, then, did pagans become Christians in the Roman
world prior to Christendom? It could not have been because
pagans found Christian meetings attractive, for after the
Neronian persecution of the mid–60s Christian churches
closed their doors to outsiders. Christianity was deemed a
superstitio, a deviation from acceptable norms of behaviour,
no longer under the protection accorded to a *religio licita* like
Judaism, so that letting anyone into worship services would
have been dangerous. Conversions came about primarily
through pagans coming into casual contact with their
Christian neighbours. They not only heard the message

about Jesus from their lips but saw that message enfleshed in a community that was truly *free*.

The catechist Justin, writing in Rome in the mid years of the second century, observed that people were turning away 'from the ways of violence and tyranny' because they were drawn to Christians as those whose lives were free of the addictions of greed, sex, xenophobia and the bondage of the magic arts. The hesitation of pagans was 'overcome by observing the consistent lives of their neighbours, or noting the strange patience of their injured acquaintances, or experiencing the way they did business with them'.[8] Justin writes of the liberating effect of the gospel on people like himself:

> Those who once rejoiced in fornication now delight in continence alone; those who made use of magic arts have dedicated themselves to the good and unbegotten God; we who once took most pleasure in the means of increasing our wealth and property now bring what we have into a common fund and share with everyone in need; we who hated and killed one another and would not associate with people of different tribes because of [their different] customs, now after the manifestation of Christ live together and pray for our enemies . . .[9]

Moreover, as Robin Lane Fox points out, 'whereas pagan cults won adherents, Christianity aimed, and contrived, to win converts. It won them by conviction and persuasion . . .'[10] Not surprisingly, the church cut across the stratifications of society, making 'the least-expected social groups articulate'[11]—slaves, women, those thrown on the local rubbish dumps as unwanted babies. While many, especially patrician males, were appalled at the social inclusivity and generosity of the Christian community, others were attracted to it.

Election and Mission

We saw in the previous chapter that the synoptic Gospels tell the story of Jesus, and especially that of his cross and resurrection, not as an historical 'quirk', a sudden and bizarre eruption of divine power into history, but as the climax to a much longer story, the story of Israel, which in turn is the pivotal focus of the story of the Creator's involvement with his world. We have seen that the Christian movement began when a group of bewildered and frightened Jews came to the conclusion that Israel's hopes (the resurrection to life, the forgiveness of sin, the return from exile and the dawning of Yahweh's rule) had all come true in the death and resurrection of Jesus of Nazareth. It cannot be emphasized too strongly that the apostles never understood themselves to be founding a 'new religion'. The lens through which they perceived reality was fundamentally a recognizable version, albeit radically transformed, of the Jewish worldview. The story of Jesus and the experience of his Spirit in the life of the Jesus community is proclaimed as the final phase of Israel's story, a story that begins with the divine calling of Abraham and the divine word of promise concerning the nations.

The Hebrew Bible sets the call of Abraham and the emergence of the people of Israel against the dramatic background of the story of creation and the alienation of all the 'families of the earth' from their Creator. All human beings share in the solidarity of sin and death. Sin has disfigured and corrupted all human relationships—with God, with the earth, and with one another. It is on the heels of a depressing narrative about collective human rebellion (Gen. 11) that we read of God's call to Abraham: to distance himself from Babylon, the archetypal city of human arrogance and wickedness, and to begin an adventure in the wilderness alone with God. The covenant that God makes with him in Gen. 12 is ultimately for the blessing of 'all the families of the earth'. The effects of sin are universal, but God's redemptive purpose is equally universal. God works with the one man and his family while his gaze, so to speak, is on all the families of the earth. God's final word on even Babylon itself is not one of judgment but of hope—but a hope that is to be mediated through the heirs of Abraham.

The God of the biblical revelation, then, is the God of universal history. But he brings that history to its goal ('salvation') through the particular history of a particular people. This interplay between the universal and the unique runs right through the Old Testament narrative. One striking example occurs in the early chapters of Deuteronomy. That Yahweh is not Israel's tribal deity but the sovereign God of the whole earth, actively involved in the histories of nations other than Israel, is the axiomatic framework within which the uniqueness of Israel is repeatedly emphasized (note, for instance, the tantalizing glimpses the narrator gives of Yahweh's sovereignty in the migrations and conquests that marked the pre-Israelite history of Canaan, 2:9–

12, 20–23).[12] But it is only within Israel that Yahweh works in terms of a redemptive covenant, initiated and preserved by his grace. The people of Israel had experienced something unparalleled 'from the day God created man on the earth' and 'from one end of the heavens to the other' (4:32): a unique revelation of Yahweh and a unique experience of his redemptive power (4: 7–8, 32–38). This was all of sheer grace, never to be construed as favouritism (e.g. 7:7–8), to which the only appropriate response was to imitate Yahweh's awesome love towards the weak and the alien (e.g. 10:14ff).

'You were shown these things so that you mght know that Yahweh is God; beside him there is no other' (4:35). This is the heart of the monotheism of Israel. It had little to do with mathematical unity, even less with a new-found conviction of a single Supreme Being beyond (or underlying) the multiplicity of gods (real or imagined)—beliefs by no means confined to ancient Israel. Israel had been vouchsafed a unique historical experience of Yahweh's character and purpose for his creation. It is this that enabled them to bear witness to *his* uniqueness as the living God (e.g. Is. 43:8–13). Israel existed as a nation at all only because of Yahweh's intention to redeem people from every nation. While Yahweh works in all nations, in no nation other than Israel did he act *for the sake of* all nations. Israel's unique experience of Yahweh issues in a unique socio-political witness to Yahweh among the nations, for their covenantal obedience to Yahweh now takes the form of imitating Yahweh's dealings with Israel. The distinctiveness of Israel's social, political and economic structures were an integral part of their theological significance in God's saving purpose for his world.[13] To choose to respond to the true God was to choose the truly human as well. This distinctiveness was the means by which God would attract the nations to himself, so that ultimately all the earth would acknowledge and experience the gracious rule of Yahweh as the only true and living God.

But in the meantime, where the universal eschatological vision impinges on the present historical situation, there is spiritual and social conflict—between Yahweh and every other claimant to deity. This is a conflict that ran through Israel's national life as well as in her dealings with her pagan neighbours. The great temptation Israel faced, and to which she repeatedly succumbed, was to think of Yahweh too as simply another tribal deity and to worship him in terms derived from an alien religious framework, thus betraying the revelation entrusted to her for the sake of the nations. Such betrayal robbed Israel of her self-identity and any claim to uniqueness. 'The whole OT (and the NT as well) is filled with descriptions of how Yahweh-Adonai, the covenant God of Israel, is waging war against those forces which try to thwart and subvert his plans for his creation. He battles against those false gods which human beings have fashioned from the created world, idolized, and used for their own purpose . . . the Baals and the Ashteroth, whose worshippers elevated nature, the tribe, the state and the nation to a divine status. God fights against magic and idolatry which, according to Deuteronomy, bend the line between God and his creation. He contends against every form of social injustice and pulls off every cloak under which it seeks to hide.'[14]

As the Old Testament scholar Christopher Wright perceptively reminds us, the calling of Israel to bear faithful witness to the revelation of the living God entrusted to her was 'not a matter of Israel's flaunting their privilege in an attitude of "Our religion is is better than yours"—as if Israel's faith was one among many brands of a commodity, "human religion". Rather what was at stake, what was so threatened by Israel compromising with the gods and worship of other nations, was the continuity of the redemptive work of the Creator God of all mankind within the unique historical and social context which he himself had chosen.'[15] Wright notes that Israel's mission as a nation was to be both holy, i.e. distinctive, and priestly, representing God (Ex 19:3–6). In the light of this calling 'for Israel to have accepted Canaanite and other religions as equally valid and acceptable alternatives to their own faith would have been no act of tolerance, kindness or maturity. It would have been an utter betrayal of the rest of mankind, for the sake of whose salvation they had been chosen and redeemed.'[16]

But what of the fact that God addressed the patriarchs of Israel and entered into covenant with them in terms of divine names and religious forms that they derived from their contemporary culture? We need to remember that the covenant between God and Abraham was grounded in God's saving initiative ('grace') and self-disclosure, and not on the

sincerity or validity of Abraham's previous worship. Moreover, as Wright observes, the Pentateuchal tradition is best
understood as a case of divine accommodation or assimilation:
the living God accommodating his self-revelation to a
human social-religious framework of concepts, myths, rites
and divine titles—'but breaking through that framework
with new and richer promises and acts'.[17] The purpose of
God's election of Abraham was not to endorse the religion of
El and the Mesopotamian pantheon, but 'to lead Abraham
and his descendants beyond it into a personal relationship
with God in *preparation* for the full experience of redemption
and thereby for full knowledge of his true name and
character.'[18]

It is precisely this biblical stress on the historical and
cultural 'particularity' (or 'situatedness') of human life, a
particularity that God takes seriously in his dealings with his
creatures, that challenges both the ancient Indian and the
post-Enlightenment Western world views. Thinkers nurtured in either tradition find the biblical teaching on divine
election troublesome, if not downright offensive. Why does
God not reveal himself directly to every individual human
soul? The biblical answer, never explicit but presupposed
from beginning to end, is simply that human beings are not
autonomous spiritual/rational 'essences', abstracted from
their location within social and material relationships that
develop through space and time. Biblical teaching about
election can be grasped only when seen as part of the
characteristically biblical way of understanding human reality.
Human life consists in mutual relationships: a mutual inter-
dependence that is not simply a temporary phase in the
journey towards salvation but one that is intrinsic to the *goal*
of salvation itself. If God's way of blessing 'all the families of
the earth' (a term, by the way, which itself expresses an
understanding of humanness in terms of personal relations)
is to be addressed to those families in their concrete situations,
and not to unreal abstractions such as 'immortal souls' or
'autonomous selves', then it must be accomplished through
election—calling and sending *some* as vehicles of that blessing
for *all*—so that human community may be freed from
fragmentation and recreated in communion with God.

The Hebrew Bible, then, presents a vision of the world
from its creation to its consummation, of the nations of the
world forming one human family under God, and the story

of a nation called by God to be the bearer of the meaning of cosmic history to the rest. That meaning cannot be 'read off' the events of history. It is not inherent to the historical process. It is not the outcome of the evolutionary unfolding of cosmic forces. It is a matter of divine *promise*. A promise concerning God's defeat of the powers of evil and death which seem to rob all life, whether the private life of the individual or the public life of nations, of any meaning. For the early disciples of Jesus that promise, first bequeathed to a nation, had seen the dawn of its fulfilment in an individual human being. They were now witnesses of that promise, in continuity with Old Testament Israel but now in fellowship with other men and women drawn from all nations. The promise was focused now in the crucified and risen Christ.

We have seen how the deep rift beween those who claimed to be the heirs of the promise on the basis of Torah, Temple, and Race, and those who claimed the same thing on the basis of Jesus and his Spirit-indwelt community, goes back behind the New Testament writings to the moment when some hitherto frightened Jews saw in the resurrected Jesus the embodiment of the hope of Israel. This did not not make Christianity anti-Jewish, any more than the Essenes, Pharisees, or any other sect or group, were anti-Jewish. But the retelling of the story of Israel in the story of Jesus, and the radical transformation of the traditional Jewish symbols, meant that the Jewish world view was subverted from within.

This is evident in all the New Testament writings, and especially in the epistles of Paul and the epistle to the Hebrews. Paul understood his own vocation, to be the apostle to the Gentiles, as part of a wider gospel framework according to which the Creator God was fulfilling his promise to Abraham. Although his preaching of the gospel subverted the narrative world of his Jewish contemporaries no less than it did the pagan stories, his claim was that it actually reinstated the true sense of the covenant promises.[19] The end of exile and the restoration of Israel are not now future events to be experienced in terms of a cleansed Land, a rebuilt Temple, an intensified Torah.

> The exile came to its catalysmic end when Jesus, Israel's representative Messiah, died outside the walls of Jerusalem, bearing the curse, which consisted of exile at the hands of the pagans, to its utmost limit. The return from exile began when

Jesus, again as the representative Messiah, emerged from the tomb three days later. As a result the whole complex of Jewish expectations as to what would happen when the exile finished had come tumbling out in a rush. Israel's God had poured out his own Spirit on all flesh; his word was going out to the nations . . .[20]

Thus for Paul, as for all the other New Testament writers, it is the universality of God's saving love which is the ground of his choosing and calling a community to be the messengers of his truth and bearers of his love for all peoples. As we have seen (in Chapter 5) all rationality is socially embodied; so that neither truth nor love can be communicated except as they are embodied in a community which reasons and loves. For the Christian community such reasoning and loving find both their starting point and criterion of truth in the self-revelation of God in Jesus Christ. The church is a particular community among other particular communities in the world. But it has a universal mission. To be elect in Christ Jesus means to be incorporated into his mission to the world, to be the bearer of God's saving purpose for his whole world.

What this means is that the particular body of people who bear the name of Jesus through history, 'this strange and often absurd company of people so feeble, so foolish, so often fatally compromised with the world, this body with all its contingency and particularity',[21] is the body which has been entrusted with the 'open secret' of God's kingdom at work through human history. As Newbigin puts it: 'The logic of election is . . . that in and through history there should be brought into being that which is symbolized in the vision with which the Bible ends—the Holy City into which all the glory of the nations will finally be gathered. But—and of course this is the crux of the matter—that consummation can only lie on the other side of death and resurrection. It is the calling of the Church to bear through history to its end the secret of the lordship of the crucified.'[22]

Incarnation and Universality

We have seen that the uniqueness of ancient Israel and the uniqueness of Yahweh, the Creator God of the covenant, flow together in the Hebrew Bible. Israel's calling was to embody in her communal life Yahweh's character and purpose for his creation. In the previous chapter we saw how, in the light of their experience of the resurrected Jesus and the unique authority with which he spoke and acted in the days of his public ministry, the early Christians under-went a radical transformation in their understanding of God and came to accord to Jesus a worship that, in their Jewish context, was due to God alone. They unconditionally ascribed lordship to him. Whenever the New Testament writers speak of Jesus Christ, with all their rich diversity, it is to point to his *theological* significance: in some way or the other he is the presence of the eternal, infinite God in time and space.[23] He embodies the identity and mission of Israel by embodying the identity and mission of Israel's God.

In the apostolic church this christological focus finds its most famous expression in the Johannine prologue: 'The Word became flesh and made his dwelling among us. We have seen his glory, the glory of the One and Only, who came from the Father, full of grace and truth' (Jn 1:14). Similarly, Paul says that in Christ 'all the fullness of the Deity lives in bodily form' (Col. 2:9); that 'God was pleased to have his fullness dwell in him and through him to reconcile to himself all things whether on earth or heaven, by making peace through his blood shed on the cross' (Col. 1:19–20). Writing about sacrifices to idols, he affirms that 'there is no God but one' and only 'one Lord, Jesus Christ, through whom are all things and through whom we live' (1 Cor. 8:4ff).[24] Even more striking are the many passages where these truths are implied, rather than explicitly stated. We noted in our critique of Samartha's use of the New Testament (Chapter 1) that even the very early Christian hymn which Paul uses in Phil. 2:6ff not only confesses the incarnation and exaltation of Jesus Christ but applies to him an Old Testament text which affirmed the uniqueness and supremacy of *Yahweh*.[25] Similarly the prophet Joel's injunc-tion 'to call on the name of Yahweh' for salvation now becomes 'to call on the name of Jesus' (Rom. 10:13, cf. Joel 2:32). The 'Spirit of God' and the 'Spirit of Christ', the 'love of God' and the 'love of Christ' are used interchangeably, for example in Romans 8.

In a book on christological method entitled *Yesterday and Today*, Professor Colin Gunton points out that the move-ment in early Christian thought was not from an abstraction called 'the Jesus of history' to the unity of Jesus with his

Father, but rather a growing understanding of Jesus' eternal significance and reality. 'What begins by seeing him oriented to the future ends by conceiving him as also the incarnation of a pre-existent Word of God'.[26] Gunton wryly observes: 'That a particular human being should, in the past, have been a unique spatio-temporal instantiation of the divine, is the most intellectually offensive of all Christian claims. Yet that is the burden of both New Testament and orthodox patristic Christology in its various forms.'[27] It is also the burden of Gunton's book, which argues that it is both necessary and possible to say this today in continuity with the ancient Christian tradition.

It is necessary because of what Gunton calls 'the logic of the saving love of God'. Something happens in time which compels interpretation as the actuality of the eternal. The link between eternal and temporal is not ideal but actual. 'God, as the Creator of the temporal order through his outgoing word, not only gives temporal and spatial form to what is other than himself (creation), but takes it also. He becomes flesh. This means that the eternal love of God locates itself in time and space, and so becomes datable. The love of God has the shape and form—the logic—of what happened in the life of Jesus: the birth as God with us; the care of the sick and the poor and outcast as the grace of God coming to us in our need; the temptation and death as the love of God meeting our hate and overcoming it; and all as one of us. That is why the logic of the story drives us, as it drove the writers of the New Testament and the theologians of the early Church to speak of the incarnation.'[28]

The doctrine is not then presupposed in the earliest confessions such as those first uttered under the impact of Jesus and faith in him. It comes to expression when the implications of that trust for our understanding of Jesus of Nazareth are worked out in different directions and dimensions. Or rather, 'It is not *logically* but *ontologically* presupposed by the confessions; and as their expressions of the meaning of the life, death and resurrection of Jesus are expanded and their reality penetrated, the logical outcome is the conviction that in the spatio-temporal life of a man God has become real among us.'[29]

Gunton recognizes the apparent absurdity of the claim: 'That our lives should be measured and healed by this lonely and suffering figure is the real reason why the ascription of uniqueness is difficult. But it is also the reason why it should be made.'[30] Jesus is unique because he is the way by which God restores his human creation, and along with it his whole creation, to a wholeness of relationship with him. This does not mean that God is met with nowhere else than in Jesus, but that Jesus confronts us with the reality of God in a manner that is unique. 'It is only when we appreciate that it is in and through Jesus of Nazareth that God meets humanity where it is, in its alienation and fallenness, and so liberates it for an imitation of that love, that we shall begin to understand that the assertion of Jesus' uniqueness, far from being immoral or illogical, is the presupposition for an understanding of the love of God for all of his creation.'[31] Borrowing PT Forsyth's famous expression, Gunton affirms that it is in the cross that we are met by God's 'holy love, which loves while taking seriously our failure to love'.

This is an important reminder, especially in the context of our dialogue with those religious pluralists who reject the classical teaching of the Incarnation on the strange grounds that it is an obstacle to genuinely loving relations with our neighbours of other faiths (secular or religious).[32] If we reject the language of pre-existence, how then do we affirm that the love which meets us in Jesus of Nazareth is one with the love which made the world? The New Testament writers are clear in their logic of the divine love: 'God demonstrates *his own love* for us in this: while we were still sinners, *Christ* died for us' (Rom. 5:8), 'This is love: not that we loved God, but that *he loved us and sent* his Son as an atoning sacrifice for our sins' (1 Jn 4:10), etc. The past tense of pre-existence relates the divine movements of creation and redemption without coalescing them. It is the reason for the progression of thought which sees Christ as active in creation from the very beginning (e.g. 1 Cor. 8:6; Col. 1:16). The love of God which became actual in this contingent, vulnerable human life is continuous with the love which operates throughout his creation.[33] Those who reject the language of pre-existence and Incarnation in the name of 'divine love' stand on shaky ground. They want to assert God's intention to redeem all peoples while denying the historical event in which that intention is made known and actualized.

Gunton goes on to argue that the belief that Jesus Christ is both man and God is not simply orthodox for its own sake, but it also involves the claim that 'we human beings both require and have received healing for the ill that distorts our humanity'.[34] Why? Because human sin is such that only God is able to deal with it, and the Incarnation is good news because it teaches that he does so in a way that respects human freedom and responsibility.

> A strong argument in defence of the doctrine, therefore, is that it enables theology to assert the fallenness, indeed radical fallenness, of humankind without in any way denying that it was created good and destined for fellowship with its Creator. Theology can thus be true to moral realities, falling neither into a life-denying pessimism nor a naive and counter-intuitive optimism.[35]

In other words, the relevance of Christian teaching for human life depends upon what it is able to say in its christology.

An incarnational christology in continuity with the New Testament and the early Fathers is possible because our cultural situation today is not as dissimilar to theirs as is commonly assumed. Even if we begin (rightly) with the preoccupations of our time, we can no more remain there than did the Fathers in their own age.[36] The difference between their age and ours requires a shift of emphasis rather than of form in christology.[37] Gunton notes a feature that the theology of the modern era shares with much ancient Greek thought (and, one may add, Hindu thought): the belief that by virtue of some feature of our being (reason, knowledge, soul, morality) we are already incipiently divine. This leads to an assumption either that Jesus' divinity *consists in* the abundant possession of certain human qualities or that, because human nature already contains the seeds of divinity, he is to be understood as simply actualizing what all of us potentially are.

Here we recall our critique of Panikkar and the Hegelian echoes of his 'theandric' language. We remarked that while Hegel did not wish to deny the factuality of Jesus, the latter disappeared in the mists of the higher synthesis of a universal self-consciousness. Hegel can be seen as a direct heir of the Cartesian tendency to divinize the human self. It is apparent in his christology: 'The idea of spirit means the unity of divine and human nature . . . Spirit is accordingly the living process by which the implicit unity of divine and human natures becomes actual and comes to have a definite existence.'[38] Kierkegaard, Hegel's most pungent intellectual critic, mocked: 'By force of lecturing they have transformed the God–Man into that speculative unity of God and man *sub specie aeternitatis* . . . whereas in truth the God–Man is the unity of God and an individual man in an actual historical situation.'[39] Kierkegaard believed that the difference between him and Hegel reflected the fundamental difference between Christianity and Christendom. The latter is actually a pagan inversion of the former, in that what it finds objectionable is not the divinity of Jesus but that divinity is given only through and with 'this lowly, poor, impotent man'.[40] Such a christology offends the established political order. Constantine and Hegel both divinize mankind rather than fall in 'fear and trembling' before the lowly Jesus of Nazareth. Gunton shows that the same distinction operates in modern theology: 'That *this* man, the lowly, crucified, impotent Jesus of Nazareth is God is true and offensive. That he reveals or teaches the divinity of mankind as a whole is false but attractive . . . .'[41]

Incarnation and *avatara*

The pinnacle of personal theism within Indian religion is found in the eleventh chapter of the *Bhagavad Gita*. The Gita itself was originally part of the great epic *Mahabharatha* which tells of the struggle between two families, the Pandavas and the Kauravas, representing the forces of *dharma* (righteousness, order) and *adharma* (unrighteousness, lawlessness) respectively. Krishna, the divine charioteer, is on the side of *dharma*, and he acts as the guardian and friend of the Pandava hero Arjuna. Just before the crucial battle with the Kauravas, Arjuna asks Krishna to reveal himself in his supreme form. Krishna responds by giving Arjuna a 'celestial eye' with which to behold his transfigured form. As Krishna throws off his human appearance, Arjuna falls to the ground in terror, unable to bear the aweful splendour of the deity. The rest of the chapter is taken up with this vision of Vishnu, the supreme One, and the hymn of praise that it evokes.

Krishna is the best known and most important of the *avatars* of Vishnu. The term means a 'descent', a 'coming down', from the prefix *ava*, down, and the verb *tr*, to come over. 'The *avatar* is an appearance of any deity on earth, or descent from heaven, but it is especially applied to the descents or appearances of Vishnu.'[42] The clearest statement of the doctrine is found in the Gita: 'For whenever the law of righteousness withers away and lawlessness arises, then do I generate Myself [on earth]. For the protection of the good, for the destruction of evildoers, for the setting up of the law of righteousness I come into being age after age.'[43] The Vaisnava tradition to which the Gita belongs recognized ten classical *avatars* of Vishnu, including various animal forms. The human manifestations, such as Krishna and Rama, are themselves the objects of popular devotional cults in India, and it has been an easy matter for the Hindu to regard the Buddha, Jesus, and even modern gurus such as Sai Baba as *avatars* of Vishnu in different generations.

It is often suggested, especially in Hindu-Christian encounter, that the concept of *avatara* is equivalent to the Christian doctrine of Incarnation, just as in the early period of the twentieth century it was popular among New Testament students influenced by the *religionsgeschichte* approach to suggest that the Incarnation was derived from the 'mystery religions' of the ancient Mediterranean world, with their myths of dying and rising gods (e.g. Adonis, Osiris) modelled on the familiar cycles of nature.[44] But the similarities are only superficial. Firstly, the concept must be interpreted within the whole *Vedanta* framework for, as Smart and Konstantine observe, 'The fact that in the Hindu tradition there is no clear dividing line between the human and the divine, as witness not just the multiplicity of *avatars*, e.g. Krishna and Rama; but also the tendency to treat gurus and other holy people as divine means that avatarhood is not an intense and unique divine commitment.'[45] It is also of a piece with the doctrine of *karma* and rebirth where different bodies (human and non-human) provide a temporary manifestation of the same identity.

Secondly, the historicity of the *avatars* is not crucial to belief in them. Indeed, there is a tendency both in popular devotion and in neo-*Vedanta* (what is sometimes called 'modern Hindu ideology') to look on the *avatars* in a somewhat docetic manner. Neo-*Vedanta*, with its ascending levels of reality and truth, sees the *avatars* as mere manifestations of the divine suitable for those not yet at the highest stages of spiritual growth.[46] The tendency to treat them as simply mythical illustrations of 'timeless truths' is clearly evident in the greatest of modern exponents of neo-*Vedanta*, Sarvapalli Radhakrishnan. In his commentary on the *Bhagavad Gita*, Radhakrishnan discounts the historicity of Krishna and makes him a symbol of the higher self in every human being. Thus: 'It is of little moment so far as the teaching is concerned, whether the author is a figure of history or the very god descended into man, for the realities of the spirit are the same now as they were thousands of years ago and the differences of race and nationality do not affect them. The essential thing is truth or significance and the historical fact is nothing more than the image of it.'[47] Even where he veers towards less monistic statements of incarnation, the historical recedes before the timeless: 'The assumption of human nature by the Divine Reality, like the creation of the world, does not take away from or add to the integrity of the Divine. Creation and incarnation both belong to the world of manifestation, and not to the Absolute Spirit.'[48]

This leads us into the third and most important difference between the concept of *avatara* and the Incarnation. In the Incarnation he who is the source and sustainer of our humanity has entered *once and for all* into our historical experience to take that humanity *for ever* into his own eternal life. We have seen that fundamental to Christian faith is the conviction that the resurrection of Jesus was not a casting off of the human and the resumption of the divine. The human is the manifestation and vehicle of the divine personality, both in the earthly life of Jesus and in his glorified humanity. The Incarnation, atoning death and resurrection of Jesus Christ decisively changed the relationship between God and humankind. It is not only that the mystery of the infinite God, discernible in the varieties of human experience in all ages and across cultures, has now come to be known personally and concretely in terms of a finite human life; but the humanity of the crucifed and risen Christ is the locus of our union and fellowship with God for ever. It is thus that God relates himself fully to us and us to him through all eternity. The risen Christ remains, in heaven, the human face of God. Although we do not understand now the manner in which the risen Christ incorporates the whole redeemed humanity, it is through the crucifed and exalted body of Christ that we continue to be embraced by the love of God.

Thus the difference between Incarnation and *avatara* is profound. It is not as if Hindus in their magnanimity affirm many incarnations while Christians, out of narrow-minded bigotry, limit it to one. The difference is logical and ontological. To translate *avatara* as incarnation is to invite confusion. It is more accurately a 'theophany', of which, of course, there are many examples in the Bible. It is also true that a number of self-sacrificing men and women can manifest in their lives more divine qualities than most, but that doesn't make them God himself in person. In Austin Farrer's well-known words, 'A good man helped by grace may do human things divinely; Christ did divine things humanly.'[49]

If God, in one of the modes of his eternal being, has expressed not only his qualities but *himself* in a particular individual and bound us in love to himself in a new, personal and eternal relationship, then that can only be once for all. That the Incarnation is necessarily unique is well expressed by the philosopher-theologian, Brian Hebblethwaite: 'Only one man can actually *be* God to us, if God himself is one. We are to posit relation in God, but not a split personality . . . To think of many human beings as incarnations of God is to think of incarnation in a different sense—a derived metaphorical sense, namely, the embodiment of general characteristics.'[50]

If in Christ our humanity is taken into God, then this solidarity of God with us, manifested in the incarnation and atoning death of Christ and continued in the exalted Christ, is what makes the liberation of humankind possible. In the shattering opening chapter of Dietrich Bonhoeffer's *Ethics*, written in defiance of the Nietzschean myth and the triumphant Nazi ideology, we read that the Incarnation now empowers the 'real man' with the liberty to be his Creator's creature. 'The quest for the superman', writes Bonhoeffer, 'the endeavour to outgrow the man within the man, the pursuit of the heroic, the cult of the demigod, all this is not the proper concern of man, for it is untrue.'[51] It is from beyond death that the new man and the new world emerges, and the Risen Christ 'bears the new humanity within himself, the final glorious "yes" which God addresses to the new man.'[52] Now, therefore, '*Man becomes man because God became man*'.[53] Thus, Bonhoeffer continues, 'Now there is no more pretence, no more hypocrisy or self-violence, no more compulsion to be something other, better and more ideal than what one is. God loves the real man. God became a real man.'[54]

Incarnation and *gnosis*

It is now time for a historical detour, the purpose of which will appear, hopefully, as we proceed.

The term gnosticism has broadly been used to cover a number of religious–philosophical worldviews which emphasised knowledge (Gk. *gnosis*) in opposition to faith as the heart of religious experience.[55] Latent gnostic ideas probably lie behind the teaching that Paul counters in Colossians, and commentators detect similar teaching in the background to the epistles of John and Jude. But full-blown gnostic systems of thought, blending together elements drawn from Christianity, Middle Platonism, hellenized Zoroastrianism and Jewish apocalyptic, first make their appearance in the middle of the second century. The most famous of the gnostic sects, principally because it stood closest to orthodox Christianity, was that associated with the Platonist Valentinus of Rome. While rival sects disliked each other as much as they did orthodox Christianity, and their philosophical systems differed widely in their degree of sophistication, they were all agreed in their views of knowledge and the human predicament. Knowledge is given by direct divine illumination; and although the content of knowledge embraces everything to do with the divine realm and the nature of the world, its primary object concerns human nature and destiny. The gnostic knows himself or herself to be, in his or her highest or essential self, divine. To know this is already to be saved. However, the gnostic awaits the final separation of the divine 'spark' from matter so that it can return to its true home in the divine realm.

For the gnostics, human beings fall into three categories. They themselves were 'pneumatic' (spiritual), possessing the divine element which is capable of knowing itself to be divine. The return to the divine realm is ensured by destiny. The second category, called 'psychics' (ensouled) do not possess the divine spirit, but they have souls. They are characterized not by knowledge but by faith, and they have free will. Although they cannot attain the salvation of the pneumatics, if they choose to incline towards the spiritual rather than the material realm, they will be rewarded in a paradise after death. The majority of Christians were classed among the psychics. The last category, the 'hylic' (material), contained the great mass of humankind, devoid of either divine spirit or soul.

This doctrine of the three classes is part of an elaborate cosmogony, remarkable in its scope, which sought to answer genuine problems which had long engaged philosophers. The revelation they claimed to 'know' consisted of a myth about the origin of the physical world as the rèsult of a pre-cosmic disaster, which accounted for the present misery of the human race, and a gnostic 'gospel' which enabled the elect few to be redeemed from their plight. The myth helped to account for the co-existence of evil and an all-powerful God. A central idea of the gnostics, which they shared with both contemporary Middle Platonist philosophers and the subsequent mainstream Christian tradition, was that God did not change. But if God causes the universe to exist, does he not change from being a non-creator to a creator? It is not only suffering and evil that are problematic, but existence itself.

The fundamental conception that underlay the bizarre imagery of the cosmic myth was that of a descending spiritual hierarchy, a great Chain of Being. They proposed a multiplicity of dispositions within 'God' which they called Aeons. Although in the language of the myth these are treated as separate, individual beings, taken together they comprise the fullness of deity (or the *Pleroma*). The absolute and transcendent divine principle was called 'Depth' (*Bythos*), unoriginated, beyond understanding and language, unchanging, invisible, and so on. *Bythos* is the subject of all the negative predications of God made by the Middle Platonists. In the great chain of being that emanates from *Bythos*, each pair of Aeons (male and female in the sexual imagery employed by the myth) is 'produced' by the pair immediately above. As *Bythos* was utterly transcendent, only *Nous* (Mind), produced directly from *Bythos*, and *Ennoia* (Purposive Thought) were capable of grasping the greatness of *Bythos*. At the other end of the chain of being was *Sophia* (Wisdom), distressed by her unfulfilled longing for the knowledge of *Bythos* which *Nous* had transmitted to all the Aeons in the *Pleroma*. This yearning gave rise to an instability within the *Pleroma*. The measures taken by the other Aeons to contain this led to the emergence of a material world outside the *Pleroma*, characterized by evil and suffering.

The gnostic myth drew on the cosmogony of Plato's *Timaeus* and the early chapters of Genesis. The Demiurge is the first of the psychic substances formed beyond the *Pleroma*—the Creator God of the Old Testament who is worshipped ignorantly by the psychics as the only God. The material world thus arises by accident, tainted by the passion and sorrow of *Sophia*, but it is still the result of divine agency through the Aeons. 'Psychic' and 'hylic' material human beings are formed by the Demiurge; but, without his knowledge, some of his human creatures (the 'pneumatics' or '*gnostikoi*', the gnostics themselves) have been impregnated by Sophia with the divine substance from the *Pleroma* itself. Thus the origin of the material world, and of evil, was 'solved' by the device of differentiating aspects or dispositions within 'God', so that while 'God' remained the cause of all things, matter and evil could not have been caused by God in his most transcendent aspect. The whole world, then, matter included, emanated from one divine principle; but the material order was so alien to the supreme Being and goodness, that it was the creation of inferior powers, either incompetent or malevolent. But it is important to note that the early gnostics did not teach the absolute metaphysical dualistism of later Manicheanism.[56] Indeed their chief concern was to bring everything under one spiritual principle, while absolving the transcendent from responsibility for the physical creation.

In some of the second-century sects Jesus, or rather the divine Christ, is regarded as a redeemer figure, one of the Aeons in the chain of being and bringing salvation through gnosis. But even in the Valentinian system, which stood closest to Christianity, a gnostic attiude to matter rules out the possibility of belief in a real incarnation. As Henry Chadwick explains, 'The divine Christ (they held) might have appeared to blinded worldlings as if he were tangible flesh and blood, but those with higher insight perceived that he was pure spirit and that the physical appearance was an optical illusion and mere semblance . . . It was inconceivable that the divine Christ could have come 'in the flesh' in any ultimately true sense.'[57]

Naturally salvation too was understood as an escape from entrapment in the world of matter and time. It was an

awakening of the divine spirits within the elect to their true
identity and destiny. After death they would begin a perilous
journey through the planetary spheres to their divine home.
Much time was therefore devoted to learning the correct
magic passwords and acquiring the most potent amulets
which would compel the powers barring their way to open
the doors they guarded and allow the spirits to make
progress towards the realm of light. The Christian gnostic
groups produced a great deal of allegorical and numerological
exegesis of the New Testament, and taught a 'secret
tradition' of the sayings of Jesus to his disciples which existed
outside the present canonical Gospels and whose meaning
was only discernible to them.

What relevance has this sketchy historical digression for
the issues dealt with in the present book? In a recent volume
on Irenaeus of Lyons (c.130–c.200), the best known of all
Christian opponents of gnosticism, the author observes that
behind the bizarre and extravagant mythology of the
gnostics there lay an impressive religious system: 'It sought
to take account of all aspects of the human condition: of
suffering and sorrow, of the distress and alienation experienced in social, familial, and sexual relationships, of the joy
and pain of mystical experience, of the achievements and and
disappointments of intellectual endeavour. It sought to
explain all these things in terms of a cosmic drama long since
finished . . . The true gnostic knows . . . that he or she does
not belong to this shadowy world of matter and soul,
multiplicity and diversity, but to the divine Pleroma of light
and spirit, where universal harmony and spirit have long
since been restored. The function of the historical Jesus in
this scheme was that of revealer of these truths.'[58]

No one familiar with the thought-world of Indian religion
can fail to observe the deep resonances with the teaching of
the *Upanishads*, the philosophy of *yoga* and the various
schools of Buddhism. All agree in seeing time as mere
temporality, a meaningless coming to be and passing away,
with no ultimate significance. Salvation is thus understood as
deliverance from the flux of time and physical embodiment,
from birth no less than death, and is accomplished through
insight (*jnana/gnosis*) into one's true condition. It is ineffable
Silence that lies at the heart of being and constitutes the goal
of the mystic's quest.[59]

In the *advaita Vedanta*, popularized in modern times by philosophers such as Radhakrishnan, the impersonal Absolute, *nirguna Brahman*, transcends the personal God *Isvara* of bhakti devotion. Not surprisingly, Radhakrishnan's religious hierarchy of being simply echoes the gnostics: 'Hinduism insists on our working steadily upwards and improving our knowledge of God. The worshippers of the Absolute are the highest in rank; second to them are the worshippers of the personal God; then come the worshippers of the incarnations like Rama, Krishna, Buddha; below them are those who worship ancestors, deities and sages, and lowest of all are the worshippers of the petty forces and spirits.'[60] On a more social-cultural level, we could point to other similarities between Hindu-Buddhist practices and those of the gnostic schools: the three-fold division of human beings, the use of secret formulas (*mantras*) in meditation and to ward off evil powers, the high esteem accorded to astrology, the role of serpents (and their association with wisdom) in mythology, and so on.

In a fascinating essay, *Buddhism and Gnosis*, Edward Conze has argued that the similarities between gnosticism and Buddhism, especially in the latter's Mahayana form, are 'remarkably close', and do not concern only fortuitous details, but 'the essential structure itself'.[61] Conze draws attention to eight basic similarities, five of which (for reasons of brevity) are shown below:

(a) In both cases salvation is only through *gnosis* or *jnana*. In both cases 'mere insight into the origination and nature of the world liberates us from it, and effects some kind of reunion with the transcendental One, which is identical with our true Self.'[62]

(b) In both cases a sharp distinction is drawn between the highest ranks of the spiritually awakened and the common herd of humankind. The saints have undergone a spiritual rebirth, have turned from the world which preoccupies ordinary people to the pure realm of spirit, and have won sufficient detachment from conditioned things to begin the journey to ultimate Silence.[63]

(c) Both are indifferent to historical facts and tend to replace them with myth. In the Mahayana, the real Buddha should not be mistaken for the historical Buddha, who is no more than a phantom body displayed by him to teach and awaken people.

(d) In both gnosticism and Mahayana, the creator god is placed at a lower level than the still and quiescent Godhead. The Buddhist counterpart to the Demiurge is to some extent the Hindu god *Brahma* ('who boasts in his stupidity about having created this cosmos, when in fact it is the automatic product of cycles of evolution and involution'[64]), while the Absolute is identifed with *Nirvana, Sunyatta,* etc.

(e) Both systems despise easy popularity and their writings are aimed at the initiates. Consequently there is a preference for the mysterious, the esoteric, the occult. This is seen especially in the Tantric and Zen schools of Buddhism, but also in the influential Yogacarin concept of 'two-level truth' (the ordinary meaning for the rank and file, and the higher-level meaning for the saint).[65]

Perhaps even more intriguing than these ancient parallels are the parallels between the assumptions of gnosticism and those that undergird the *ideology of religious pluralism.* We have already observed, at many points in our critique of Asian and European pluralists, the following tendencies which can now be seen to have close affinities with the gnostics: the denigration (in practice, if not always explicitly in theory) of the personal Creator of biblical revelation in favour of an unknowable Absolute/Mystery; a concept of salvation that is essentially individual and 'spiritual' in some vague sense (e.g. Hick's 'transformation of self-centredness to reality-centredness', Samartha's and Panikkar's diffuse *advaitic* framework); a view of Jesus as essentially a teacher of divine truths, never as one whose death and resurrection have decisively altered the condition of humankind in any way; an elevation of 'religious experience' over and above belief, doctrine and scripture in all the world's faiths; a downgrading of the historical and literal elements in the scriptures of all faiths in favour of mythological re-interpretations; the positing of a universal, unifying spiritual principle (e.g. Panikkar's 'cosmotheandrism', Pieris' 'salvific principle'), coming to expression in many saviour-figures who all stand in varying distance from the source; and an incipient elitism which distinguishes between the devout but misguided faithful in all religions and the select few (the pluralists, drawn from within all) who alone grasp the true meaning of all religion and are the vanguard of the future.

Irenaeus and the Gnostics

Irenaeus' major work, *Adversus Haereses* (or Against Heresies) is dominated by one central thesis: there is only one God, one creation, and one saving purpose for his creation, which is accomplished by the one God.[66] In uniting redemption and creation (without collapsing one on to the other) Irenaeus struck at the heart of both the Valentinian system and the teaching of Marcion which, in their different ways, drove a wedge between the creator God of the Old Testament and the God revealed by Jesus in the New.[67] In both Marcion and the gnostics redemption is *from* creation, the redeemer God delivering the spiritual beings from the material realm of the creator God.

Impressive as the gnostics' sense of the transcendence of God was, that of Irenaeus was even more profound. For the gnostics, despite their aversion towards the material realm, God and matter stand in the same continuum, the one great Chain of Being. To borrow an illustration from Denis Minns, 'Just as light from the sun falls more weakly on the surface of the planet Jupiter than it does on the earth, so, in the Valentinian system, the further removed anything in the continuum of being is from the source of being the weaker will be its hold on being.' Minns goes on to note that the alienation which was a marked feature of this world view was only relative: 'One might suffer a terrible dislocation, of being far removed from the source of one's being and from one's proper place in relation to that source, but there was some comfort to be had in the thought that, wherever one was, one was in the same continuum of being as everything else, including the source of being. Even more comforting was the hope of reversing the outward movement, of turning back to the centre and source of one's existence.'[68]

Irenaeus' exposition of the bibical doctrine of creation was one of his most significant theological contributions to the developing orthodox Christian tradition. He rejects the concept of a Chain of Being, of any kind of substantial continuity between God and his creation. He sweeps aside the elaborate gnostic universe by denying that there is anything which links our world to its Creator. There is no substance or essence or being common to all creatures, much less to creatures and God. Creatures are called into existence by the word of God, and held in being, suspended over non-existence. Whatever 'exists' does so not in virtue of sharing in the being that is God, but because God creates it, bestows existence upon it by an act of grace. God alone is the only reality, the only being who really *is*. All else is in a state of *becoming*, coming into or passing out of being, and under-pinned by the sovereign, loving will of God. Minns observes that 'paradoxically, just because God's transcendence over creation is absolute, he is immediately present to his creation in a way impossible within the Valentinian scheme . . . All existing things, instead of occupying different grades in a hierarchy or chain of being, are immediately present to the God who creates them, or, as Irenaeus likes to say, they are in his hands.'[69]

The details of Irenaeus' refutation of the gnostics need not detain us.[70] But a summary of his rich theology of the divine 'economy' of salvation is in order, as it is set forth as a counter-story to the pre-cosmic drama of the gnostic myth. The whole biblical drama of creation to consummation is encapsulated in Ephesians 1:9–10; and Irenaeus' doctrine of salvation can be understood as a commentary on these verses: '[God] has made known to us the mystery of his will, according to his good pleasure that he set forth in Christ, as a plan (Gk. *oikonomia*) for the fullness of time, to gather up all things in him, things in heaven and things on earth' (New RSV). For Irenaeus the verb translated 'gather up', or 'sum up' (it occurs again in Rom 13:9) led to a theory of 'recapitulation' as the heart of the divine economy of salvation. Building on the Adam/Christ typology of Romans 5 and 1 Corinthians 15, Irenaeus taught that Christ, the second Adam, recapitulates Adam and his progeny in his own incarnate human life, retraces the temptation and defeat in his own death and reverses that defeat in the victory of his obedience and resurrection. His obedience is thus Adam's renewal, the perfection of the glory God intended for him.

It is thus in Christ that the uncreated divinity and the created order meet and are reconciled. For Irenaeus the wonder of the economy of our salvation lies in the fact that the transcendent God intended from the beginning that this gulf be bridged, in the perfecting of the earth-creature (Adam) in his own image and likeness, and in lifting up of that creature to fellowship and friendship with himself.[71] Jesus of Nazareth is God made visible and touchable, God speaking to human beings and seeking them in order to carry his own creation home on his shoulders.[72] On the cross, the unseen God who upholds creation is himself held up by his own creation.[73] Irenaeus does not show the caution later theologians would show in speaking of God, or even the Word of God, suffering on the cross. For him, if Christ is God made visible, so that to see or hear him is to see or hear God, to kill him is to kill God.[74] Christ's humanity does not conceal his divinity, but rather makes that divinity available to human apprehension.

This has deep implications for his understanding of human nature. Our humanity is not something that comes between us and God. On the contrary, it is precisely in our humanity that we are called to be bearers of the divine glory, the means by which God is made known. 'For the glory of God is a living man,' he writes, 'and the life of man consists in beholding God.'[75] Adam is never just an individual for Irenaeus; he is both an individual and the symbol of all humanity in its relationship with God. What makes us human is that we share the same flesh and blood derived from Adam, which in turn was formed from the mud/earth by the hand of God. Adam's humanity bears the stamp of Christ, for it is the incarnate Word, God made visible in flesh, that is the image of God. Adam is thus defined in relation to Christ's humanity. When God declared at the beginning his intention to make 'an earth creature in our own image and likeness', he began a process embracing the whole history of humankind until the consummation of the kingdom of his Son. Thus the incarnation of the Word is integral to the history of salvation.[76]

Irenaeus' understanding of Gen. 1:26, then, is that Adam was not created perfect (complete) but with a view to his growth into perfection—the likeness of God, summed up in the person of Christ—at the end of a long process of training in the school of God. God will not be hurried into the fulfilment of his plan.[77] Indeed, for Irenaeus the sin of Adam and Eve was the root sin of disobedience, and precisely the disobedience of *rejecting the divine economy itself*. It was the refusal to wait on God as creatures and not gods, to accept that likeness to God was to be had only as a gift from God, and only when they had grown strong enough to bear it.[78]

Disobedience is the archetypal sin. As Minns, in his commentary on Irenaeus, expresses it: 'The only proper attitude of the creature before God is one of receptivity and acceptance of all the goodness that God will bestow. This preparedness to receive from God is what Irenaeus means by faith: it is a question of *listening*, which is what the word obedience [in Greek] means.'[79] The same disobedience lies behind the gnostics' attempt to invent a plan of salvation for themselves. God cannot create us in his own image and likeness unless we fully embrace our creatureliness, unless we accept that we can never be perfect but can be drawn ever closer to the glory of God, unless we abandon all attempts at making something of ourselves and learn to relax in the obedience of faith, to be responsive to the gentle touch of his creative fingers as he fashions us after the pattern of Christ. In other words, to echo Luther thirteen hundred years later, to let God be God.[80]

Thus the gnostic belief that the real and essential element of our human being is something spiritual, temporarily associated with our physical frame and awaiting its freedom in an other-worldly spiritual realm, is exposed as pathetically escapist. Escapism is childish, it is not an option for an intelligent adult. For Irenaeus the redemption the Christian Gospel offers is not a matter of the release of the spirit from a malignant body, but of the body being made whole again in Christ, who, 'in Adam's own flesh, re-engaged the conflict with Satan, defeated the ancient enemy of humankind, despoiled him of all those he had taken captive, bestowed on them the victor's prize of incorruptibility, and led them back to friendship with God.'[81]

We need not endorse every aspect of Irenaeus' theology to appreciate the fact that here is a refreshing attempt to proclaim the biblical drama of salvation in a way that is coherent and challenging to those who live in an environment, religious or secular, moulded by alternative images of salvation. Indeed, there are lessons we can learn from Irenaeus in our own quest to develop a theological framework for Christian witness in our own pluralistic world.

First, his stress on the *unity* of the divine economy, from creation to consummation. It is this that undergirds his sense of universal history as well as the continuity of the old and the new covenants in Scripture. In the Western theological tradition that derives from Augustine, there has often been a

tendency to stress the incarnation and redemption of Christ
in such a way as to divorce it from the stream of human
history. Christ does represent a new and gracious intervention of God in history, but this intervention is often
depicted as taking the history of the redeemed in a direction
totally disconnected from the rest of Adam's progeny. For
Augustine, there are two histories. There are those whose
fate was sealed, by an act of predestination, when they
sinned 'in Adam'; and there are those whose sin is dealt with
by the saving grace of God, so that they can become part of
salvation history. For Irenaeus, it is all humankind who were
'predestined' to share in the true humanity of Christ. But this
does not rob them of their free will—indeed Irenaeus affirms
and defends human free will in the teeth of gnostic determinism
—nor does it lead to an unbiblical universalism. The tragedy
of sin is that human beings do choose perversely. For those
who refuse to be part of God's purpose in human history,
there is no other history. To reject the divine economy is to
destroy one's humanity. Though sin does not call the divine
economy into existence, it does have catastrophic consequences for those who persist in it.[82]

Secondly, his passionate *Christ-centredness*. The divine
economy finds its origin, pivot and goal in Jesus Christ.
Irenaeus reaffirms the apostolic teaching that Christ is the
agent of both creation and redemption. And his distinctive
emphases on Christ's humanity as both the vehicle of his
divinity and the paradigm for our own (emphases that
tended to be neglected in the subsequent tradition), are
valuable. In the risen Jesus our humanity exists in an
infinitely more glorious state than it ever did in Adam. And
although his doctrine of Christ's recapitulation of Adam's
path involves him in some forced and extravagant exegesis
of Scripture, he draws our attention to the important biblical
truth that through his contact with every human experience
from within, God is able to heal every condition of human
life.

Irenaeus' description of faith as a relaxing in the hands of
the Creator so that he can form Christ in us is a moving
picture of God's justifying and sanctifying work in the
believer's life. Equally appealing, especially to those nurtured in a traditional Asian environment, is his picture of the
unhurried patience of God, loving, forming and guiding his
handiwork through all the twists and detours of history.

Salvation is progressively realized, reaching its culmination in the triumphant Kingdom of the Son (and not in the church in her pilgrimage through history). The Spirit needs time to grow accustomed to dwelling in humankind, even as humankind needs time to grow accustomed to bearing divinity.[83]

Thirdly, his vision of the *wholeness* of human life. Irenaeus stands out among patristic and medieval theologians for his celebration of the material creation and the place he accords it in the economy of salvation. He felt nothing of the embarrassment towards the human body that marked even prominent churchmen of his own day, not to mention later theological heavyweights such as Origen and Augustine who were influenced by Neo-Platonic ideas. His whole theological outlook militates against any view of the life to come as a state of blissful union between the individual soul and God. For Irenaeus the fact that we are embodied creatures means that we are inherently social and political beings. In the last book of *Adversus Haereses* he shares an eschatological vision, drawn from the Old Testament and the Book of Revelation, of a this-worldly reign of the just with Christ, which is a social and political reality.[84] Such views were an embarrassment to the medieval church, which tended to spiritualize or allegorize such texts.

Irenaeus sees change as intrinsic to creaturely existence. But far from drawing negative and pessimistic conclusions from this, as Augustine and other Christian Platonists subsequently did, he envisages the possibility of an unending growth towards Christlikeness and communion with God, a growth that continues even within the millenarian kingdom —for as the creature will always remain the creature, he or she can never cease to belong to the world of Becoming rather than Being. Irenaeus does not make the mistake of seeing this progressive growth as something self-driven or automatic. That would be to deny his strong emphasis on the *gifts* of God. Growth is possible only because God is always forming the creature, always drawing him or her from Becoming towards his Being.[85] Though God can draw near to his creature in all his awesome glory, he chooses instead to adapt himself to the stages of the creature's growth.[86]

Finally, his fine balance of biblical *conviction* and biblical *agnosticism*. On the one hand, Irenaeus accurately perceived the threat the gnostics posed, especially within the Christian community, to the apostolic tradition which he took as the normal and true form of the Christian faith. He was thus determined to show, from as wide a groundwork as possible, that they were wrong. For him the task of church leaders, and especially those in churches founded by the apostles, was to witness faithfully to the deposit of truth made known in the apostolic witness to Christ. He would have been horrified if he had been praised for being 'original'. The quest for originality as an end in itself was idolatry. The original thinkers of his day were the gnostics, Marcion and other heretics. Irenaeus spoke out of a deep-seated conviction that the incarnate, crucified and risen Jesus Christ was the centre of God's purposive dealings with his creation.

But, on the other hand, we cannot fail to be struck by his intellectual humility. Unlike the Valentinians, whose system represented an attempt to embrace everything under a single principle, including the problem of evil, Irenaeus felt no compulsion to provide an answer for everything. He admitted that he himself did not know everything.[87] Unlike some early (and modern) Christians he does not preoccupy himself with the nature of hell. He sarcastically pointed out that the Valentinians go to great lengths to claim that God is totally unknowable and then set about describing him in great detail, fracturing him into multiple dispositions, often based on human psychology.[88]

For Irenaeus the ultimate object of all knowledge is God himself. But how God is in himself, abstracted from his relationship to us, is not a proper subject for intellectual inquiry.[89] Christians worship God as Trinity because God has revealed himself to us in love. It is only because of the way his economy of salvation unfolds that we are able to distinguish Father, Son and Spirit.[90] We need to ponder the intractable questions about the eternal relationships between Father, Son and Spirit only in order to avoid misunderstandings concerning the mystery of our salvation. It is the God of salvation that Irenaeus consistently points to: the ineffable, transcendent God who reveals himself to us as the God of mercy and justice, who enters his own creatures' lives to the extent of being brutalized and murdered by them, who seeks them as a good shepherd seeks his wayward sheep and invites them to share in his own divine life.

Notes to Chapter Seven

1. BF Meyer, *The Early Christians: Their World Mission and Self-Discovery*, quoted in NT Wright, *The New Testament and the People of God* (London: SPCK, 1992) p. 360.
2. See further L. Sanneh, *Translating the Message: the Missionary Impact on Culture* (Maryknoll, NY: Orbis, 1991); 'The Gospel, Language and Culture: the Theological Method in Cultural Analysis', *International Review of Mission*, vol. LXXXIV Nos. 332/333, pp. 47–64; 'Pluralism and Commitment', *Theology Today*, vol. 45, April 1988, pp. 21–33.
3. Wright, op. cit. pp. 360, 361.
4. Cicero, *Pro Rabirio* V.16. Elsewhere Cicero calls crucifixion the most gross, cruel, and hideous manner of execution. *In Verrem* V.64, 66). Quoted in Martin Hengel, *Crucifixion in the Ancient World and the Folly of the Message of the Cross* (Eng. trans. J Bowden, London: SCM, 1977).
5. For the sociological distinctiveness of the early Christian church, see,e.g., WA Meeks, *The First Urban Christians: The Social World of the Apostle Paul* (New Haven: Yale University Press, 1983); J Stambaugh and D Balch, *The Social World of the First Christians* (London: SPCK, 1986).
6. See e.g. 1 Cor 10:32; Gal 3:28; Eph 2:14ff.
7. Wright, op. cit. p. 360.
8. Justin, *First Apology*. 16, in *Early Christian Fathers*, vol.1 (Library of Christian Classics, ed. CC Richardson, Philadelphia: Westminster and London: SCM, 1953).
9. Justin, *First Apology*.14, ibid.
10. Robin Lane Fox, *Pagans and Christians* (New York: Alfred Knopf, 1986) p. 330.
11. Ibid.
12. For Yahweh's sovereign activity in the histories of other nations, see also Ex. 9:13–16; Is. 10:5–19; Jer. 27:5–7; Amos 9:7; Is. 44:28–45:13. It is interesting to note, too, that Israel's destruction of the Canaanites and occupation of the land was held back by Yahweh for four hundred years until the sins of the Canaanites had 'reached their full measure' (Gen. 15:16).
13. E.g. Deut. 10:14ff; Lev. 19:1,2; Lev. 25. For the revolutionary distinctiveness of Israel's social system (rooted in her religious self-awareness) from both the Canaanite system she displaced and other ancient West Asian cultures, see the classic study by NK Gottwald, *The Tribes of Yahweh: a Sociology of the Religion of Liberated Israel, 1250–1050 BCE* (London: SCM, 1980), and the (more readable) works by the British Old Testament scholar CJH Wright, e.g. *Living as the People of God: the Relevance of Old Testament Ethics* (Leicester: IVP, 1983).
14. J Verkuyl, *Contemporary Missiology, An Introduction* (Grand Rapids: Eermans, 1978) p. 95, quoted in CJH Wright, 'The Christian and other religions: the biblical evidence', *Themelios*, January 1984, vol. 9, no 2, p. 9.
15. Wright, Ibid. p. 7.

16. Ibid. p. 8.
17. Ibid. p. 6.
18. Ibid. p. 7 (Italics in text).
19. Cf. esp. Rom. 4; Rom. 10:1–4; Gal. 3:1–4:7.
20. NT Wright, op. cit. p. 406. It is also worth quoting Wright's pertinent observations concerning anti-Christian persecution by Jews: 'What evokes persecution is precisely that which challenges a worldview, that which up-ends a symbolic universe . . . No new Temple would replace Herod's, since the real and final replacement was Jesus and his people. No intensified Torah would define this community, since its sole definition was Jesus-belief. No Land claimed its allegiance, and no Holy City could function for it as Jerusalem did for mainline Jews; Land had been transposed into World, and the Holy City was the new Jerusalem . . . Racial identity was irrelevant; the story of this new community was traced back to Adam, not just to Abraham . . . Once we understand how world-views function, we can see that the Jewish neighbours of early Christians must have regarded them, not as a lover of Monet regards a lover of Picasso, but as a lover of painting regards one who deliberately sets fire to art galleries—and who claims to do so in the service of Art.' (p. 451).
21. L Newbigin, *The Gospel in a Pluralist Society* (Grand Rapids: Eerdmans and Geneva: WCC, 1989) p. 87.
22. Ibid.
23. Whatever other significance he possesses, e.g. as a moral examplar, is presupposed by the theological. Cf. e.g. the ethical purpose for which Paul quotes the hymn confessing the pre-existence of Jesus, Phil 2:5–11.
24. On this verse, Gordon Fee comments bluntly: 'Although Paul does not here call Christ God, the formula is so constructed that only the most obdurate would deny its Trinitarian implications. In the same breath that he can assert that there is only one God, he equally asserts that the designation 'Lord', which in the OT belongs to the one God, is the proper designation of the divine Son. One should note especially that Paul feels no tension between the affirmation of monotheism and the clear distinction between the two persons of Father and Jesus Christ. As with other such statements in the NT, Jesus is the one through whom God both created and redeemed. Thus together the two sentences embrace the whole of human existence', *The First Epistle to the Corinthians*, NICNT (Grand Rapids:Eerdmans, 1987, pp. 375–6). James Dunn has made a brave attempt to see only Adam Christology, stemming from the resurrection (and not pre-existence), and no incarnational Christology in the Pauline corpus *Christology in the Making: a New Testament Inquiry into the Origins of the Doctrine of the Incarnation* (London: SCM, 1980, esp. pp. 125–28, 254–56). For a refutation of Dunn's arguments, see, e.g., S Kim, *The Origin of Paul's Gospel* (Grand Rapids: Eerdmans, 1982, pp. 137–268).
25. Is 45:21–23. Interestingly, both Old and New Testament texts are voiced against a backdrop of religious pluralism. Is. 40–55 asserts, in the midst of the polytheistic culture of sixth-century BC Babylon,

the uniqueness of *Yahweh* as the sovereign ruler and saviour of the nations. The same terms and language are used to assert the sovereignty of *Jesus* in the midst of the Greco-Roman pluralism of the first century CE.

26. C Gunton, *Yesterday and Today: A Study of Continuities in Christology* (London: Darton, Longman and Todd, 1983) p. 70.
27. Ibid. p. 132.
28. Ibid. p. 134.
29. Ibid. p. 134 (italics in text).
30. Ibid. p. 165.
31. Ibid. p. 164.
32. So, for instance, Samartha: 'Christology from above makes it impossible for Christians to relate themselves, their faith in God through Jesus Christ . . . to neighbours of other faiths', *One Christ—Many Religions* (Bangalore: SATHRI, 1992) p. 134. Samartha presents this as a matter of logical necessity; but, since the logic is specious, we must conclude that he is making an empirical judgment about the Christians he knows.
33. Cf. Athanasius' well-known words in *De Incarnatione*, 8: 'For this reason the incorporeal and incorruptible and immaterial Word of God came to our realm; not that he was previously distant, for no part of creation is left deprived of him, but he fills the universe, being in union with his Father. But in his benevolence towards us he condescended to come and be made manifest.' (Translated and edited by RW Thomson, Oxford University Press, 1971).
34. Gunton, op. cit. p. 178.
35. Ibid. p. 180. Note also his comment, adapting Gregory of Nazianzus: 'If Jesus Christ is not fully man, the human condition is not restored *from within*—"the unassumed is the unhealed"; if he is not also God, we are not healed, for only God can, by reconciling us to himself, restore to authenticity our deeply alienated lives.' (p. 181).
36. Gunton draws interesting parallels between Platonic and post-Kantian dualisms. Kant encapsulated the Enlightenment's tendency to make absolute the temporal, just as Plato represents Hellenism's tendency to conceive of the eternal as timeless. While recognizing how the Fathers sometimes failed, crowding out the temporal figure of Jesus in their christology, Gunton nevertheless points out that 'The wonder is, rather, that so often the Fathers were able to break through the axioms of their world to produce what, as orthodox Christology, came to assert the co-presence of both eternity and time in this one historical figure. Against this background it is possible to see orthodox Christology as not the slave but the critic of Hellenistic philosophy.' (p. 105). He also notes Cochrane's observation that Athanasius' doctrine of coinherence (or *perichoresis* within the Trinity) was the basis for an understanding of reality that at once transcended and demolished Hellenistic ontology.
37. Here is a good example of the way classical theological concepts can be reinterpreted in modern context while remaining true to the reality they express: 'Many difficulties with transcendence derive from the way in which visual patterns of perception dominate our understanding of space. The things we see are mutually exclusive.

For example, a patch of blue in a painting excludes the presence of any other colour . . . But do the phenomena of hearing enable us to trancend the alienation of absolute space? The answer, of course, is in music. When, for example, the notes of a major triad are played simultaneously, we hear in one and the same place three tones which retain their identity and create a new reality, the chord. That is in itself an interesting parallel to the statement that in Jesus Christ there are two co-present realities—what Chalcedon called the human and divine natures—which in their association, the "hypostatic union", form a new reality which yet does not do away with the specific characteristics of the old: "without confusion, without change".' (Ibid, p. 115).

38. GWF Hegel, *Lectures on the Philosophy of Religion*, 1895, quoted in ibid. p. 42.
39. S Kierkegaard, *Training in Christianity* (Eng.trans. W.Lowrie, Princeton University Press, 1941) p. 123.
40. Ibid. p. 105.
41. Gunton, op. cit. p. 194.
42. G Parrinder, *Avatars and Incarnations* (London: Faber & Faber, 1970) p. 19.
43. *Bhagavad Gita, 4:7–8,* trans. R.C. Zaehner (Oxford University Press, 1973).
44. One of the best refutations of this latter view, combined with a thoughtful exposition of the Incarnation against the backdrop of God's revelation in the created order, remains that of CS Lewis in Chapter 14 of *Miracles* (London: Collins, 1947).
45. N Smart and S Konstantine, *Christian Systematic Theology in a World Context* (London: Marshall Pickering, 1991) pp. 255–6.
46. Smart and Konstantine also note that the Incarnation differs greatly from the Mahayana Buddhist concept of a multiplicity of *bodhisattvas* and of the idea of the Transformation-body (*nirmana-kaya*) of the Buddha in the *Trikaya* doctrine of the Yogacara school. While the latter notion may have 'some superficial resemblances to the Trinity idea', 'many Buddhists, among them distinguished modern scholars such as Edward Conze and DT Suzuki, regard celestial Buddhas and *bodhisattvas* essentially as objects of meditation. It is argued by some too that this fact of the virtually fictional character of such great beings is an advantage, for Buddhism does not, like Christianity, have to depend on the nitty-gritty of history.' (p. 257).
47. S Radhakrishnan, *The Bhagavadgita: Introductory Essay* (London: Allen & Unwin, 1949) p. 37.
48. Ibid. p. 32.
49. A Farrer, *Saving Belief* (London: Hodder, 1964) p. 75. Note also his wonderful description of the Incarnation: 'What then did God do for his people's redemption? . . . He set divine life in human neighbourhood. Men discovered it in struggling with it and were captured by it in crucifying it.' (p. 99).
50. B Hebblethwaite, *The Incarnation: Collected Essays in Christology* (Cambridge University Press, 1987) p. 50.
51. D Bonhoeffer, *Ethics* (Eng. trans. London: SCM, 1955) p. 18.
52. Ibid. p. 17.

53. Ibid. p. 20 (My emphasis).

54. Ibid. p. 19.

55. The classic work on Gnosticism is by Hans Jonas, *The Gnostic Religion* (2nd ed, Boston, 1963). See also Kurt Rudolph, Gnosis (New York, 1983); Edwin Yamauchi, *Pre-Christian Gnosticism* (Grand Rapids, 1983); and the essays by Birger Pearson, Jacques-E Menard and Gordon Macrae in EP Sanders (ed), *Jewish and Christian Self-Definition*, vol.1 (SCM,1980). All standard works on early Church history and doctrine contain summaries of gnostic teachings, e.g. JND Kelly, *Early Christian Doctrines* (London: A & C Black, 5th rev.ed. 1977, pp. 22–8).

56. Manicheanism was the religion founded by Mani (212–276); its most famous convert was Augustine prior to his turning to Christianity. Hans Jonas describes Mani's syncretistic world religion as 'the most monumental single embodiment of the gnostic religious principle, for whose doctrinal and mythological representation the elements of older religions were consciously employed' (op. cit. p. 207), and observes that 'Mani's is the only gnostic system which became a broad historical force, and the religion based on it must in spite of its eventual downfall be ranked among the great religions of mankind. Mani indeed, alone among the gnostic system-builders, intended to found, not a select group of initiates, but a new universal religion; and so his doctrine, unlike the teaching of other Gnostics with the exception of Marcion, has nothing esoteric about it' (ibid. p. 206). Mani was successful in his intention to a remarkable degree— beginning in Iraq, the Manichean religion spread West into North Africa and Italy and in the East as far as China. After its extinction in the West, following Zoroastrian persecution, it survived for a millenium in Central Asia and the East.

57. H Chadwick, *The Early Church* (London: Penguin, 1967) pp. 37–8.

58. D Minns, *Irenaeus* (London: Geoffrey Chapman, 1994) p. 24.

59. Cf. also J-E Menard, 'No matter how authentically mystical they may be, most Gnostic texts leave next to no place either to a divine intervention from outside or to a God who knows and loves man first, the way Paul understands it for example in Gal. 4:8–9 and 1 Cor. 8:1–3. On the contrary, the *Gospel of Truth* of Codex 1 [Nag Hammadi Library] claims that man knows the Divine first and is known by it in a mutual and reciprocal identification (19.30–33). Phenomenologically speaking, true Gnosis could easily be defined as being a mystical theology of the identification of God with the Self', ('Normative Self-Definition in Gnosticism' in EP Sanders (ed), *Jewish and Christian Self-Definition*, vol.1 (London: SCM, 1980) p. 149).

60. S Radhakrishnan, *The Hindu View of Life* (New York: Macmillan, 1969) p. 24.

61. E Conze, *Further Buddhist Studies* (London: Cassirer, 1975) pp. 15–32.

62. Ibid. p. 17. Conze recognizes the fact that, unlike the gnostics, classical Buddhism showed no interest in what may have preceded ignorance. All that was necessary to know was how salvation could

be achieved. But he adds the proviso that the later Yogacarins, particularly in China, devoted much attention to the stages by which the world is derived from an original pure 'store-consciousness' (*alayavi-jnana*). (p. 27).

63. Con7e notes that the division between 'saints' and 'foolish world-lings' is found in all Buddhist sects and go back a long time. After about A.D. 200 some Mahayanists superimposed upon it another division which distinguishes three classes (*rasi*) of people, viz. those destined for salvation (*samyaktva-niyata*), those destined for perdition (*mithyatva-niyata*) and those destiny is not fixed either way (*aniyata*) (Ibid. p. 19). But it must be emphasized that this not part of the mainstream Buddhist tradition.

64. Ibid. p. 25. Conze also notes that 'however the world may have come about, at present it is, in any case, the domain of an evil force, of Satan or of Mara the Evil One'.

65. How do we account for these kinships? Conze only states the problem and admits that there is no definite historical solution. He points out that we have abundant evidence of the close contact between the Buddhist and Hellenistic world and the possibility of much mutual borrowing is strong. However the mode of trans-mission remains obscure. He also notes that the Buddhists were in contact with the Manicheans of Persia and Central Asia and that 'it is indeed remarkable that Gnostic texts often invoke Jewish, Babylonian, Iranian, Egyptian, etc. authorities, but very rarely Buddhist ones.' (p. 31).

66. 'The affirmation of the oneness of God, imperilled by Gnostic speculation of every sort, was the indispensable premiss for refuting the Gnostic separation of the Testaments, and to demonstrate this oneness was the principal task of Irenaeus and his contemporaries', JND Kelly, *Early Christian Doctrines*, op. cit. p. 69.

67. Marcion (c.80–c.160) should not be classed among the gnostics though he shared some things in common with them. He is best known for his rejection of all Old Testament and Jewish influences in the New Testament, opposing the God of law, justice and wrath in Judaism with the hitherto unknown Father of Jesus Christ who brought mercy and salvation. While for Marcion the two gods had nothing to do with each other and vied for the allegiance of humankind, the gnostic sects had a more sophisticated view of differentiation and harmony among the gods.

68. Minns, op. cit. pp. 32–3.

69. Ibid. p. 33.

70. His philosophical arguments against them are found in Book II of *Adversus Haereses*, while the theological-scriptural arguments follow in Book III. Some scholars regard the former as the weakest aspect of his case, e.g., G Vallee, 'Theological and Non-Theological Motives in Irenaeus' Refutation of the Gnostics' in EP Sanders (ed), *Jewish and Christian Self-Definition*, *Vol. 1* (London: SCM, 1980). But see Minns, op. cit.

71. E.g. *Adv. Haer.* IV.13.1, 4; 14.1–2; 16.3–4; 20.4; 40.1.

72. *Adv. Haer.* V.15.2.

73. *Adv. Haer.* V.18.1–2.

74. E.g. *Adv. Haer.* III.18.6; V.18.3.

75. *Adv. Haer.* IV.20.7. All translations are from *The Ante-Nicene Fathers* trans. A. Roberts and J. Donaldson (Eerdmans, 1987 reprint).

76. It was the Word, Irenaeus says, who walked in the garden with Adam; the Word, and not the Father, whom the prophets saw in their visions (*Adv. Haer.* IV.20.7–8). Although the Word/Son who reveals the Father co-exists eternally with the Father, for Irenaeus the theophanies of the Old Testament were anticipatory visions of the Word incarnate.

77. 'With Him is nothing incomplete or out of due season, just as with the Father there is nothing incongruous. For all these things were foreknown by the Father; but the Son works them out at the proper time in perfect order and sequence.' (*Adv. Haer.* III.16.7).

78. *Adv. Haer.* IV.38.4.

79. Minns, op. cit. p. 62.

80. E.g. *Adv. Haer.* IV.38.4; 39.2–3.

81. Minns, op. cit. p. 137.

82. 'According to nature, then—that is, according to creation, so to speak—we are all sons of God, because we have all been created by God. But with respect to obedience and doctrine we are not all the sons of God: only those are so who believe in Him and do His will. And those who do not believe, and do not obey His will, are sons and angels of the devil, because they do the works of the devil.' (*Adv. Haer.* IV.41.2) For his belief in the reality of judgment and hell, cf. *Adv. Haer.* V.26.2, V.27.1–2, V.35.1–2, V.36.1–3.

83. E.g. *Adv. Haer.* III.20.2.

84. *Adv.Haer.* V.36.1–3.

85. E.g. *Adv. Haer.* IV.11.1–2. Note also V.2.3: '. . . because the strength of God is made perfect in weakness, in order that we may never become puffed up, as if we had life from ourselves, and exalted against God our minds, becoming ungrateful; but learning by experience that we possess eternal duration from the excelling power of this Being, not from our own nature, we may neither undervalue that glory which surrounds God as He is, nor be ignorant of our own nature . . .'

86. E.g. *Adv. Haer.* IV.38.2.

87. *Adv. Haer.* II.28.1–2.

88. *Adv. Haer.* II.13.3. For Irenaeus, in contrast, God is entirely simple: he has no parts, his acts cannot be distinguished and classified. For God, unlike us humans, thinking, planning, willing, and performing are all one act.

89. *Adv. Haer.* II.28.1–3.

90. Modern theologians distinguish between an *immanent* and an *economic* theology of Trinity. The former refers to attempts to express how God is in himself: how the essential oneness is related to the distinctiveness of Father, Son and Spirit. We have seen that the word 'economy' was used by Greek-speaking theologians such as Irenaeus to refer to God's plan of salvation. So economic theologies of the

Trinity explore the way God reveals himself in and to his creation. Irenaeus lived at a time before the necessity to develop an immanent theology became a pressing issue in combating false views of Christ's salvation. In the orthodox Christian tradition, immanent theologies have always been subservient to the economic.

[8]

Gospel Praxis

'In former generations this mystery was not made known to humankind, as it has now been revealed to his holy apostles and prophets by the Spirit: that is, the Gentiles have become fellow heirs, members of the same body, and sharers in the promise in Christ Jesus through the gospel' (Ephesians 3:5–6).

We have seen that the unique story which the Bible tells reaches its climax in the incarnation, ministry, crucifixion and resurrection of Jesus of Nazareth, the Son of God. The 'religious' stories of other cultures, even stories of dying and rising gods, illustrate an unchanging human condition, obviously rooted in the universal human experiences of birth, suffering and death. They make no claim to be datable events in world history nor to have affected irrevocably the course of that history. If the biblical story is true in the sense that it claims to be true, then it is true for all. Its very uniqueness constitutes its universality. The universal purpose of God, embodying his gracious love towards all his creation, is communicated in and through the particular events which centre in Jesus of Nazareth.

We have seen how these events also became the controlling reality for a new world view which challenged the reigning world views of the ancient world and which continue to do the same in the world of modernity (and, if one accepts the rigid distinction, post-modernity). This gospel has been a cause of offence from the very beginnings of the Christian movement. Those who have found it most offensive have been the official guardians of the dominant plausibility structures and the socio–political structures associated with the latter. As in ancient Israel, so in the modern

265

world, new world views and new socio-political practices go hand in hand.

Gospel Humanity

The gospel creates new human community, and that new human community is itself part of the gospel to be pro-claimed. All proposals for building human community presuppose some particular understanding of the human condition and have as their unifying centre some particular programme or person. The form such community takes (whether, say, in the Nazi party, a scientific institution or a multinational corporation) will depend on the nature of that unifying centre. The opening chapters of Paul's letter to the Ephesians are an exposition of the cross of Jesus Christ as the centre of history, as the means by which God's way of peace is effected. It is through the 'blood of Christ' (2:13, cf. 1:7) that both Jew and Gentile are made one—with God and with each other. The vertical and the horizontal dimensions of peace are interwoven in such a way that *it is impossible to speak of one without referring to the other*. The death of Christ breaks down the 'dividing wall, that is, the hostility between us' (2:14b) so that the 'new humanity' that is created in its place may be 'reconciled to God in one body through the cross' and thus 'have access in one Spirit to the Father' (2:15ff).

The fact that this is all God's work, and not the result of human effort, is the secret both of its efficacy and also of its 'offence'. The dividing wall between Jew and Gentile in Paul's day was 'the law with its commandments and ordinances' (2:15). As long as the Jew found his self-identity in the possession of the Torah, and thus looked down on those who did not either possess the Torah or keep the Torah within Israel, he was separated from his fellow human beings. Similarly, we could say in general that if our self-identity is rooted in anything we *possess*, whether it be our racial or cultural heritage, educational ability, theological scholarship, wealth, social prestige, religious devotion, 'meritorious works', political power, moral achievements, or whatever, that identity will always divide us from others who lack that particular possession. Language, Culture, Religion, Education, Science . . . all these, while either neutral or good in themselves, become causes of human division whenever they are sources of human identity. And they become sources of human identity when we reject the identity God confers on us. The attempt to 'make ourselves' through what we do, in whatever area of human action, stands in contradiction to divine *grace*.

Thus it is that 'law' must be abolished as a means of human self-identity if true reconciliation between God and humankind and within humankind can be realised. The Cross brings all human beings, men and women, rich and poor, religious and secular, to the same level before God. It confronts us with the claim that when the Son of God entered his world the highest representatives of religious wisdom and the highest representives of secular law put him to death. It is at the foot of the cross that all human beings, without exception, are exposed as sinners deserving of God's wrath. But it is also at the foot of the cross, that all human beings, without exception, are revealed as the objects of God's forgiving and re-creating love. This is all of grace: 'the gift of God—not the result of works, so that no one may boast. For we are what he has made us, created in Christ Jesus for good works, which God prepared beforehand to be our way of life.' (2:10).

The cross, in other words, humbles every form of human pride. It tells us that it is not the 'good Christian' or the 'sincere Hindu' or the 'devout Buddhist' or the 'men and women of good will' who are assured places in the kingdom of God. But, rather, that it is the bad Christian, the bad Hindu, the bad Buddhist—those who know themselves to be moral failures, that they have fallen hopelessly short of the kind of life they know (in their better moments) they should be living—it is these who are closer to the kingdom of God. This can be so precisely because salvation is through grace, mediated in the cross of Christ, received in faith. From the perspective of the cross, then, it appears that there are only two kinds of human being: those who, accepting their wretchednesss, lift their eyes to God for mercy; and those who, seeking to establish their own identity, spurn God's mercy and look down on others (cf. Lk. 18:9–14). True humanness, as Irenaeus reminded us, *is* salvation, and it can be received only as *gift*.

This, then, is the logic of the cross: the very act that binds me to God in grace binds me, *simultaneously*, to my neighbour in acceptance. The working out of that double-sided act in every dimension of my personal experience will, of course, take time. It is what we mean by 'conversion'. But this life-long process of conversion is not an addition to the gospel of God's grace; it is rather a matter of allowing the Holy Spirit to lead us deeper into the truth of the gospel and the transforming power of that truth. Within the pages of the New Testament the best-known example of this is provided by Peter's encounter with the Roman centurion Cornelius (Acts 10–11). The narrative records a process of 'double conversion'. On the one side, we see Peter repenting of his racial prejudice under the deepening impact of the gospel on his thinking and as a result of witnessing the same gospel at work in another's life. On the other side, Cornelius, upright and God-fearing though he was, still needed to hear the gospel from Peter's lips (not even from those of an angel!) in order to receive forgiveness of sin and the gift of the Holy Spirit.[1] The result is the stupendous sight, unimaginable in their contemporary world, of a Jewish peasant and a Roman centurion living together under one roof.

Returning to Paul and his letter to the Ephesians, it is this 'revealed secret' that Paul is constrained to share as an apostle of Christ. He himself is the recipient of mercy (3:7–8). The gospel has been entrusted to him, as it has been to the church, 'to bring to the Gentiles the news of the boundless riches of Christ' (3:8b). Once again we see the logic of election, incarnation and salvation working itself out through a particular human community to embrace all within its scope. Those who have received become the servants of those who have not, and thus true human community emerges. Grace, truth, mission and servanthood are inextricably interwoven in the gospel message itself; and it is these that form the basis of true human community.

It is important to affirm that this human community endorses a *cultural pluralism*. Paul campaigned vigorously against any attempt to impose Jewish cultural standards on Gentile believers, arguing that the unity which the gospel makes possible also serves to safeguard human diversity, precisely because salvation is a matter of divine grace not of human works. The West African scholar Lamin Sanneh has rebutted the popular charge that Christian mission in Africa and Asia has always led to the destruction of other cultures in the form of Western cultural hegemony. Sanneh points out that the major plank in Protestant mission strategy was always Bible translation. This often involved writing down a vernacular for the very first time, and the creation of grammars and local literatures. Translation of the Bible into over 2000 languages has been the chief instrument of indigenous cultural renewal in many parts of the world. By believing that the vernacular was adequate for participation in the Christian movement, the more serious-minded missionaries and translators have preserved a great variety of languages and cultures from extinction, and lifted obscure tribes and ethnic groups into the stream of universal history.

Sanneh writes,

> In many significant cases, these languages received their first breath of life from Christian interest. This is true whether we are speaking of Calvin and the birth of modern French, Luther and German, Tyndale and English, Robert de Nobili or William Carey and the Indian vernaculars, Miles Brunson and Assamese, Johannes Christaller and Akan in Ghana, Moffatt and Sichuana in Botswana, Ajayi Crowther and Yorruba in Nigeria, and Krapf and Swahili in East Africa, to take a random list from many examples . . . vernacular translation excites vernacular self-confidence, which in turn foments the national sentiment.[2]

Saneh observes that the Christian view that all cultures may serve God's purpose 'stripped culture of idolatrous liability, emancipating it with the force of translation and usage'.[3] It is perhaps another of the many ironies of church history that such indigenous renewal should have turned into anti-missionary stridency and later into nationalism.

Saneh invites us to contrast this attitude to culture with that of Hinduism or Islam. To the Hindu and Muslim alike, sacred texts are untranslatable. Sanskrit and Arabic are the divine tongues, and the culture of origin becomes the universal paradigm. Until quite late into this century, many high-caste Hindus believed that in venturing beyond India one became ritually contaminated. While Islam has practised social pluralism, it is 'through tolerance rather than the substitution by the vernacular of Arabic'.[4] The missionary success of Islam is in effect the universalization of Arabic as the language of faith. Every Muslim must step into Arabic on entering the mosque to perform his rites, a daily passage that for many reaches its climax in the annual *hajj*, the pilgrimage to Mecca. When one considers that three out of every four Muslims in the world are non-Arabs, it is clear that this implies a down-grading of their mother tongues in the fundamental acts of piety and devotion. Cultural diversity is regarded, at best, irrelevant or, at worst, a hindrance to faith.

Given the homogenizing pressures of modernity and the massive assault on our societies of ugly American 'mass culture', it is surely an important part of our Christian calling to encourage local peoples to recover the riches of their own cultural heritages; and for Christian artists, musicians, architects and theologians to make them appropriate vehicles for the glory of Christ.

✝ Gospel Integrity

How then should the gospel travel among the nations? If Christian mission is a matter of bearing witness to the unique story that has its centre the incarnation, atoning death and bodily resurrection of Jesus Christ, how are we testify to that story before those who believe otherwise? Once again, it is to the heart of the gospel itself that we must turn for guidance. The argument outlined in the remainder of this book is simply that the manner in which we witness to the gospel must be consistent with its content.

(a) Since the gospel affirms all human beings as created in the image of God and as the objects of their Creator's seeking love, we must accord them the *respect* that their created dignity requires. Thus we shall welcome and rejoice in every sign of God's grace at work in the lives of people who do not know Jesus as Lord. There are struggles for justice and human dignity in which we can (and must) cooperate with those of other worldviews in order to achieve specific goals which conform to our vision of God's kingdom. Obviously we shall differ on our respective visions of the ultimate meaning and goal of history, as well as in our motivations for the struggle. There will be points in our common journey with others where we shall find that our ways must part. But such points of divergence are real opportunities for genuine dialogue and faithful witness. As Jürgen Moltmann observes, while the real motivation in dialogue is 'to change conditions that are life-threatening, in other words, directed towards practical consequences', nevertheless 'a dialogue that does not revolve around the question of truth remains irrelevant.'[5] To work alongside people of all faiths and ideologies, without losing the critical questioning and radical challenge that the gospel poses to all faiths and ideologies, requires a breath of vision and courage that the gospel itself can impart.

I take it for granted that no genuine conversion of mind and will can ever be brought about by coercion or financial inducements, and that respect involves a rejection of any emotional manipulation in the presentation of the gospel. I also assume that it is intrinsic to the nature of love that it allows the object of its love to go his or her own way, even if that way is a passage to hell. It is here that genuine respect for the other is far more virtuous than the easy tolerance advocated by many in our pluralist societies. Whoever boasts of being 'tolerant' towards other beliefs while, at the same time, asserting either that such beliefs are fundamentally no different to any other sets of beliefs or that, even if they were, they do not make any decisive difference to a person's life now or ever, is simply emptying the word tolerance of any moral value. At worst, it is simply a narcissistic endorsement of one's own worldview. Conceptual and ethical relativists, religious pluralists and the 'politically correct' ideologues of the post-modern world have never experienced the pain involved in an act of genuine tolerance. To believe that my neighbour is wrong in her beliefs and that as long as she clings to her beliefs she will suffer eternal ruin, and yet at the same time to defend and protect her freedom to hold those beliefs . . . this, surely, is the real meaning of tolerance.

But Christian respect goes beyond social tolerance to servant-hood. My fellow human being, of whatever persuasion, has a claim on my life simply by virtue of being human. The church (as William Temple pointed out) is probably the only society on earth which exists for the sake of those who do not belong to it. In a pluralist world, the church is called by the gospel to champion not her own 'rights' but the 'rights' of other communities and individuals, indeed to be willing even to lay aside her own 'rights' in order to do so. And in doing so, she will come into confrontation with political authorities and the chauvinisms of many 'religious' people even within her own ranks.

It is a fact that while Christians are treated as second-class citizens in many Islamic countries, to the point of being denied basic civil liberties, Muslim immigrants in the West expect and demand equality in all areas of national life. This fact must never be used by Christians in the West to justify discrimination against Muslims or to oppose the building of mosques on what was formerly church land; for to do so would be to deny the very gospel that calls us to lay down our lives for even our enemies. I cannot help feeling that the indifference of many Western Christians and their governments to the genocide of Muslims in Bosnia has severely damaged, for many generations to come, the credibility of Christian witness in the Islamic world.

Respect for people means that we do not regard them as primarily Buddhists or Muslims or as members of some other abstract class, but rather as unique individuals. What a person really believes and treasures in life can be discovered only through personal engagement. Often many in the rural areas of Asia who are labelled Buddhists have more in common with primal religions than with the rationalism of Theravadin scholars or the mysticism of the Mahayanists. Much urban 'Buddhism' is centred on popular Hindu gurus and personal astrologers. Similarly many Christians in the older churches of the Indian subcontinent wear their Christianity as simply a sociological label, with little, if any, biblical shaping of their outlook and behaviour. Willingness to explore the sacred texts of the religious traditions of others is, of course, a necessary aspect of showing respect; but these can never be a substitute for the more costly demands of friendship. As an old Chinese proverb reminds us, 'He who comes with the odour of enmity will invite the clash of weapons, he who comes with the fragrance of friendship will be loved like a brother.'[6]

Respect for people thus involves the readiness to listen. Any attempt to 'read into' other people's beliefs a content that is congenial to my own is to fail to respect them. Sometimes the differences may be less important than we thought, at other times the similarities we assumed to exist turn out on closer inspection to be very superficial. The foregoing pages offer several examples of how distortions arise when concepts are prised apart from the worldview and social practices in which they are embedded. Listening will lead, at times, to new appreciation; at other times, profound disagreement and vigorous debate. Intellectual persuasion through debate is itself an act of respect for the integrity of the other.

(b) Since the gospel announces the sheer grace of God towards unworthy sinners, it can be commended to others only in a spirit of *humility*. Why I should have been chosen to bear witness to this gospel has nothing to do with my personal qualities, let alone merit. It is all of grace. This forbids me from thinking of the gospel as my possession and of evangelism as a matter of demonstrating the superiority of my 'religion' over all others. Salvation is not through any religion, and the Christ who is the world's Saviour stands also as Judge over every religious practice, institution and ideology, including the empirical church and what is known historically as 'Christianity'. The Christian is a forgiven sinner among other sinners; and she has no need to defend every perversion of the gospel and every atrocity committed in the name of Christianity in the history of her nation. Indeed it is the gospel that enbables her to humbly ask forgiveness from non-Christians for the sins of the Christian church. Asking forgiveness *from* others is as much an outflow of the gospel as is the offer of divine forgiveness *to* others.

The other aspect of the gospel that makes humility a distinctive mark of Christian witness is that salvation is not only 'now' but 'not yet'. Salvation is the glorious completion of God's work in creation and redemption, the summing up of all things with Christ as head (Eph. 1:10). Until that day when all hostile powers are subject to Christ and we share in the resurrection of the dead (1 Cor. 15:24–28), we see 'in a mirror, dimly' (1 Cor. 13:12). I am *simul justus et peccator* (saint and sinner). I have been grasped by the truth as it is in Christ Jesus, yet am ever growing into the fullness of that truth. In this pilgrimage, even as I share the story of Jesus with others, I find myself drawn deeper into the story and given fresh insights into it. It is humility that enables me to see the ways in which I may be prone to use my 'Christianity' to conceal inconvenient truths about God and myself or to bolster my own ego in self-justification. Evangelism, if authentic, changes the bearers as well as the recipients of the gospel.

In our discussion of Irenaeus we noted the attractive balance of conviction and agnosticism in his theological outlook. Perhaps we modern Christians need to meditate more than we do on the closing words of Deuteronomy 29: 'The secret things belong to the Lord our God, but the revealed things belong to us and to our children for ever . . .' (29:29). Christian wisdom distinguishes between what can be clearly known, as a result of God's initiative in revealing himself to his world, and what is still obscure because they lie outside that revelation. It is as arrogant to suppress revealed truth as it is to elevate speculation to the status of truth.

Questions such as the final destiny of people who, through no fault of their own, have never had a chance to hear the good news of Jesus Christ, can safely be left in the hands of a God who the gospel reveals to be both just and gracious in his dealings with humankind. Both 'fundamentalists' and 'liberals' have been guilty of arrogance in this regard. To argue that all who do not make a verbal confession of faith in Jesus as Lord are eternally lost is not only to go beyond the biblical evidence, it is to deny salvation to the Old Testament people of God, the mentally handicapped and little children. Similarly, to argue that all men and women are saved, irrespective of Christ, is to contradict the entire biblical testimony. All we can say, humbly yet boldly, is that if anyone *is* saved it will not be through any religion or human attainment, but solely through the objective, atoning death and resurrection of Jesus Christ, whether consciously appropriated or not.

Once again it is to Lesslie Newbigin that we turn for a sharp and eloquent rejoinder to both the 'exclusivist' and the 'universalist' positions within the contemporary church. He points out that all true thinking must be held within the 'magnetic field' set up between the twin poles of the 'amazing grace of God and the appalling sin of the world'.[7] For Newbigin,

> The same revelation in Jesus Christ, with its burning centre in the agony and death of Calvary, compels me to acknowledge that this world which God made and loves is in a state of alienation, rejection and rebellion against him. Calvary is the central unveiling of the infinite love of God and at the same time the unmasking of the dark horror of sin. Here not the dregs of humanity, not the scoundrels whom all good people condemn, but the revered leaders in church, state, and culture, combine in one murderous intent to destroy the holy one by whose mercy they exist and were created.[8]

One can slacken the tension between these two poles by either invoking some form of universalism or by limiting the operation of God's grace to one's own understanding and experience. In both cases, genuine encounter is impossible with those outside the church. In the first case 'dialogue' becomes vacuous because nothing vital is at stake; in the second case 'dialogue' is irrelevant because the other is simply someone to be rescued. Newbigin observes that 'Nothing could be more remote from the whole thrust of Jesus' teaching than the idea that we are in a position to know in advance the final judgment of God. It would be tedious to repeat again the innumerable warnings of Jesus in this matter, his repeated statements that the last day will be a day of surprises, of reversals, of astonishment.'[9]

This kind of theological position, which seeks a biblical balance of confidence and humility, defies classification under the customary categories of exclusivist, pluralist and inclusivist where Christian views on the world religions are concerned.[10] It is exclusivist in the sense that it 'affirms the unique truth of the revelation in Jesus Christ', but it is not exclusivist in the sense of 'denying the possibility of the salvation of the non-Christian'.

> It is inclusivist in the sense that it refuses to limit the saving grace of God to the members of the Christian Church, but it rejects the inclusivism which regards the non-Christian religions as vehicles of salvation. It is pluralist in the sense of acknowledging the gracious work of God in the lives of all human beings, but it rejects a pluralism which denies the uniqueness and decisiveness of what God has done in Jesus Christ.[11]

(c) Since the heart of the gospel concerns God incarnate, it can only be communicated in an *incarnational* way. The good news of the saving love of God was embodied in a human life, finding its climax in that life poured out in death. The legitimate fear that many have of any claim to absolute truth derives from the historical observation that such claims have led to intellectual tyranny and social repression. But enough has been said to indicate that the logic of the gospel leads us in a different direction. We have seen how the claim of Jesus to absolute truth and, therefore, an absolute authority, was expressed in the form of lowly, sacrificial service. The community that has been brought into being by this truth and entrusted with it for the sake of others can only proclaim that truth in the way of Jesus. Truth is not only embodied in a community, but in a community that reliquishes power in identification with the powerless.

It is salutary to remember that Jesus never taught his disciples any techniques or methodologies of mission. But he did leave with them two abiding missionary principles, both of which are sadly absent from most modern discussions of global evangelization. They are both found in the Fourth Gospel as part of the teaching of Jesus in the last week prior to the crucifixion. The first is the principle of *loving*: 'By this everyone will know that you are my disciples, if you have love for one another' (Jn 13:35). First stated following his symbolic act of foot-washing, it is repeated in Jesus' final prayer for them as he launches them into a hostile world: 'I in them and you in me, that they may become completely one, so that the world may know that you have sent me and have loved them even as you have loved me.' (17:23). It is the growing unity of the disciple–community, drawing together people of all cultural and social backgrounds, which will convince sceptics not only that Christ is the supreme locus of divine revelation but that Christians have been caught up into the eternal love of the Father for his unique Son.

If the church is part of the gospel, then it follows that authentic witness can only be ecumenical witness.[12] The world must see as well as hear the gospel. The communication of the gospel is not the work of some roving evangelist who drops in for a brief, slickly organized 'crusade'; rather it is the work of local Christian communities who patiently articulate to others what Christ is doing so obviously in their own collective life. Christians who come from outside the local situation must first seek out local believers and identify with them. Where there is a local church, the incarnational missionary puts himself and his special skills at the disposal of the church and is accountable primarily to its leaders and not to his home church.

At the end of his wonderfully comprehensive survey of the early history of the Christian movement in Asia, Sam Moffett explores some of the possible causes for the decline and near-total disappearance of the church at the start of the colonial age. He observes, for instance, how, while 'sharp persecution breaks off only the tips of the branches', 'never-ending social and political repression' (as under the various Islamic empires) 'starves the roots' and stifles evangelism.[13] He wisely desists from offering any 'definitive answer' to the question of the church's decline, confessing that there are often times when 'history can only be described, not explained' and that he is content to leave it as 'one of the mysteries of the providence of God'.[14] But not before declaring that 'in Asia, as everywhere, Christians have always been their own worst enemies'. Moffett rightly notes that the deadliest obstacles to mission are found within, not outside the church: 'The School of Nisibis, for example, was almost destroyed not by Zoroastrian priests but by dissension in its own Christian faculty. Pride and rivalry among quarrelling bishops were as much to blame for state interference in the government of the Church as the ambition of Zoroastrian shahs and Muslim caliphs to control it.'[15] This sad story continues in Asia right through to the closing decade of the second millenium.

This leads us into the second great principle of missionary fruitfulness, namely *dying*: 'Unless a grain of wheat falls into the earth and dies, it remains just a single grain; but if it dies, it bears much fruit' (John 12:24). This is spoken in the context of the Son of Man's imminent 'glorification' on the cross (12:23,27), and it applies to the disciples' mission what is true of the biological order: there is no life without death. The grain of wheat (rice in an Asian context) falls into the soil and is buried, disappears from view for many months, and then emerges as a fruitful stalk. Likewise the disciple-community of Jesus, walking in the footsteps of their Master, must be prepared to be buried—buried in a world of cruelty, poverty, bigotry, violence, hopelessness . . . the same world which crucified their Master. The church that seeks security, prestige and worldly power is no longer the church of the crucified Jesus. In this regard, it is a striking fact that whenever Paul was challenged to prove his apostolic credentials, it was to his sufferings that he always pointed.[16] The power of the gospel can only be demonstrated through weakness and humiliation. It seems that the apostolic church is recognized in the world not only by her verbal profession of the apostolic gospel but by her sharing in apostolic suffering.[17]

Why is suffering the mark of the authentic church? Because the gospel it bears for the world is the story of a God who suffered and was brutalized at the hands of his creatures. Such a gospel, we have seen, is deeply subversive of all other stories, whether religious or secular. It calls for a conversion of mind and will that is far-reaching in its implications. It challenges the false gods that men and women erect in every society as substitutes for the living God, substitutes that can be manipulated to protect the vested interests of the rich and the powerful. It exposes the demonic elements in the 'highest' religions and much-vaunted culture of modernity. It demonstrates a new way of being truly human, a way that calls into question all other definitions of humanness. It declares a higher claim and loyalty on our lives than those of family, ethnic group or nation; and it calls those who bear the name of Christ not only to suffer for that name, but to embrace willingly the pain and suffering of others who do not profess the name of Christ. The church, in the name of the crucified Jesus and in the power of his Spirit, make an unflinching challenge to all the powers of evil that control the present world-order, but it does so in total vulnerability.

The church in Asia is still deeply divided and, in many places, still bears the crippling legacy of the colonial experience. But, outside the pockets of comfortable affluence and 'respectability' that we find in some Asian city churches, the great majority of Asian Christians today are economically poor (though not destitute), politically marginalized and socially insignificant. This is especially true of evangelical Christians in China and the Indian subcontinent. What this means is that, for the first time in her history, the church can no longer be identifed with the power blocs of West and East. The gospel goes out, as it did at its inception, not from the 'top' downwards but from the 'bottom' upwards. Perhaps the evangelization of Asia, which some religious pluralists have dismissed as a total failure after four hundred years of Western missionary endeavour, has only just begun. . . . And, may we not envisage the possibility that as Western Christians learn to disentangle the gospel of Christ from the assumptions, values and practices of pagan Western society, they too will experience the social ostracism and suffering that the gospel brings, so that the evangelization of Europe and North America will have begun afresh?

In his book *Hindu and Christian in Vrindaban* the German missionary Klaus Klostermaier, who spent many years in an ashram in India, writes scathingly of what he calls 'the 70 degF theologians'. They are those who 'settle down in some library and find enough books there by means of which it can be proved that the non-Christian religions are the normal way to salvation for the non-Christian, that each one finds God even without mission—that one should not disturb the conscience of the non-Christian.' Klostermeier contrasts this attitude with the incarnate Christ who 'tired himself out, exposed himself to heat and cold'. He continues, ' How strange that he did not rely on the fact that God would redeem the world in any case, that he himself should go through the fire of death and find his God in the ultimate solitude of agony! How strange that he should have asked his disciples to do as he had done . . .'[18]

Gospel Radicalness

We noted in the opening section of the previous chapter that what attracted many pagans to the Christian faith in the first few centuries, before the church came to be identified with power and privilege, was the new way of humanness embodied in the Christian communities. Moreover, the manner in which Christians went to their deaths was a perpetual source of wonder and bewilderment to their pagan neighbours. In a stimulating essay on evangelism in this period, Alan Kreider reminds us that often the initial encounter between non-Christians and Christians came through witnessing a martyrdom, 'which brought these communities a notoriety that they would have preferred to avoid'.[19] Their endurance in the amphitheatre, their trans-parent love for each other, caused those who had previously given no thought to the Christian movement to ask questions. 'What profit has their religion brought them, which they have preferred to their own life?' asked incredulous onlookers in the Lyons pogrom.[20] Many Christians testified that it was the fidelity of the martyrs that had first attracted their attention to the faith. In Tertullian's words, faithfulness in public suffering 'is the bait that wins men for our school.'[21]

But Kreider also notes that 'no teaching was more repeated by the Christians, or more pondered by the pagans, than Jesus' command to love the enemy.'[22] This could have been part of an extremely early fixed catechetical tradition within the Church.[23] In any case, the way Christians provided not only for the material needs of their own community but also for that of their hostile neighbours often dumbfounded contemporaries. Pagans received poor relief and hospitality at the hands of Christians who were often as poor as themselves. Eloquent testimony to this practice comes from an unlikely source, the ex-Christian emperor Julian ('the Apostate') who, finding it difficult in the 360s to reinstitute paganism as the official religion of the Empire, complained against Christians that it was 'their benevolence to strangers, their care for the graves of the dead and the pretended holiness of their lives that has done most to increase their atheism . . . the impious Galileans support not only their own poor but ours as well'.[24] Kreider comments: 'However, his attempts to get the pagan priests to stir their adherents to comparable practices were, like his brief reign, barren. For all his contention that 'this was our practice of old', nobody believed him. The pagans had neither the living traditions, nor the theological understandings, nor the communal disciplines, nor the appropriate rites to make this practice live among them.'[25]

Kreider gives two interesting examples of radical Christian service from the third century. The first relates to how Christians in Alexandria intervened, on both sides, in a civil war to attempt to mediate a dispute and to bring relief to the victims of both warring parties.[26] The second, taken from the life of Bishop Cyprian of Carthage as reported by his biographer Pontius, relates to the great plague which followed on the heels of the Decian persecution of 250–51.[27] In this situation of great danger, when wealthy pagans were fleeing Carthage, Cyprian preached to his congregation from Matthew 5:43–48, urging them not to save their own lives, not even to seek the survival of their Christian community, but to love their enemies who had recently been persecuting them. This was an opportunity to show the love of Jesus by staying in the city and nursing pagan and Christian alike. A recent study has shown that, not only did the minority Christian community which did not flee but stayed to provide nursing have a higher survival rate than their pagan neighbours, but that the pagans who had been cared for through the crisis by Christians were likely to be open to a faith that, unlike their own, had demonstrably worked.[28]

Thus, in an age of social fragmentation, political disorder and psychological bondages of various kinds, the newness of life that the Christian communities practised towards non-members was 'intriguing, inviting, question-posing'.[29] Why, people asked, did they live like that? Kreider has no hesitation in ascribing the spread of the gospel in this way to the quality of worship experienced in the church. Worship was significant, not because it was attractive to pagans (who were, in any event, prohibited from attending Christian services), but because 'its rites and practices were designed to re-form those pagans who joined the Church into Christians, into distinctive people who lived in a way that individually and corporately looked like Jesus Christ. As such these people, re-formed, would be attractive'.[30]

Hence the importance given in Christian catechetical instruction (such as Irenaeus' *Proof of the Apostolic Preaching*, for instance, or Origen's daily Old Testament expositions) to imparting a living narrative, a history which finds its culmination in Jesus Christ, which would supersede other narratives and equip these new-born Christians with life-giving precedents for the journey on which they had embarked. Men and women undergoing catechism and experiencing worship in the Christian churches were being 'rehabituated', so that they would 'react to situations of tension and difficulty in a distinctive way, not like pagans, but like members of a Christian community, and ideally like Jesus'.[31]

I am reminded here of Dietrich Bonhoeffer's passionate insistence that 'to be conformed to the Incarnate—that is to be a real man'.[32] The primary concern of the Scriptures, Bonhoeffer pointed out, was 'not the forming of a world by means of plans and programmes', but, rather, 'with the one form which has overcome the world, the form of Jesus Christ.'[33] Formation was not a matter of applying Christian values and teaching to the world, least of all was Christ 'a principle' in accordance with which the world must be shaped. Christian ethics was not an abstract system but, on the contrary, the living process of 'being drawn into the form of Jesus Christ . . . as *conformation* with the unique form of Him who was made man, was crucified, and rose again.'[34]

For Bonhoeffer, the point of departure for Christian ethics is 'the body of Christ, the form of Christ in the form of the Church, and the formation of the Church in conformity with the form of Christ.'[35] The church bears the form which is in truth the proper form of all humanity.

> The Church is the man in Christ, incarnate, sentenced and awakened to new life. In the first instance, therefore, she has essentially nothing whatever to do with the so-called religious functions of man, but with the whole man in his existence in the world and all its implications. What matters in the Church is

not religion but the form of Christ, and its taking form amidst a band of men.[36]

Thus, 'It is not Christian men who shape the world with their ideas, but it is Christ who shapes men in conformity with Himself.'[37]

Alan Kreider rightly observes that Christians today are separated from pre-Christendom Christians not only by a gulf of seventeen hundred years but also by Christendom itself. 'In my experience most people today view Christians not as advocates of something new and exciting but rather as blinkered defenders of views that are old, which have been tried, and which have failed.'[38] In any case, the early Christians are not our models, and there may be good reasons why we may not wish to copy them. But, Kreider points out, the early Christians do put to us some pertinent and challenging questions:

> At work or at home . . . are you known to your neighbours? Are you known as members of a *superstitio*, a deviation from the norms of accepted behaviour? Are you distinctive because of Jesus, whose teachings and way offer you perspectives and ways of living that are new? And how about your congregations? In the way that they function and worship, are they becoming communities of peace and freedom which are evidences of the truth of the gospel? . . . Are your rites strong and living, enabling you to address the issues that really trouble your communities? Do you evaluate your worship primarily by how it makes you feel, or by the extent to which it shapes your character—as communities of faith and as individual Christians —so you look like Jesus Christ?[39]

Through humble conversation with the early Christians we shall perhaps discover resources that equip us to face the challenges of interaction with the worldviews and ideologies of our world at the end of the twentieth century, and to bear witness to Jesus Christ with integrity and radicalness.

Notes to Chapter Eight

1. Thus Wesley Ariarajah completely ignores this double thrust of the story in his insistence (part of the pre-understanding he brings to the text) that 'there is no need to "channel" God to people. God has a direct access to people, and they stand in a relationship to God' (*The Bible and People of Other Faiths*, Geneva: World Council of Churches, 1985, p. 17). He admits that Cornelius became a disciple of Christ, but goes beyond the text in assuming that 'the special relationship

with God' in which he stood prior to his hearing of the message was salvific. Why then the need to hear the message, let alone baptism and discipleship to Christ?

2. L Sanneh, 'Pluralism and Christian Commitment' in *Theology Today*, vol. 45, April 1988, pp. 21–33.

3. Ibid. p. 27.

4. Ibid. p. 23.

5. J Moltmann, 'Is Pluralistic Theology Useful for the Dialogue of World Religions?' in G D'Costa (ed), *Christian Uniqueness Reconsidered* (London: SCM, 1990) p. 154.

6. Quoted in J Needham, *Within the Four Seas: Dialogue of East and West* (London: Allen & Unwin, 1964) p. 159.

7. L Newbigin, *The Gospel in a Pluralist Society* (Grand Rapids: Eerdmans and Geneva: WCC, 1989) p. 175.

8. Ibid.

9. Ibid. p. 177. Newbigin also challenges the 'unspoken assumption' that 'religion' is the primary medium of human contact with the divine (p. 172). He points out that 'When the New Testament affirms that God had nowhere left himself without witness, there is no suggestion that this witness is necessarily to be found in the sphere of what we call religion'. He continues, 'When the Fourth Gospel affirms that the light of the Logos who came into the world in Jesus shines on every human being, there is no suggestion that this light is identified with human religion. The text goes on to say that this light shines in the darkness, and the ensuing story constantly suggests that it is religion which is the primary area of darkness, while the common people, unlearned in religious matters, are the ones who respond to the light' (p. 172).

10. The three terms were used by Alan Race in his book *Christians and Religious Pluralism* (Maryknoll, NY: Orbis, 1982). They were taken up by Gavin D'Costa who argues for a Rahner-like inclusivism in *Theology and Religious Pluralism* (Oxford: Blackwell, 1986).

11. Ibid. pp. 182–3.

12. Of course the ecumenism that Jesus envisages is a far cry from the ecumenism understood today as a vague notion of uniting 'all people of faith'. In the preceding verses which form the context of Jesus' prayer for unity, he assumes that the basis of their unity is acceptance of his word as 'truth' and faith in him as the one whom the Father has sent into the world (cf. 17:6–8, 17–18) and who knows the Father in a way the world does not (25, 26). This is an evangelical ecumenism, evangelical because it arises from a common allegiance to the evangel.

13. S. H. Moffett, *A History of Christianity in Asia, Vol 1: Beginnings to 1500* (San Francisco: HarperSan Francisco, 1992) p. 504.

14. Ibid. p. 509.

15. Ibid. p. 506.

16. Cf. Gal 5:11, 6:17; 1 Cor 4:8–13; 2 Cor 5:7–12; 6:3–10; 11:22–33.

17. e.g. Phil 1:29; Rom 8:17, 1 Thess 3:3, 4; Acts 14:22.

18. K Klostermeier, *Hindu and Christian in Vrindaban* (London: SCM, 1969) pp. 47–8.

19. A Kreider, 'Worship and Evangelism in Pre-Christendom', *Vox Evangelica*, vol. XXIV, 1994, p. 11.
20. Eusebius, *HE* 5.1.60, cited in Kreider, p. 12.
21. Tertullian, *Apol.*50.13, cited in Kreider, op. cit. p. 12.
22. Kreider, op. cit. p. 11.
23. Cf. CEB. Cranfield, *The Epistle to the Romans* (Edinburgh: T&T Clark, 1979), II, p. 645 (cf. Rom 12:17 with 1 Thess 5:15 and 1 Pet 3:9: 'The close similarity . . . suggests that we have here the fixed formulation of the catechetical tradition.'). Athenagoras: 'What then are the teachings on which we are brought up? I say to you, love them who curse you, pray for them who persecute you, that you may be the sons of your Father in heaven' (*Legatio*. 11.2); Aristeides: 'Now the Christians . . . have the commandments of the Lord Jesus Christ himself engraven on their hearts, and these they observe' (*Apol.*15)—both cited in Kreider, Ibid. p. 20.
24. Julian, *Ep.*22, cited in Kreider, op. cit. p. 16.
25. Op. cit. pp. 16–17.
26. Eusebius, *HE*, 7.32.7–12.
27. Pontius, *Vita Cypriani*, 9. A similar event, this time in Alexandria in 256, is reported by Eusebius, *HE*, 7.22.2–10.
28. R Stark, 'Epidemics, Networks, and the Rise of Christianity', *Semeia*, 56, 1992, pp. 159–75. For the remarkable contribution of Christian medical missions in the past two hundred years to the development of medical education, community health and national health services in many countries of the Third World, see Stanley G Browne (ed), *Heralds of health: The Saga of Christian Medical Initiatives* (London: Christian Medical Fellowship, 1985).
29. Kreider, op. cit. p. 10.
30. Ibid.
31. Ibid. p. 19.
32. D. Bonhoeffer, *Ethics* (eng. trans. London: SCM, 1955) p. 18. In my quotations, I have retained the non-inclusive language of the translation!
33. Ibid.
34. Ibid (Italics in text).
35. Ibid. p. 21.
36. Ibid. p. 21.
37. Ibid. p. 18.
38. Kreider, op. cit. p. 30.
39. Ibid.

Bibliography

Austin, J.L., *How to do Things With Words* (Oxford: Clarendon Press, 1961)

Ariarajah, W., *The Bible and People of Other Faiths* (Geneva: WCC, 1985)

Barr, J., ' "Abba" isn't "Daddy" '*Journal of Theological Studies, vol.39*, 1988, pp.28–47.

Bauckham, R.J., 'The Sonship of the Historical Jesus in Christology', *Scottish Journal of Theology*, vol.31, 1978, pp.245–60

——'The Worship of Jesus in Apocalyptic Christianity', *New Testament Studies*, vol.27, 1981

——'God Who Raises the Dead: the Resurrection of Jesus and Early Christian Faith in God', in P. Avis (Ed.), *The Resurrection of Jesus Christ* (London: Darton, Longman & Todd, 1993)

Barth, Karl, *Anselm: Fides Quaerens Intellectum* (Eng.trans. London: SCM, 1960)

——*Protestant Theology in the Nineteenth Century* (Eng.trans. London: SCM, 1972)

Bediako, K., Christianity in Africa: the Renewal of a Non-Western Religion (Edinburgh: Edinburgh University Press & Maryknoll, NY: Orbis, 1995).

Berger, P.L., Berger, B. & Kellner, H., *The Homeless Mind:Modernization and Consciousness* (Harmondsworth: Penguin, 1973)

Bevan, E., *Hellenism and Christianity* (London: George Allen & Unwin, 1921)

Blomberg, C.L., *Interpreting the Parables* (Downers Grove, Ill: Inter-Varsity Press, 1990)

Boff, Leonardo & Clodovis, *Salvation and Liberation* (Maryknoll,NY: Orbis, 1984)

Bonhoeffer, D., *Ethics* (Eng.trans. London: SCM, 1955)

Browne, S.G., Davey, F., and Thompson, W.A.R., (Eds.) *Heralds of Health: The Saga of Christian Medical Initiatives* (London: Christian Medical Fellowship, 1985)

Buckley, Michael, *At the Origins of Modern Atheism* (New Haven and London: Yale University Press, 1987)

Bultmann, R., 'New Testament and Mythology' in Hans Werner Bartsch (Ed.) *Kerygma and Myth* (2 vols) (Eng.trans. London: SPCK, 1962)

Caird, G.B., *The Language and Imagery of the Bible* (London: Duckworth, 1980)

Chadwick, H., *The Early Church* (London: Penguin, 1967)

Chaudhuri, N., *Hinduism* (London: Chatto and Windus, 1979)

Conze, F., *Further Buddhist Studies* (London: Cassirer, 1975)

Cochrane, C.N., *Christianity and Classical Culture* (Oxford: Clarendon, 1940)

Collins, Steven, *Selfless Persons: Imagery and Thought in Theravada Buddhism* (Cambridge: Cambridge University Press, 1982)

Cox, Harvey, *Religion in the Secular City: Towards a Postmodern Theology* (New York: Simon and Shuster, 1984)

——*Many Mansions: A Christian's Encounter With Other Faiths* (Boston, 1988, London: Collins, 1989)

Cranfield, C.E.B., *The Epistle to the Romans,* Vol.II (Edinburgh: T & T Clark, 1979)

Cronin, Richard, *Imagining India* (London:Macmillan, 1989)

Crossan, J., *The Historical Jesus: The Life of a Mediterranean Jewish Peasant* (San Francisco: Harper, 1991)

Cupitt, Don, *The Debate About Christ* (London: SCM, 1979)

——'A Final Comment' in J. Hick (Ed.) *The Myth of God Incarnate* (London: SCM, 1977)

Davies, Brian, *The Thought of Thomas Aquinas* (Oxford: Clarendon, 1992)

D'Costa, Gavin, *Theology and Religious Pluralism* (Oxford: Blackwell, 1986)

——(ed.), *Christian Uniqueness Reconsidered* (London: SCM, 1990)

Dunn, J.D.G., *Jesus and the Spirit* (London: SCM, 1975)

——*Christology in the Making: A New testament Inquiry into the Origins of the Doctrine of the Incarnation* (London: SCM, 1980)

——*Unity and Diversity in the New Testament* (London: SCM & Philadelphia: Trinity Press, 2nd edn., 1990)

——'Pharisees, Sinners, and Jesus' in *Jesus, Paul and the Law* (London: SPCK, 1990)

Durrant, Michael, *Theology and Intelligibility* (London: Routledge & Kegan Paul, 1973)

Farrer, A., *Saving Belief* (London: Hodder, 1964)

Fee, Gordon, *The First Epistle to the Corinthians* (NICNT, Grand Rapids: Eerdmans, 1987)

Fischer, K.P., 'John Locke in the German Enlightenment: an Interpretation', *Journal of the History of Ideas*, vol.36:3, 1975

Fitzmeyer, J., *The Gospel According to Luke (X–XXIV)* (The Anchor Bible, New York: Doubleday, 1985)

Fox, Robin Lane, *Pagans and Christians* (New York: Alfred Knopf, 1986)

France, R.T., *Jesus and the Old Testament* (London: Tyndale Press, 1971)

——*The Gospel According to Matthew: An Introduction and Commentary* (Leicester: InterVarsity Press & Grand Rapids: Eerdmans, 1985)

——'Jesus. the Baptist?' in J. Green and M. Turner (Eds.) *Jesus of Nazareth: Lord and Christ.*

Frege, Gottlob, 'On Sense and Meaning' in Brian MacGuiness (Ed.), *Collected Papers on Mathematics, Logic and Philosophy* (Oxford, 1984)

Geertz, Clifford, *Islam Observed* (Chicago, Chicago University Press, 1971)

Giddens, A., *The Consequences of Modernity* (Cambridge: Polity Press, 1991)

Gilson, E., *History of Christian Philosophy in the Middle Ages* (London: Sheed and Ward, 1955)

Gombrich, Richard, 'Introduction: The Buddhist Way' in H. Bechert and R. Gombrich (Eds.), *The World of Buddhism: Buddhist Monks and Nuns in Society and Culture* (London, 1984)

——*Theravada Buddhism: A Social History From Ancient Benares to Modern Colombo* (London: Routledge & Kegan Paul, 1988)

——'Reflections of an Indologist' in Ian Hamnet (Ed.), *Religious Pluralism and Unbelief: Studies Critical and Comparative* (London: Routledge, 1990)

Gorringe, T.J., 'Not Assumed is Not Healed', *Scottish Journal of Theology*, vol.38, 1985

Gottwald, N.K., *The Tribes of Yahweh: A Sociology of the Religion of Liberated Israel, 1250–1050 BCE* (London: SCM, 1980)

Gray, S., *The Least of My Brothers: Matt25:31–46 A History of Interpretation* (Atlanta: Scholars Press, 1989)

Green, Joel and Turner, Max (Eds.), *Jesus of Nazareth: Lord and Christ* (Grand Rapids: Eerdmans and Carlisle: Paternoster Press, 1994)

Green, Joel, 'Good News to Whom? Jesus and the 'Poor' in the Gospel of Luke' in J. Green and M. Turner (eds.) *Jesus of Nazareth: Lord and Christ*.

Grillmeier, A., *Christ in Christian Tradition, Vol.1: From the Apostolic Age to Chalcedon* (Eng.trans. London: Mowbrays, 1975)

Gunton, Colin, *Yesterday and Today: A Study of Continuities in Christology* (London: Darton, Longman & Todd, 1983)

Gutierrez, Gustavo, *A Theology of Liberation* (Eng.trans. London: SCM, 1974, revised edn. 1988)

Harvey, A.E., *Jesus and the Constraints of History* (Philadelphia: Westminster Press, 1982)

Hebblethwaite, B., *The Incarnation: Collected Essays in Christology* (Cambridge: Cambridge University Press, 1987)

Hengel, Martin, *The Son of God: The Origin of Christology and the History of Jewish-Hellenistic Religion* (Eng.trans. London: SCM, 1976)

—— *Crucifixion* (Eng.trans. London: SCM, 1977)

——*Between Jesus and Paul: Studies in the Earliest History of Christianity* (Eng.trans. London: SCM, 1983)

——*The 'Hellenization' of Judaea in the First Century After Christ* (London: SCM and Philadelphia: Trinity Press International, 1989)

Hick, John and Knitter, Paul (Eds.), *The Myth of Christian Uniqueness* (London: SCM, 1987)

Hick, John, *Problems of Religious Pluralism (London: Macmillan, 1985)*

——*An Interpretation of Religion* (London: Macmillan, 1989)

——*Disputed Questions in Theology and the Philosophy of Religion* (London: Macmillan, 1993)

Hodgson, L., *The Doctrine of the Trinity* (London: Nisbet, 1943)

Hodgson, P.C., 'Hegel' in Ninian Smart et al. (eds.) *Nineteenth-Century Religious Thought in the West*, 3 Vols. (Cambridge: Cambridge University Press, 1985), Vol.1

Hurtado, L.W., *One God, One Lord: Early Christian Devotion and Ancient Jewish Monotheism* (Philadelphia: Fortress Press, 1988)

Irenaeus, *Adversus Haereses (Against Heresies)*, in *The Ante-Nicene Fathers*, vol.1, trans. A. Roberts & J. Donaldson (Grand Rapids: Eerdmans, 1987 reprint)

Jeremias, J., *The Prayers of Jesus* (Eng.trans. London: SCM, 1967)
——*Jerusalem in the Time of Jesus* (Eng.trans. Philadelphia: Fortress, 1969)

Jonas, Hans, *The Gnostic Religion* (2nd ed, Boston, 1963)

Jungel, E., *God as the Mystery of the World* (Edinburgh: T & T Clark, 1983)

Kaiser, C., *Creation and the History of Science* (Basingstoke: Marshall Pickering/Grand Rapids: Eerdmans, 1987)

Kant, Immanuel, *Religion Within the Limits of Reason Alone* (trans. T. Greene and H. Hudson, New York: Harper and Row, 1960)

Katz, Steven, 'Language, Epistemology and Mysticism' in S. Katz (ed.), *Mysticism and Philsophical Analysis* (New York: Oxford University Press)

Kaufman, Gordon, 'Religious Diversity, Historical Consciousness, and Christian Theology' in J. Hick and P. Knitter (eds.) *The Myth of Christian Uniqueness*.

Kelly, J.N.D., *Early Christian Doctrines* (London: A & C Black, 5th rev.edn. 1977)

Kierkegaard, S., *Training in Christianity* (Eng.trans. Walter Lowrie, Princeton University Press, 1941)

Kim, S., *The Origins of Paul's Gospel* (Grand Rapids: Eerdmans, 1982)

Kirk, A. J., *Liberation Theology: An Evangelical View From the Third World* (London: Marshall, Morgan and Scott, 1979)

Klostermeier, K., *Hindu and Christian in Vrindaban* (London: SCM, 1969)

Knitter, Paul, *No Other Name?: A Critical Survey of Christian Attitudes Towards the World Religions* (Maryknoll, NY: Orbis, 1985)

Kreider, Alan, 'Worship and Evangelism in Pre-Christendom', *Vox Evangelica*, Vol.XXIV, 1994

Lane, W., *The Gospel of Mark* (London: Marshall, Morgan and Scott, 1974)

Lannoy, Richard, *The Speaking Tree: A Study of Indian Culture and Society* (Oxford, 1971)

Lessing, G.E., 'On the Proof of the Spirit and of Power' in H. Chadwick (ed.) *Lessing's Theological Writings* (Stanford: Stanford University Press and London: A. & C. Black, 1957)

Lewis, C.S., *Miracles* (London: Collins, 1947)

Lindbeck, George, *The Nature of Doctrine: Religion and Theology in a Post-Liberal Age* (London: SPCK, 1984)

Ling, Trevor, (ed.), *Buddhist Trends in Southeast Asia* (Singapore: Institute of Southeast Asian Studies, 1993)

Locke, John, *Essay Concerning Human Understanding* (Book IV), ed. P. Niddich (Oxford: Clarendon, 1975)

Mackintosh, H.R., *Types of Modern Theology: Schleiermacher to Barth* (1937, London: Collins, 1964)

Marshall, I.H., *The Origins of New Testament Christology* (Leicester: InterVarsity, 1976)

——*The Gospel of Luke: A Commentary on the Greek Text* (Exeter: Paternoster, 1978)

——*I and 2 Thessalonians* (Grand Rapids: Eerdmans, 1983)

Mascall, Eric, *Existence and Analogy* (London, 1949)

Mbiti, John, 'Theological Impotence and the Universality of the Church', in G.H. Anderson and T.F. Stransky, *Mission Trends No.3: Third World Theologies* (New York: Paulist Press & Grand Rapids: Eerdmans, 1976)

McGrath, Alister, *The Genesis of Doctrine: a Study in the Foundations of Doctrinal Criticism* (Oxford: Blackwell, 1990)

——*The Making of Modern German Christology, 1750–1990* (Leicester: Apollos, 2nd ed., 1994)

Meeks, W.A., *The First Urban Christians: The Social World of the Apostle Paul* (New Haven: Yale University Press, 1983)

Meier, J.P., *The Vision of Matthew: Christ, Church and Morality in the First Gospel* (New York: Paulist Press, 1979)

Menard, J.E., 'Normative Self-Definition in Gnosticism', in E.P. Sanders (ed.), *Jewish and Christian Self-Definition*, Vol.1.

Meyer, Ben F., *The Aims of Jesus* (London: SCM, 1979)

——'Resurrection as Humanly Intelligible Destiny', *Ex Auditu*, 1993

Michalson Jr., G.E., *Lessing's 'Ugly Ditch': A Study of Theology and History* (Pennsylvania State University Press, 1985)

Milbank, John, 'The End of Dialogue' in G. D'Costa (ed.), *Christian Uniqueness Reconsidered* (1990)

Minns, D., *Irenaeus* (London: Geoffrey Chapman, 1994)

Moffett, Samuel, *A History of Christianity in Asia, Vol.1* (San Francisco: HarperSan Francisco, 1992)

Moltmann, J., *The Way of Jesus Christ: Christology in Messianic Dimension* (San Francisco: Harper, 1990)

——'Is Pluralistic Theology Useful for the Dialogue of World Religions?' in G. D'Costa (Ed.), *Christian Uniqueness Reconsidered* (1990).

Moule, C.F.D., *The Origin of Christology* (Cambridge: Cambridge University Press, 1977)

Murti, T.R.V., *The Central Philosophy of Buddhism* (London: George Allen & Unwin, 1955)

Myers, Bryant, *The Changing Shape of World Mission* (Monrovia, California: MARC, 1993)

Nandy, A., *Traditions, Tyranny, and Utopias: Essays on the Politics of Awareness* (Delhi: Oxford University Press, 1992)

Needham, J., *Within the Four Seas: Dialogue of East and West* (London: Allen & Unwin, 1964)

Neil, S., *Christian Faith and Other Faiths* (Oxford: Oxford University Press, 1970)

Neil, S., and Wright, N.T., *The Interpretation of the New Testament, 1861–1986* (new edn., Oxford: Oxford University Press, 1988)

Netlund, Harold, *Dissonant Voices: Religious Pluralism and the Question of Truth* (Grand Rapids: Eerdmans, 1992)

——'Truth, Authority and Modernity' in P. Sampson, V. Samuel and C. Sugden, *Faith and Modernity* (Oxford: Regnum Lynx, 1994)

Neusner, J., *The Rabbinic Traditions About the Pharisees Before 70* (Leiden: E.J. Brill, 1971)

——*From Politics to Piety: The Emergence of Pharisaic Judaism* (Englewood Cliffs, NJ: Prentice-Hall, 1973)

——'Mr.Sanders' Pharisees and Mine', *Scottish Journal of Theology*, vol.44:1, 1991

Newbigin, Lesslie, *The Other Side of 1984* (Geneva:WCC, 1983)

——*The Gospel in a Pluralist Society* (Grand Rapids: Eerdmans/Geneva: WCC, 1989)

——*Truth to Tell: The Gospel as Public Truth* (Grand Rapids: Eerdmans, 1991)

——'Truth and Authority in Modernity' in P. Sampson, V. Samuel and C. Sugden (eds.) *Faith and Modernity* (Oxford: Regnum Lynx, 1994)

Nicholson, R.A., *Rumi: Poet and Mystic* (1950, London: George Allen & Unwin, 1978)

Oestreich, G., *Neo-Stocism and the Early Modern State* (Cambridge: Cambridge University Press, 1983)

Osborne, Grant, 'Structure and Christology in Mark 1:21–45' in J. Green and M. Turner, *Jesus of Nazareth: Lord and Christ.*

Otto, R., *The Idea of the Holy* (Oxford: Oxford University Press, 1958)

Panikkar, Raimundo, *Myth, Faith and Hermeneutics* (London: Darton, Longman & Todd, 1970)

——*The Silence of God: the Answer of the Buddha* (Madrid, 1970; Eng.trans. Maryknoll, NY: Orbis, 1989)

——*The Trinity and the Religious Experience of Man* (London: Darton, Longman & Todd, 1973)

——*The Unknown Christ of Hinduism* (London: Darton, Longman & Todd, rev.edn.1981)

——'The Jordan, The Tigris and the Ganges: Three Kairological Moments of Christic Self-Awareness' in J. Hick & P. Knitter (eds.) *The Myth of Christian Uniqueness (1988)*

Pannenberg, W., Jesus—God and Man (Eng.trans. London:SCM, 1968)

——*Christianity in a Secularized World* (Eng.trans. London: SCM, 1988)

Parrinder, G., *Avatars and Incarnations* (London: Faber & Faber, 1970)

Pascal, Blaise, *Pensees* (trans. A. Krailsheimer, London: Penguin, 1966)

Pelikan, J., *The Christian Tradition, Vol.1: The Emergence of the Catholic Tradition (100–600)* (Chicago: University of Chicago Press, 1971)

——*Jesus Through the Centuries* (New Haven and London: Yale University Press, 1985)

Perkins, P., *Resurrection: New Testament Witness and Contemporary Reflection* (New York: Doubleday, 1984)

Perrin, N., *Rediscovering the Teaching of Jesus* (New York: Harper and Row, 1967)

Pieris, Aloysius, *An Asian Theology of Liberation* (Edinburgh: T & T Clark, 1988)

——*Love Meets Wisdom: a Christian Experience of Buddhism* (Maryknoll, NY: Orbis, 1988)

Polanyi, Michael, *Personal Knowledge: Towards a Post-Critical Philosophy* (Chicago: University of Chicago Press, 1958)

Polanyi, Michael, and Prosch, Harry, *Meaning* (Chicago: University of Chicago Press, 1975)

Proudfoot, Wayne, *Religious Experience* (University of California Press, 1985)

Race, A., *Christians and Religious Pluralism* (Maryknoll, NY: Orbis, 1982)

Radhakrishnan, S., *The Bhagavadgita: Introductory Essay* (London: Allen & Unwin, 1949)

——*The Hindu View of Life* (New York: Macmillan, 1969)

Reventlow, H.G., *The Bible and the Rise of the Modern World* (Eng.trans. London: SCM, 1984)

Ricoer, P., *The Symbolism of Evil* (Eng.trans. Boston: Beacon, 1967)

Robinson, J.A.T., *Truth is Two-Eyed* (Philadelphia: Westminster, 1979)

Sanders, E.P., (Ed.), *Jewish and Christian Self-Definition*, Vol.1 (London: SCM, 1980)

Sanders, E.P., *Jesus and Judaism* (Philadelphia: Fortress Press, 1985)

——*Judaism: Practice and Belief, 63 BCE-66 CE* (London: SCM and Philadelphia: Trinity Press International, 1992)

Sanneh, Lamin, 'Pluralism and Commitment', *Theology Today*, Vol.45, 1988, pp.21–33.

——*Translating the Message: The Missionary Impact on Culture* (Maryknoll, New York: Orbis, 1991)

——'Africa' in J.M. Phillips and R.J. Coote (eds) *Towards the Twenty-first Century in Christian Mission* (Grand Rapids: Eerdmans, 1993)

——'The Gospel, Language and Culture: The Theological Method in Cultural Analysis', *International Review of Mission*, Vol.LXXXIV, Nos. 332/333, 1995, pp.47–64.

Samartha, Stanley J., 'Reply', in G.H. Anderson and T.F. Stransky (eds.), *Christ's Lordship and Religious Pluralism* (Maryknoll, NY: Orbis, 1981)

——'The Cross and the Rainbow' in J. Hick & P. Knitter (eds.), *The Myth of Christian Uniqueness.*

——*One Christ—Many Religions: toward a Revised Christology* (Maryknoll, NY: Orbis,1991; Indian edn. Bangalore: SATHRI, 1992)

Schillebeeckx, E., *Jesus: An Experiment in Christology* (New York: Crossroad, 1979)

Schouls, Peter, *Descartes and the Enlightenment* (Edinburgh: Edinburgh University Press, 1989)

Schurer, E., *The History of the Jewish People in the Age of Jesus Christ*, rev. and ed. G. Vermes et.al., Vol.2 (Edinburgh: T & T Clark, 1979)

Searle, J.R., *Expression and Meaning: Studies in the Theory of Speech-Acts* (Cambridge: Cambridge University Press, 1979)

Smart, N., *Beyond Ideology: Religion and the Future of Western Civilization* (San Francisco: Harper and Row, 1981)

Smart, N., and Konstantine, S., *Christian Systematic Theology in a World Context* (London: Marshall Pickering, 1991)

Smith, W. Cantwell, *The Meaning and End of Religion* (New York: New American Library, 1964)

——*The Faith of Other Men* (New York: Mentor, 1965)

Song, C.S., 'New China and Salvation History—a Methodological Inquiry', in S.J. Samartha (Ed.), *Living Faiths and Ultimate Goals* (Geneva: WCC, 1974)

Soskice, Janet Martin, *Metaphor and Religious Language* (Oxford: Clarendon, 1985)

Stanton, Graham N., *A Gospel for a New People: Studies in Matthew* (Edinburgh: T & T Clark, 1992)

Stambaugh, J., and Balch, D., *The Social World of the First Christians* (London: SPCK, 1986)

Stark, R., 'Epidemics, Networks, and the Rise of Christianity', *Semeia*, 56, pp.159–75, 1992

Surin, Kenneth, *Theology and the Problem of Evil* (Oxford: Blackwell, 1986)

Suzuki, D.T., 'The Buddhist Conception of Reality' in F. Frank (ed.), *The Buddha Eye* (New York: Crossroad, 1982)

Taylor, Charles, *Sources of the Self: The Making of the Modern Identity* (Cambridge: Cambridge University Press, 1989)

Thiselton, A.C., *The Two Horizons* (Exeter: Paternoster Press, 1980)

——*New Horizons in Hermeneutics* (Grand Rapids: Zondervan/HarperCollins, 1992)

——'Christology in Luke, Speech-Act Theory and the Problem of Dualism After Kant' in J. Green & M. Turner (eds.) *Jesus of Nazareth: Lord and Christ*

Thomas, M.M., *Salvation and Humanization* (Madras: CLS, 1971)

——*The Acknowledged Christ of the Indian Renaissance* (Madras: C.L.S, 2nd edn. 1976)

Tillich, Paul, *The Dynamics of Faith* (New York: Harper and Row, 1957)

Torrance, T.F., *Karl Barth: An Introduction to His Early Theology, 1910–31* (London: SCM, 1962)

——(Ed.) *Belief in Science and in Christian Life* (Edinburgh: Academic Press, 1980)

Vallee, G., 'Theological and Non-Theological Motives in Irenaeus' Refutation of the Gnostics' in E.P. Sanders (ed.) *Jewish and Christian Self-Definition*, Vol.1 (London: SCM, 1980)

Vermes, Geza, *Jesus the Jew* (London: Collins, 1973)

Wiesel, Elie, *The Town Beyond the Wall* (Eng.trans. New York: Avon, 1970)

——*Night* (Eng trans. London: Fontana Collins, 1972)

Williams, Rowan, 'Trinity and Pluralism' in G. D'Costa (ed.), *Christian Uniqueness Reconsidered*

Williams, Stephen, 'John Locke on the Status of Faith', *Scottish Journal of Theology*, vol.40:4, 1987

——*Revelation and Reconciliation: A Window on Modernity*, Ch.2 (Cambridge: Cambridge University Press, 1995)

Wittgenstein, Ludwig, *Philosophical Investigations* (1936–1949) (Oxford: Blackwell, 3rd edn., 1967)

Wright, C.J.H., *Living as the People of God: The Relevance of Old Testament Ethics* (Leicester: InterVarsity Press, 1983)
——'The Christian and other religions: the biblical evidence', *Themelios*, vol.9:2, 1984
Wright, N.T., *Who Was Jesus?* (London: Hodder, 1992)
——*The New Testament and the People of God* (London: SPCK, 1992)
Yamauchi, Edwin, *Pre-Christian Gnosticism* (Grand Rapids: Eerdmans, 1983)
Yerkes, J., *The Christology of Hegel* (Albany, NY: State University of New York Press, 1983)
Zaehner, R.C., *Concordant Discord: Gifford Lectures on Natural Religion, 1967–69* (Oxford: Oxford University Press, 1970)
——(trans. and introd.) *The Bhagavad Gita* (Oxford: Oxford University Press, 1973)